MW01617194

THE CHURCH OF CATHEDRAL AND CRUSADE

VOLUME 1

THE CHURCH OF
CATHEDRAL AND CRUSADE

VOLUME I

Henri Daniel-Rops

Translated from the French
L'ÉGLISE DE LA CATHÉDRALE ET DE LA CROISADE
by JOHN WARRINGTON

CLUNY
Providence, Rhode Island

HENRI DANIEL-ROPS

THE HISTORY OF THE CHURCH OF CHRIST

CLUNY MEDIA EDITION, 2023

This Cluny edition is a republication of the 1957 edition of Chapters I–VII of
Cathedral and Crusade, published by E. P. Dutton & Co., Inc.
....
For this Cluny edition, citation and reference styles
have been updated and developed, as needed,
for the purposes of clarity and accessibility.

For more information regarding this title
or any other Cluny Media publication,
please write to info@clunymedia.com, or to
Cluny Media, P.O. Box 1664, Providence, RI 02901

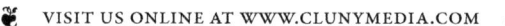 VISIT US ONLINE AT WWW.CLUNYMEDIA.COM

Cluny edition copyright © 2023 Cluny Media LLC

All rights reserved.

ISBN (paperback) | 978-1685952129
ISBN (hardcover) | 978-1685952167

NIHIL OBSTAT: Joannes M. T. Barton, S.T.D., *Censor deputatus*
IMPRIMATUR: Georgius L. Craven, *Epus Sebastopolis, Vic. Cap. Westmon.*
WESTMONASTERII, DIE 31 DECEMBER, 1956

The *Nihil obstat* and *Imprimatur* are a declaration that a book or pamphlet is considered
to be free from doctrinal or moral error. It is not implied that those who have granted the
Nihil obstat and *Imprimatur* agree with the contents, opinions or statements expressed.

Cover design by Clarke & Clarke
Cover image: Albrecht Dürer, *The Emperor Charlemagne*,
1511/1513, painting on lime wood
Courtesy of Wikimedia Commons

CONTENTS

NOTE TO THE TEXT

This is a translation of *L'Eglise de la Cathédrale et de la Croisade*, the third volume of M. Daniel-Rops's *Histoire de l'Eglise du Christ*. It covers the period 1050–1350. (THE TRANSLATOR)

CHAPTER I

Three Centuries of Christendom

I. A FLORENTINE FRESCO

IN the chapter-house of the Dominican convent of Santa Maria Novella at Florence there is a mural painting known as "The Hounds of God." It appears to attract the notice of few visitors, but might provide food for endless meditation. At the foot of the picture some hunting dogs, mottled black and white, are fighting with a pack of wolves; they symbolize those other Hounds of the Lord, *Domini canes*, the sons of St. Dominic, who do battle with the monstrous hordes of heresy, of temptation, and of sin, that ever prowl about our poor humanity.

The painter, Andrea da Firenze, cannot be said to rank with the great masters of his art: he will not stand comparison, for example, with Duccio, Ghirlandaio, Orcagna, or the astonishing Paolo Ucello, whose work is to be seen nearby in all its glory. But it is perhaps true to say that no Christian artist ever learned so well as did Andrea to crowd within a few square yards all that a society dreamed, and willed, and strove to realize upon earth. In that one picture he gave expression to the whole ideal of medieval society.

There in the foreground is the Pope, serene, majestic. Close to him stands the Emperor; he is almost as tall, and we might believe him the pontiff's equal were it not that the skull he carries in his hand reminds us that the governments of earth must pass away while Heaven's law endures. On either side, in strict order of precedence, are aligned the dignitaries of Church and State: cardinals, bishops, and doctors on the right hand; on the left kings, noblemen, and knights. Behind them stretches a vast multitude of the faithful,

2   rich and poor, good and bad—all who have started out on life's adventure and who contend from day to day for the appointed prize. Men of all social grades are to be seen, each one in his destined place, each one with his part to play. And what is that part? The artist has used a symbol to describe its twofold character. In the natural order, man must endeavour to build up the Church militant, as represented by the newly completed Duomo of Florence soaring skyward in the background. On the supernatural plane, he must participate in the Mystical Body, transcend the misery of this passing world, and climb the steep path whereby these ranks of the redeemed toil upward to a blinding light. There, amid the song of angels and the prayer of saints, Christ is enthroned, the Plenitude of Being, the Living God.

Curiously enough, Andrea's fresco was painted in the middle of the fourteenth century, by which time it had ceased to correspond with fact. Nevertheless, ten generations had borne that noble image in their hearts, recognizing it as the ideal of their existence, both as pattern and as promise, and had striven with their tears and with their blood to make it a reality. That vision of the world had taught them all they wished to know: what they were to do on earth, and what they might expect hereafter. It had revealed to them the perfect organization of society, with man subject to God, directed by His mandate, and governed by just laws. It had enabled them to understand that there is no worthy institution outside God's design, none but has some function in raising man to his Creator. Wherefore, all things had a goal, had a meaning, had some final cause. Life's journey was no longer aimless, was no longer without hope. Each individual knew the reason why he worked and suffered, why he lived, and why he must inevitably die.

A noble image, indeed, on which humanity may gaze with yearning; for we have lost the idea of end and means. We struggle vainly to re-establish order; but it is precisely our rejection of the hierarchic system which has landed us in tragedy and ruin.[1]

---

1.   It was with reference to this painting in S. Maria Novella that Ernest Lavisse, a great historian but a determined anti-clerical, lamented the passing of "an institution founded on belief in the fraternal unity of mankind under the fatherhood of God." (Preface to the French translation of Bryce's *Holy Roman Empire*, 1890.)

2. THE SPRINGTIME OF CHRISTENDOM

SUCH, for about three hundred years, was mankind's vision of the world. Before 1050 it had been evolving gradually, in tears and blood; after 1350 it was doomed to disappear. For three long centuries its law held sway; nor can we assign to chance the fact that, between those years, society enjoyed what may be considered the richest, most fruitful, most harmonious epoch in all the history of Europe, an epoch which may be likened to spring after the barbarian winter.

When we survey those centuries, we are struck, first, by their wealth of illustrious names and great events. Just as the sap in springtime leaps in every plant, so, in that soil watered by the grace of Christ, all seems to germinate and put forth abundant foliage. The fervour of creative instinct is manifest on all sides, everywhere a deep-seated urge to take the road and journey towards the future. No chronological table, however detailed, can afford an adequate idea of that awakening.

The cathedrals were rising, and men were setting out to recover the Holy Sepulchre, to free Spain from the Moorish yoke, to preach the gospel in the Baltic lands. Grave questions were debated in the universities; epic poetry flowered, and there were born legends that will never die. While new political forms were in the crucible, millions left home on pilgrimage, others to explore the world, even to the secret heart of Asia. All that, it must be remembered, was going on simultaneously; there was an upsurge of activity wherein each event influenced and was influenced by the others, and of which we cannot hope to analyse the complexity.

That prodigious stirring, on the other hand, was no mere freak of nature. It was not simply the premature revival of a tree whose leaves are blown away by the first blast of April; for it bore fruit in some of the imperishable triumphs of European genius, compared with which our modern works of art too often seem absurd. It was an era which bequeathed to us the Royal Porch at Chartres, the façades of Amiens and Rheims, the windows of La Sainte Chapelle, and the frescoes of Giotto; which begot the mystical writings of St. Bernard and St. Bonaventure, the *Summa Theologica* of St.

4   Thomas, the prophetic works of Roger Bacon and of Dante; which saw the birth of those religious and secular institutions which were to serve as bases for posterity. Only the ages of Pericles, Augustus, and Le Roi Soleil can rival in creative energy the period which elapsed from the death of Louis VII of France to that of his great-grandson St. Louis, from the election of Innocent II to that of Pope St. Celestine.[2]

An achievement of such magnitude presupposes corresponding talent, and Europe at that time seems to have produced innumerable men of outstanding ability in every walk of life. Such were the great saints and scholars; such too were the artists, and those master-craftsmen whose names are buried in oblivion; while statesmanship and military science were represented by such rulers as Philip Augustus and St. Louis, Barbarossa and Frederick II, William the Conqueror and the great crusaders. There was no sphere of human activity devoid of names held in veneration to this day; and at the head of these splendid cohorts stand the popes, above whom tower the figures of Gregory VII and Innocent III.

The ventures, even the tragic conflicts and catastrophes, in which these men took part, bear the stamp of greatness. True, there are certain periods (that, for example, of the Merovingian kings, or the break-up of Charlemagne's empire) whose history is one of petty squabbling and base intrigue; not so the three hundred years with which we have to deal. The crusades form a stupendous episode, as do the Mongol invasion (for all its violence and cruelty) and the appearance of the Almoravids in Spain. Even those disastrous clashes between the Papacy and the Powers are relieved by a dramatic quality which emphasizes the significance of a contest between two irreconcilable ideals.

---

2.   Another fact not seldom overlooked is the material achievement of that epoch. It was then that houses were first equipped with chimneys instead of the old central hearth, and that transparent glass began to be used in windows. The clock-spring was invented in the thirteenth century; so was the compass described by Pérignon de Maricourt in 1269. Other inventions, e.g., the horse-collar, the horse-shoe, and the ship's rudder, were to have important consequences. (See Chapter VII, section 2.) The story of the missions will enable us to appreciate how much geography owed to travellers of the twelfth, thirteenth, and fourteenth centuries. (See Volume 2, Chapter XII, section 5.)

The three centuries under review disclose a state of order and equilib-
rium no less than of vigour and vitality. Their political institutions, as well
as their economic system, are solid, down-to-earth, man-sized: there is no
trace of that unwieldiness and inhuman abstraction so characteristic of the
modern world. Rather, we are studying an age reminiscent of its own creation, the cathedral. Though of infinite complexity, its countless elements
disclose a wellnigh inexhaustible fount of inspiration; yet they are clearly
subordinate to an established pattern which gives meaning to the whole
while it recognizes the value of each part.

Many philosophers of history, from Spengler to Toynbee, maintain that
human societies no less than individuals are subject to an unalterable cyclic
law and pass through stages analogous to those which govern the physiolog-
ical being: infancy, youth, maturity, old age. In so far as such comparisons
are valid, it is impossible to doubt that between 1050 and 1350 Western
Christendom enjoyed the springtime of its youth, with all that youth entails
of creative energy, generous impetuosity that was sometimes vain, violence,
faith, sublimity.

3. THE "MIDDLE AGES"

THE expression "Middle Ages," when used to designate the period 1050–
1350 and the following century, is open to objection. The phrase itself and
the notion it is intended to convey were alike unknown to the men of that
epoch. Unconscious of any break in continuity between themselves and
their predecessors of the ancient world, they had no sense of living, so to
speak, in an historical parenthesis. No such idea would ever have occurred to
them; their existence was too full to admit the mournful prospect of a tran-
sitory age. Their sense of kinship with and loyalty to the past was infinitely
stronger than that of the present generation, whose faith is pinned upon the
years to come, and who glibly assume that because a thing belongs to the
future it is more valuable than its present counterpart. In the "Middle Ages"
the opposite was true: every legacy of the past was viewed with respect and

6 received as a model; for until the fourteenth century most Europeans considered themselves lineal heirs to all that was best in ancient civilization.

This term "Middle Ages" was used first in 1469 by the papal librarian Giovanni Andrea, who distinguished "the ancients of the Middle Ages from the moderns of our time." Similar expressions were employed by Joachim von Watt, John Heerwagen, and Adrian Junius in the sixteenth century, and later, during the classical period, by Cellarius, Canisius, Goldast, Voss, and Horn, as well as by Du Cange, the celebrated author of a *Glossary of Medieval Literature*. The notion gradually became widespread; but it was only in 1829 that there was published the first *General History of the Middle Ages* by Desmichels, rector of Aix-en-Provence.

Moreover, the term implied a measure of reproach. Ronsard speaks of the "monstrous ignorance" of the past. Heinsius affirms that culture had had to be "re-born." The Italian polygraph Paolo Giovio would remind us of those "gothic tombs wherein art and letters had been miserably laid to rest." There is contempt in that word "gothic."[3]

In their unreasoning enthusiasm for antiquity, the leaders of the Renaissance were outrageously unfair towards the preceding age. Many of them, too, were adherents of the "reformed" religion, and religious motives are perceptible through their aesthetic utterances. To disparage an era when the Catholic Church inspired and led society was to denigrate the Church herself. At the very height of the Renaissance, however, there were not lacking those who formed a more equitable judgment: the learned Pico della Mirandola, for example, and the sculptor Ghiberti. In the first years of the eighteenth century, when "the barbarity of gothic" had become almost a truism, an honest German professor, Polycarp Leyser, wrote a lengthy pamphlet on the "pretended barbarism of the Middle Ages," and followed it up in 1721 with a *History of Medieval Poetry*. Somewhat later the Benedictines undertook their monumental *History of French Literature*, and paid homage to the century of St. Bernard, of the *Chansons de Geste*, and of the *Roman de la Rose*. It is to the honour of the Romantics, especially of Chateaubriand,

---

3. See Volume 2, Chapter IX, section 6.

that they restored to the "Middle Ages" their dignity, their pride of place in European history; and it is significant that the decisive work, which confirmed this change of outlook, was none other than *Le Génie du christianisme*, dedicated to the glory of the Church.

Today, no one would begrudge recognition of the medieval achievement. The history, art, and literature of those generations, all alike, are objects of close study and detailed research; while their spirituality is practised with a devotion far more enduring than the raptures of romanticism. Johan Nordström, the great historian of Sweden, has remarked that "if ever an epoch deserves praise as one of regeneration and revival, it is this"; and when we look upon the glories of Rheims, Amiens, and Chartres, to a better appreciation of which the camera is continually assisting us, who will not endorse the truth of Nordström's word, and feel himself in presence of the human mind at what was perhaps its finest hour?

Yet, if today the word "medieval" no longer implies contempt, it remains open to misinterpretation upon several grounds. Considered etymologically, it assumes that we have to deal with a threefold division of time, a succession of three periods in terms of Hegelian dialectic. Viewed thus, the "Middle Ages" are a transition from antiquity to modern times; but if by that phrase we mean that they form a chronological link between the two, we convey exactly nothing. "What age is not the link between that which goes before and that which follows? Every age is a 'middle age,' and we ourselves shall one day be regarded as medieval by posterity."[4] If, on the other hand, we mean to describe an era of preparation, of quest, and of elaboration, which is to perfect the social order, then, it is to be feared, we are still farther from the truth; for the present scene affords scant evidence of progress, in the moral or the social sphere.

The whole concept of the "Middle Ages" has been falsified. The medieval period was in no sense an age of transition, uncertain of its goal and of the means thereto. It was a starting-point of history, when society, profoundly conscious of itself and of its destiny, accomplished a task the like of

---

4.   Joseph Calmette, *Trilogie de l'histoire de France*, 1948.

which has not been equaled and may never be; when humanity attained a unity and balance never since achieved. We cannot now abandon so well-established an expression as "the Middle Ages," however misleading it may be; but its use here is intended simply to evoke the splendour of that period.

We must also determine the limits of an era denoted by so elastic a phrase. Most historians agree that the Middle Ages start with the great Germanic invasions at the beginning of the fifth century, and end with the fall of Constantinople in 1453; but within those ten centuries it is not difficult to discern periods of violent contrast. When, for example, we speak of the "masterpieces of medieval art" we refer to the central part of the millennium; and when we conjure up the "Dark Ages" and the horrors associated with that time, we are thinking of the Merovingians or of the Carolingian Empire in decay. Again, is Joan of Arc to be reckoned a "medieval" figure? Her saintly patriotism belongs rather to the rising flood of national consciousness; her troops employed the cannon, a modern instrument of war. There are, in fact, within those thousand years three different stages: tentative effort, poise, and finally the drift to ruin. The first of these is the barbarian epoch; the third coincides with the late fourteenth and early fifteenth century. How, then, can we best describe the period of full bloom? Perhaps by two of its most striking achievements: the Cathedral and the Crusade.

It is, of course, true that even within this period there was change. No age is altogether static. Just as French history in the seventeenth century opens with the coarseness of Henri IV's reign and closes amid the exquisite refinement of the Regency, so between 1050 and 1350 there is an equally remarkable development. Western Christendom becomes conscious of what its immediate forbears have achieved; this is followed by the solid simplicity of the twelfth century; and the summit is reached a hundred years later with the cathedrals, the *Summa* of St. Thomas, and the triumph of the papacy. The magnificent edifice is seen thereafter to contain cracks which will soon become lines of cleavage. Now between those four stages there are very real contrasts, and much valuable information may be derived from asking which was the more fruitful or more Christian, the twelfth or

the thirteenth century, the age of St. Bernard or that of St. Francis and St.
Dominic, the age of romanesque or that of gothic? While recognizing the
differences, however, we must not lose sight of an essential unity: it is more
important to take account of those features which unified so many diverse
elements, and wove ten generations of mankind into one gorgeous tapestry.
There was a common view of life and of life's purpose, an acknowledgment
of common principles, an undivided faith, and hearts directed to a single
goal.

4. CHRISTIAN EUROPE IN 1050

THE splendid era of the Cathedrals and Crusades opened about 1050.
During the fifth century the Church had stood alone against the forces of
disruption. Through St. Augustine she had laid the foundation-stone of
reconstruction; through St. Benedict she had formed a spiritual and intellectual aristocracy. During six hundred years of labour in God's service, she
had worked unceasingly to prepare the rebirth of civilization. By sending
missionaries into the heart of the barbarian world, and by converting its
heathen princes, she had begun that racial fusion whence modern Europe
was to spring. In her religious houses she had preserved the embryos of art
and manners. Unwearied, never despairing, the Church had pursued her
task from age to age; and when, after the short-lived brilliance of Charlemagne's reign, darkness fell once more upon the West, it was she who saved
Europe from the lethal tide of anarchy. During six hundred years of fiery
trial her patience and her courage had matched her faith and constant hope,
until the year 1050 which marks the turning-point.

In the East, Byzantium was in decline. Assailed by the Turks, and a prey
to those internal dissensions which ruined the powerful Macedonian dynasty, she chose to isolate herself in priestly formalism and caesaropapism at the
very hour when day dawned in the West.

Two factors were decisive. First, the invasions ceased: the cloud of barbarian aggression, which had hung continuously on the horizons of the

Western world, now rolled away. The causes are no less obscure than those which had opened the flood-gates; they were probably linked with domestic policies in far distant lands whence the invaders came. But there were other reasons. The Church had not hesitated to baptize the newcomers, and had thereby roused their zeal for incorporation in civilized society. Her courage in this respect was of paramount importance, especially in the case of the Normans and Hungarians. At all events, the passing of so dire a menace had much to do with the flowering of Christendom.

No less decisive, though more difficult to follow in detail, was a second phenomenon, this time in the social and moral sphere. The end of Carolingian rule had inevitably given place to chaos. The feudal system, based upon an inevitable appeal to force of arms, had gradually emerged; but there was danger that it would in turn beget a society devoid of culture—a community of warriors, the very opposite of civilized mankind. The Church, however, had found a remedy for this state of affairs. At the beginning of the tenth century it had seemed probable that she herself would be more or less overwhelmed by violence, engulfed in feudal anarchy. Nevertheless, an astonishing effort had enabled her, under the leadership of the popes and the monastic orders, and with the aid of a few loyal princes, to ride out the storm. Now she was dictating to, and even punishing, the warrior caste, opposing to brute force the principles of charity and justice. It might at one time have been feared that western Europe would divide into two groups: on one side the military clique, on the other a more cultured caste of clergy and bourgeoisie. But, thanks to the Church, their synthesis was virtually complete before 1050.

By the middle of the eleventh century Christendom was an accomplished fact, though its boundaries at that date are not easy to determine. In the south and east of the Mediterranean it had lost considerable areas to Islam; but Christian communities continued to exist in regions that were mainly infidel. Elsewhere the Gospel seed was taking root, particularly in southern and western Europe. The Byzantines held Asia Minor for no more than a quarter of a century, but they controlled Thrace, Macedonia, the Aegean Isles, and Greece. The Normans evicted them from southern

Italy; but those hardy conquerors were too sagacious to continue in the role
of pirates. In 1059 Robert Guiscard, the most adventurous of their leaders, proclaimed his membership of the Christian flock by enrolling himself
among the "protégés" of St. Peter. Central and northern Italy, the country
between the Rhone and the Alps, as well as Germany from the Meuse to the
Elbe, were dependents of the Holy Roman and Germanic Empire which
had been formed by Otto the Great in 962, and which, by the year 1000,
was on excellent terms with the Church.

Two countries had extended the frontiers of Christendom as far as the
Atlantic Ocean. The Faith had struck deep roots in France, and since 987
the house of Capet had been writing the first pages of a history that was to
continue for eight hundred years. In France also, Robert the Pious (d. 1031)
had lately shown that it was possible to be at once a temporal ruler and a
servant of Christ. England was still governed by Anglo-Saxon kings, and
the Church there was renowned for its devotion to the Holy See; while in
Scotland, Ireland, and Wales the old Celtic monachism, which had done so
much to propagate the Faith overseas, continued to flourish.

It is clear, then, that Italy and Germany, France and England were the
strongholds of Christianity in the West; in those four countries the hierarchy was firmly established. Italy contained numerous small dioceses, whose
boundaries were practically identical with those of the ancient Roman cities.
Chief among these were Rome, Milan, Ravenna, Aquileia, Capua, Benevento, Salerno, Naples, and Amalfi. Beyond the Alps, the kingdom of Burgundy
stretched along the Rhone, and was well organized into about thirty-five
episcopal sees, the most important of which were at Lyons, Vienne, Arles,
and Besançon. North of the Loire, the principal cathedral cities were Sens
(of which Paris was only a suffragan), Rheims, Rouen, and Tours; while the
dukes of Brittany took care to have their own metropolitan at Dol. South of
the river, jurisdiction was shared by the four bishoprics of Bordeaux, Bourges, Narbonne, and Auch. Finally, Lotharingia and Germany were divided
into six provinces and forty dioceses.

These facts help us to appreciate how solid, coherent, and permanent
was the Church's organization. We may add that in 1050 the majority of

bishops were of Roman origin; but as the fusion of races continued, Teutonic elements began to appear in the ranks of the episcopate, especially in Germany where the successors of Otho appointed many native bishops.

One other point calls for notice: monastic influence was strong throughout Christian Europe, and in this respect there was little to choose between the East and the West. After the suppression of iconoclasm, with which the Orientals had been preoccupied for more than a century, monastic life became so popular that the government at Constantinople felt obliged to limit the number of vocations.

We have already alluded to the pre-eminence of Celtic monachism in certain parts of the British Isles; but everywhere, in Italy as in France, the monasteries were famous both as power-houses of prayer, as schools and libraries, and as economic and commercial centres. At the turn of the eleventh century, indeed, monachism, animated by a lively spirit of reform, was the driving force of Christian society; and religious houses were bastions of the Faith in missionary lands.

Christianity had also made some recent gains outside the territories subject to episcopal jurisdiction, where spiritual life was nourished by the monastic Orders. Preachers from Hamburg had journeyed through heathen Scandinavia under safe-conducts issued by Gundhild of Denmark, St. Olaf of Norway, and Olaf of Sweden. The earliest bishoprics of Schleswig (Ribe and Aarhus, which were founded in the middle of the tenth century) had been abolished, but a new evangelical offensive had quickly restored them. And during the reign of Canute the Great (1017–1035) Christianity had reached the isles of Denmark and of Sweden, while the Vikings bore the Gospel to Iceland and Greenland.

East of the Elbe was Slav territory. Within a quadrilateral represented by the Elbe, the Oder, the Baltic, and the mountains of Bohemia, various peoples known generically as "Wends" caused the German monks some understandable anxiety. While the bishops of Brandenburg held theoretical jurisdiction as far as the Oder, paganism remained a formidable opponent, as was shown on more than one occasion; and in Saxony it was not before the very end of the eleventh century that missionaries dared venture to the right bank of the Saale. This unpromising situation, however, was offset by the conversion of other Slavonic groups, which had enlarged the Christian frontiers to include central and eastern Europe. Much hidden labour and not a few set-backs had preceded the decisive work of the ninth century, which had taken a variety of forms. The Carolingian and Byzantine rulers alike had sponsored rival missionary undertakings. The bases of this activity in the West were the frontier-dioceses of Salzburg and Ratisbon. In the East, Sts. Cyril and Methodius, the apostles of Bohemia, were famed for their efforts to win souls for Christ by persuasion instead of by force. Again, there was the influence of troops and traders, the effects of intermarriage, and the conduct of such temporal rulers as St. Wenceslaus and St. Ludmilla.

In this way the Slavonic peoples of central Europe had received the Christian Faith. Spiritual jurisdiction was divided between Byzantium and Rome, though it is not easy to determine exactly what the position was in 1050. Roughly speaking, Bohemia and Moravia had owed allegiance to Rome since Pope John VIII (872–882) permitted the use of Slavonic in the liturgy. The bishopric of Prague, established in 973, had been somewhat unwisely attached to the archdiocese of Mainz.

Farther east, Poland had become Christian largely owing to the marriage of the Bohemian St. Dombrovska to Duke Mieczslaw, but also to the preaching of Teutonic missionaries. The first Polish bishopric was erected at Posen, and was originally subject to Magdeburg; but King Boleslav the Mighty (d. 1025) had obtained the establishment of a national metropolitan see at Gniezno, and had invited the Benedictines and Camaldolese to come and strengthen the faith of his subjects. In 1033 there was a violent pagan reaction, during which priests were massacred and convents burned; but this persecution was ended by Casimir I, "the Restorer."

On the middle Danube, the Hungarians, wedged between the northern and southern Slavs, had become an outpost of Christianity, looking toward the Balkans. Their ruler, St. Stephen, had been nominated "Apostolic Sovereign" in 1001, and had placed his subjects under the protection of Christ and the Holy See. The first Hungarian diocese was created at Gran in 1007, and numerous convents were established. These were the headquarters of missionaries who, led by St. Bruno of Querfurt, penetrated to the wilds of Transylvania.

Christianity had long since begun to flourish in the north-west region of the Balkans—as early, indeed, as the lifetime of St. Paul. A narrow fringe of Latin bishoprics was dependent on the patriarchate of Aquileia and the archdiocese of Spalato; while the Roman liturgy was in general use as far north as the Save. The Byzantine rite prevailed in the mountains of Serbia and Montenegro, in Bulgaria (where King Boris had been converted in 863), and in Russia. Here, the little church of Kiev, which was founded in the middle of the ninth century and became the national church on the conversion of St. Vladimir in 987, was governed by a Greek metropolitan; while a number of scattered churches stood amid the forests and steppes right away to the Volga.

It must, however, be admitted that the constancy of these newly baptized masses, stretching from Denmark to the Ukraine, was not yet assured. The often spectacular submission of their chiefs could not at once destroy superstition and savage custom, and fierce pagan revivals sometimes swept away those early Christian harvests. The ancient priesthood still had its following; there were still sacred trees, secret ceremonies, and heathen sacrifices. What, too, are we to think of a conversion like that which Vladimir imposed upon his subjects? They were ordered on pain of death to plunge into the Dnieper and there receive the sacrament of baptism; after which the idols were thrown down, and the great god Peroun, with his golden head and silver beard was flogged to the accompaniment of indignant cries.

On the eastern limits of Christendom, Islam was once more restive. Meanwhile, the Seljuk Turks exerted continual pressure on Byzantine territory in Asia Minor, which they were very soon to overrun. The Empire still held the Anatolian plateau of Armenia, the upper Euphrates, Cilicia, Antioch, and the coast of Syria; but not for long. Her splendid fortresses were garrisoned by cowards when the Turks occupied Melitene (1057) and launched their first great offensive against Armenia, which was monophysite and therefore hostile to the orthodox Byzantines.

Monophysitism was likewise the faith of the Syrian Jacobites; and   15
although the Melchite Church on the coast adhered to Rome, the Maronites
of Lebanon acknowledged obedience to none. Conflicting creeds and racial
antagonism were a grave menace on the eve of the Turkish grand assault.

The whole Mediterranean was overshadowed by the Muslims, whose
pirates harried the Aegean and Tyrrhenian shores. Sicily and northern Africa were in their hands; and they had occupied all the Iberian peninsula,
except for a number of heroic principalities which for three hundred years
had remained impregnable in their mountain fastnesses. Among these, one
city before all others represented Christendom. Santiago di Compostella, in
the extreme north-west, was the religious capital of Spain. The Moors had
besieged it, but without success, and in 950 it had welcomed a French pilgrimage led by Gottschalk, Bishop of Puy.[5] But it was not only in the high
valleys of northern Spain and among the little communities of the east that
the Cross stood firm against the Crescent; there were flourishing Christian
centres in occupied Spain, which had even won official recognition from the
conqueror. Many such continued to exist also in Sicily; and there were others
in Africa, descended from those once ruled by St. Cyprian and St. Augustine.

In order to complete our sketch-map of Christendom in 1050 we have
still to notice those other far-flung communities which, though infected
with heresy and in many cases hopelessly decadent,[6] remained true to the
Gospel. Such were the Copts in Egypt, riddled with monophysitism and
monothelitism; such too were the monophysite Ethiopians, nestling in the
steep folds of the Abyssinian massif. Above all, there were the Nestorians
with headquarters at Bagdad, dominating Persia and Mesopotamia. This
Church continued to flourish notwithstanding its corruption; it provided
the caliphs with doctors, scholars, and men of letters, while its missionaries accomplished the astounding feat of travelling along the caravan routes
right across Asia to Mongolia and China.[7]

---

5. See Volume 2, Chapter XII, section 2.
6. See Volume 2, Chapter XII, sections 5, 7.
7. See Volume 2, Chapter XI, section 9.

Thus far, after one thousand years, the Gospel tree had spread its foliage. It was a glorious achievement; but things far more glorious were yet to come. By the middle of the eleventh century Christendom was conscious of herself and of her own strength; she longed to expand and to realize her potentiality. During the barbarian epoch she had been obliged to turn inward upon herself; now the position was reversed.

About 1050 there were many signs of renewed vigour. First, in the territorial and political sphere, Christian Spain arose and prepared, with foreign aid, to steal a march upon weakling caliphs at Cordova. The naval powers of Genoa and Pisa, too, were sweeping the corsairs of Islam from the Mediterranean and re-establishing themselves in Sardinia. The Normans swooped on Sicily, and in 1060 won back from Muhammad that most beautiful of isles. Here and there men talked of an expedition to free the Holy Sepulchre. Northward, Christianity was active in Scandinavia, making ready to occupy the Baltic lands. A few years later the Norman Conquest severed England from the Nordic world and attached her to the West. Everywhere Christendom was stirring or about to stir.

The same was true in other fields; an irresistible enthusiasm spread in all directions, particularly in the spiritual domain. Here the spirit of reform, inspired by Cluny and her rivals, was communicated in turn to the popes, and soon effected a thorough transformation in the Church. It is no less evident in the artistic and intellectual sphere: Raoul Glaber's "white mantle of churches" flowered, and culture was once more held in high esteem. We cannot, indeed, but recognize that in 1050 Christendom was on the threshold of great achievements; new dangers, however, as well as triumph lay ahead.

5. THE TREE BEARS FRUIT

THE resurrection of Europe, especially in the West, was due in part to material causes. The first of these, although undeniable in the light of such evidence as we have, is a matter of racial statistics which have not so far been the object of systematic investigation. Between the eleventh and the fourteenth century Europe's population increased, steadily and upon an enormous scale. In some cases we possess definite figures. Thus in England, the Exchequer Rolls enable us to affirm that the population grew from one million one hundred thousand in 1086 to three million seven hundred thousand in 1346; i.e., it was more than trebled. On the Continent such documents are fewer, but external evidence (e.g., the genealogies of noble families) points to a similar increase. Continuous expansion of the towns is marked, as at Paris, by the remains of successive lines of wall erected to enclose an ever-widening space. Urban parishes were multiplied, and larger churches built. There is no question of a general exodus from the country-side; for at that very period we find the old family estates divided among numerous sons; forest receding before newly cultivated fields; and new towns with such names as Villeneuve or Villefranche springing up all over Europe to house peasants for whom no land was available.

The cause of this phenomenon remains obscure. Why should a population increase at certain periods, and at others decline? Economic and political reasons do not account for everything. It was not merely because the Saracens, Normans, and Hungarians had ceased their depredations that the population of the West multiplied threefold within a period of thirty decades. There can be no doubt of the influence exerted by the Christian view of marriage. At that time abortion was extremely rare, and "birth-control" unknown. On the other hand, it may be that the whole matter should be referred to those cyclic laws which are said to govern the lives of communities no less than of individuals.

At all events, the rise of the birth-rate was to have notable repercussions. As ancient zones of habitation became more and more populous the tempo of life increased. Those teeming masses required living-space; and, not finding it in Christian Europe, they naturally looked farther afield. They swelled the ranks of the Reconquista in Spain, joined the armies of the crusade, or colonized the Baltic lands. The same cause explains the vast manpower of which the cathedral builders seem to have disposed. It was responsible too for the growth of monasticism and the huge areas covered by conventual buildings. Whatever aspect of the period we are considering, we must never lose sight of the fact that it was an age in which the Western world yielded a rich harvest of men.

Some historians remind us of the disasters and misery which must have been endured. We should, however, take care not to confuse our dates and attribute to the twelfth and thirteenth centuries what was true of an earlier period; and even then there has been some exaggeration. For example, was the celebrated famine of 1037, described by Raoul Glaber, really so terrible or so widespread as is commonly believed? Glaber, that good monk who so often saw the Devil in his cell, had a lively imagination. Besides, his narrative is not always simple affirmation; the horrid tale is sometimes qualified by a cautious phrase, e.g., "as it is said." But that is not to deny that there were famines in the twelfth and thirteenth centuries. Such calamities were unavoidable at a time when communications were bad and there were no means of transporting reserves of food quickly from one place to another. In the absence of anything like central administration, a diocese or even a whole province might well starve in consequence of the slightest drought. But the evil was most often localized, as has happened in our own day in certain occupied countries during the Second World War, and in various parts of India and China since 1945.

It is no less certain that some areas of Christendom were ravaged by disease; but, with a few exceptions,[8] those epidemics appear not to have been widespread. The plague, leprosy, epilepsy, a sort of gangrenous ergotism, and other afflictions were serious enough, especially as medicine was powerless to check them. But there was far less tuberculosis, venereal disease, and cancer than at present. If the expectation of life was shorter than it is today, particularly in consequence of infant mortality, it is equally true that the men of that period were physically strong, mentally alert, robust, and vigorous.

8.   The most terrible of these was the Black Death in 1348, of which we shall speak later.

6. FROM FEUDALISM TO MONARCHY

MEDIEVAL civilization, whose glory we are about to view, was both healthy and fertile; it also enjoyed social and political stability in a high degree. But here again we must be careful with regard to dates. A well-worn phrase like "feudal" may fairly describe the close of the barbarian epoch; for the disruption of Charlemagne's empire in the ninth and tenth centuries left a trail of confusion in the West that lasted until the balance of contending forces was restored. The same expression, however, is quite false when applied to the system that prevailed in Europe from the eleventh to the fourteenth century—an age of universal reawakening and of creative venture.

Under the barbarians, society was founded to some extent upon a twofold partition of power and even upon racial differences. I refer, of course, to the threefold classification of mankind. Over the mass of agriculturists and traders, who formed the backbone of the community, were the military and ecclesiastical castes. The first of these two had developed from the accidents of war, and later became an aristocracy, while the churchmen rested their claim to authority upon spiritual grounds alone. But such a classification, although fundamental in theory, is in fact no more than superficial. It explains the grouping and division of a people, but tells us nothing as to the sources from which the several grades were drawn, and provides no evidence of their mutual relations. Class distinctions were not at that period so well defined as they afterwards became, for instance, in France under Louis XIV. The highest ranks of the clergy were recruited from all levels of society, and nobility was accessible to anyone who could prove his worth. At the same time, we are in the presence of a coherent system wherein respective groups recognized themselves as owing certain duties to the public good rather than to private interests. This outlook is admirably summed up in the *Poème de Carité* by the Recluse of Mollieu:

> The sword says, "my office is to protect the clerks of Holy Church and those who win us our daily bread."

There, in that harmony of three distinct elements, we have the ideal formula of society: one class devoted to prayer, another to arms, and a third to manual labour.

Command lay with the sword, as in the dark years when all men lived in dread, when central government had proved itself unequal to the maintenance of order and public safety. One after another the invading hordes— Lombards, Arabs, Normans, and Hungarians—had swept down upon the civilized world. The weak took refuge with the strong; the humble begged protection from the great. Thus there had evolved those social strata within which power was exactly proportioned to the protector's efficiency. The system grew; its customs became legal institutions, and the consequent feudal regime was to be the mainstay of Christendom long after its original cause had vanished.

This regime was based upon a twofold relationship affecting not only the person, but also landed property, which at that time was the only possession of real value. A man in fear of his life entrusted himself to some more powerful neighbour who could and would defend him. Hence the dependence of the weak upon the strong, called "vassalage." The vassal put himself at the disposal of his "suzerain" or overlord, who gave him in return that measure of security which the central authority could no longer guarantee. The suzerain, in his turn, became dependent on another yet more powerful, and the result was a kind of hierarchy, a pyramid, as it were, based upon material security and personal obligation. Theoretically there might still be "free men" with the king alone as suzerain; but in practice there were very few of these.

In order to protect his land the vassal surrendered its legal ownership to his overlord, retaining only the usufruct for himself and for his heirs; but such was not the only means whereby land was brought within the feudal system. With a view to ensuring his vassal's loyalty, the overlord sometimes gave him a "benefice" as reward for his service. At first the benefice was granted for life, but it soon became hereditary. Generally speaking, all land enjoyed the same status, irrespective of who was the original owner; it was a status of dependence, something between legal ownership and

usufruct, which is described by the word "fief."[9] There were, however, exceptions known as "freeholds"; a certain number of these existed in the south
of France, but in the north they were few and far between. One such was the
famous "Kingdom of Yvetot."

This subordination of person and property affected only the upper
classes, those whose duty involved military service. But among the rural
masses, who formed the vast majority of the population, there was likewise
a hierarchic organization known as seignory, which is often, though erro-
neously, identified with feudalism. Its origins go back to the great estates
of the later Roman Empire, or to those which came into being at the time
of the barbarian invasions, and it had to do with the occupation of land. A
landowner divided his property into two parts, one of which, the "reserve,"
was cultivated for his immediate use; the other was let out to tenants, free-
men or serfs. Whoever dwelt within the lordship had not only to pay rent
for his land, but also to put in a certain amount of unpaid work—sowing,
reaping, carting, etc.—on the owner's reserve. Finally, he had to pay for the
compulsory use of the lord's mill, kiln, winepress, and forge. Seignory, in
fact, completed the subordination of property by extending it to cover the
lowest strata of society; and though distinct from feudalism in origin and
essence, it dovetailed therewith, because every noble, were he suzerain or
vassal, was at the same time a landowner.

There was a personal hierarchy, too, within the limits of the lordship;
for the peasants were juridically subject to the owner, and their dependence gradually received official recognition as the practice of "immuni-
ty" increased little by little from the ninth century onwards. Even the most
powerful sovereigns, like Charlemagne, found it suited them to govern
through successive grades of officials. The monarch exercised immediate
control, at least in theory, over his most powerful subjects, under whom
were others claiming obedience in turn from their subordinates down to the
humblest vassal and even the very peasants. The scheme was in the long run

---

9. Latin *foedum*, from German *Vieh* meaning "cattle" and then "fortune." Cf. *pecunia*
from *pecus*.

disastrous, for the central government was soon rendered powerless by this widespread delegation of authority; but so well did it accord with the spirit of the age, that it was the guiding principle of almost every king. High officials and military leaders had been allowed to act within the boundaries of their jurisdiction as if their territories were their own benefice, and they had in fact annexed them outright. More than one sovereign, also, had granted a majority of his vassals privileges that formed part of the royal prerogative; e.g., the control of roads and bridges, the supervision of markets, the right to make police regulations, to administer justice, and even to mint coinage. A baron was thus virtually his own master inside his fief, except for those personal ties which bound him to his overlord; the state had been dissolved into a multitude of petty kingdoms.

During the twelfth century, which marks the apogee of the feudal system, we find a series of titles used to denote the various grades of personal dignity and territorial jurisdiction. Allowing for local differences, they were approximately as follows: first came knights and vavasours; above them the lords castellan, or barons who possessed fortified castles; over these again, though in an order which might vary from one locality to another, viscounts, earls, marquesses, and dukes, who governed, or were supposed to govern, the ancient administrative districts of the kingdom. At the summit was the king, the nominal suzerain of all. Between one grade and the next there were correlative duties of protection and fealty. The suzerain owed his vassal justice and assistance, and must go to his help on all occasions. A vassal owed his overlord *consilium* and *auxilium*. The first of these involved attendance at court to assist in the affairs of government and administration; the second, military service (*l'ost et la chevauchée*) and provision of troops in the event of hostilities. He was also obliged to pay four "aids," or monetary contributions when the suzerain knighted his son, married his eldest daughter, went on crusade, or was taken prisoner.

The outward sign of these mutual undertakings between overlord and vassal was an impressive ceremony obligatory upon all who, whether by grant or by inheritance, came within the feudal system. The vassal did homage in this form: kneeling before his overlord, in whose hands he placed his own, he swore to fulfil the duties of his state and acknowledged himself to be his "man." The overlord then "invested" him with his goods, stating what they comprised, and delivering some symbolic object—a clod of earth or a vine branch in the case of lay homage, the church-door key or the bell-rope in that of a religious fief.

Such, then, were the main principles of the feudal and seignorial regime which prevailed throughout most of Europe, though it varied from country to country according to such historical circumstances as the strength of royal authority or the personal position of the overlord. As regards France, the feudal link was much stronger in the north, where the power of the Capetians was an ever-present reality, than in the south, where it was often little more than nominal. In Germany, the great feudal barons were not seldom more powerful than the emperors themselves. In England, on the other hand, feudalism scarcely existed so long as the monarchy remained supreme; and even the restriction of its authority left the baronage without exclusive right of control.

These differences enable us to understand that, if there were inherent flaws in the system, it was no less subject to external attack. All the same, it was an efficient piece of machinery, well suited to the economic framework and to the deepest human aspirations. It was rooted in the land, and closely linked both with man's personal dignity and his political significance—two factors of decisive importance in an age of violence. Its more serious defects were twofold. In the first place, if a single unit, at any stage of the pyramid, failed in his duty, there was immediate danger of anarchy; and secondly, if uncontrolled passions led to a clash between two vassals, and their common suzerain could not or would not call his men to order, there was war. While these defects were overlooked in face of more ominous threats, e.g., from the Normans or Hungarians, it remained true that unemployed soldiers were very dangerous masters.

Between the years 1050 and 1350 the stability of the feudal system underwent constant change. On the seigniorial level the "reserve" tended to diminish; money took the place of personal service; and authority became less extensive. In certain countries new forces sprang up in opposition to feudal custom, principally in the towns, the development of which had been interrupted by the great invasions. Huddled within their walls, urban populations had lagged behind those rural communities whose prosperity had been fostered by the landowners. A movement originating in Italy early in the twelfth century, and known as the "urban revolution," was connected with a phenomenal growth of free towns. About two hundred years before that date, Venice, availing herself of the internal dissensions of Islam and the troubles of Byzantium, had built a navy, and had steadily increased her wealth. Genoa and Pisa had taken a new lease of life, capturing Sardinia from the Muslims in 1015; and the great crusading movement towards the close of the eleventh century hastened the general reawakening of the West. From Lombardy, Tuscany, Provence, and Marseilles the urban revolution spread to Champagne and Flanders, up the Rhone valley to the Rhine, and across the Brenner Pass to the Danubian provinces. Industry began to flourish, and with it the great commercial centres of Ghent, Ypres, and Arras. Fairs were established at Messina, Lille, Cologne, and Mainz, as well as in the neighbourhood of Paris, at Beaucaire, and at Lyons. The consequences of this marvellous prosperity were easy to foresee; they had already become apparent in Italy, where the inhabitants of fortified cities and townships were opposed both to ecclesiastical and to secular overlords. All these places became nests of individualism, of liberty, and of law as against the authoritarian feudal hierarchy which relied on force. The belfry frowned across at the castle keep, while city councils, who incidentally despised the common folk, hurled defiance at the nobility. The towns of Italy, of France, and of Flanders were in the grip of a vast movement towards emancipation; and the urban revolution, which was economic in origin, became political and communal.

But this was not the only danger to the feudal system. In countries where royal authority was either remote, as in Italy, or limited by election, as in Germany, the barons managed to sustain their power, but only at the cost of compromise with the towns, which had themselves meanwhile become overlords. Elsewhere, especially in France, the situation was different. As the Capetian sovereigns became conscious of their strength, and their purpose more clearly defined, they grew more and more intolerant of opposition

from the feudal barons. They insisted upon two points in particular—their
right to dispense justice and, later, to control finance. Having resolved to
establish their authority upon a firmer basis than the hierarchic system,
the French kings enlisted the support of their people, who desired nothing
more than central government. Above all, they won approval from the middle classes, whose interests coincided with their own and who would one
day provide the monarchy with a civil service.

The urban revolution and the strengthening of royal authority contributed to the revival of jurisprudence. The old regime of force was gradually
displaced by those principles of law which grew from commercial intercourse between the towns. It was these same principles that the kings of
France sought to impose; and indeed the middle-class jurists exercised an
important influence under the great Capetians. The substitution of monarchical for feudal government between the eleventh and thirteenth centuries
reflects a profound change in the approach to human relationships.

7. THE KINGDOMS OF THE EARTH

WE have now described the framework within which the Church had to
function, and it is impossible to understand her story without reference
thereto. The dignity of her position brought the supernatural body into
close contact with the institutions and individual elements of secular society. Her Master's kingdom might not be of this world; but its frontiers
marched with those of earthly realms. Their subjects were members of her
flock; and since all baptized persons were numbered in that fold, she could
not be indifferent to the forms of civil government. The secular and ecclesiastical history of this period are so closely interwoven as to be sometimes
almost indistinguishable.

About 1050 France, England, Germany, and Italy formed, as it were, the
central piers of Christendom. During the next three hundred years all but
the last of these four western territories achieved a political integration that
gave promise of their future glory. Italy long remained in a state of wellnigh

hopeless confusion. The period in question represents a splendid epoch of French history under the "direct Capetians"[10] and may be summarized as follows. In 987, Hugh, Duke of France, later surnamed Capet, had adopted the style and insignia of royalty together with the overlordship of fifteen feudal principalities, several of which were far more powerful than himself; yet by 1300 France was a united kingdom whose monarch commanded universal respect. It was the good fortune of the Capets to produce a line of extraordinarily able sovereigns who, with the possible exception of Louis VII, were endowed with an abundance of common sense and far-sightedness. Their realistic outlook is clear also from the fact that they turned a deaf ear to the calls of overweening ambition and concentrated their efforts upon France alone. They took care to impose the principle of hereditary succession, and were thereby enabled to establish a dynasty whose male line continued unbroken from 987 to 1328. A homely attachment to their family possessions helped to convince them that the kingdom was their primary concern. France must be consolidated and, with her capital at Paris, become the nucleus of those semi-independent fiefs. Keenly aware of their great mission, they adapted the feudal system to their needs, exacting homage from all, but doing it to none. At the same time, they rejected the more dangerous elements of the regime, especially the multiplication of fiefs by legal inheritance. Accordingly they bequeathed the entire kingdom to their eldest sons, while the younger were provided for by grants of appanages.

As landowners, as feudal overlords, and as kings the "direct Capetians" had a single interest—to build France. Their history falls into five distinct periods, each of which produced an outstanding figure: Hugh Capet (987–96), Robert the Pious (996–1031), and Henri I (1031–1060) neglected the heart and centre of the realm for the sake of outlying territories. Henri, indeed, went so far as to curtail the Crown lands by conferring Burgundy upon one of his brothers, a princeling who, after his defeat by the Duke

---

10. The house of Capet was represented by three families: the "direct Capetians," Hugh Capet to Charles IV (987–1328); the Valois, Philip VI to Henry III (1328–1589); the Bourbons, Henry IV to Louis Philippe (1589–1848).

of Normandy at Mortemer in 1054, made himself even more ridiculous by
trying to substantiate his title to Lorraine upon the grounds that he was heir
of Charlemagne!

Philip I (1060–1108) adopted an entirely different policy. This monstrous, miserly glutton was at pains to steer his little kingdom clear of those
rocks upon which so many of his countrymen were then meeting with disaster in England, Sicily, Portugal, Syria, or Palestine. He strove, rather, to unite
the fair lands of France as well as to strengthen his authority. His son Louis
the Fat (1108–1137) was the reincarnation of his father. Pasty-faced and
of gigantic stature, he was obese in early manhood; but his tireless energy
earned for him the nickname "Sleepless." During his reign the kingdom was
swept clear of brigand-chiefs; the foundations of stable government were
laid by Suger; and the royal power rested secure on popular good will.

The matrimonial whims of young Louis VII (1137–1180) were a source
of anxiety to the State; for he allowed his divorced wife, Eleanor of Aquitaine, to carry an enormous dowry to the English Crown. But in spite of this
embarrassment, the French monarchy was now too strong to be imperilled,
as became apparent on the accession of Philip Augustus (1180–1223), that
handsome prince, whose physical beauty made so deep an impression on the
masses, and whose reign inaugurated the noblest traditions of the house of
Capet. The royal domains were increased threefold by the incorporation of
Vermandois, Valois, Normandy, Maine, Anjou, and Poitou; the leading feudal families were broken up, forced into submission, and allied by marriage
with younger members of the Royal House; while the Anglo-German coa-
lition was smashed in 1214 at the battle of Bouvines. Such were the more
important consequences of a reign that must be counted among the most
glorious in French history.

The short rule of Louis VIII (1223–1226) forms, as it were, a corollary to that of his predecessor. It was during these years that the Capetians
extended their sway over the south of France, a solid advantage of far greater
importance than dreams of foreign conquest in England and Italy.

We come at last to the climax of our period, to that pure flame which
soared, from 1226 to 1270, before the astonished gaze of France and of the

world; a man in whom was realized the triple concept of Christian, king, and warrior. The prestige of St. Louis, which dominated the whole European stage, was literally supernatural. Though he never forgot the duties of his exalted station, he was able to reconcile them with the Christian view of politics. He worked hard in the interests of the Crown; and if he called a halt to the conquests of his father and grandfather, he consolidated their gains, strengthened the monarchy on a basis of improved administration, and, above all, left his subjects in no doubt that Capet's rule spelled justice for all men.

The descendants of St. Louis were destined to perfect his achievement in the sphere of government; but they could not preserve untarnished the splendour wherewith he had covered his escutcheon. Philip III, "the Hardy" (1270–1285), carried the organization of his dominions one step further. Philip IV, "the Fair" (1285–1314), was a fine athlete, a living statue; but his heart was of stone, and worse. It was under him that the sovereign's domain became at last co-extensive with the kingdom, that the drive to the east began, and that administrative reforms made vital progress. But his glory is obscured by a succession of deplorable events which could not fail to lower posterity's esteem for the last of Hugh Capet's immediate and great descendants. The brief reigns of his three sons, Louis X, "the Quarrelsome" (1314–1316), Philip V, "the Tall" (1316–1322), and Charles IV, "the Fair" (1322–1328), appeared even to their contemporaries as warnings or as punishment from Heaven.

Considered, therefore, as a whole, the "direct Capetians" accomplished much. They not only created the body-politic of France, but also inspired her with a fundamental sense of justice founded upon law and administered by the supreme authority. From the complex of feudalism they had forged a nation. To them, in large measure, France owed her position at the head of European culture, as "the oven," to quote a contemporary author, "in which the bread of all the Western world is baked." Though less advanced, from the economic point of view, than Italy or Flanders, she stood intellectually as well as geographically at the cross-roads. She was the privileged home of art and of ideas, and therefore of Christian initiative.

While the French kingdom was evolving under the guidance of a strong central government whose power increased from reign to reign, her two Christian neighbours followed a very different course. In 1066 William the Bastard and his "international brigades," armed with the dreaded battle-axe, set sail across the Channel, landed at Pevensey near Hastings, destroyed the Anglo-Saxon rule by slaying the Pretender Harold, and founded a new dynasty of his own. William I (1066–1087) ascended the throne of England by right of conquest. He ruled accordingly. Obedience was required of everyone alike; all property was registered in Domesday Book for the convenience of the Exchequer; but there was no racial conflict between victors and vanquished, for all were subject to the king.

This order did not survive the monarch's death. He made the fatal error of dividing his possessions among his sons; and England paid for his mistake with close on seventy years of unstable government, throughout the reigns of William II, "Rufus" (1087–1100), Henry I, "Beauclerk" (1100–1135), and Stephen of Blois (1135–1154). The only advantage gained during that period was the enlargement of English territory by the acquisition of Plantagenet Anjou.

The situation improved with the accession of Henry II (1154–1189), a red-headed giant, fat and sensual but unusually intelligent, who resumed and carried on the Conqueror's work. Eleanor of Aquitaine, divorced wife of Louis VII, brought him her extensive dominions; so that he held undisputed sway over territories reaching from Scotland to the Pyrenees. He might have been tempted to cross swords with the Capetian kings, but was prevented by serious difficulties with his sons, by an even more painful episode with the Church in the person of St. Thomas à Becket, and above all by the appearance of Philip Augustus on the throne of France.

After Henry's death, the sky was once more overcast. Richard Coeur de Lion (1189–1199), an improvident hero, was followed by the incompetent John "Lackland" (1199–1216), who threw away the opportunity of the Crown. England rose against the despot who had gone to war and lost his French dominions; the nobility and clergy joined forces and obliged him to sign the Great Charter (1215); while an assembly soon to be called "Parliament" admitted representatives of the upper classes to a share in government. Thereafter it was in vain that the Crown endeavoured to reassert absolute authority. The pious yet frivolous Henry III (1216–1272) attempted to do so, but managed only to rouse the opposition of his subjects who, under the leadership of Simon de Montfort, imposed upon him a more rigid system of control embodied in the Provisions of Oxford (1258). Edward I (1272–1307) saw the wisdom of recognizing an accomplished fact; he strove in concert with his people for the good of all, and even permitted them to vote their own taxes. The royal prerogative had been curtailed, but the Crown had rallied to its side those free elements that most truly represented England. The system thus inaugurated was so deeply rooted in the national consciousness, that when the worthless Edward II (1307–1327) sought to reject it, Parliament rejected him in no uncertain terms. His death marks the end of England's growth, much in advance of her contemporaries, from absolute monarchy to parliamentary government.

Wise statesmanship, an innate sense of what is possible and what impossible, characterized the great French and English monarchs, though with different results. It was sadly lacking in the rulers of that Italian-German compound known as the Holy Roman and Germanic Empire. Instead of facing squarely the very serious problems which confronted them, even in Germany—the barbarian menace on their frontiers, and the ambition of feudal lords ever on the watch for an opportunity to make themselves petty kings—the emperors wasted time dreaming of Italy and her boundless wealth, of Charlemagne's vanished might, and even of worldwide dominion. But their foundations were too weak to uphold such vast designs. The imperial crown had been hereditary since the death of Henry II in 1024, which meant that they were ultimately dependent upon the great lords who begrudged them obedience. Italy, torn by conflicting passions, where the papal power was steadily increasing and where the Normans were establishing a kingdom by force of arms, was no asset; it was a liability which obliged them to disperse their forces. All the Germanic emperors had to contend with the same difficulties; all alike suffered disappointment.

Their chief problem was that of relations with the papacy,[11] and it was
in conflict with the spiritual arm that the empire exhausted her strength.
Henry IV (1050–1106), Frederick Barbarossa (1152–1190), Henry VI
(1190–1197), and Frederick II (1218–1250) all had ability, and at least
two of them were men of genius; but each in turn squandered his resources
upon too widespread and extravagant enterprises. Germany and Italy were
subject to alternations of rigid discipline and bloodstained anarchy, from
which a few great cities might derive some advantage, but which, in the
long run, proved disastrous. The Hohenstaufen dynasty ended with Conrad
and the tragic Conradin (1268); during the Great Interregnum of twenty-
three years the empire had no ruler. Several great families tried and failed
to restore peace and order in their country and to re-establish succession
to the throne; but neither the Austrian Hapsburgs, Rudolph (1273–1291)
and Albert I (1298–1308), nor the house of Luxembourg in the person of
Henry VII (1308–1313), nor the Bavarian Louis IV (1314–1347) could
achieve their purpose. The middle of the fourteenth century found the
Holy Roman Empire in a deplorable state of weakness that was to endure
for some considerable time.

8. UNITED EUROPE

THESE states whose growth, as we have seen, had resulted in such different
forms, could not live side by side and yet in isolation; they were enemies or
allies as circumstances might dictate. At that time, as in our own day, there
were wars due to the reaction of home politics upon international affairs.
During the twelfth and thirteenth centuries there was an earlier version of
the Hundred Years War between France and England. It was caused by the
French kings' refusal to recognize England's claim to half the soil of France,
and was contested no less bitterly than the great conflict of the fourteenth
and fifteenth centuries. Between France and the Germanic Empire relations

---

11. This question will be discussed at length in Chapter V.

were on the whole more friendly; but there were periods of violent antagonism. Thus in 1214, Otto IV, supported by John "Lackland" and some rebellious French nobles, attempted to destroy the power of Philip Augustus, who defeated them at Bouvines.

Externally, then, Europe in the twelfth and thirteenth centuries seemed much as today. Their wars were not fought upon so vast a scale as ours; but if we consider the dimensions of the world at that time, they will appear proportionately great. There was, however, one fundamental difference between international relations then and now. Hostility between two kings or princes represented no dramatic clash of whole peoples to decide their destiny. There was certainly an element of patriotism, as was shown by the enthusiasm of the French at Bouvines; but nationalism had not yet endowed war with its modern relentlessness. Europe might be sundered politically, and sometimes torn by bitter strife; but Europe remained one. This truth dominates the whole international scene at the period under review. In spite of intermittent antagonisms, that unity was manifest in many ways; for three hundred years Europe sailed the seas of mutual understanding, a thing which she had never done since the end of the *Pax Romana*, and which she would never do again. The brutal game of politics had not yet blinded Europeans to their being members of a family, to their representing a unique standard of culture. Of that they were keenly though subconsciously aware, and without recourse to such terms as "United States of Europe" or "the European Community."

There are innumerable evidences of this truth. Even in time of war, it never occurred to the governments of belligerent countries to arrest enemy aliens and throw them into concentration camps. Foreign travel was not hedged about with ridiculous complications of passports, exchange permits, and other vexatious documents with which the twentieth century is blessed. Pilgrims could visit any country to pray to their favourite saint without government interference, and even without the necessity of government protection. The passage of enormous armies, like those of the crusades, not infrequently caused minor "incidents"; but that was only because particular groups of military footpads overstepped the bounds of moderation. On the

general principle of free passage no government entertained the slightest
doubt. War did not prevent merchants travelling with their commodities
to the international fairs; French and Lombard bankers were still free to
exchange letters of credit. If hostilities did any harm to trade, it was due
simply to the hazards of war and not to any government decree that forbade
"trading with the enemy."

On numerous occasions men from different lands united in a common
enterprise. The crusades are an outstanding example. French and English
fought side by side with Spaniards and Portuguese to liberate the Iberian
Peninsula; Germans and Hungarians joined hands to penetrate the wilds of
Transylvania; while Polish troops reinforced the German armies. Moreover,
we find princes or cities seeking arbitration rather than recourse to arms,
and settling their differences under the guidance of some great saint or of
the Pope.

The essential oneness of Europe is apparent in every sphere of activity. Italians, French, and Englishmen succeeded one another on the throne
of St. Peter. The great monastic orders transferred their subjects from one
country to another regardless of international frontiers. A Cistercian statute provides that in the election of superiors no account must be taken of
nationality. Bishops and abbots were often complete strangers to the community or diocese which they were called upon to govern; thus St. Anselm,
a Piedmontese, was Abbot of Bec in Normandy, and then Archbishop
of Canterbury; St. Hugh, a Savoyard, became Bishop of Lincoln; and an
Englishman, John of Salisbury, occupied the see of Chartres.

An equal cosmopolitanism is found in the domain of thought and culture. No one dreamed of forbidding a scholar to teach in a particular country
just because he was a foreigner, and there were many such in the University
of Paris. Sigier of Brabant was a Belgian, Albert the Great a German, St.
Thomas Aquinas and St. Bonaventure Italians. The same was true of their
pupils: at Paris there were English, German, Scandinavian, Portuguese, even
Byzantine and Levantine students; and the exclusive use of Latin, an international language, enabled those heterogeneous assemblies to understand the
master's words. In consequence, Europe possessed a fund of philosophical

and theological learning, as well as a common literature, in which all countries shared, upon whose treasures all were free to draw. Intellectual activity was orientated to a single end, it had both meaning and order.

So too with the arts. Master-craftsmen found a welcome far from their own lands; Frenchmen worked in England, in Hungary, and in Spain. Stone-masons plied their trade across the whole Catholic world, so that their works were constantly subject to innumerable and subtle influences. Modern man, prone to imagine that the exchange of ideas began with the invention of mechanical transport, finds it difficult to grasp the rich achievement of an earlier age.

9. CHRISTENDOM

THE meaning of all this is plain: there were fewer subdivisions of society than today. Christian Europe was mindful of her unity, because all men were subject to a universal order. Now this organic whole, inspired by common principles, owed its existence to a single cause—the profound influence of the Faith and the overriding authority of the Church.

The Christian world had profited by her manifold triumph in the temporal domain. During the years of peril, the Church had played so decisive a part in determining the fate of Europe, that no one dreamed of refusing her obedience. She had won recognition for her teaching as the very basis of civilization, and her representatives were active everywhere. She was clearly the guide of nations, for it was she who imparted to mankind the notion of their common destiny; in proclaiming them sons of God redeemed by the Precious Blood of Christ she convinced them that they were brothers one of another, raised above the conflict of private interests.

But there was more than solidarity; there was vitality and the consciousness of human endeavour. Each man knew that God had set him down in a particular station of life, where he had a definite task to fulfil with a perfectly clear end in view. Each man, therefore, had his appointed place, and enjoyed the certainty that his labour formed part of a much greater and

transcendent work. The universe appeared like some vast but single entity
foreseen and ordained by a superior Power; nothing, therefore, could be
trivial or in vain. It is indeed no small advantage for a society to know its
destination.

Thus for three hundred years the Augustinian thesis strove to attain
actuality. The "City of the World" was merely a preparation for the "City
of God," and we find the two united in that fresco at Santa Maria Novella.
All the baptized constitute on earth a living and fraternal body, enlivened by
the same principles, linked in a common effort. In future we shall designate
this body by its proper name and call it "Christendom."

The first and fundamental meaning of that term appeared towards the
end of the ninth century when the aged Pope John VIII, in a moment of
rare insight and in face of dire peril, tried to inspire the Christian world with
a sense of its common interests. *Christianitas* had hitherto been used in an
abstract sense, to signify the Faith of Christ, or the fact of being a Christian.
By applying it to a concrete entity, the temporal society of mankind, the
Pope had given it a new and deeper meaning.

From the eleventh century onwards the term was in current usage. Henceforward we find frequent reference to Christendom, to the dangers which
beset it, and to its obligations. A similar meaning attached to such phrases
as "the Christian People," "the Christian Community," "the Christian Brotherhood." One great pontiff after another enriched its significance. Gregory
VII first used it to denote the sum total of those territories where Christians
dwelled; in his view, wherever the Cross of Christ was planted, there is Christendom. Urban II, preaching the crusade, emphasized the unity of Christendom, and directed it as a single body towards a shining goal. Alexander III
introduced the juridical sense, which requires peaceful relations between all
baptized peoples in the interests of the Christian world. Finally, Innocent III
completed the idea of Christendom, which he sought to make a true society
of Christian states, an "Internationale" of the Cross, with the Gospel precepts
as law and Christ's Vicar upon earth as the sole fount of authority.

How then should Christendom be described at the moment of its full
flower in the twelfth century? According as we look at it from the viewpoint

36   of heaven or of earth, it has two definitions, each complementary of the other. In a broad sense, Christendom is the whole body of mankind redeemed
by Christ, aspiring to His kingdom; in a narrower sense, it is the Christian
society living on earth and engaged in temporal activities which have their
fulfilment in Almighty God. Christendom, then, is a people, a race born of
Christ, nourished upon Him, quenching its thirst with His Blood. It is a
"nation," a community, confined by no geographical framework; a community whose members feel at home. It is a society, *populus Christianus*, where
all social and professional inequalities should be resolved in a single harmony. It is, in fact, a fatherland, for whom each member must be ready to sacrifice his life. The religious Orders were its international brigades. Palestine,
as Étienne Gilson has so aptly remarked, "was to be the Alsace-Lorraine of
Christendom." "Christendom" is not to be identified with any particular territory; Christians are fully aware that our Lord's message is addressed to all
alike, that Christendom is virtually worldwide, and that the term cannot be
used exclusively of Europe, or even of the East or West. Nevertheless, human
frailty is such that only part of the earth has seen the good grain flourish,
that part which is at a given moment Christian and which must therefore
be strengthened and defended.[12] The frontiers of Christendom are defined
by baptism: wherever there are baptized Christians, there is Christendom.
Differences arising from schism and heresy could never prevail against this
deep-rooted feeling. Even the insults which Byzantium was to hurl against
the Holy See would not deter the popes from assisting the Greeks against
the Turks. The remotest communities of heretical Christians, buried in the
heart of Asia, were looked upon as brothers by the sons of Christendom;
and St. Louis himself dispatched ambassadors to the Mongol Nestorians.

Such, then, was the concept which gave to the baptized their sense of
fundamental unity, an ideal which had never ceased to haunt the Western

---

12. We find a similar idea in the conception which the Communists make today of the
role of the U.S.S.R. For them, too, the Marxist revolution is international and must
end by embracing the whole world; but since here and now only the U.S.S.R. is fully
Communist, she must be considered as the Promised Land, the pattern of all Communist states.

mind since the Roman Empire collapsed. Charlemagne and Otto, each in turn, had relied upon it for the fulfilment of their grandiose designs; but with the eleventh century there began a noticeable change. The Holy Roman and Germanic Empire could no longer serve as the framework of these ambitions; there were important areas to which its authority did not extend, nor was it possible to perpetuate the fiction that West and East were parts of a single whole. But if the empire was no longer one, Christendom was so beyond a doubt; and in place of a world subject to imperial rule there was substituted a new idea—the commonwealth of Christian peoples with the Church as its governor.

The Church, however, was distinct from Christendom; as mistress and teacher she could not be identified with that body which it was her duty to instruct, to guide, and to control. Considered even as the sum total of baptized persons, she must not be confused with Christendom; for membership of Christ's mystical Body and membership of a temporal institution have different ends. The Church and Christendom are two Christian societies in close alliance; but the purpose of one is to secure its members in possession of eternal life, and of the other to help them towards the attainment of an earthly goal. As a member of Holy Church, the Christian is subject to ecclesiastical jurisdiction; but as a unit of Christendom, he is ruled by secular authority.

The distinction is clear-cut, and was universally recognized. It is apparent, for example, in the phrase "Christian people, kings, and clergy"; though confusion was always possible—and sometimes tempting. The Church may not be *identical with* Christendom, but she it is who furnishes those principles upon which Christendom is based. Do away with the Church, and Christendom is no longer conceivable. Moreover, if the *ultimate* goal of temporal society is supernatural, that society could not be independent of the Church which guards the supernatural treasury. "Christendom," says Jean Rupp, "is not the Church considered as a hierarchy, but it owes its very being to the Church"[13]; and therein lies the root of all those troubles to which the period was prey.

---

13. *L'idée de Chrétienté dans la pensée pontificale*, 1939.

We shall discover a tendency to confuse "Christendom" with "the Church." Instead of allowing each to operate in its respective sphere, human interests came to regard them as synonymous. In their anxiety to strengthen the force of Christian principles and to impose the Christian order upon men, churchmen too frequently stepped down from the spiritual to the temporal plane. The fundamental distinction between the City of God and the City of the World was more or less forgotten; it was believed, or pretended, or at any rate devoutly hoped, that ecclesiastical interference in the secular domain would bring about on earth a foretaste of celestial order, a "theocratic Utopia" as Maritain has described it.

Utopia indeed; for the dream, splendid as it may have been, could not come true, and there was a rude awakening. The Kingdom of God is not of this world, the stain of sin mars all man's endeavour here below. But the fact remains, so lofty a conception raised whole generations above themselves, deepened the significance of Christian life, and left behind imperishable monuments. Can that be rightly called a dream which wrought so much? Are the great achievements of mankind aught but Utopias realized by determination, sacrifice, and faith?

CHAPTER II

Faith the Foundation of Society

1. "DYED IN HIS BLOOD"

THE structure of medieval society rested upon the Christian faith. To lose sight of that truth leads to a misunderstanding of the whole period. Faith was the cornerstone; religion exerted an influence upon the minds of men as something absolute, which no one called in question. There was no trace of indifference, still less of atheism; from the lowest to the highest, society *believed*. The twentieth century finds it difficult to grasp that fact and the consequences which followed, in every department of life, upon submission to supernatural claims.

The Church had managed to preserve the light of faith throughout the barbarian epoch. It was the only comfort, the only guide, the only hope of civilization at a time when Europe lay drowned in blood and intellectual darkness. Let us be frank: the field was as yet untilled, as yet intermingled with the tares of savagery and superstition. The best still grew together with the worst. One need scarcely remark that the transition from one era to another did not at once effect a change in this state of affairs. The faith of the Middle Ages, the faith of St. Bernard, St. Francis of Assisi, or St. Louis, did not spring fully armed from the chaos of the year 1000, like Athena from the head of Zeus. It long retained those elements of crudity and violence which the Church unceasingly opposed. From beginning to end of the three centuries with which we have to deal, the story of the Faith is by no means one of static calm or unalloyed success. It is a tale of effort, evolution, and not infrequently of storm. Hence its vigour.

A general picture of medieval religion, therefore, reveals sharp chronological divisions. At the beginning of the eleventh century it was still largely selfish, and not always exemplary. That must appear inevitable when we remember that society had for generations been deprived of security and even of structure. It was not long, however, before a change set in. While the feudal system was being consolidated and monarchies were being born, the Church both purified herself and increased her influence upon the souls of men largely through the Cluniac and Gregorian reforms. By the twelfth century society was fully organized, and the Church was seen in all her glory: the religious Orders had begun to flourish, she had terminated the Quarrel of Investitures, her authority was on the way to supremacy, she was the guide of speculative inquiry, and the cathedrals had begun to rise. The Faith itself attained new depths as its quality improved; and St. Bernard represents the climax of an epoch which was brought to a close by Pope Innocent III. At the same time, however, there were heard discordant sounds to mar the beauty of such harmony, and disquieting cracks appeared in the social edifice. Such were the birth of nationalism, the failure of the crusades, an intellectual ferment, and a number of heretical undercurrents. The Church counter-attacked with the mendicant Orders, the *Summa* of St. Thomas, and the Inquisition; but she was obliged to relinquish her hold upon certain parts of that immense domain which she had previously ruled. She remained all-powerful in the realms of art and private life, but not in those of politics and material civilization. The faith of her children, too, was in obscure but painful labour, heralding the crisis of the fourteenth century.

Thus for three hundred years there is clear evidence of evolution; but this did not affect the unanimity of faith, which was never called in question. The Faith was a decisive factor in every sphere of human activity; and nothing was done on earth which had not God as its end, its means, its witness, or its judge. Medieval civilization was wholly consecrate.

Proof of an undivided faith is manifold, and will be found in every chapter of this work. I refer to those saints and Christian heroes, men and women, for whom love of Christ was the sole reality which gave life meaning, and which sometimes required the sacrifice of life itself on His behalf.

There is also the evidence of those who bore witness to Christ although their conduct was an insult to His Precious Blood. Such was the brutal soldier who, having divorced and remarried, confronted a bishop, sword in hand, and cried: "Give me absolution or I'll kill you!" When the prelate merely stretched out his neck and said "Strike!" he was answered in these extraordinary words: "No, I don't like you well enough to send you straight to heaven!" For all his violence and for all his sins, that man *believed*.

An example of this kind disposes of the hackneyed argument that the Christian faith cannot have been so unanimously and so firmly entertained, since it was betrayed at every step by man's perversity. Nothing could be more absurd than to regard the Middle Ages as a heavenly period of universal grace and gentleness. Men remained human even after baptism; but in the very act of sin they *recognized* the sin, for their eyes were ever on more lofty principles. This respect for established hierarchies is the basis of world order. For all his monstrous iniquities, his more or less superstitious credulity, and his doctrine of cheap salvation, medieval man was on the royal road of Christianity, because he was humble before God and had unshakable confidence in the Redemption. No one at that period could have foreseen the major heresy of today, which is not to fight against God but simply to ignore Him, to think and behave as if He did not exist. In those days God was far from dead; He was very much alive.

And so the Faith was part and parcel of the age. It shed a peaceful light over civilization, a light that was nothing else than Christian hope; it underlay the remarkable vitality to which I have already alluded; and it was in large measure responsible for an increase of the population, as well as for much creative energy. Believing firmly in Almighty God and in His providence, man was courageous, enterprising, ready to take risks. There is nothing gloomy about medieval culture; it radiates joy and a spirit of bold originality. A contemporary poet, Eustache Deschamps, gives us the reason in a lovely line which occurs as the refrain of a ballad: "I hold God made all for the best...." There you have that tranquillity and sublime confidence which alone could have produced the cathedrals and crusades.

Now is the time God comes to look for us

With arms outstretched; we are dyed in His Blood.

These two lines of Ruteboeuf, a contemporary of St. Louis, apply not only to the crusaders, but to the whole of medieval society, which knew that God seeks man in everything, that Jesus is King of Kings, and that every man, be he never so wretched, is dyed in the Precious Blood of Christ.

2. THE SUPERNATURAL AND ITS BOUNDS

FIRM faith entails an attitude towards knowledge and scientific methods which it is necessary to appreciate in order properly to understand those factors which may well appear as shocking aberrations. We of the twentieth century, even those of us who are Christians, live in an atmosphere of scientific demonstration. We are penetrated with the idea that all things are governed by natural laws; we think in terms of the principle of causality. Now medieval man had quite a different outlook. Granted God's existence and almighty power, earthly phenomena follow human logic only in so far as God permits and does not intervene to change the course of events; and because it is certain that the ultimate explanation of life is supernatural and lies beyond our ken, it is not surprising that mystery should obtrude at every point, that the supernatural should be manifest in everything. How different a mentality from ours![1] "The visible rests on the invisible, the knowable on the unknowable." Those words sum up the medieval mind, explaining in particular its "credulity" which has been found so disconcerting. Yet long before Baudelaire, our ancestors of the twelfth and thirteenth centuries looked on the world and all that is therein as a foreshadowing of heaven.

---

1.   There were some, e.g., Roger Bacon, who asked questions in terms analagous to our own and recognized the existence of natural laws. I shall have more to say about them later on. (Volume 2, Chapter VIII.)

Let me take an example, the attitude of a medieval Christian towards miracles. Whenever we are told that a miracle has taken place, our first inclination is to doubt, pending a critical examination of the facts. In the Middle Ages it was not so. The Church, however, was by no means indifferent to the veracity of witnesses or to the accuracy of what they reported, and we have records of several miracles investigated by order of the religious authorities. Nor did the more learned theologians ignore the element of danger in a popular faith founded upon miraculous occurrences. Thus St. Thomas Aquinas considered miracles as *signs* rather than as *proofs* of faith. It is no less true, on the other hand, that in the vast majority of cases men accepted the prodigy without question, and welcomed it as one more convincing proof of God's care for His creatures.

In such an atmosphere it was not unnatural that miracles should abound, and there were frequent apparitions of our Lord, of His blessed Mother, and of the saints. Further, it is possible to trace a connection between these miracles and current forms of devotion. We shall see, for instance, that one of the characteristics of medieval piety was devotion to the Humanity of Christ, and, as a corollary of this, adoration of the Sacred Host, in which Catholic dogma recognizes the Real Presence of the Incarnate Word. Hence it is not surprising that there occurred during the Middle Ages a number of Eucharistic miracles. In 1229, during Mass at Sant' Ambrogio in Florence, a drop of the Precious Blood which had been left at the bottom of the chalice floated to the top of the ablution water and took on the *accidents* of blood. At Bolsena, in 1263, there was a priest whose mind was troubled during Mass by doubts as to the Real Presence. He had just broken the host when he saw blood flow from it, stain the corporal, and trickle from the altar. Pope Urban IV appointed St. Bonaventure and St. Thomas Aquinas to investigate this claim; they declared it authentic, and St. Thomas described it as the "miracle of miracles."[2] It was largely responsible for the institution of the feast of Corpus Christi; while the magnificent cathedral of Orvieto

---

2. Raphael has portrayed the scene in a celebrated fresco in the Sala Eliodoro at the Vatican.

44 was built to house the linen and sacred vessels which had been the instruments of so signal a favour. Catholics may not deny those miracles which have been recognized by the Church; but the rule does not apply to all the innumerable wonders recorded by chroniclers, poets, and hagiographers.

Belief in the supernatural is certainly one of the most admirable qualities of the medieval mentality. It exalted man by assuring him he could rise above himself and attain to greatness. It caused him also to dwell in that atmosphere of poetry and wonder from which the arts derived considerable benefit. But there are limits beyond which genuine supernatural faith begins to fade. They are not easy to determine; the frontiers of divine truth and the realm of marvel are but ill defined, and at no time (least of all in the Middle Ages) have the common folk been gifted with much critical acumen.

Hence the blind acceptance of legendary tales, whose origin is often suspect and to which the Church has never lent the weight of her authority. How explain the popularity of these traditions? The reason, surely, is not far to seek; they give piquancy to the sober narrative of Holy Writ by mixing therewith an element of marvel that tickles the imagination. Scripture, for example, says nothing about our Lord's childhood; so it was exciting to tell tales of miracles which He was supposed to have performed at the age of eight or nine years, giving life to birds which He had fashioned out of clay, or changing one of His playmates into a mule for teasing Him! Again the Acts are silent about our Lady in old age; it was therefore told how an angel came to warn her of approaching death, and how all the apostles, miraculously informed, found themselves gathered at her bedside. This love of the marvellous was not seldom productive of excesses which can only be deplored (e.g., the outrageous story of a midwife present at our Lord's Nativity).

The principal source of these curious interpolations was the Apocrypha, a collection of fanciful writings which appear to have originated between the first and the fifth century. The Church wisely omitted them from her canon[3]; but they were handed on from one generation to another, through

---

3. See Daniel-Rops, *Les Évangiles de la Vierge*, 1948, and *Évangiles Apocryphes*, eds. F. Amiot and Daniel-Rops, 1953.

the agency of pilgrims and crusaders, until their contents were confused with
scriptural history. Émile Mâle[4] has shown that they exerted much influence
upon the decoration of our churches. The presence of an ox and an ass at the
Nativity, for instance, is apocryphal; so is the royalty of the Magi, and the
miracles which were believed to have occurred during the Flight into Egypt.
These texts are not false in every detail, for the Church has preserved in her
liturgy, and even in her dogma, some of the events which they relate, e.g.,
the story of Sts. Joachim and Anne, the descent of Christ into hell, and the
Assumption of our Blessed Lady. The Middle Ages, however, took little care
to distinguish what is acceptable from what is not.

The same admixture of fact and fiction is no less evident in the *Lives
of the Saints.* There is no reason to doubt that many of the saints worked
miracles, though not, perhaps, to the extent that was formerly believed; and
while Jacobus de Voragine, Dominican Archbishop of Genoa, devoted all
his leisure hours to compiling the *Golden Legend* (c. 1270), he applied no
critical test to any of his sources. It must also be remembered that a variety of
reasons called for a large measure of generosity towards the saints in respect
of their miracles. Every one of them was, so to speak, domiciled in the place
where he or she had lived and where their relics lay. The local inhabitants
had a major interest in guaranteeing that "their" saint had worked miracles
in life no less than after death; and certain *Lives* reveal all too plainly the
determination of their authors.

It was at this period also that there took root in many dioceses traditions more venerable than reliable, according to which the first bishop was
someone mentioned in the Gospel. Limoges believed its patron, St. Martial,
to have been the child whom our Lord embraced; Toulouse entertained no
doubt at all that St. Sernin had held our Lord's garments during His baptism; and Rocamadour, a celebrated place of pilgrimage, was quick to see
in its founder, St. Amadour, the publican Zacchaeus! Most remarkable was
the tradition of Compostella, whose extraordinary success appears to have
rested upon a wellnigh incredible episode in the life of the apostle St. James.

---

4.   *L'Art religieux en France an XIIe siècle* and *L'Art religieux au France au XIIIe siècle.*

46 (I say "appears to have," because I shall presently show that the celebrated pilgrimage may have been due to other and more probable causes.)

Genuine supernatural faith, popular credulity, love of the marvellous, and material interests all coalesced to play their part in certain forms of medieval piety. This fact is nowhere better illustrated than in the cult of relics. To reverence the tangible remains of God's devoted servants is perfectly wholesome and legitimate in principle. The knight carried a relic in the pommel of his sword, the traveller in a little bag strung round his neck, and crowds would flock to some venerable shrine. Why not, indeed? Such practices were in no sense *bound* to become idolatrous; it was not *inevitable* that interest in the effective properties of a relic should exclude consideration of the saint's example. But such was undoubtedly the popular *tendency*: to possess a relic was to have at one's disposal a supernatural weapon, a sovereign talisman.

From its beginning in the third century, devotion to relics had stumbled on the slope of fetishism. It had slipped still farther during the barbarian age, which was rife with tales (some deplorable, some wholly laughable) of relics faked, or stolen, or transferred from place to place.

The Middle Ages were hardly different in this respect. If a church or monastery possessed a wealth of relics, it could be sure of drawing crowds; and no stone was left unturned in order to obtain them. There were regular centres of trade in these commodities, above all Constantinople, which prospered wonderfully well; for to satisfy their wealthy customers the Orientals did not hesitate to divide the bodies of the saints! If honest dealing could not procure the relics one desired, other methods were employed. The monks of Conques, disappointed at their failure to obtain the bones of St. Vincent of Saragossa, chose one of their community to go to Agen and get himself appointed guardian of the shrine of St. Faith, which he was to break open, and bring back the body. The religious entrusted with this astonishing embassy tells us that although it took him ten years to perform, it was an unqualified success! We read also of the stratagems employed by the sailors of Bari and of Venice in their race for the port of Myra in Asia, where lay the body of St. Nicholas.

These coveted relics were of several kinds, but the most popular were naturally those of Christ Himself. The True Cross, which had been removed to Constantinople when the Arabs overran Palestine, was broken up in the course of ages, and pieces were distributed among churches, monasteries, and foreign princes, enclosed in small but richly ornamented reliquaries known as "staurotheks." The Latin Emperor Baldwin II, being short of money, sold the Crown of Thorns to St. Louis, who built for its reception that glorious "casket of glass," La Sainte-Chapelle.[5] In default of objects which had touched Our Lord, the next best were those connected with our Lady, the apostles, and the saints.

Who, then, guaranteed the authenticity of these relics? As a rule, no one; the public was often deceived. We have documentary evidence that there were exposed for veneration a reliquary containing what purported to be a piece of bread chewed by our Lord, the sponge that was offered to Him on the Cross, the baskets used at the multiplication of loaves, His swaddling clothes, some drops of His bloody sweat (at Vienne), and even one of His teeth—which, as some grave sceptics observed, was a little surprising, for His Body must have ascended into heaven whole and entire! On the other hand, it must not be forgotten that the Church frequently expressed her disapproval of these follies, denounced the so-called "pardoners" who trafficked in bogus relics, and, at the Lateran Council in 1215, forbade the veneration of any object without express permission of the ecclesiastical authorities.

It is not only God, the Blessed Virgin, and the saints who are active among men. Faith assures us that invisible beings with natures superior to our own play their part on earth. They are often mentioned in the Bible; so here was an attractive theme combining the supernatural with the marvellous, and the angels occupied an important place in popular tradition. Their existence was, of course, unquestionable. But it meant far more to the

---

5. According to some writers, the famous shroud of Christ, known as the "Holy Shroud of Turin," made its appearance early in the thirteenth century. (See Daniel-Rops: *Jésus en son temps.*)

medieval mind than to the majority of Christians of our own day; and there is no book whose miniatures, no cathedral whose sculpture and stained glass, do not portray these beautiful, winged forms. Such are the famous smiling angel on the façade of Rheims, and those on the left-hand tympanum of the Royal Porch at Chartres, flying so gracefully with Christ at His Ascension. The angels are God's messengers: they protect man in peril; they assist the dying to cross the dreaded threshold; one of them weighs good and evil; and a whole battalion is employed to escort the elect to Paradise. How comforting, therefore, it must have been to know that these excellent creatures were always ready to fight under the banner of St. Michael; for was there not the ever-present threat of Satan, with all his wicked spirits, "going about like a roaring lion seeking whom he may devour"?

Fear of the Devil is characteristic of the medieval mind, characteristic of its taste for the marvellous as well as for the supernatural. Hell is part of Catholic dogma, and as such, part of Christian belief. But here too faith may run riot. We shall have occasion later on to speak of the medieval attitude towards sin, and its emphasis upon the virtue of penance. Now fear of hell was a natural consequence of this attitude, and Émile Mâle has demonstrated with much learning the importance of the Devil in medieval psychology. It is enough to read Peter the Venerable's *De Miraculis* in order to understand the power of imagination when applied to the havoc wrought by Satan. He it is who comes to torment faithful souls, his fury proportioned to their virtue; he it is who, in hideous or alluring guise, prowls about the monasteries. As incubus, he forces virgins to his will, and procreates foul offspring in their wombs. As succubus, he tempts men vowed to God. Could one doubt the truth of this when St. Augustine[6] said that it is so? Representations of the Devil are numerous. In churches he grimaces from the capitals or assists with his fell legions at the day of doom; he appears in frescoes, in miniatures, and even on the stage.

But if Satan is found everywhere, his figure is not always repulsive; evil may lurk behind a pretty face. Woman is often associated with the Devil,

6. *De Civitate Dei*, XV. 23.

reminding us of Eve's iniquity. At Vézelay, and at Autun, we see the temptress go unrobed, save for an ineffectual streamer that seems to float upon the wind. A young man watches her, absorbed, while Satan lurks in the background.[7] Still, the Immaculate Virgin protects her faithful servants; an *Ave* saves us from the spell of Eve. If woman is a thorn in our flesh, the Rose of Heaven is not far away.

It is not to be denied that popular demonology included a substratum of fun, and the Middle Ages sometimes laughed at these unholy, monstrous forms. It has been said that whereas the twelfth century depicted demons as horrible deformities, the thirteenth saw them rather as grotesque. All the same, medieval obsession with the powers of darkness, together with an ancient heritage of primitive superstition, was responsible for much psychoneurosis among the credulous.

Superstition, indeed, had been a spiritual leprosy in the barbarian age, and it continued to menace the whole of this otherwise enlightened period. Its origins were many: remote ancestral beliefs, vestiges of Roman mythology, Druidic survivals, Germanic and even Arabic traditions. At the beginning of the eleventh century Burchard of Worms wrote a treatise against those who venerated springs and sacred trees, and who consulted magicians and spellbinders. His book remained in use for many generations. In the twelfth and thirteenth centuries there were still people who dedicated Thursday to Jupiter, who celebrated the new year in pagan fashion, who believed in the Fates and set out banquets for them. When a gale of wind shook porch and roof, it was said the "Mesnie Hellequin" passed by, the fantastic ride of the Valkyrie; and the Breton legends of Death may yet preserve some memory of ancient fears.

---

7.   Let us be fair; the Middle Ages knew full well in what handsome guise Lucifer would visit a young woman. Thus in the *Jeu d'Adam*, looking just like Don Juan, he whispers in a charming and too ready ear:
      "You are a sweet and tender thing,
      Fresher than any rose;
      You are whiter than rock-crystal,
      Or snow that falls on ice down in the vale."

Superstition, a degraded form of supernatural faith, can have dire consequences, by perpetuating the practice of witchcraft and exploiting cowardice. This is where demonology joins hands with age-long magical beliefs which the Church has never managed wholly to eradicate. Strange as it may appear, trust in the efficacy of these rites took on a new lease of life rather than decayed between the twelfth and the fourteenth century. Witch, sorceress, and poisoner were never out of work. It was firmly maintained that one could direct the powers of hell against an enemy by making a small wax image in his likeness and running it through with a bodkin; the practice is called "imitative magic." There were also stories of men changing themselves into beasts and running about the countryside intent on every sort of crime; such were lycanthropes and werewolves. Finally, it was thought that old hags flew by night to assist at Satan's sabbath!

The Church never ceased to deplore such absurdities. We find Gregory VII rebuking Haakon of Denmark for having burned some women who had been accused of sorcery. A Benedictine monk of Weihenstephan near Freising protested at the execution of three unfortunate women who had been condemned on a similar charge, and he proclaimed them "martyrs to popular fanaticism." John of Salisbury, who was Bishop of Chartres at the end of the twelfth century, wrote, not without a touch of humour, that the only way of combating witchcraft was—not to talk about it! Arnaud de Villeneuve, at the request of the Bishop of Valencia in Spain, compiled a treatise (c. 1280) against these aberrations; but they have not yet quite disappeared. They represent the sombre side of that taste for marvel so characteristic of a childlike people.

3. SPIRITUAL GUIDES: SAINTS AND MYSTICS

To recognize only debased forms of religion, and look no farther, would be completely to misrepresent the spiritual climate of the Middle Ages. To insist, as many "lay" historians have done, upon superstition and witchcraft trials, and to ignore the brighter side of the picture, is a betrayal of the truth.

Distortions of Christian faith and practice cannot refute that splendid
cloud of witnesses who testify to a creed which has no streak of facile credulity. The true guides of medieval society were the saints and mystics.

Sanctity in the Middle Ages was a commonplace; it flowered throughout
the Christian world. There were saints in every land, in every class, at every
level of society: monks and priests, popes and bishops, kings and princes,
labourers and peasants, scholars and soldiers, contemplatives and men of
action. In their search for God some fled the world, to dwell as cenobites, as
hermits, and even as recluses.[8] They renounced all hope of tangible success
that they might labour for the salvation of mankind through prayer and
the merit of their sacrifice. But there were also those who grappled directly
with the world, its evil and its unbelief; who spread the word of God, and
were even called on to lay down their lives for Christ. It is remarkable that
both forms of Christian effort were often realized in a single individual, who
successfully combined the twofold life of action and contemplation. Those
who see in every mystic an abnormality—an eccentric dreamer, a "schizo-
phrenic"—and who look on all contemplatives as "deserters," are confounded by a host of medieval saints. Consider St. Bernard, St. Dominic, and St.

---

8. The eremitical life is one of the most extraordinary aspects of God's appeal to the
    human soul. It answers to a mysterious craving for solitude as experienced by the pio-
    neers of monachism, St. Paul of the Desert and St. Anthony. St. Benedict himself
    at one time dreamed of following their example. In the days of St. Honoratus and
    St. Martin, monastic communities included hermits, and we find them today in the
    "Republic" of Mount Athos. A hermit is one who, urged by the longing to do pen-
    ance, or to practise contemplation, withdraws from the society of his fellow men and
    lives in solitude. Following the tradition of Lérins and Ligugé, later foundations, e.g.,
    Vallombrosa, had sought to *organize* this anarchical form of the spiritual life. The
    hermit's cell was open and accessible. He could come and go at will; he could wander
    about in silent meditation through the woods, or visit a brother hermit. A recluse,
    on the contrary, was walled up in an impenetrable cell, a little room of one hundred
    square feet, communicating with the outside world by a narrow slit through which
    the "prisoner" received his food. One may say that from the eleventh to the four-
    teenth century every city in Europe had its reclusery. Remains of one have been dis-
    covered at the Tour-Roland in Paris, where the Châtelaine adopted this form of life
    after her husband's death on the crusade. At Lyons eighteen have been traced. Among
    these recluses of either sex some may have been *illuminati*, but many appear to have
    been normal men and women who wished only to live more fully in God, praying for
    their fellow men. Many have been beatified and even canonized.

Louis; is it possible to imagine more balanced personalities? Were souls ever lodged more nobly in flesh? "The great mystics," says Bergson, "have generally been men and women of action, of superior common sense."

In this section I have only touched upon the subject of medieval holiness. Later on I shall have occasion to treat it in more detail by reference to particular saints. At the root of their heroic endeavour lay a single motive cause—the love of God. The medieval period was above all a mystical age, understanding that word in its proper sense, which is far removed from the material and even sensual connotation with which modern writers have endowed it. Mysticism, strictly speaking, is the act of love whereby a man "touches" and "tastes" God. That is its essential element; ignore it, and you distort the whole picture. The faithful in that age observed the mystical act with profound insight, and defined it with extraordinary precision. They recognized and affirmed that this crowning activity of the human intellect does not depend on man alone; it is a grace whose first cause is none other than God Himself, revealing in a very special manner His presence and perfection, and calling the soul unto Himself. They explained that while self-discipline and active prayer are indispensable to all who would attain these heights, neither *constitutes* the mystical act; mortification belongs to an inferior, almost elementary, level of the spiritual life. Though they were models of asceticism, the medieval mystics considered self-denial as a means, not as an end. Medieval society was all too prone to confuse the supernatural with base irrational forms of affectivity or with doubtful probing into the mysterious; yet there are numerous writings which repeatedly emphasize that mystical activity is *not* an extension or, as it were, an overflow of sentimentality, but that it attains its end only outside the sensible, in "that utter silence, that absolute tranquillity" to which John of Fécamp refers. External manifestations of mystical activity there assuredly were[9];

---

9. Mention, however, must be made, in any sketch of medieval spirituality, of the seers and prophets who were so numerous, and whose message may seem to us mere raving. Towards the end of the eleventh century Joachim of Flora, a profound mystic but an austere and worthy monk, interpreted the Apocalypse in the light of visions with which he claimed to have been favoured. He announced the imminent coming of the Holy Spirit, and for two centuries his writings exercised considerable influence.

but men like St. Bernard and St. Francis, though they enjoyed such favours, employed the utmost caution when speaking of them. The medieval mystics wrote of the ascent to God and its several degrees in a manner which subsequent ages have amply confirmed. "There are four things," says Hugh of St. Victor, "whereby the footsteps of the just are led, four stages whereby they are raised to ultimate perfection: reading, meditation, affective prayer, and the prayer of quiet (that loving disposition which, so to speak, cries out to God). Finally there is contemplation, which we may call the fruit of what has gone before, and by means of which we enjoy in this life a foretaste of eternal happiness." Such an analysis is sufficient to convince us that as regards the spiritual life the Middle Ages left little for posterity to discover.

This wealth of mystical experience revealed itself in a wide variety of forms. Just as the great composers have written many melodies upon a single theme, so, on the single motif of God's love, several schools have enacted the most diverse codes. Benedictines, Cistercians, Franciscans, and Dominicans follow different roads to perfection. The Benedictines laid great emphasis upon obedience to the Holy Rule; Choral Office was the centre of a peaceful and well-ordered community—life within the monastic enclosure; nor did manual labour, though it occupied an important place in their daily task, interfere with spiritual reading or hinder the love of beauty in God's service. The reform of Citeaux introduced a different stamp of monasticism. Contemplation occupied a more important place among the White Monks; asceticism was more highly valued; manual labour occupied a large part of their time; while formal beauty yielded to restraint and lack of ornament.

(See Volume 2, Chapter XIV, section 2.) St. Hildegard and St. Elizabeth of Schönau, in the twelfth century, declared that they had received revelations in which our Lord had directed them to call their generation to an amendment of life. Blessed Angela of Foligno, a somewhat later visionary, considered her ecstasies rather as lessons in self-improvement. In the thirteenth century, St. Mechtild of Magdeburg wrote some most interesting accounts of her mystical experiences. It is to be noted that the number of visionaries increased from one century to the next; it grew in proportion as the perfect equilibrium of the Middle Ages gradually failed and ultimately gave place to the troubled decades of the fourteenth century. In the twelfth century St. Hildegard was almost an exception; in the thirteenth we have a regular avalanche of female visionaries; and at the turn of the century Joachim of Flora's influence had terminated in positive aberrations which the Church resolutely opposed.

54   But this austerity was counterbalanced by increased devotion to the person of our Lord and to His Blessed Mother. There were similar divergences between the Orders established almost simultaneously at the beginning of the thirteenth century and classed together as "Mendicant." Among the Franciscans, the accent was on renunciation, absolute poverty, passionate love of Christ, and an exquisite reverence for the created world as an image of God. Franciscan spirituality, in fact, was watered with streams of tenderness. That of the Dominicans appears at first sight more austere, directed rather to intellectual achievement. Nevertheless, St. Dominic himself was a great contemplative, and it was under Dominican auspices that the Rosary became so popular. The outstanding characteristic of the Dominican way of life was study (considered as a means of self-improvement), and the apostolate (charity in action) regarded as a means of achieving union with God.

We cannot here take account of all the spiritual wealth; the men and their writings are far too numerous, nor is the dividing line always clear between speculative and mystical theology. The most we can do is to cite the more important names in each of the principal schools.

Among the Black Monks there was *Peter the Venerable* (d. 1156), the most celebrated of the abbots of Cluny, who vigorously defended the ideals of his Order. *St. Anselm* (1033–1109), a Doctor of the Church, was in turn Abbot of Bec and Archbishop of Canterbury; his influence is apparent in many contemporary events and in several trends of thought. At Citeaux the giants crowd one upon another: first, of course, St. Bernard, whom we shall consider presently[10]; then *William of Saint-Thierry* (d. 1147), whose magnificent *Golden Letter* is one of the most acute and substantial works on mystical theology ever written. The holy life of *Blessed Joachim of Flora* (d. 1202) was perhaps of more importance than his apocalyptic visions. *St. Gertrude* (1256–1341) was a great German mystic whose spirituality (both affective and practical), as expressed in her *Exercises*, had a profound effect

---

10. See Chapter III. Other great figures named in this paragraph—St. Norbert, St. Francis of Assisi, St. Dominic, and St. Thomas Aquinas—will also be studied at greater length in subsequent chapters.

on her generation; while *St. Bridget of Sweden*, princess of the blood royal, who entered a convent after the death of her husband, had much to do with ecclesiastical reform. And in the school of St. Victor, established by William of Champeaux at the foot of Mont Sainte-Geneviève, a number of eminent scholars revived the Augustinian system and combined the practice of asceticism with sacred studies, two indispensable prerequisites of the mystic state. The most celebrated member of this school was *Hugh of St. Victor* (1099–1141). He wrote an important work on the Sacraments; and every Christian intellectual should bear in mind his twin formulae: "To be ignorant is to be weak," but "Love surpasseth knowledge." Such figures abound in medieval Christendom. Among the Carthusians were the two *Guigo* (twelfth century), one of whom was author of the *Scale of Paradise*. The Premonstratensians include *St. Norbert* with his immediate disciples *Hugh de Fosses*, *Walter of Saint-Maurice*, and *Philip of Bonne Espérance*, who wrote one of the greatest medieval syntheses. Both *St. Francis of Assisi* (1181–1226) and *St. Dominic* (1170–1221) inspired a host of mystics; the Franciscan *St. Bonaventure* (d. 1274), known as the "Seraphic Doctor" was renowned no less for his theological learning than for his loyalty to the spirit of his master. There were also the anonymous author of a *Meditation on the Life of Christ*; *David of Augsburg*; and *Blessed Angela of Foligno* (d. 1309), a fashionable lady who joined the Third Order of St. Francis and whose voice still seems so close to us. *St. Thomas Aquinas* (1225–1274) and *St. Albert the Great* (d. 1280) are the most outstanding of several great Dominicans. And still the list is incomplete; scores of secular priests and laymen likewise enjoyed and bore witness to the sublime experience. In Germany these "friends of God" included Henry of Langerstein and Rulman Merswin; in France Honorius of Autun, Richard of Saint-Laurent, and, even more illustrious, St. Louis, that king whose *Instructions to his Son* form a veritable treatise on the spiritual life. The religion of the masses always reflects the teaching of those who represent the noblest elements of Christian faith.[11] Judged by these and similar examples,

---

11.   One need only call to mind, for example, the influence upon their contemporaries of St. Francis of Sales, of Cardinal Berulle, and of M. Olier, in whose image and likeness the literary and artistic genius of France has at various times expressed itself.

the medieval soul was far from superstitious, credulous, and intellectually blind. It shone with the bright flame of understanding and supernatural faith, the very light of God.

4. FOUR CHARACTERISTICS OF MEDIEVAL RELIGION

THE Christian religion has at all times been consistent with itself and loyal to its tradition. But that has not prevented it taking on a different colour, so to speak, from one generation to another. The emphasis nowadays, at any rate among French Catholics, is on the social aspect of the Creed, on the necessity of recourse to biblical and patristic sources, and on deeper acquaintance with the liturgy. During the great centuries of the Middle Ages, there were four main characteristics.

The first and most fundamental of these was the profound influence of Holy Scripture. It is certain that the Bible, considered as a whole, was familiar to all. Many other books were read in the monasteries and universities, particularly the Fathers, and above all St. Augustine; but what the masses of the faithful knew best was the Gospel—Christ Himself manifested through the written word. The remainder of the New Testament recalled the earliest beginnings of Christian history or, in the Apocalypse, looked forward to the mysterious dawn of eternity. The popularity of the Old Testament was founded upon a notion inherited from the Fathers of the Church and universally accepted—that the persons and events described therein are prophetic of the later dispensation.

Proof that medieval Christians were thoroughly conversant with the Scriptures is furnished by the glass and sculpture which adorn the great French cathedrals. No craftsman would have troubled to multiply the pages of these "bibles in stone" of these "transparent gospels" if those who used the buildings had regarded them merely as picture-puzzles. It has been said that the cathedral "spoke to the illiterate"; and, we might add, the illiterate understood their language.

Men were familiar with Holy Writ because it was studied and taught;
not only in religious houses, where the Rule of St. Benedict ordained that
"spiritual reading" should occupy one-third of the day; not only among exe-
getes and scholars, many of whom were so deeply versed in Scripture that
their very thought and literary style were moulded by the Bible. The Sacred
Books were not reserved to clerics who could read Latin. Educated laymen
had translations made of those parts which interested them, and many such
vernacular renderings were produced between the eleventh and thirteenth
centuries. The four Books of Kings were done into French (c. 1100), and
the Proverbs of Solomon into Anglo-Norman (c. 1150). The Oxford and
Cambridge Psalters followed not long afterwards, and in 1190 one Herman,
a worthy canon of Valenciennes, published a complete edition of the Bible
in Alexandrine verses!

This passion for the Bible became, in fact, so strong that the authorities grew uneasy at the prospect of simple folk nourishing their faith upon
obscure and often misleading texts.[12] Nor were these apprehensions unjustified; for even the Waldenses and Albigensian heretics based their arguments
upon passages of Holy Writ. The fact remains, however, that the faithful
drank at the wells of Scripture, which is the Word of God; and that, no
doubt, explains the freshness and vigour of their belief.

The second characteristic was devotion to the saints. Though rooted
in the deepest soil of Christian teaching, it flourished upon a scale unpar-
allelled before or since. It was, of course, wide open to the abuses of credulity and superstition; but at the same time it was profoundly significant.
Medieval man experienced a sense of humility and helplessness in presence
of his Creator; he felt the need of intermediaries between himself and the
Almighty, intermediaries who should be men like himself, and who had
won their way to heaven by perfecting a nature similar to his own. Nietzsche
has formulated this need in celebrated words: "Man is a creature who likes
to be outstripped"; and the Middle Ages satisfied their craving by devotion

---

12. Innocent III took steps to meet this danger; somewhat later, Alexander III called
attention to the fate of those who turn Scripture to their private ends.

to the saints—which at any rate is no more unreasonable than to idolize a boxing champion or a film star.

Lives of the saints vied in importance with Holy Scripture, from which, in fact, they were hardly distinguished by the rank and file. The history of God's faithful servants was looked upon as all of a piece with the Old and New Testaments, and enjoyed almost equal authority. These biographies were innumerable; and although very few of them were admitted to the official literature of the Church, many formed part of the stock-in-trade of *jongleurs* and wandering minstrels, as did the *chansons de geste*, to which indeed they sometimes bore a striking resemblance. Vincent of Beauvais, in the *Mirror of History*, begins his narrative with the saints of the Old and New Testaments; while the Benedictine Guy of Chartres, and the two Dominicans Peter Calo and Bernard Guy, compiled vast hagiographical tomes which covered every period of history and enjoyed no small degree of popularity. Contemporary lives were not overlooked; and no sooner had Thomas à Becket fallen by the swords of Henry's knights than a French cleric, one Guernes of Pont-Sainte-Maxence, wrote his life in phrases of impassioned eloquence. It is true that in the *Golden Legend* of Voragine we find a good deal of fiction mixed with fact; but his famous collection breathes none the less a moving reverence toward the saints.

One could not fail to meet at every turn the countless legions of the Blessed. Every province, every diocese, counted them by the score; every place, every aspect of daily life, was under their protection. The new-born child received his "patron's" name, and owed him a particular devotion. In later life he relied upon the saints rather than the doctor for his continued health: St. Geneviève was well known to cure fever, Sts. Apollonia and Blaise the toothache, while St. Hubert was the guardian against madness. The peasant at his daily toil invoked St. Medard to protect his vine against the frost, St. Anthony to watch over his pigs, and many another for such useful purposes. The journeyman-stonemason prayed to the apostle St. Thomas, the wool-carder to St. Blaise, the tanner to St. Bartholomew, the shoemaker to St. Crispin; and no traveller would dare to start his journey except under the protection of the archangel Michael or of St. John the

Hospitaller. Moreover, every season of the year was under saintly patronage. Springtime enjoyed the favour of St. Mark and St. George; summer of St. John the Baptist; winter of St. John the Evangelist; autumn of St. Martin. Memories of these and other things still linger in the countryside.

Saints of both sexes are prominent also in the sculpture and stained glass of our cathedrals. They mount guard at the doors side by side with the great figures of the Bible; episodes from their lives are depicted along with scenes from Holy Scripture, and Christian folk knew every one of them by heart. The presence of a saint in their midst formed a communal link among the faithful. Whole towns, whole countries even, are known to have poured out their wealth in order that some venerable bones might be laid up in a worthy casket; and the enamellers, maybe of renowned Limoges, expended all the treasures of their cunning craft upon these reliquaries. At certain times of the year, or perhaps to ward off the ravages of a plague, the relic, or sometimes a statue of the saint, was carried in procession; and there was much rejoicing as the sacred object passed from street to street on the back of a well-caparisoned horse, surrounded by young clerks clashing cymbals, or blowing ivory horns!

Devotion to the saints was more than simple piety. First, there was a continual lesson in faith and moral progress; for each of these heroic souls afforded a sublime example of Christian principles in action. As the dogma of the Communion of Saints was better understood, so did the cult increase. St. Bernard describes the spiritual chain which binds together the Church militant and triumphant, and which unites them both with Christ, their head; St. Bonaventure lays stress upon the theological bases of this exalted doctrine; the visions of St. Mechtild of Hackeborn contain a noble image of the Church forgathered beyond the frontiers of death; while the *Divine Comedy* of Dante is simply "an epic on the Communion of Saints." It is of faith that good works, performed in a state of grace and augmented by the infinite merits of Christ with which they are conjoined, form, as it were, a reserve fund against the immeasurable debt of sin. This doctrine of the "reversion of merit" is the background to and the justification of a cult which might appear ingenuous and even vulgar, but which was in fact one of the most efficacious means employed by the Church to raise the standards of morality and faith.

Love of Holy Scripture and devotion to the saints had been outstanding factors in the religion of an earlier epoch; but the remarkable tenderness of medieval Christianity arose from two other characteristics—devotion to our Lord's humanity and cult of the Virgin Mary. We must not, of course, exaggerate the importance of this trend to the exclusion of other aspects of the faith, nor must we overestimate its originality. The outlook of the Middle Ages was certainly Christo-centric, but it did not on that account ignore the other Persons of the Godhead. The Three Divine Persons were often represented together in works of art, and it was during this period that John XXII instituted the feast of the Holy Trinity. Significant also is the great popularity enjoyed by such hymns as the *Veni Creator*, inherited from an earlier century, and the *Veni, Sancte Spiritus*, written about 1200 by Stephen Langton, Archbishop of Canterbury. I have said, we must not overestimate the *originality* of medieval devotion to Christ as man; for something like it is already apparent even in the early Fathers, e.g., St. Ignatius. It is none the less true that a new note is discernible. "Hail, Jesus whom I love. Thou knowest how I long to be nailed with Thee to the cross. Give Thyself to me! Look down upon me from Thy Cross, beloved; draw me wholly to Thee, and say to me: 'I heal thee, I forgive thee!' Meanwhile, though filled with shame, I embrace Thee in a surge of love." These phrases, typical of the new devotion, were spoken by St. Bernard, who may be truly said to have introduced it. Before him, St. Anselm and John of Fécamp had already given utterance to fine "surges of love" towards God made Man, but not with such intensity, nor with the same heart-rending pathos. Christianity has never forgotten this poignant song of faith; innumerable devout souls have repeated it, and St. Francis of Assisi, who was above all else "the friend of Jesus" has sent it echoing down the centuries.

The purpose of this devotion is clearly analogous to that which we recognized in the cult of saints; for insistence on the human side of Christ brings Him closer to man, and emphasizes the fact that He is the supreme intermediary between the sinner and the Judge. Men spoke of the Babe of Bethlehem, whose very swaddling clothes are mentioned by St. Bernard; of

the twelve-year-old Boy, upon whom St. Aelred of Rievaulx wrote a whole
treatise of exquisite beauty; and His conduct during the years of public ministry was analysed in order to discover and expound its lesson. Above all,
there was the contemplation of His agony and death—"the passion for His
sacred Passion."[13]

The flowering of love towards the humanity of Jesus bore fruit of several kinds. In the liturgy, for example, the consecrated host, as symbol of
Christ's body immolated, became the object of very special fervour. As soon
as Christendom learned of the celebrated miracle of Bolsena, St. Juliana (a
Premonstratensian nun) proposed the eucharistic feast of Corpus Christi.
Instituted in the diocese of Limoges in 1246, it was soon afterwards extended to the universal Church by Pope Urban IV; and it was for the office of
this festival that St. Thomas Aquinas wrote his masterpiece, the *Lauda Sion*.
To the same current of devotion belongs the familiar monogram of Christ,
IXP, which the Swedish order of Seraphins wore upon their breasts. The
Jesuits use the Holy Name itself to designate their Society.

But this cult of Christ's humanity found perhaps its noblest expression
in the arts. Every scene in our Lord's life is found depicted in sculpture and
stained glass; and the Royal Porch at Chartres is one of many such façades
designed with Jesus as its centre, reminding us in turn of His Incarnation, of
His death, and finally of His glorious Resurrection and Ascension. When
we admire the intimate humanism of romanesque and gothic sculpture, we
should not forget that it was inspired by a faith which taught the love of
man in God.[14]

Another facet of medieval religion was an overwhelming devotion to
Mary, the mother of Christ. This was not, as has been suggested, a medieval innovation denounced by some as "mariolatry." Old almost as the
Church herself,[15] it had developed in the course of centuries, particularly

---

13. It is possible to discover in some of the followers of St. Bernard the remote origin of
    devotion to the Sacred Heart. Guerric of Igny, for instance, speaks with much feeling
    of the wound opened by the lance in our Lord's side.
14. See H. Daniel-Rops, *Le Porche du Dieu fait homme*.
15. See H. Daniel-Rops, *Les Évangiles de la Vierge*.

in the East where the scurrilous attacks of Nestorius served only to increase the public fervour. But in the West also, from the eleventh century, there was an ever-flowing stream of love towards the mother of Jesus. Why? For the same reason that underlay devotion to the saints and accentuated the human side of Christ: man's longing for a mediator between himself and the dread majesty of God. Who better than the Mother could intercede with her own Son? The cult of Mary is, at all events, closely bound up with that of Jesus. "All praise of the Mother," says St. Bernard, "redounds to the honour of her Son"; and Conrad of Saxony remarks that "there is no better way of praising our Lord than to praise His most glorious and gentle Mother." It is usual to attribute this devotion to the efforts of St. Bernard, to the writings of St. Bonaventure, and to the preaching of the mendicant Orders. In point of fact, however, nearly all the great figures in the spiritual life of these three centuries laboured for its propagation. St. Anselm, his disciple Eadmer, Richard and Adam of St. Victor, Philip of Bonne Espérance, Blessed Hermann Joseph, St. Francis, and St. Dominic all contributed their share. But in order properly to understand the feelings of the twelfth and thirteenth centuries towards our Lady, we must go to the sermons of St. Bernard, to Conrad of Saxony's *Mirror of the Blessed Virgin Mary*, or, again, to the twelve books of Richard of Saint-Laurent's *Praises of the Blessed Virgin Mary*, which might be described as a "Summa" of Marian devotion.

This period witnessed also the composition of two celebrated anthems, the *Salve Regina* and the *Alma Redemptoris Mater*.[16] It was the period in which the Cistercians began referring to Mary as "our Lady" (a title borrowed from the usages of chivalry and courtly love) and in which *jongleurs* and troubadours sang of her miracles. It was the age in which the "Hail Mary" first became popular and the Rosary was instituted. Finally, it was during this period that the feast of the Blessed Virgin's Conception, which had been observed in Ireland since the ninth century, took root in England and spread from there all over Europe.

---

16. The *Salve Regina* appears to be the work of Adhemar of Monteil, Bishop of Puy and preacher of the first crusade. It was sung by the crusaders at their entry into Jerusalem. The *Alma Redemptoris Mater* is by Hermann Contract, a monk of Reichenau.

Mary, mother of Christ, held a unique place in the hearts of men: as a mother who listened to her children's woe, as an advocate who would obtain forgiveness of their sins, almost as a supernatural lover. The Franciscan James of Milan, in his *Goad of Love*, calls her "the ravisher of hearts." The Old Testament was searched for figures that foreshadowed her. *Eva, Ave!* In that reversal of a name was seen the cancellation of our first parent's fault by yet another woman. But if her joys were hymned, so too were her sorrows; and close by Mary at the Crib stood Mary of the Seven Dolours. *Stabat Mater.*

The extent of devotion to our Lady is revealed in splendid works of art. Innumerable churches are dedicated to her; and the cathedral of Notre Dame at Paris is surrounded by seven other sanctuaries of the same title, arranged not unlike the petals of a flower. Artists, too, vied with one another to depict her with exquisite grace, and the Virgin Mother appears more and more frequently amid the sculptures of both porch and tympanum. At first she is seen only with her Son, then alone, and even at the last "in majesty"—an attitude reserved until that time to Christ. From its high place in popular esteem her cult shed upon Christianity a tenderness which has never been surpassed, and which ranks among the fairest of medieval flowers.

5. THE SPOKEN WORD

How did the Church manage to diffuse the great dogmatic concepts which underlie these several devotions? Chiefly by means of preaching, to grasp the importance of which we must forget the pattern of our present world. The twentieth century has at its disposal many sources of information and amusement; but the Middle Ages possessed no radio, no cinema, no newspapers, and there were no political meetings. All these things, which occupy so much of our time and attention, were represented by the rites and ceremonies of the Church. Surprising as it may seem, the medieval substitute for instructive recreation was the Mass and the sermon!

64   During those troubled times which followed the break-up of Charlemagne's empire, the pulpit had been almost abandoned. While we possess numerous sermons of the fourth, fifth, and sixth centuries, it is hard to find so much as one between this latter date and the twelfth century, when preaching regained some of its importance. The revival was no doubt due to the same impulse which had begun to elevate the human spirit in every domain, a thirst for knowledge of the things of God. It began in ecclesiastical circles. At the beginning of the twelfth century, teachers addressed themselves mainly to a clerical élite; but their voices were soon heard beyond the walls of monasteries and chapter-houses. Peter the Bald (d. 1197), Maurice de Sully, Bishop of Paris (d. 1196), and Raoul Ardent (d. 1101), whose "word was a sword," all spoke to the masses.[17]

Henceforward preaching made rapid strides, and to it more than one celebrated churchman owed his reputation. St. Norbert, St. Bernard, St. Francis of Assisi, St. Dominic, and, above all, the Portuguese St. Anthony of Padua, held enormous congregations spellbound. Other famous orators were St. Bonaventure, St. Thomas Aquinas, Peter the Hermit, Fulk of Neuilly, Guibert of Nogent, Urban II, Innocent III, and Guichard of Beaujeu, who was styled by an indulgent congregation "the layman's Homer." Collections of sermons—most of which seem to have been heavy going—were read, studied, and commented upon. Such was the *Mirror of the Church* by Honorius of Autun (d. 1129), a collection of sermons for every day of the year. It was written in doggerel and vaguely rhyming Latin, but has been shown by Émile Mâle to have exerted considerable influence among artists.

From the twelfth century onwards there was a sermon on any and every occasion: during Mass, on pilgrimage, at religious ceremonies, clothings, and consecrations of churches; but also at civil functions—coronations, burials, peace conferences, and even tournaments. Preachers spoke on bridges and at

---

17. The pulpit as a piece of furniture seems to have been introduced by the Dominicans of Toulouse. Previously there were *ambos*, slightly raised platforms set up in the choir, from which the epistle and gospel were read. It was only in the fourteenth century that the pulpit (movable or immovable) came into general use, a fact of which many liturgists are still unaware. (See G. A. Leccy de la Marche, *La Chaire française au Moyen Âge*, 1886.)

street corners, and a stone pulpit or temporary wooden platform was often
erected in the public squares.

What was a medieval sermon like? It would certainly not bear comparison with Bossuet's stately art; it was more like those vivid, vigorous discourses which Caesar of Arles or St. Hilary of Poitiers had once delivered before enthusiastic audiences. The style was animated, familiar, uninhibited, and sometimes little more than trivial or clownish; for in order to stimulate the interest of his hearers, a speaker would not hesitate to throw in such pieces of news, or mere gossip, as he had picked up in the course of his travels. He might announce the capture of Jerusalem by the crusaders, or the humiliation of the Emperor at Canossa; but he would not disdain to tell of some comic incident that had caused trouble in the neighbouring market-town, or to inform his congregation that a cow had dropped four calves! And if he were the parish priest addressing his own flock, he would not gloss over petty scandals or even grave ones. What man but loves a veiled allusion to his neighbour?

The general public, too, enjoyed the same liberty as the preacher. A sermon was a kind of melodrama at which the audience wept or laughed, or (not seldom) interrupted. If the speaker introduced some unfamiliar theme, he was stopped and questioned. Nor was that all. On one occasion a Dominican was insisting that Pilate's wife, so far from having played a creditable part during our Lord's trial, had, by her intervention, risked preventing the crucifixion and thereby placing an obstacle in the way of our salvation. Whereupon the Lady of the Manor rose, indignant, and stalked out declaring she would not listen to this revilement of her sex!

Such piquant sauce, however, helped down the main dish, which, in all truth, was a tax on the digestion. The preacher's aim was to convey the truths of faith; but he had scant regard for their methodical presentation. Most of the sermon consisted of biblical texts thrown off higgledy-piggledy, of patriotic or personal commentaries thereon, of allegories and anecdotes. Pride of place in this hotch-potch was enjoyed by Holy Scripture: "The Old and New Testaments," cried Hildebert, "are twin breasts; ye preachers, drink from them!" Quotations from the Bible were put forward as decisive arguments, and each one was allowed to have at least four meanings. Thus, when a preacher spoke of Jerusalem, he referred to the city itself; to the Church, of which it is a figure; to the faithful soul, which longs to possess God as the Jewish capital possessed the Temple; and finally to heaven, where the elect behold God face to face. This complicated symbolism may sometimes have confused the audience; for, although quite familiar,[18] it was rendered yet more elaborate by a host of subtle allusions to the secret significance of plants and beasts, of precious stones and the heavenly bodies, and by a thousand other curiosities.

By way of light relief, there were, fortunately, "examples" in the form of anecdotes and apologues. The former were taken from history, contemporary events, or legend. The latter were fables: *The Crow and the Fox*, *The Cobbler and the Moneylender*, *The Milkmaid and the Milk Jar*, all occur in medieval sermons. Anecdotes and apologues alike were full of colour, and ended with an edifying moral that was easily understood. It is surely not surprising, in these circumstances, that a good sermon often lasted for two hours.

6. THE SEVEN SACRAMENTS

I⊤ was not, however, sacred doctrine alone with which the Church provided her children. The sacraments offered them supernatural means of union with God. The meaning of the word "sacrament" was defined in the twelfth century. Until then it often referred to ecclesiastical rites which are not of divine institution; thus the reception of holy water or of ashes is described even by Hugh of St. Victor as "sacraments." The necessity of refuting heresy

---

18. Manuals large as encyclopaedias were compiled to assist inexperienced preachers, e.g., by Alan of Lille, Peter of Limoges, St. Anthony of Padua; and somewhat later by William of Mailly, Nicholas of Gorran, and John of San Gimigniano (author of a *Universum praedicabile*). So many would-be orators strove to acquire these books from the library of Paris University that a decree was issued by the Rector, in 1303, appointing a fee payable by each borrower.

caused theologians to cast their thought in language more precise than hitherto. The recognition of seven sacraments is discovered first in the *Life of Otto of Bamberg* (1139); but it is mainly to *Peter Lombard* that we owe the clarification of this dogma which was sanctioned by the Council of Trent in the sixteenth century, and which has remained the official teaching of the Catholic Church.

Baptism was conferred upon the new-born child. The practice of adult baptism was extremely rare; for the Church had long ago emphasized the importance of baptizing infants with the least possible delay,[19] and it was no longer necessary to wait for the canonical seasons when baptism was traditionally conferred. How then was the sacrament administered? The Greeks still followed the ancient rite of triple immersion; the Latin Church authorized a threefold infusion of water. The older custom, which is more complicated and may be objectionable on grounds of health or public decency, was rarely practised except at Milan and in a few German dioceses. Baptisteries were gradually replaced with fonts, and the ceremony was accompanied with those simple but beautiful prayers which are now recited at the church door.

The act of faith which the god-parents had pronounced on his behalf was later repeated by the child himself, with full knowledge of his responsibility, in the sacrament of *Confirmation*. It was only in cases of danger that this sacrament was administered immediately after baptism. Ordinarily it was postponed at least until adolescence; and to mark its importance it was reserved to the bishop, except in cases where the Pope granted special faculties to a priest.

The *Eucharist* is a sacrament whereby men participate in the Flesh and Blood of Christ crucified; it was considered as the most sacred of all rites, and layfolk were not admitted to frequent communion. The ancient practice of receiving a morsel of leavened bread in the palm of the hand continued in the East. In the West, however, a small disk known as a "host" was received, as now, upon the tongue; it is unleavened in memory of that

---

19. A maximum of forty days was the rule in Italy.

which Christ ate at the Last Supper. As to the practice of communion under the species of wine, the precious liquid was at first taken through a reed in order to avoid excess and indelicacy, but was later suppressed altogether.

If communion was rare, the sacrament of *Penance* was extremely popular; for medieval man, as I have said, was acutely conscious of sin. Peter Lombard and Gratian, among many theologians, dwell at great length on this sacrament. Since man is a sinner and knows himself as such, what more valuable rite, they ask, than that which reconciles him with God? It was actually held that in imminent danger of death confession might and ought to be made to anyone available, even to a layman; and we find examples of this practice in the *Gestes* as well as in the *Chronicle of Joinville*. Confession was made in one of two ways. It was public for such as had given scandal; but this custom was already dying out, and its full rigour was mitigated by commutation, acts of atonement, and indulgences. Private confession, on the other hand, became increasingly common, and was gladly frequented by the faithful. Auricular confession, which had been encouraged by Irish monks during the barbarian epoch, became the general rule. It was made to a priest, upon whom the Lateran Council of 1215 imposed a rule of absolute secrecy; and handbooks known as "Penitentials" supplied confessors with numerous cases of conscience together with the manner of resolving them. Popular as it became, this sacrament was treated with the utmost respect, and was certainly one of the principal means of the Church's action upon souls.

Those who wished to serve God more directly received *Holy Orders* according to a rite which has never since varied. The solemn ceremonial which attends the conferment of each order, no less than the *interstices*, or intervals, that must normally elapse between the reception of the sub-diaconate, diaconate, and priesthood, are eloquent proof of their importance.

Matrimony, the sacrament wherein the Church both hallows and confirms the union of husband and wife, was hedged about with guarantees. The priest's blessing was then, as it is now, of obligation; and the indissolubility of the bond was unqualified, even in cases of adultery. The Church in her wisdom required express consent of the parties. She never allowed parental opposition to invalidate the union; but she would not recognize

a marriage between persons related by ties of consanguinity.[20] The dignity   69
attached by Holy Church to this sacrament was, in fact, one of the principal
foundations of society.

When at last the hour struck for a man to depart out of this life, the
Church afforded him one last chance in the sacrament of *Extreme Unction*,
which, sanctifying his body doomed to speedy dissolution, and accompany-
ing his soul with exhortations and prayers for deliverance from evil, constituted the supreme viaticum. Many councils, too, enjoined the clergy to see
that it was conferred at all costs upon the dying.

Thus, from birth to death, the whole cycle of events which mark man's
passage through the world was sanctified.

7. THE FAITH OF THE COMMON MAN

To what extent, it may be asked, did medieval man embrace this doctrine;
and to what extent did he follow the sacramental road to salvation? What
was the religious life of the people, of all that unrecorded mass of folk whose
names have not come down to us, and who performed no signal deeds? It
cannot surely have been mere formality: that those who built the cathedrals
and shed their blood in the crusades drank deep at the Fount of Living
Water is proved by documentary evidence; but it is rather more difficult to
say exactly how they did so.

Certain aspects of medieval faith remind us of the barbarian age, an
admixture of light with shadow, and marked by striking contrasts. The
superstitious practices to which the cult of saints gave rise might lead us to
pronounce it shallow, conventional, and without much foundation. Nothing could be farther from the truth. Side by side with these aberrations there
were not lacking examples of intelligent and deep-rooted belief. Prior to
the twelfth century, the accent had been rather upon moral conduct and

---

20. Until the fourth Lateran Council the prohibition extended to the seventh degree in
the collateral line; it was then limited to the first four degrees.

obedience to set principles; but from that time onward the interior life of the soul came to be regarded as all-important in a religious scheme which later found expression in *The Imitation of Christ.*

It is absurd to generalize about medieval religion, to describe it as "commonplace" or "naïve." Then, as now, the Christian faith was one in essence, though its attributes differed according to the intellectual gifts of its adherents; but to say that popular faith was "gross" and "devoid of intellectual basis" is to forget that many of the great mystics and theologians came from the lower levels of society, and that traces of those ideological conflicts which troubled the learned world may be detected in medieval folklore. Differences of opinion among speculative theologians were no less striking. They were, if anything, more pronounced than in our day; for the foundations of faith had not been called in question, and a greater margin of freedom was permissible than in present circumstances. Today the fundamental dogmas of Christianity are under attack, and require stricter interpretation through the mouth of an infallible pontiff. But during the Middle Ages, when society as a whole was proof against erroneous teaching, there was more scope for the philosophical ventures of Abélard and St. Thomas Aquinas. Both were firm believers, yet differed widely in their points of view, which were in turn as poles apart from the standpoint of St. Bernard.

These variations are not without significance: they show that in the Middle Ages faith was by no means naïve, over-simple, and narrowminded. So far from "clouding the mind," it was a source of understanding—*fides quaerens intellectum,* as St. Augustine says—and the enthusiastic search for divine truth which it encouraged produced a ferment of intellectual activity in the form of some remarkable debates among the theologians of Paris, Chartres, and Oxford. But while the Faith thus acted as a leaven, its unchanging principles maintained order amid the clash of ideas and prevented them dissolving into anarchy. All Christians, at whatever intellectual or social level they might be, and however different temperamentally, recognized one overriding purpose—union with God in Jesus Christ.

The spirituality of the Middle Ages expressed itself first and foremost in frequent prayer. There are numerous examples in medieval literature of prayer in time of danger or at some critical stage of life. It consisted mainly of such traditional formulae as the "Our Father" and Creed (which many councils urged that all should know by heart). There was also the "Hail Mary," of which the second part was written during the twelfth century, and which was officially recognized for the first time by Sully, Bishop of Paris, c. 1196. It had been a common practice since the tenth century to recite a series of *Paters*, counting them on a knotted cord. During the twelfth and thirteenth centuries the custom was gradually transferred to the "Hail Mary" under the twofold influence of Citeaux and the Dominicans; and this "chaplet" was the origin of the Rosary.[21]

Medieval Christians, however, were not content with oral prayer alone. Mystical authors explain that there is another and more interior form, which they describe as "mental prayer"; nor is it uncommon to find, even in such profane works as the *Chansons de Geste*, the hero "praying in silence." Geoffrey of Vendome (d. 1132) even speaks of the "prayer of tears," which seems to have been widely practised.

The importance of prayer in daily life is attested by the large number of books providing samples for every occasion. To the older *Manuals* of Fleury and the Venerable Bede, to the collections of Alcuin, and John of Fécamp's *Meditations*, there were added the devotional writings of St. Anselm and the *Exercises* of St. Gertrude, together with prayers by St. Francis of Assisi, St. Bonaventure, St. Thomas Aquinas, and Raymond Lull. We have reliable evidence of the popularity enjoyed by these works; they were, in fact, what we should call today "best sellers."

Prayer was accompanied by gestures that were so ancient as to be considered almost obligatory.[22] The custom of turning eastward, towards Jerusalem, was still observed. Arms were stretched out so that the body formed a

---

21. The Rosary (French, *Rosaire*; German, *Rosenkranz*) derived its name from a charming legend. A monk (a Cistercian according to some; others say a Dominican) had just recited fifty "Hail Marys," when our Lady appeared to him, crowned with roses. At first it was called "our Lady's psalter" because it included one hundred fifty "Hail Marys," corresponding to the number of the Psalms.

22. St. Dominic attached a good deal of importance to the externals of prayer.

cross, or were raised in supplication like the *orantes* of the catacombs. There were frequent signs of the Cross, genuflexions, prostrations (known as *veniae*, i.e., afflictions); and many a statue in our cathedrals preserves the memory of these dignified postures.

Why did men pray? Chiefly to ask God's protection and benefits. The prayer of praise was not unknown, but it was less widespread than that of petition. Ulric of Strasbourg defines prayer as a "lifting up of the mind to God as the giver of all good gifts"; and even the great mystic Hugh of St. Victor explains that, although the Psalms include few petitions, they are a useful form of prayer because they "obtain so much from God." We shall have occasion to notice other examples of this realistic outlook of the Middle Ages.

A secondary motive of prayer was man's consciousness of his own misery. John of Montmédy, analysing the two sorts of prayer, emphasizes that the prayer of praise "is permeated with spiritual joy"; and he goes on to say that "the prayer of petition springs from penitence." Herein lies one of the more attractive features of medieval religion. Man felt the heavy weight of sin; mindful of his wretchedness, he humbled himself before Almighty God; and this fact lends a certain charm even to the worst of sinners. Such a one was the "Knight of the Tub," a nobleman who had indulged in every form of blasphemy and violence. Having sought out a hermit, he made his confession and was ordered, by way of penance, to fill a little tub with water. He tried for weeks to carry out this apparently simple task, but all in vain; no matter into what spring or well he plunged the vessel, it immediately became empty. One day, however, he let fall a tear of true contrition, and at that moment the tub was filled to overflowing! It was their sense of sin and their innate humility that brought men to repentance and confession,[23] that drove forth innumerable pilgrims on the roads, and furnished the cathedral building-sites with an endless stream of voluntary workers.

---

23. The penitential spirit was often carried to excess. The "discipline" was of ancient usage; but the practice of self-flagellation in public bordered on exhibitionism. The first processions of flagellants took place in Italy, at Perugia in 1260. (See Volume 2, Chapter XIV.)

Notwithstanding his faults, the medieval Christian lived in the full light
of Christ.

The Holy Eucharist, strangely enough, was seldom approached by the laity, though priests communicated of necessity whenever they said Mass. In the eleventh century St. Peter Damian and Gregory VII had recommended daily communion as "a principal means of preserving chastity"; their advice went unheeded. The fourth Lateran Council (1215) imposed the obligation to confess and receive Holy Communion at least once a year, and as a general rule the faithful communicated at Easter, Pentecost, and Christmas. St. Louis did so six times a year; but it was not until the fourteenth century, when the *Imitation of Christ* was published, that the Blessed Sacrament came to be looked upon as a source of strength against the powers of darkness. Surprising as this abstention from communion may be, it was a sign not of indifference but of profound respect; it was due to fear of sacrilege.

All things considered, the religious life of the common folk seems to have attained a fairly high standard, as is shown also by the custom of "spiritual direction" which was becoming fashionable at this period. St. Bernard gives it explicit approval[24]; and several Chapters of the Dominican order complained that some reverend fathers were so busy directing souls that they had time for nothing else! These facts may be accepted as evidence of an intense religious fervour.

8. THE CHRISTIAN YEAR

SPIRITUAL life was fostered during the Middle Ages by the intellectual climate of that period. Herein modern man is at a serious disadvantage; for today, in almost every land, the atmosphere is laden with materialism. God is no longer welcome, unless it be surreptitiously and almost in the teeth of society. Even the most obvious traces of religion, such as the dates of public holidays, are commonly overlooked, so entirely has the world been

---

24. "He who appoints himself his own guide will listen to a fool."

secularized—Yuletide revellers scarcely recognize the meaning of a feast which they celebrate with plum-pudding and champagne.

In the Middle Ages things were very different; the whole air was Christian, and no one but could feel himself wrapped round, sustained, and guided by the Faith. The day was regulated by the sound of bells, particularly by the *Angelus*, that lovely prayer which had recently been introduced. The year itself followed the liturgical cycle; holidays coincided with the great religious festivals; and work was sanctified by the religious solemnities of the guilds. Says Paul Claudel, remembering "the latent murmurs, the eloquent silences, the inexhaustible lesson" of the French cathedrals: "Christian soul, such is thine inner world, and such thy silence." It was not only the cathedral, but the entire social scheme, which confronted man with the truths of religion and thereby kept alive the flame of his belief.

Our modern calendar bears the stamp of Christ on every page. The year was filled with Him, with reminders of His life and of His death. In December, when nature lies asleep, the Church proclaimed the coming of a Saviour who would triumph over death. The four Sundays of Advent heralded His approach; Christmas Day, marked by solemn rites, was loud with hymns of joy; and the first crib, made by St. Francis of Assisi in 1223, was soon copied throughout the Christian world. The feasts of the Circumcision (January 1) and Epiphany (January 6) recalled our Lord's public manifestation, an event which was commemorated during several weeks. But then the central mystery of our Redemption became foremost in the thoughts of men. On Ash Wednesday there began a forty days' fast in memory of Christ's act of self-denial at the opening of His public ministry, and from that date the approaching drama dominated the liturgical scene. Only on the feast of the Annunciation (March 25), which was instituted in the West during this period, did the sad countenance of Mother Church light up with an angelic smile. Next came Holy Week: on Palm Sunday Jesus entered into His city; and step by step, from Wednesday evening, the faithful walked with Him towards Good Friday, a day of dereliction and overwhelming sadness. The Resurrection was accompanied with such joy and such magnificent ceremonial, that in some countries, particularly in France under the Capetian

kings, Easter Sunday was observed as New Year's Day. The Paschal festivities
lasted forty days and offset the sombre hues of Lent. Finally, our Lord rose
into heaven, and ten days later sent the Holy Spirit at Pentecost to comfort
and confirm His brethren.

The whole year was thus planned according to the festivals of the
Church. Besides the major feasts of our Lord, many saints' days were kept
with solemn rites, and those of our Lady took rank above them all. There
was the feast of her Nativity on September 8, the Purification, or Candle-
mas, on February 2, and the Assumption on August 15.

These landmarks in the ecclesiastical calendar, as well as Sundays, were
official days of rest. Public holidays are now regulated by the law of the
land, and even when they happen to coincide with Christian festivals, as
at Christmas, Easter, or Whitsun, the majority of people are ignorant of
their religious origin and significance. The medieval worker, on the other
hand, rested on Sunday *because that day was set apart for God*, and on certain
other days *because they were appointed for the honouring of saints*. We shall
have occasion to notice the importance of this fact when dealing with the
Church as a social influence.

Servile work and other profane activities were forbidden on Sundays
and holy days of obligation. These latter steadily increased, and a council
held at Oxford in 1222 mentions fifty-three, which together with Sundays,
the Ascension, and Assumption, gives a minimum total of one hundred sev-
en days. A reaction then set in, tending to diminish their number.

At certain times of the year, also, the duty of fasting sanctified one of
man's humblest and purely animal characteristics; I mean the need of food.
This venerable custom, inherited from the Jews and widely practised in the
early Church, was held in great esteem. To take only one full meal a day was
to deny the body for God's sake, and thereby to teach it submission to His
will. Fasting was of obligation during Lent, on ember days, on the Vigils of
certain feasts, and on Fridays (in commemoration of our Lord's Passion).
The Advent and Saturday fasts, common in the preceding era, were gradually abandoned; but no one thought of shirking those which remained in
force.

The religious framework of daily life supplied an important psychological requirement. Medieval man, though not in the least standardized, was
conscious that he formed part of a whole. The monk in his monastery, the
craftsman in his workshop, the burgess in his town, each one laboured for
the common good of all; and this communal outlook existed likewise in
the religious sphere. Unlike ourselves, every individual realized that he was
not alone in the battle for salvation, but was acutely conscious of belonging to the Church. That consciousness was born in early Christian times; it
was strengthened in the heroic age of persecution; it cemented the unity of
Christendom in face of the barbarian invaders; and in the eleventh, twelfth,
and thirteenth centuries it took shape in those great Christian enterprises,
the Cathedral and Crusade. But the sense of solidarity with one's fellow men
found its noblest utterance and deepest spiritual significance in the liturgy.

9. THE LITURGY

THE offices of the Church were no less popular than the pulpit. As is still
the case in certain Swiss cantons (e.g., Valais) and in French Canada, the
entire population attended Mass and took part in the procession. No one,
indeed, could neglect this duty without grave scandal. It was not only to
Mass on Sundays and holy days of obligation that the people flocked, but to
such offices as vespers which are today sadly neglected.

Medieval men, feeling at home in church, went there regularly; and
Christians were thus brought into contact with that lofty, all-embracing
expression of the faith which is the liturgy. Better than the best sermon, better than the most learned treatise, it was the liturgy that made God's presence most keenly felt. This association of voice and gesture, wherewith the
Church conducts her public worship and accompanies the most important
events of private life, occupied the forefront of medieval religion. A modern
Catholic will find it almost impossible to appreciate this truth if his participation in the liturgy is confined to attendance at a late Mass on Sunday
morning.

The external beauty of the liturgy formed a large part of its appeal. The
gorgeous vestments, the unhurried pomp of ceremonial, the organ, and the
moving simplicity of plain-chant, all these things conspired to elevate the
minds and hearts of those who saw and heard them. There, in that huge
casket of stone, with coloured light pouring from the windows, how could a
man not feel himself to have reached "the heavenly Jerusalem, with walls of
precious stone, adorned as a bride for her bridegroom"?[25] And yet this outward splendour was as nothing compared with what lay beneath the words
and gestures, if he would but meditate thereon. The rites themselves were
part of an age-long tradition; each time he went to Mass he was reminded
of some event in sacred history or of his ancestors' loyalty to the faith. He
found himself confronted with the very drama of his own salvation, with
mysteries that matter more than life itself—the Incarnation, the Redemption, and the Resurrection. It is not to be wondered at that a mystic like St.
Louis was so penetrated with the grandeur of the liturgy that he once fell
into ecstasy while hearing Mass.

Love of the liturgy, however, went hand in hand with a good deal of
carelessness; and the behaviour of priest and congregations sometimes left
much to be desired. Cats, dogs, and hawks were taken into church; men
remained covered throughout the service; and the time was even spent
in dubious conversation. The Holy Sacrifice itself was in certain cases an
object of blasphemous parody, like the Burgundian "Mass of Bacchus." The
Church had not only to combat these abuses; she had even to lay down rules
for the celebration of Mass. The presence of at least one server was required;
and after 1065 no priest was allowed to say more than one Mass a day,[26]
except on specified occasions, as at Christmas. The failure of some priests
to exercise their sacred office at all caused the Councils of Ravenna (1314)
and Toledo (1324) to decree respectively that every priest must say Mass at
least once and four times a year. Such customs, far removed from those of

---

25. The words are used in the office for the dedication of a church.
26. Some priests, in order to increase their income from stipends, were in the habit of
celebrating twelve times a day.

our own day, show that medieval religion, for all its admirable qualities, had serious defects. Of these we shall have more to say.[27]

The Roman liturgy had been accepted by the whole Latin Church during the Carolingian era, and allowed of very few exceptions. Variant forms were tolerated in a few dioceses (e.g., Milan, Lyons, and Toledo) on the grounds of immemorial custom, and the Dominicans enjoyed similar privileges. Although the main structure of the Roman rite is of great antiquity, medieval liturgists made a few additions to the missal—notably the three sequences, *Stabat Mater, Lauda Sion,* and *Dies Irae*—and assigned the final blessing to the priest instead of reserving it to the bishop as hitherto. Now that the sexes were no longer segregated, it was judged wise to abandon the kiss of peace; and the practice of genuflecting at the words "et incarnatus est" in the Creed was taken over from St. Louis, who had introduced the custom in his private chapel. The most important liturgical innovation dating from the Middle Ages was the elevation of the Host, a courteous gesture which also enabled those present to see and adore Christ's Body under its sacramental veils. This rubric was intended as a protest against the heresy of Berengar,[28] who denied the Real Presence.[29]

The beauty of the Roman rite lies in its straightforward simplicity; Oriental liturgies involve much complicated ceremonial and an air of secrecy. The Syriac, Coptic, and Byzantine rites[30] seem overcharged with symbolism and protracted ritual, which are apt to confuse the uninitiated. Moreover, the "eikonostasis," a screen hiding the altar from the congregation, causes the central act of the sacred drama to take place unseen, in what is known as the "ritual of silence." Although the hymns and introductory processions are no doubt of great beauty, they make no direct spiritual impression on the

---

27. Chapter IV.

28. See Volume 2, Chapter XIII.

29. On the history of the liturgy see Daniel-Rops, *Missa est* (1951). At this period also there grew up the custom of Solemn Exposition and of carrying the Blessed Sacrament in procession. The purpose in each case was to afford the congregation a better view of the Sacred Host.

30. The Byzantine rite includes that of St. Basil, that of St. John Chrysostom, and a Mass of the Presanctified.

mind, evoking the eternal Logos surrounded by celestial hierarchies rather than Christ crucified. In the West, Mass was a real drama whose familiar stages all could follow and understand; and although the ceremonial has been simplified to some extent since the Middle Ages, many features of our liturgical year still preserve a strong dramatic content; those of Holy Week, for example, or the ceremonies of Christmas and Easter. The alternate responses, the chant, and even the vestments, all tend to arouse in the mind a sense of theatre; and even the sacred text lends itself directly to this treatment.

It was therefore not unnatural that, from the second half of the eleventh century, there developed a sort of dramatized liturgy. The events of Christmas, Epiphany, Holy Week, and Easter were actually represented "on the stage," though a certain amount of liberty was taken with the gospel narrative in order to heighten the effect. For example, a sermon wrongly attributed to St. Augustine, in which the Apostles are described as having to render an account of their conduct, gave rise to that "drama of the prophets" which inaugurated the Christmas festivities at Saint-Martial in the diocese of Limoges. Again, to the sober account of the Magi's visit there were added many picturesque details from the Apocrypha. Nor was symbolism overlooked. The disciples at Emmaus were thought of as figures of medieval pilgrims journeying in search of God; they were dressed, as was our Lord Himself, in the familiar habit of pilgrims with hat, scrip, cockle-shell, and bourdon.

Despite their familiarity, these performances made an irresistible appeal to ordinary folk, who watched them for hours with undivided attention. The cast was composed of clerics, and each character had his traditional garments and make-up. Christ always wore a beard, a diadem, and a red robe; Moses was immediately recognizable by the horns on his brow, symbols of the beams of light; John the Baptist was invariably clothed in camel-hair; and (a lasting source of fun) St. Joseph was certain to be dressed in yellow. Before long, "stage-properties" were introduced: Balaam's ass consisted of two men hidden under a skin, which enabled the beast to speak as in the Bible; and Daniel's lions had formidable jaws that really moved. When the

Magi spoke in picturesque gibberish that was supposed to be Persian, or when the little publican Zacchaeus climbed up the sycamore tree, then the crowd would roar with laughter. But there was a solemn silence broken only by sobs as our Lord died upon the Cross.

At the end of the thirteenth century, fashions changed: the play moved from the body of the church and was acted in front of the west doors; episodes and "effects" were multiplied; and the cast was no longer made up exclusively of clerics. The "Mystery Plays" of the fourteenth and fifteenth centuries were on the way to becoming a reality. Social historians may discover in these facts undeniable proof of the religious origins of tragedy. The revival of the theatre, which had been buried in oblivion since the fall of the Graeco-Roman Empire, was due to the medieval Church, and is one of the most striking examples of her influence upon all forms of human activity, as well as of her astonishing creative power.

10. THE PILGRIMS

No picture of medieval Christianity is complete without some account of pilgrimages, which were among the most picturesque phenomena of that age. The custom of travelling in groups to some venerable shrine is found in all religions and in every land; it is as old as the Church herself. The Israelites, a nomad people, used to "go up to Jerusalem" at the great festivals, walking in long files and chanting psalms. Christianity took over this custom, and from the second century onwards pious folk journeyed at considerable risk to pray at the tombs of St. Peter and St. Paul in Rome. In the fourth century many travelled to the Holy Land, among whom was Silvia Etheria, an enterprising Spanish nun who has left a fascinating account of her journey. Not even the tide of barbarian and Islamic invasion had prevented the satisfaction of this urge. During the whole of that unsettled period thousands of Christians were prepared to face danger in order to kneel at the Holy Sepulchre or at the "Confession" of St. Peter; and with the return of peaceful conditions pilgrimages became still more frequent.

It is hard to imagine the endless flow of those enormous caravans; indeed, such figures as we possess are wellnigh incredible. Half a million people made their way each year to Compostella. Rome was visited by more than two million pilgrims in the first Holy Year; and at no time were there fewer than two hundred thousand in the Eternal City. In 1064, notwithstanding that Jerusalem was then in Muslim hands, seven thousand pilgrims led by Bishop Gunther of Bamberg undertook the long, difficult journey to the Holy Places. It was considered a moral obligation to go on one of the major pilgrimages at least once in a lifetime, but many did so more than once. Blessed Thierry, abbot of Saint-Hubert in Ardenne, travelled to Rome seven times, and Geoffrey of Vêndome on no fewer than twelve occasions.[31]

God was the final cause of every pilgrimage. The journey was undertaken to obtain from Him some favour, e.g., cure from bodily sickness; to atone for some grave fault; to fulfil a sacramental penance; perhaps merely to express one's faith and happiness; or even, as in the case of Anne Vercors, to tell God of one's restlessness. All these reasons led the "Jacquots" or "Jacobites" to Compostella, the "Romieux" or "Romites" to the Eternal City, the "Palmers" to Jerusalem, or—more modest but no less fervent of purpose— the "Miquelots" to Mont Saint-Michel. Pilgrimage was an act whereby a

31. The material organization of medieval pilgrimages would repay detailed study. The question of passage by sea has been discussed by the French naval historian Charles de la Roncière, and the following is his account of their embarkation. "When a group of pilgrims arrived on the quaysides at Venice, Genoa, or Marseilles, a tremendous clamour rose from the ships, whose destination was written on a scarlet cross upon the sails. The unfortunate travellers were besieged from every side with offers and imprecations, while employees of the various shipmasters strove to obtain possession of their baggage, swore at one another, cursed their rivals, and protested their willingness to be of service. Bewildered and undecided, the pilgrims allowed themselves to be enticed by the display of dainties set out in the stern—Cretan wines and sweetmeats from Alexandria, which the captain himself handed round." (*Histoire de la Marine française*, vol. 1, p. 273). There were regular agencies for the transport of pilgrims; and on board every ship was a *cargator*, the equivalent of our purser, who sold provisions. Etymologists who trace a connection between the word *cargator* and the French *gargotier* (a bad cook) suggest a not improbable picture of conditions on board ship. The *cargator* was not to be trusted; neither he nor any member of his family was allowed to make ship's biscuit, and, in order to prevent him making a profit by issuing short rations, he was obliged on reaching port to throw overboard all unused supplies.

man placed himself for the time being entirely at the service of Almighty God. It was the highest form of outward prayer and penance, and the whole Christian people was held to benefit thereby: the Church militant, through its suffering *en route*; the dead, who had once travelled the same road and now waited in hope of heaven through the merits of their children; and finally the Church triumphant, in whose honour the laborious journey was made. Every pilgrim, too, was regarded as an object of God's special favour. On the tympanum at Autun Cathedral there is a Doom showing the dead rising from their graves, naked as Adam, all except two pilgrims, each of whom carries a scrip slung from his shoulder. One of these is marked with the cross of the Holy Land, the other with St. James's cockle-shell. With such insigna they had no fear of Judgment Day.

Everyone, therefore, went on pilgrimage, or at least meant so to do: high and low, prelates and princes, craftsmen and labourers. There was no class distinction in that vast crowd. Nor was age a bar; for we have record of pilgrimages for twelve-year-old children and of octogenarians undaunted by the long, weary march. Difficulty and danger lay in wait for pilgrims; for, although their sacred character should have afforded them a measure of protection, there were infidel bandits always ready to attack. The long journey on foot, fatigue, and cold were themselves penitential. No doubt there were generous souls who would always welcome a Jacquot or Romite—and even kill a swan in his honour, as in the ballad of *Roland de Cambrai*. No doubt, too, the wayfarer would find shelter in the monasteries and hospices erected for that purpose by means of charitable gifts. All the same, pilgrimage was an arduous undertaking and meritorious in the sight of God.

Let us picture a man starting out on the great adventure. The time has come when he must fulfil his vow, but his wife and family view the whole business with profound mistrust, and protest against his going. Why should he? Surely God does not expect it of him. If the journey is really necessary, why not visit some place nearer home? What about Conques, Vézelay, or Le Puy? Why not take ship and go to Mont Saint-Michel? Compostella is so far away! Our "Jacquot" takes no notice; in spirit he is already on the road. His friends have told him of the marvels he will see: the stained glass

and sculpture, the huge altars, the famous statue of St. James on its silver
throne, the magnificent ceremonial, and, above all, the very body of the
Saint "ablaze with heavenly carbuncles, wrapped in the brightness of celestial torches." No, he is not to be deterred. Besides, he has been to confession
and has received a diploma which not only certifies that he starts at peace
with God and with the Church, but will enable him on his return to use the
glorious title "Confrère of St. James." More than that, he has been received
in audience by the bishop, who has given him a letter of introduction to the
authorities *en route*. This will prove that he is no impostor, one of those ras-
cals who mix with the holy company—God knows for what nefarious ends!
Lastly, he has also made his will—one never can be sure.

The pilgrim's dress is simple, as prescribed by custom. It consists of a
large hat with upturned brim and a band of cockle-shells (symbolic of St.
James), a leather hood, a voluminous cloak, and a "scrip" or wallet hanging
from his belt. He carries a crooked staff or "bourdon."[32]

It is now about Eastertide; the day of departure has come, and the happy
pilgrims forgather, say, at the Tour Saint-Jacques in Paris. They hear Mass,
and special prayers are recited over them. The priest sprinkles them with
holy water, and hands each one his staff and scrip. The remaining hours of
daylight are spent in farewell visits, and at nightfall the caravan gets under
way. A great shout of "Alleluia!" goes up, and gradually there is heard along
the road that inspiring hymn "Forward, pilgrim, ever forward!"

The pilgrim routes were established by tradition. Men, women, and
children travelled on foot and observed no particular order; very few were
able to afford the modest luxury of a horse or donkey. They were escorted

---

32. If he is wise, he will also have learned something about the road. There were handbooks for this purpose, ancestors of *Baedeker* and the French *Guides Bleus*. The
best-known of these manuals was one, written in 1140 for pilgrims to Compostella,
by Aimcry Picaud of Poitou. It gave full particulars of all places of interest through
which the reader would have to pass, of the difficulties he might expect to encounter,
of rest houses, and danger-points. "Travel light," says Aimery. "When crossing the
Landes beware of bogs and horse-flies; and don't touch fried food, it's absolute poison!" He also has something to say about money, which was never safe: "Don't be too
lavish; the journey may last longer than you think. And don't hesitate to sleep out of
doors with a view to economy."

by minstrels, whose songs alternated with the pilgrims' chorus; only public penitents (recognizable by their dark gowns marked with a red cross) walked in silent prayer and meditation. The convoy moved from place to place, finding in every town some memorial of ancient belief[33]; for the map of Christendom was in their eyes but a network of cathedrals, tombs, basilicas. These journeys lasted many weeks. Compostella was a nine months' march; Rome was not quite so far; but it sometimes took three years to reach the Holy Sepulchre.

The first great centre of pilgrimage, both in dignity and in the merit it conferred, was Jerusalem. It had enjoyed this primacy since the fourth century. The Caliph Hakim in a fit of rage had destroyed the church of the Holy Sepulchre and rendered travel in Palestine extremely dangerous. Even so, Jerusalem had lost none of its pre-eminence; and some bold individuals, Count Fulk of Anjou among them, had made several journeys to seek the grace of repentance—of which, it cannot be denied, they stood in urgent need. But pilgrimage to the Holy Places was still beset with difficulties in the eleventh century; for the Seljuk Turks did not hesitate, when they felt so inclined, to massacre the Christian caravans, or sell them into slavery. The indignation roused by this maltreatment of "God's travellers" was one of the principal motives urged by the Church in support of the first crusade; and the pilgrimage remained a formidable undertaking, even after the establishment of a Christian kingdom at Jerusalem in 1099.

Having travelled across Italy by the Aemilian Way, the pilgrim embarked at Brindisi; not, however, before paying his respects to the Archangel Michael on Monte Gargano. He might, perhaps, decide to take ship at Pisa, Genoa, or Venice; but the distance was still considerable. Once on board, he was faced

---

33. It is curious to note that these Christian memorials on the great pilgrim routes were found side by side with relics of legendary heroes. In Gironde, for example, on the road to Compostella, both Roland and St. Romanus were venerated at Blaye; at Bordeaux, Roland's horn was preserved in the church of St. Seurin; while in the Alyscamps at Arles the first Gallic martyrs were commemorated together with the warriors who fell at Roncevaux. In Italy too, on the road to Jerusalem, there are many echoes of the *Chansons de Geste*. Thus at Modena we find a picture of King Arthur and the Knights of the Round Table; and on the façade of Verona Cathedral is a statue holding a sword upon which is carved the word "Durandarla"—Durandal, Roland's sword.

with a voyage of several weeks in an overcrowded vessel; and after disembarking at a Syrian port, several days' journey lay between him and his destination. But that did not matter; his joy would be all the greater when he knelt at the Holy Places mentioned in the Gospel. There was Bethlehem, where a silver star marked the exact spot of our Lord's birth; the lovely lakeside which had once heard the Master speak; and, above all, the Sepulchre where His Body had rested for three days. He would have so much to tell on his return: he would describe the basilica which was then in course of construction; he would display his precious souvenirs—a little dust from the Tomb, a spray of olive from the Garden of Gethsemane, a medal, a statuette, or better still a palm like those of which the "palmers" wore an image round their necks.

The journey to Rome, though not so difficult, was considered almost as meritorious. It has been called the "pilgrimage of the heart," for a great surge of love carried faithful Christians toward the Eternal City which is the very nerve-centre of the Church. The road, however, was not without its perils; for in proportion as the pilgrims were more numerous, so did a host of robbers lie in wait for them amid the wild passes of the Alps. But such was the unending flow of travellers along every road, that St. Bernard of Menthon was moved by charity to build hospices for their reception at the most dangerous points. The French pilgrims, indeed, were so many, that more than one of the routes they followed came to be known as *via francigena* or *via francesca*. In every town there were relics of the saints to venerate, famous churches to visit; but no one failed to turn aside and adore the "Holy Face" at Lucca. This was a great statue of Christ to which many miracles were attributed; it had eyes of crystal, which gave it an appearance of awful majesty. After a journey of about one thousand two hundred fifty miles the travellers arrived at the summit of Monte Mario, which was also called the Mount of Joy—Montjoie of the old battle-cry. From here they could see Rome spread out at their feet. Caught up on a mighty wave of emotion at the sight of houses, palaces, churches, and vast ruins, all bathed in golden light, they intoned the famous canticle: "Hail, Rome! Mistress of the world, red with the blood of martyrs, white with the lily of virginity; be thou for ever blessed!"

86   The first visit was to St. Peter's, the most ancient church in the city. Here
was the statue of St. Peter whose big toe they kissed; here was his tomb and
that sublime relic, whose authenticity no one questioned, Veronica's veil,
with its imprint of our Divine Lord's countenance. They might even be able
to greet the Pope himself and kiss his pastoral ring. But there were other
places scarcely less venerable: St. Paul outside the Walls, where the Apostle was buried after his martyrdom; St. John Lateran; the Church of the
Holy Sepulchre, reminding them of another at Jerusalem; the Colosseum,
with its memories of the early martyrs; and Santa Maria della Rotonda, the
ancient Pantheon. Among some excellent guide-books, which told the pilgrim all that he should see, was the *Itinerary of Einsiedeln*. More interesting,
however, was the *Complete Description of the City*; it had something to say
about every monument and legend, not forgetting the lodging houses, one
of which (the Albergo d'Orso) may still be seen on the banks of the Tiber.

Rome's importance as a place of pilgrimage increased steadily throughout the Middle Ages, and was linked with the growing power of the papacy.
It attained its zenith in 1300, when Boniface VIII revived the old Jewish
tradition of the Jubilee by proclaiming a "Holy Year." Responding to the
Pope's invitation and the promise of special graces, pilgrims flocked to the
city in their thousands. It was difficult to find accommodation for them all;
and Dante, who was there, tells us that it became necessary to turn the Pon-
te Sant' Angelo into a one-way street! These pilgrims were drawn from every
land and from every level of society. They included whole delegations representing various nations and cities, that of Florence being distinguished from
the rest by its magnificence. What was the result? Evil tongues whispered
that the only true beneficiaries of Holy Year were the Roman tradesfolk;
but it can hardly be denied that such a demonstration of piety must have
strengthened the links of Christendom and spread devotion to the Church
and her supreme head on earth.[34]

---

34. The Jubilee of 1300 initiated a custom which has lasted ever since. In 1343 Clement
VI decreed that the celebration of Holy Year should take place every fifty years as
from 1350. In 1389 Urban VI reduced the interval to thirty-three years in memory of
the years of our Lord's earthly life.

The pilgrimages to Jerusalem and Rome were based on such historical facts as the life and death of Christ, or the arrival and martyrdom of St. Peter. That Compostella should have attained a position such that its pilgrimage rivalled the other two is not easy to explain. Nevertheless, it did so; and in the *Vita Nuova* Dante goes so far as to say that, "strictly speaking, a pilgrim is one who travels to the House of St. James." It is odd that the spotlight of history should be focused on the humble fisherman of Bethsaida, son of Zebedee and brother of St. John the Evangelist, who, according to the Acts, was first of the Twelve to receive the crown of martyrdom. An apocryphal work informs us that he had visited Spain as a missionary; but it was not until long after his death that his name passed into legend.

Tradition says that in the year 45 a ship from some distant land ran ashore on the coast of Galicia. On board were seven men with a cedarwood coffin; they were disciples of St. James seeking a burial place for the holy relics of their master. Nearby was a city surrounded with strong walls and ruled over by a Druid princess known as the "She-Wolf." These seven Christians endured many trials, during which the terrible princess was on the point of denouncing them to the Roman governor; but at last, overwhelmed by numerous divine prodigies, she submitted, received baptism, and offered the disciples two bulls to draw the hearse, together with some land on which to build a tomb. Such was the supposed origin of the cult of St. James in Galicia. The place was called Compostella, "Field of the Star," because the tomb, which had disappeared during the barbarian invasions, was rediscovered by a hermit who dreamed that he was led to it by a star. It is impossible to understand how such traditions could set up so powerful a wave of devotion, unless we associate the pilgrimage with historical fact—the determination of the Christians of Spain to rid their country of the Muslims. St. James was reported to have appeared on the battlefield of Clarijo and to have led the Christian charge, on which account he was styled "Matamore," slayer of the Moors. There can be no doubt but that the pilgrimage to Compostella was part of the Church's keen interest in Spain, an interest which resulted in the Reconquista. Though it originated in the ninth century,[35] it was not organized on any large scale until three hundred forty years later, by Diego Gelmirez, first archbishop of the new see; but it remained popular throughout the Middle Ages.

Pilgrims came in thousands to Compostella from every part of the Western world. They included Germans, Flemings, English, Poles, and Hungarians; but so numerous were the French, that here, as in Italy, the highways along which they travelled were known as "French roads." Four main routes, on all of which there were regular stopping places, led across France. The first of these, starting from the Tour St. Jacques in Paris, ran via St. Jacques-du-Haut-Pas to Tours, where it was joined by another road from Chartres. The Burgundian route commenced at Vézelay; that of Auvergne at Clermont; while the southern route ran from the Alyscamps at Arles, with Toulouse as its most important halt. All these roads met at Puenta la Reina south of the Pyrenees, from which place the pilgrims journeyed to Compostella by way of Burgos, Leon, and Villafranca. Everywhere there are reminders of their passage, and the Jacobites appear in many a sculptured group, wearing the cockle-shell badge. To the ritual cry of "Outrée! Susée!" they moved in long columns across scorched plains and frozen plateaux.

Jerusalem, Rome, and Compostella, then, were the three main centres of pilgrimage, but there were others almost as important. Such was the shrine of St. Thomas at Canterbury and that of the Magi at Cologne. Places of less renown also drew enormous crowds. The relics of St. Mary Magdalen were believed to have been hidden by St. Maximin at Saint-Baume in Provence. No one doubted this tradition after 1279, when Charles of Salerno exhumed a body whose tongue was found to be incorrupt, and the place was visited by popes and princes. There was another shrine of the Magdalen at Vézelay in Burgundy, where some of her bones and hair were said to be preserved. The tomb of St. Martin of Tours enjoyed considerable prestige; it was a popular place of pilgrimage, especially on the anniversary of his death (November 11) and on the feast of the translation of his relics (July 4). In Normandy, on

---

35. The stone sarcophagus had been identified as that of St. James about 870; the first great pilgrimage, led by Gottschalk, took place in 950.

the very borders of Brittany, stood Mont Saint-Michel, the inviolable sanctuary of that archangel who is represented in the Apocalypse as protecting the woman's Son against the fury of a seven-headed dragon. He was the patron saint of warriors, and the "first baron of France"[36]; but the pilgrims who flocked to his chosen isle included artisans, merchants, and even children (the "Pastoureaux" of 1333), all of whom were fanatically proud of their title, "miquelots." In Italy the most popular places of pilgrimage were associated with St. Francis, particularly Assisi with San Damiano and the Carceri nearby. There were also Monte Alverno, where he received the stigmata, Gubbio, and indeed countless places immortalized by some event in his life.

Innumerable shrines, of course, were dedicated to our Lady: Notre-Dame of Chartres, a venerable foundation in whose crypt stood the Virgin of the Underworld; Notre-Dame of Puy, built to commemorate a miraculous cure; Notre-Dame of Fourvière, set on a hill-top over Lyons; Notre-Dame of Garde, erected by Peter of Accoules about 1210 as a spiritual "lighthouse" above the port of Marseilles; Notre-Dame of Liesse, the glory of north-eastern France, which was built by the crusaders and became famous when our Lady helped Enguerrand de Coucy to find his two little sons who had been kidnapped by robbers. Notre-Dame of Dusenbach and Notre-Dame of Marienthal were centres of devotion in Alsace. In the south-west, Notre-Dame of Rocamadour, Notre-Dame of Font-Romen, and Notre-Dame of Bécharram were forerunners of Lourdes. The ancient Norman sanctuary of Notre-Dame de la Délivrande was not far from Auray. Here the shrine of St. Anne did honour likewise to Mary, whom the Bretons venerated in person at Rumengol, Folgoat, and elsewhere.

These international, national, provincial, and local pilgrimages constituted, in the words of Jacques Madaule,[37] "a vast arterial system which kept alive the people's fervour and exerted an influence even upon those who never took part in them. The unity of Christendom was evident in the perpetual movement which inspired artists and craftsmen, and provided the

---

36. The three fleur-de-lis appear in the arms attributed to St. Michael.
37. *Pèlerins comme nos pères*, 1950.

minstrels with their songs." The pilgrimages, indeed, exemplify the driving force of medieval religion, with its passionate craving for the infinite and its intolerance of boundaries.

II. THE SPIRITUAL ARMOURY OF THE CHURCH

THE outstanding characteristic of the Middle Ages was its unanimous, living, and inspiring faith; a faith whose virtue persisted in spite of blemishes, a faith which explains the determining influence of the Church upon the social and political history of that age. We cannot fail to recognize that secular and ecclesiastical history were more closely linked during these three centuries than in the barbarian epoch.

How was it possible for an essentially spiritual power to dominate the temporal scene? The answer is not far to seek if we bear in mind the unanimous acceptance of the faith. What were the psychological foundations of ecclesiastical authority? First, respect for God's representative on earth. When Pope Innocent IV, speaking as Vicar of Christ, declared all secular power subject to his own, "as the soul is superior to the body, and the sun to the moon," he was merely giving utterance to an idea that had long been admitted throughout the Western world.

Moreover, public opinion tended to equate, if not actually to identify, obedience to the law of the land with submission to the law of God. Just as heresy, an offence against religion, was considered tantamount to the civil crime of treason, so, conversely, many misdemeanours which would today incur penalties in the civil courts were punished by ecclesiastical tribunals with a "penance," e.g., an order to go on pilgrimage. There are few offences in the modern calendar which even a professed Christian would consider as involving sin; but in the Middle Ages life's drama was played out on a stage whose limits were defined by God Himself, and those who overstepped the mark incurred religious guilt. The Church, in fact, controlled the entire mechanism of society; and it was this universal recognition of ecclesiastical authority which had enabled her, since barbarian times, to operate in the

twofold character of a spiritual and temporal ruler. The latter may be seen
in her creation of new institutions and in her contact with the civil powers;
her spiritual function is more difficult to analyse, for it concerned the souls
of men. At all events, this dual role produced, as it were, a distinctive human
type, a civilization which, in spite of its undeniable weaknesses, does honour
to our race.

How, then, did the Church enforce her authority? By means of religious
sanctions; those who disobeyed her precepts met with public or with private
chastisement, which at that time it was very difficult to escape. But if the
Church could order pilgrimages, scourging, almsgiving, fasting, or prayers,
she had equal power to mitigate the severity of justice. For our Lord had said:
"Whatsoever you shall bind or loose on earth shall be bound or loosed in
heaven." Hence the principle of substitution, which corresponded more or
less to the German *Wehrgeld*: a sinner might avoid the full rigour of the law
by the merits of a third person, or by almsgiving. Moreover in the eleventh
century the Church began to grant "indulgences," i.e., the partial or plenary
remission of canonical penances, to anyone who rendered outstanding service to the Christian cause, or even, in certain circumstances, gave evidence
of extraordinary piety. One could, for example, cite numerous instances of
an indulgence granted for helping in the construction of cathedrals and hospitals, bridges and dikes, for joining the crusade or fighting with the armies
in Spain, or for confessing at some venerable shrine. It is also known that
during Holy Year, in 1300, a plenary indulgence was granted to all pilgrims
to the Eternal City who complied with the regulations governing visits to the
basilicas, the recitation of certain prayers, and reception of the sacraments.

The execution of an ecclesiastical sentence depended upon no *direct*
means of coercion. The Church had no police force; but she could generally
rely upon the support of the civil authorities, since they too were subject
to her commands. Her immediate weapons were exclusively spiritual; that
they were effective was due to the faith of her subjects, who believed in hell
fire and dreaded the awful consequences of Heaven's wrath.

No one, not even the most hardened sinner, was undaunted by the tide
of sacred eloquence. When a preacher in the pulpit named the guilty person

and threatened him with eternal damnation, the most cynical became uneasy. "Ye are devouring wolves," thundered Jacques de Vitry to some looting lords; "ay, and in hell ye'll howl like wolves!" To Peter de Courtenay, who had insulted the Bishop of Auxerre, Innocent III publicly addressed this awful warning: "Your conscience will bear witness against you. Bound hand and foot, you will be cast into exterior darkness to be consumed by the avenging flames. In vain then will you plead with the Bishop of Auxerre to dip the end of his finger into water and refresh your tongue. Wretched man, what will you say in your defence when you hear the voice of Christ: 'Whatsoever you have done to the least of these my little ones, you have done it unto me'?"

Besides private admonitions of this kind, there were three public sanctions. The first was the *anathema*, or solemn curse, which was directed against the malefactor in person and did not affect his relations with other men. Here is the sentence pronounced by the Chapter of Saint-Julien at Brionde upon a thief who stole the priceless reliquary given them by Charlemagne: "Cursed may he be in life and death, eating and drinking, standing and sitting! May his life be short, and his goods pillaged by his enemies! May an incurable paralysis assail his eyes, his brow, his beard (?), his throat, his tongue, his mouth, his neck, his breast, his lungs, his ears..." (and so on for four more lines). "May he be as a weary stag pursued by hunters; may his children be made orphans, and his wife a demented widow...!" The medieval outlook was such that the poor fellow could not help feeling somewhat anxious as to his future.

Excommunication and *interdict* involved serious consequences in the social and political order. The first of these measures deprived the criminal of association with his fellow Christians. The Church rejected him, and, since the social link was essentially religious, he no longer enjoyed a place in the community. His wife could leave him; his children could defy his orders with impunity. His servants fled the house; and if his property were threatened, no one would lift a finger to protect it, for he was now under the ban of society. The dramatic ceremonial of excommunication was designed to impress the victim with his unhappy state. It was a kind of burial service,

read over a living being, and intended not to open for him the gates of heav-
en, but to bind him fast in death; and no Christian could remain unmoved
as the black-clad priests blew out their candles, pronouncing meanwhile the
culprit's name. And these measures applied no less if the excommunicated
person were the greatest monarch on earth. If he entered one of his cities the
churches were closed, the bells were silent, and the streets empty; he might,
indeed, have been the plague.

An interdict was even worse, applying as it did to a whole region; and
if the guilty party were a king, the entire realm suffered in consequence of
his sin. Not only were the churches closed, but the crosses reversed, and no
sacrament, except baptism, might be administered. There were no marriages, no burials with religious rites; and since the Church at that time was the
equivalent of our public registrar, the very bases of legal existence were thus
undermined. Social life came to a standstill, for there were no Sundays or
feast days; and the people found it a heavy burden to be deprived of goods
which they valued more than life itself. On all sides there were murmurs of
rebellion; and if the guilty ruler would not submit, his subjects threw off
their allegiance. No wonder that these sanctions proved effective.

Against whom, and in what circumstances were they employed? High
and low were subject to excommunication for such crimes as unlawful marriage, brigandage, physical violence upon the persons of clerics, and offences against the law of nations. Among numerous sovereigns who incurred
the penalty were Philip I of France, Godfrey of Lorraine, Philip Augustus,
Louis VII, and Alfonso IX of Leon. Interdict was applied in cases of recidi-
vism and categorical refusal to obey the laws of the Church. Louis VII, John
"Lackland," and Frederic II of Hohenstaufen were all punished in this way.
It was extremely rare that persons so condemned did not eventually come to
a better frame of mind.[38] Their submission might not always be prompt, and
might even be accompanied at first with mental reservation; but in the last

---

38. There were cases, however, in which ecclesiastical leaders perished for having used
these spiritual arms. Thus, in 1220, Bishop Robert de Meung was assassinated by a
knight whom he had excommunicated.

resort the sense of their own interests and the desire for pardon combined, as in the case of Henry IV at Canossa, to bring them to their knees.

12. SUMMARY

So long as men believed firmly in the gospel teaching, society was dominated by the Christian faith. Practically no aspect of the Middle Ages can be properly understood except by reference to Christian principles. Everyone felt himself to be "dyed in Christ's blood"; every facet of human life, indeed, bore the sign of the Cross.

Political organization was inseparably bound up with Christianity; for even the feudal chain itself was forged on the anvil of religion in the form of an oath taken on the Holy Gospels. The successors of Charlemagne owed their prestige as delegates of God on earth to their coronation, the repetition of that august ceremony first performed on Christmas Eve in the year 800; and the "Most Christian Kings" of France, Spain, and England were anointed for no other reason than to lay solemn emphasis upon the fact that they owed their power to God rather than to the accident of birth or the fortune of war. This religious element which underlay the structure of civil authority was the Church's justification for intervening on the political plane, and for exercising her control in matters which might have seemed to lie outside her province.

In the social sphere, Christianity assigned each grade its function in the common task, enabled the lowly to ascend the ladder of success, and relieved the destitute through charitable works, thereby saving them from desperation and rebellion. Christianity alone, we might almost say, stood for the principles of social justice.

Economic life itself was subject to the immediate control of Christian morality, and not on the material plane alone. It is true that the monasteries were centres of production and exchange; and the rising fabric of the cathedrals was the most evident sign of prosperity. But the Church's mistrust of wealth, her condemnation of usury, and her idea of a "fair wage" produced a

spiritual outlook quite different from ours, an outlook whose consequences
in the practical affairs of life were immense, notwithstanding widespread
indifference to her teaching.

This leads us to the moral influence of Christianity, a decisive factor in
the Middle Ages. Men's lives were governed by the faith, by the Ten Commandments, and by the precepts of the Church. Christ's representatives on
earth had never ceased from the beginning to insist upon the principles of
perfection; and in spite of error, excess, and outright transgression, Christianity had kept alive the highest standards of conduct by imposing on all
alike an irrefutable code of morality.

The catholicity of the Church roused in mankind that longing for
expansion—that resolute determination in God's cause, which later manifested itself in the Spanish Reconquista, in the missions of St. Francis,
Raymond Lull, and John of Plan-Carpin, but above all in the crusade, that
wonderful epic renewed time and again during a period of two hundred
years.

The Church was also the light and guide of man's intelligence; for, as
St. Bernard says, "The Word was made flesh and dwelt amongst us; ay, and
in our memory and in our thought." It was Christian doctrine that supplied
the theses of philosophy and poetry, that inspired all that was best in the
spiritual domain. Nor need we dwell upon its creative function in the realm
of art; it is demonstrated before our very eyes by the cathedral, an unchal-
lengeable fruit of faith, "a great ship towering to the sky."

Such, then, was medieval faith, and such its works. But we must do
more than analyse its several elements; the limbs are not the living body.
We must try to see Christianity at work in the stream of life, to understand
its influence upon those who for three centuries bore witness for mankind
before the Lord. It is difficult to choose one from among so many whose
sole purpose was to "seek the kingdom of God and His justice," and who,
according to the promise, were endowed with gifts that gave them power to
determine the fate of their contemporaries.

In choosing St. Bernard of Clairvaux, I do so not because I consider him
in every way superior to men like St. Francis and St. Dominic, not because

96   I regard him as having left a deeper mark upon the Church, but because he
      appears to sum up in himself those numerous aspects under which medie-
      val Christianity is revealed. He laboured with pre-eminent success in many
      walks of life; and so well does he embody the aspiration of the Middle Ages,
      that his personality may be taken as representative of the whole epoch.

CHAPTER III

Saint Bernard of Clairvaux

1. THE CALL OF CHRIST

NORTH of Dijon stands the ridge of Fontaines, a spur of Mons Affricus upon which Caesar once encamped his legions. Although not very high, it is fairly steep; from its summit one obtains a bird's-eye view of the Saône valley, the Jura mountains, and, far away on the horizon, the gleaming Alpine snows. A little to the south-west are the hills of Burgundy with their famous vineyards—Richebourg, Pommard, and Corton. But the young man who looked down from his father's terraces upon this countryside in the late summer of 1111 was interested not so much in the splendid panorama, with its harmonious blend of mountain-range and valley, as in a dark forest-patch which concealed a monastery.

He was just twenty-one years old, having been born in 1090, third of the seven sons of Tescelin, lord of Fontaines, and of Aleth, daughter of the powerful lord of Montbard. Both families belonged to the Burgundian nobility; and through his mother, who was descended from the counts of Tonnarre, he had inherited some ducal blood. His ancestry, of which modesty never permitted him to boast, explains some of his outstanding characteristics: his impulsiveness, his courage in face of danger, and his outward bearing, which was ever that of a true knight. Tescelin was a prominent figure in Burgundy,[1]

---

1. The role of Burgundy has been well described by Pierre Gaxotte in his *Histoire des Français* (Paris, 1950), vol. 1, p. 247: "I would draw attention to one fact of historical geography: the two monastic capitals of Cluny and Citeaux are situated in Burgundy. Is this a mere coincidence? It may be; but the coincidence enables us to understand

that region of sharp contrasts, and synthesis of the many diverse elements which go to make up France. He seems to have owned large estates, and to have held high office at the court of Duke Eudes; at all events he brought up his children according to the most lofty ideals, and, above all, set before them the example of his own unblemished life.

Bernard's mother, Aleth, was not only a saint, but a beautiful woman and perfect mistress of a home. Fulfilling with grace and dignity the duties of her rank, she never disdained more humble tasks about the scullery or kitchen; and her charity to the poor was boundless. Her children could not, in fact, have had a more accomplished mother. If she entertained a secret preference for one, it was for her third son, Bernard. One of her biographers relates that while carrying this child in her womb, Aleth had a dream: she saw a white puppy barking furiously, and recognized it as a sign that her child was destined to become a famous preacher of God's word. This charming story is found also in the lives of St. Stephen Harding and St. Dominic; it need be taken no more seriously than the honey-bees on Plato's lips.

When the time came for her sons to begin their studies, Aleth moved to Châtillon-sur-Seine, where her family owned a house, and where there was a celebrated capitular school attached to the church of Saint-Vorles in the diocese of Langres. If one may judge a master by his pupils, the canons regular who taught young Bernard must have been excellent of their kind; "for nowhere else could he have acquired that clear, incisive style, which makes him one of the most charming and original Latin prose-writers of the

---

the soul and nature of that province. It is a region of varied characteristics, a crossroads, a land of highways, a place of passage and encounter. It is quite the reverse of a barrier, uniting far more than it divides; and the peoples of the West have felt themselves in Burgundy to be on common ground. In this sense it is the key-point of France, whose geographical and historical importance lies in the easy access it affords between the Mediterranean, the Channel, and countries bordering the North Sea. If Burgundy had remained outside the French kingdom, France would not have played so decisive a part in the destinies of Europe. As it was, there were few areas of Christendom so well suited to become a centre of the apostolate, a centre from which men and new ideas were to radiate in all directions." This observation should not be forgotten when considering St. Bernard, a Burgundian who was at once the greatest Frenchman of his age, perhaps the greatest Christian, and the most influential figure of medieval Europe.

Middle Ages."[2] At Châtillon he followed what we should call "secondary studies." Besides the "trivium," which included grammar, rhetoric, and dialectic, he read and expounded Horace, Virgil, Ovid, Cicero, Lucan, Statius, Boethius, and, of course, the Fathers of the Church, especially St. Augustine. He did little in the way of higher studies (the *quadrivium*), excepting music; his biographer, however, assures us that at Saint-Vorles he proved himself an attentive scholar, a retiring but obedient pupil, and a friend of delicate susceptibilities. His love of solitude was already apparent, and he was an eager student of Holy Scripture.

Bernard returned to Fontaines in time to be present at his mother's deathbed, and he learned from her one final lesson. Knowing that her end was near, Aleth wished to die in absolute simplicity. She forbade the curtailment of some parochial festivities which had been arranged, and extended the usual invitation for the clergy to come and dine at the castle. Having received extreme unction and viaticum, she made the responses to the Litany of the Saints, and, as the prayer concluded, fell asleep in Christ. No young man could forget such a scene.[3]

In his twenty-second year, Bernard was a noble figure of manhood: slender and dignified, with deep blue eyes that were full of gentleness. His broad forehead proclaimed the keenness of his intellect; and his contemporaries recognized in him that distinguished bearing possessed by most men in whom physical beauty is allied with greatness of soul. Despite these natural gifts, however, there was no trace of arrogance or vanity. The passing years had changed his youthful shyness to that "extraordinary reserve" of which one biographer speaks, but which never prevented him from asserting his authority whenever circumstances required. He was gentle, modest, and refined; so refined, indeed, that the least impropriety touched him on the raw. But a modest exterior concealed a soul of fire which no fetters could

---

2. Étienne Gilson.

3. Aleth richly deserved the honour paid to her by St. Bernard's successors when in 1250, her body was moved from the crypt of St. Benignus at Dijon to their abbey church. Her reputation, which rivals that of Blanche of Castile (a lady of far different temperament), has been honoured by the Church with the title "Blessed."

restrain. Though the world had many snares for a young man thus endowed by nature and by grace, his biographers are no doubt guilty of some exaggeration when they tell, for instance, of a lady introducing herself into Bernard's bed, or of Bernard throwing himself into the icy waters of a lake in order to subdue temptation excited by the mental image of a girl. These tales were invented to illustrate the gravity of the danger to which he was exposed; but the truth seems to have been less romantic, the struggle of a more interior kind.

Intellectual temptations are the worst that can assail a brilliant youth; they are not conquered by cold baths. Bernard was torn between the attraction of profane studies and his growing preoccupation with things divine, a conflict in which the warrior-blood of Tescelin may have played some part. For a while he suffered the torments of uncertainty; but having confided in his uncle Gaudry, a man of profound insight, he was convinced that God called him to join the company of those who had abandoned all things for Christ's sake.

At this juncture fresh difficulties arose from without. It was not the first or the last time that a young man in search of his true vocation has found the decision complicated by parental opposition. Should he go to Germany and continue his studies? Why not allow his father's influence to obtain for him some lucrative situation half-way between religion and the world? During those long hours on the terrace at Fontaines, he stood gazing down upon the dense forest, seeing in his mind's eye the humble dwelling of the monks.

In order to appreciate the spiritual conflict whose issue was to determine a soul's fate, we should remember that it was fought out in the unsettled years of youth. And even when the decision had been reached, Bernard's life continued to the end a battle-field. He would always have to choose between contraries; there were no half measures and no compromise.

The spring of 1112 was a period of uncertainty and wretchedness, through which every great soul must pass, and from which it cannot emerge except by the narrow gate of an irrevocable choice. On one side there was "divine discontent," and on the other a thousand contrary aspirations, a thousand hopes, upon which he would have to turn his back. He must decide one way or the other, and accordingly set out for Citeaux.[4] Bossuet, in a famous passage of the *Panegyric*, has depicted Bernard at this time. "Behold a young man in his twenty-second year, filled with ardour, impatience, and the impetuosity of desire! That force, that vigour, that hot, boiling blood, like a heady wine, allows him no rest or relaxation." Others may turn the restlessness of youth to very different ends; Bernard realized that, since Christ had called him, his gifts would run to seed unless he employed them for the one purpose that ultimately matters. He therefore resolved the forces of contradiction that raged within him by embracing the folly of the Cross.

Fourteen years earlier, on March 21, Palm Sunday and the feast of St. Benedict, a group of novices, moved by the spirit of reform, had left the Cluniac abbey of Molesmes for a dreary solitude among the *cistels* or reeds of the Saône, and established a house of new observance, Citeaux.[5] Since 1098 the foundation had managed to survive under the direction of St. Robert, St. Alberic, and St. Stephen Harding; but they had had the utmost difficulty in obtaining vocations and providing for their material wants. In 1112 this first Cistercian community deserved its reputation for terrible austerity and extreme poverty which bordered upon destitution, and in these circumstances Tescelin's resistance is not hard to understand; a monastery where the brethren lived like serfs at forced labour, digging the ground and clearing drains, seemed at variance with a nobleman's ambition for his son.

But St. Bernard now revealed that extraordinary power of persuasion which characterized his entire life. He enlisted the support of his uncle Gaudry, who afterwards followed him into the cloister; and every one of his brothers was gradually won over to his project. Most of them were soldiers,

---

4. "The Lord spoke to the heart of a young man named Bernard, and although he was young, noble, refined, and learned, he conceived so great a fire of divine love, that, despising all the pleasures and delights of the world, no less than ecclesiastical dignities, he proposed in the fervour of his soul to embrace the rigorous life of the Cistercians" (*Great Exordium of the Cistercian Order*).

5. We shall study the origins of the Cistercian order in the next chapter.

and one was married; but Bernard predicted that God would contrive a means to gain them all. Gerard was wounded in battle; at the sight of his blood he cried out, as if baptized again: "Henceforward I am a monk of Citeaux!" Guy, the young husband, left his wife, who in turn took the veil with their two daughters. There was left only Nivard, the youngest, who at fifteen was below the canonical age for admission. "See how rich you'll be," said his elder brothers, referring to the inheritance which they left behind. "What, you take heaven and leave me the earth?" replied the boy; "I won't agree to any such arrangement." And later on he too left for Citeaux. Tescelin was powerless to stem the tide, and only warned his sons: "Don't overdo it. I know you so well, it will be difficult to restrain your zeal."[6]

In April 1112 a troop of about thirty knights (for many of their friends had followed the example of the young men from Fontaines) knocked at the gate of Citeaux. "What do you ask?" inquired the abbot, Stephen Harding. And Bernard, in the name of all, fell on his knees and answered in the ritual formula: "The mercy of God and of the Order."

2. THE MONK

ON entering Citeaux, Bernard experienced that almost indescribable gladness which reaches to the very roots of a man's being when he has discovered his true calling. From the first he delighted in the stern asceticism of the new observance. In accordance with the Holy Rule, he underwent a year's novitiate, although there could be no doubt as to his vocation. Those first twelve months were not so much a period of physical testing as a spiritual apprenticeship, during which there was born in him a craving that was never satisfied until his death. He prayed unceasingly and devoted much time to scriptural and patristic literature. "I used in those days" he said in later life, "to gather and set up in my heart a sheaf made of our Lord's sufferings, His agony and all His bitterness of soul."

---

6.   Tescelin himself subsequently joined the Order.

One fact stands out: Bernard was a monk before all else. Notwithstanding long journeys, arduous political negotiations, the clash of speculative ideas, and the power and glory of this world, he remained always a monk. Titles and honours, even the tiara itself, were offered to him; but he refused them all, preferring the humble dignity of a Cistercian. "St. Bernard was no mere writer locked away in his own individuality; he was a monk in a community of monks, praying as they prayed, working as they worked, adhering strictly to the spirit of the Rule and all that it prescribed."[7]

So, at the age of twenty-two, Bernard was a monk—for ever. He had donned the plain knee-length tunic of serge and the white woollen cowl, whose hood protected his shaven head against the sun and rain. In his humility he desired nothing better than to live as the most obscure member of the flock; but this was not to be for very long.

One might almost say that Bernard's arrival had attracted God's attention to Citeaux; for after a somewhat precarious existence the community started rapidly to increase, and twelve months later had grown so large that it was able to found La Ferté, followed by Pontigny, in 1113. Young Bernard had brought new blood into the Order; his holiness and intellectual gifts endowed him with qualities of leadership that were recognized by all. When, therefore, in 1115, the Count of Troyes invited the Cistercians to establish a house in his territory, Bernard was made superior of the little community which set out for a high plateau near the headwaters of the Aube. He was no more than twenty-five years of age, and his appointment might have seemed unwise. But the selection was that of no less a man than Stephen Harding, and bore witness to the qualities of Aleth's son.

The foundation of this new monastery was the work of several years. The twelve monks from Citeaux reached their destination towards the end of June 1115, and chose an extensive clearing in the woods at a place called Val d'Absinthe, to which they gave the beautiful name Clairvaux. A cemetery was marked out, an altar set up, and some huts erected. William of Champeaux, Bishop of Châlons-sur-Marne, approved the foundation and

---

7.   V. Berlière, *L'Ascèse bénédictine*, p. 101.

raised Bernard to the priesthood. Before long, permanent buildings began to rise, simple and devoid of ornament. There was nothing on the walls, not even on those of the church, and no lamp hung in the sanctuary. The refectory was unpaved, and narrow windows let in a few rays of light. The dormitory was like a row of coffins, for the beds were mere boxes consisting of four planks. As for the abbot's cell, it was a cupboard under the stairs, illuminated by a wretched slit, a hollow in the wall to serve as seat of government.

Bernard had acted upon our Lord's advice and entered by the narrow gate. To conquer his animal nature, according to the precept of St. Paul, was in his view the first and indispensable stage on the road to heaven. The monastic vocation involved a total sacrifice: a life of renunciation, fasting, work, and perpetual self-denial. The monastery was a school of sanctity where every monk must forget himself for love of God.

Bernard was to lead this sacrificial existence to the very last. In spite of his exhausting labours, he practised the most extraordinary forms of austerity, which soon began to undermine his health. In the early days of Clairvaux the diet consisted of nothing but bread made of barley, millet, or vetch, together with boiled nettle-leaves, roots, and beechmast. Salt and oil were the only seasoning. It is not to be wondered at that a regime of this kind proved too much for a young man whose health had never been robust. Since Bernard was unwilling to submit to treatment, William of Champeaux intervened, and the chapter was requested to relieve the abbot of his duties for one year so that he might rest. But the doctor engaged to look after him was no better than a quack, whose "remedies" only increased the suffering of his unfortunate patient; and it was said that the dishes ordered for the sick man were so horrible that they would have turned a healthy stomach. That, however, did not deter the abbot from accepting them with perfect indifference.[8] So far from improving his health, his physical condition deteriorated, and he remained an invalid all his life. It might, indeed, have been

---

8. One painful detail will give some idea of St. Bernard's constant weakness: whenever he occupied the abbatial chair, a hole was dug in the ground so that he could relieve an irresistible impulse to vomit.

said of him, in the words of St. Paul, that God confounds the strong by the weakness of His saints.

A man who had obtained such mastery of himself could not but influence others, and there was no one at Clairvaux who did not hold him in admiration. He had proved himself a leader at the age of twenty-one, and a leader he remained throughout his life. He looked upon his exalted situation as one more reason for taxing his own strength; and he never failed to practise that "purity of heart," that "ever right intention," that determination to set a high example, which typify the religious superior as described in his own sermons.

It was to be expected that one so eager to triumph over the limitations of human nature would demand much of his subjects, and might perhaps require too much. He laid a heavy burden on himself, and there can be no doubt that his monks loved him in return. He spoke of them as a mother of her children, and he used no metaphorical language when he said that they were dearer to him than his own heart. It is impossible to read without emotion those letters which he wrote to the community at Clairvaux, who were always foremost in his thoughts: "If you find my absence hard to endure, yours is still harder for me to bear. Your lot and mine can never be the same; for whilst you are deprived of me alone, I long for each and all of you."

But it was not for their sake or for his own that Bernard held his sons so dear. It was for God. The happiness he desired for them was such as will never fade. He asked of them the absolute oblation of their instincts, pleasures, and personal tastes, admitting frankly that the effort was "above unaided human strength, uncommon, and even contrary to nature." But the real difficulty in these cases is to see the line where excess begins and where rigour can turn only to frustration. Did the Abbot of Clairvaux overstep that mark?

At first, yes. Seeing in the principle of absolute self-renunciation the only means of achieving the necessary "reform" of the Church, Bernard imposed upon his monks an existence of undue hardship. St. Francis of Sales, who wrote on the subject with his usual perspicacity, says that "so keenly did he spur these poor aspirants to perfection, that in the endeavour to get them there he merely held them back; for they lost heart, finding themselves driven so hard up the steep and narrow slope." But Bernard was far too intelligent not to detect faint-heartedness among his own. He questioned himself, asked the advice of his friend, William of Champeaux, and realized that he had gone too far. Some years after the foundation of Clairvaux he discovered the happy medium between extreme asceticism and the requirements of human nature, and this was later embodied in the *Charter of Charity*. St. Francis of Sales says that he became "gentle, amiable, gracious, and condescending—all things to all men in order that he might gain all to Christ." It is easy to understand that material conditions in the monasteries under Bernard's crozier would have terrified most of our contemporaries!

The marvel is (and it demonstrates the medieval thirst for God) that Bernard's reputation for austerity, far from driving away souls, drew them to him in hundreds. Clairvaux exercised an enormous attraction almost from the date of its foundation. In 1116 the school at Châlons-sur-Marne was half emptied by departures for the Val d'Absinthe. Next came a Benedictine from Chaise-Dieu, followed by the canons regular of Honicourt. Clairvaux might have been described as a heavenly ambush from which Bernard struck down, one after the other, a highwayman, a party of knights on their way to a tourney, as well as numerous monks and priests. Of the saint's family, there now remained in the world only his sister, Humbeline. One day, accompanied by a brilliant retinue, she came to see her brother. Struck by the poverty of the conventual buildings, and suddenly disgusted with her own absurd luxury, she cried out: "I am nothing but a sinner; but it was for sinners that Jesus died. Bernard may despise my body, but not my soul. Let him come, let him command: I will obey...."

Bernard had but to leave the walls of Clairvaux for this round-up of souls to assume even more astonishing dimensions. His radiance spread everywhere. He appeared, he spoke; and, as at the call of that magic flute in the German fable, thousands were spellbound. Wibald, abbot of Stavelot, has described him preaching: "...his visage pale, emaciated by fatigue and fasting, seeming almost ethereal, and so impressive that the mere sight of him convinced his hearers before he had even opened his mouth." Or again:

"his deep emotion, his incomparable art (fruit of long exercise), his clear
voice, his gestures always appropriate to his words."

The result was "a miraculous draught repeated ever and again." When he preached at St. Quentin, thirty members of his audience begged to accompany him. He visited the students at Paris, and twenty of them left Mont Saint-Geneviève for the Val d'Absinthe. His renown crossed the Channel, and English postulants soon began to arrive at Clairvaux, where the brethren included not a few illustrious persons. Henry, brother of the King of France, came to ask Bernard's advice, but dismissed his retinue and embraced the austere conventual life, as did Philip, Archdeacon of Liége, and Alexander, a canon of Cologne, who later became abbot of Citeaux (c. 1167). When St. Bernard died there were seven hundred monks at Clairvaux.

Nor was that all. Clairvaux had sown as well as she had reaped. The first daughter-house was established at Trois-Fontaines in the diocese of Châlons (1118); it was followed soon afterwards by Fontenay near Montbard, and Foigny near Vervins. More distant regions too were colonized: Igny in Champagne, Boumont in Vaud, Eberbach near Mainz on the Rhine, Chiaravalle in Italy, and Fountains in England. By 1153 there were one hundred sixty offshoots of Clairvaux, some of them in Ireland, Hungary, Scandinavia, Spain; and these too multiplied in course of time.

Bernard indeed left his mark upon the face of Europe. Think of the weight on those frail shoulders! Abbot of Clairvaux until his death in 1153, he never ceased to fulfil the duties of his office, finding time, even amid the cares of state, to decide a question of farming, of enclosure, or of the sale of cattle. Not only did he personally administer the charity of his house, which relieved thousands of poor people, but, as head of the Order, he kept an eye on all its members, restoring peace to a troubled community, helping another to surmount its difficulties, showing his tireless solicitude for all. These tremendous labours presuppose, apart from heroic virtue and unflagging energy, unequalled powers of organization, of observation, and of understanding, no less than an abiding determination to rise above himself. It is the glory of our race that there are a few souls who thirst for "more," as there are legions who enjoy an unalterable taste for "less."

3. THE PERFECT STATURE OF A MAN

THE foregoing account of St. Bernard's youth and monastic vocation reveals in him a curious admixture of gentleness and passion, of tenderness and fervour, of sensitiveness and forcefulness. These contradictions, reconciled in God, endowed his personality with rare charm. He has been not seldom represented as his own executioner, and torturer of his fellow men; he has even been described as "a wicked man." Actually, he was human in every sense of the word.

We have already noticed St. Bernard's affection for his community. This, like many another facet of his character, is frequently misunderstood. He was no fanatical prophet, no unyielding polemist, as, for example, was St. Peter Damian. In this respect also he was the embodiment of his age: outwardly rough and even violent, but full of that interior sweetness which is known as charity.

True son of the gentle, saintly Aleth, he was devoted to his brothers; and there is no finer instance of fraternal love than his anguish at the death of Gerard, one of his first companions in religion and a close collaborator in his work. One morning in Chapter, as he was explaining a passage from the Canticle of Canticles, the thought of Gerard welled up in his heart, obliging him to pause. To the amazement of those present he burst into tears, and then continued: "You tell me not to weep? My bowels are torn out; shall I have no feeling? Nay, if I suffer, I do so with my whole being. I am not made of stone; my heart is not a heart of bronze. I confess my woe. It is carnal, you say? I know that well, for I know that I am a creature of flesh and blood, sold under sin, delivered unto death, and subject to suffering. What would you? I am not insensible to grief; I have a horror of death, both for myself and for my own. Gerard has left me, and I am in pain; I am wounded unto death." Is that the cry of an inhuman soul, of a deluded and fanatical ascetic?

Numerous examples of this kind might be adduced to demonstrate St. Bernard's tenderness toward his friends no less than toward his brothers. "Let us rest in the heart of those we love, as they rest in ours," he would often say; and he practised what he preached. Some of his friendships were models of their kind. Such was the tie that bound him to William of Saint-Thierry: when the latter fell sick, Bernard laid aside even the most urgent business, hurried to the bedside of his friend, and offered to look after him for as long as might be necessary. Nor did he fail in charity towards those with whom he disagreed. At the height of an acrimonious dispute with Peter the Venerable on the subject of Benedictine tradition and the new Cistercian observance, he proved himself so generous that the Abbot of Cluny wrote in a tone of gentle mockery: "Candid and terrible friend, what could destroy my love for you?" In the famous duel with Abélard, when he felt obliged to discard the last vestiges of pity because the issue was far more important than any human consideration, his final gesture towards his defeated enemy was, as we shall see, one of perfect charity.

It is simply not true that Bernard's austerity prevented the development of his natural gifts, or limited his capacity for love and fellow-feeling. His life provides the answer to those many critics who imagine that the least restraint of natural appetites is detrimental to human character. The farther he travelled on the road of self-renunciation, the greater became his influence for good. The more firmly he controlled himself, the more truly human he was found to be; and that is so, from whatever standpoint his personality is viewed. The famous line of Terence, "I am a man, and nothing human is alien to me," might have been written by St. Bernard; and in point of fact, though his eyes were ever upon God, the great mystic used similar words.

To treat Bernard exclusively as the warrior of Christ would be to distort his image beyond recognition. There were many facets to his character: ceaseless curiosity, a deep-rooted but sober craving for knowledge, and the "sense of time," that indefinable quality whereby a man not only *belongs* to his age, but understands and gives it expression. St. Bernard's interest in human affairs—politics, literature, art, and a thousand commonplaces of daily existence—is among the most attractive elements in his manifold nature. It affected his very outlook upon life, which was always realistic, broad, and sound.

Nevertheless, in common with all who really love mankind, he entertained no illusion about human nature. He knew those shadows which hang over the deep waters of man's heart. This, of course, does not mean that he looked upon our wretchedness as incurable; Bernard was no Calvin. He often alludes to the unhappy fate of Adam's children since the Fall; he points to the sadness of their lives and to the depth of their humiliation; but he never forgets that this wounded and corrupt nature is stamped with the divine image and likeness, that the lamp of God is ever ready to dispel our darkness. This association of clear thinking and supernatural confidence in respect of man is characteristic of St. Bernard's humanism. "Consider thy nobility," he says, "and be ashamed at thine own shortcoming. Forget not thy beauty, lest thou be confounded by thy deformity."

St. Bernard has been described as a "Christian Socrates"; but while the expression is not contradictory in terms, the emphasis must lie upon the adjective rather than the noun. According to him, faith is the means of knowledge and right judgment, and the power directing man's potentialities to their final cause. He realized that in and through God alone can man attain his goal.

4. LIFE IN GOD

It would be misleading to recognize in St. Bernard's character and thought only those features which make him like ourselves, for they were magnified by faith and love of God. If he was of the full stature of a man, it was mainly because the human element was illuminated by the light of the Holy Spirit. "It was almost in spite of himself," says Montalembert, "that he was a great orator, a great writer, a great personality. He was, as he desired above all to be, something else besides—a monk and a saint."

Bernard was a saint in no ordinary sense of the word. His brand of holiness consisted not merely in his refinement of the basic virtues, in his extraordinary humility, in his unfailing charity, or in his continual effort at self-conquest. Sanctity has a more inclusive meaning, which can be applied only in the case of one whose whole being, whose every act and thought, is directed to God who is both End and Way.

The fullness of St. Bernard's life and its impact upon his contemporaries   III
stamp him as a mystic. His mystical activity is apparent as the determining
factor in all that he did and in every word he uttered. Here again, he is representative of his age, of its profound and unanimous faith, of its submission
to the will of God. He is one of the high peaks in medieval society; but a
mountain is, after all, part of the surrounding plain, and has its roots therein.

The mystical urge permeated St. Bernard's life. Hence his cry: "My
God! My love! How Thou lovest me! How Thou lovest me!" and: "Oh,
incomparable, vehement, burning, and impetuous Love! Thou wilt let me
think of nothing but of Thee; Thou disdainest all things else; and despising all, art sufficient unto Thyself!" The immensity of that love, and of that
ineffable exchange of hearts, is nowhere better described than in these few
words: "Understand with what measure, or rather how immeasurably, God
is worthy to be loved. He who is so great hath loved us first, gratuitously
and entirely, though we are small and miserable! ... Since our love is related
to God, it is related to the boundless, to the infinite, for God is infinite and
hath no limits. What then, I ask, should be the measure and the term of our
love?"

This man, who has been represented as hard, unfeeling, bases his doctrine upon the notion of God's love for him in spite of his mortality. Mabillon bestowed upon him the title Doctor Mellifluus; and it aptly describes
that happy union of tenderness, ingratiating manner, and unvarying politeness which typify his conduct at every stage, and which we might call "unction," had not that word come to denote a quality which we abhor. He was
bathed in, penetrated and moulded by, a love compared with which all other sentiments are vain.

St. Bernard is likewise typical of his age in the fundamentals of his religious outlook. Since God is the *alpha* and *omega*, what other knowledge
can there be that does not proceed from Him? Reading, study, and work
for the sake of knowledge as such is idle curiosity. The only school is that
of Christ. "Peter, Andrew, the sons of Zebedee, and their companions were
not chosen from a school of rhetoric or philosophy; yet it was through them
that our Lord accomplished His purpose of salvation." Hence that almost

exclusively scriptural tinge of Bernard's thought and eloquence, which was so prominent an aspect of medieval faith. The Bible was his favourite, if not his only book; he studied it in great detail, and spent some twenty years commenting upon the Canticle of Canticles, comparing one passage with another and endeavouring to elucidate their many problems. If he gave much time also to the early Christian writers, it was only because St. Ambrose, St. Augustine, St. Gregory, and others were themselves steeped in Holy Scripture, and form part of the mainstream of Biblical tradition. His devotion to the Bible was so intense, that a number of his sermons consist entirely of scriptural quotations arranged in a rhythmical order which is itself derived from the Psalmist and the Prophets.

His strong mystical tendencies enable us to recognize St. Bernard as the source of a current which bore medieval religion towards devotion to our Lord's humanity. "He who is filled with the love of God is easily stirred by all that concerns the Word made Flesh. When he prays, the sacred image of the God-Man stands before him: he is present at Christ's birth, watches Him grow up, hears Him preach, witnesses His death, His glorious Resurrection, and His Ascension...." Such phrases are a perfect summary of the origin and scope of this devotion, which is so closely associated with the Middle Ages. Christ is not only the supreme model, the archetype; but the Word is truly flesh, our Brother and our Friend. So thought Bernard, who pondered deeply upon every detail of our Lord's human life; and his sermons, taken as a whole, form a complete mystical biography of the Saviour. Speaking of the new-born Babe of Bethlehem, he chooses simple, poignant words, suited to that Babe's humility. The stable, the straw, and even the poor swaddling-clothes, he treats as so many symbols for our edification. But when referring to Christ crucified, his manner becomes stark; his anguished tongue can do more than tell one by one the sufferings of Jesus; and he moves our imagination by the sheer simplicity of his account.

At the centre of St. Bernard's spiritual life stood Christ, the God-Man, so near to us and yet so far removed. The great preacher must have carried his hearers along with him, and stirred them to the very depths with this description of our Lord: "He was beautiful among all the sons of men, both within and without. He, the glory of eternal light, outshone the splendour of the angels. To set eyes on Him was to recognize Him as a man without blemish, flesh without sin, Lamb without spot. O human soul! To think there is conferred upon thee so inestimable a privilege that thou mayest be the spouse of One who is the object of angelic contemplation; that thou mayest gaze upon Him whose beauty the sun and moon adore, and at whose nod the universe obeys!" In order to appreciate how well St. Bernard's method was suited to his period, we need only glance at that unforgettable image of the Messiah, known as *Le Beau Dieu*, on the porch of Amiens cathedral. Or again, that window in the basilica of Notre-Dame du Sacré Coeur at Issoudun. It shows our Lord and St. Bernard standing face to face; and in order to express their mutual love, the artist has written above the Heart of Christ the one word "Bernard," and on the White Monk's breast the Holy Name.

While on the subject of artistic representation, it is worthwhile to recall a somewhat different work, illustrating another side of the great abbot's piety. I refer to Murillo's celebrated canvas known as the *Lactation of Saint Bernard*, a symbolic idea which is found also in a window of the church at Laines-au-Bois in the diocese of Troyes. St. Bernard kneels with outstretched arms, his eyes fixed on the Virgin Mary. She is in the act of uncovering her breast (as would a mother for her child) to quench the thirst of her devoted servant. This gracious imagery conveys some idea of Bernard's impassioned reverence for the Mother of Jesus, whom he was, perhaps, the first to call "our Lady" and who was never far from his thoughts. There is a tradition that one day, as the community were chanting the *Salve Regina*, the torrent of love which leaped up in his heart overflowed and caused him to cry out: "*O clemens! O dulcis! O pia!*" Those words now form part of the noble anthem, and perpetuate his memory. Whether or not the story is true, he is known to have composed the *Memorare*. Medieval devotion to Mary is, in fact, inseparable from Saint Bernard.

It would be false, however, to imagine that he set no limit to his veneration. He was strictly orthodox, and never transgressed the boundaries at which Holy Scripture seemed to call a halt. He wisely ignored the apocryphal writings; nor would he call Mary "Mother," because the patristic tradition reserved that title to the Church and to sanctifying grace.[9] It was within the strict limits of Catholic dogma and Holy Scripture that Bernard's flaming soul sought out the raw material for those treasures of Christian doctrine which were taken over and recast by later generations. The mystic of Clairvaux rises to his greatest heights in this respect when he discusses Mary's role as mediatrix: "Needest thou an advocate with Jesus? Fly, then, to Mary. I say without hesitation, Mary will be heard because of the consideration due to her. The Son will hear His Mother, and the Father His Son. Confidence, unflinching confidence, is the stairway of sinners; that is the foundation of my hope."

The idea of intercession, of man's instinctive longing for a mediator with the Almighty Judge, is an essential mark of medieval piety. Nor, in St. Bernard's view, is Mary our sole advocate; for he often speaks of the part played by the Church triumphant. More than one panegyric has survived, preached by him in honour of some saint, wherein he rouses the faith of his hearers by pointing out those of the elect who will represent man's need before the throne of mercy. From this point of view also Bernard was of his time. But he never indulged in those flights of exaggerated fancy to which his contemporaries were so prone; he spoke little on the subject of miracles,[10] and he attached no undue importance to relics.

All these manifestations of Bernard's devouring thirst for God, all his saintly life, culminated in what is certainly the crown of mystical activity—an absolutely pure and disinterested love of God. It is not my purpose here to enlarge upon his mysticism, which combined the two extremes of sweetness and austerity. Nor shall I delay to examine those peculiarities which differentiate it from other schools. I shall merely refer to his insistence that

---

9. On St. Bernard's devotion to the Mother of God, see Aubron, *L'Oeuvre Mariale de Saint Bernard* (Paris, 1935).

10. There is no doubt whatever that St. Bernard wrought a number of miracles in his lifetime, although his fourth biographer, the author of *The Book of Miracles*, seems to have overstepped the mark. He healed the sick and vanquished demons; but his biographers take care to emphasize that he disliked these appeals made by simple folk for the exercise of supernatural power. He was torn between humility and charity.

all forms of devotion are meaningless unless directed to Almighty God, and that man's end is "to love God no longer for one's own sake but for Himself alone." He brought to the supernatural life that urge to seek ever more distant horizons which, as I have said, was among the finest characteristics of the medieval mind. There can be no doubt that he enjoyed at certain rare and privileged moments of his life the ineffable experience of God's presence; but he expressed himself upon this subject with the utmost reserve.[11] But this flight to the summits never caused Bernard to lose sight of earth and human realities. Mystic though he be, your Burgundian has both feet planted firmly on the ground. "His mysticism," writes Étienne Gilson, "was wholly interior and psychological; it was based on self-knowledge and the analysis of our spiritual poverty." This fact explains how it was that so great a contemplative managed to lead a life of such astonishing activity.

Bernard's impact upon the religion of his contemporaries was enormous. All medieval mysticism derives more or less from him; many writers borrowed from him unashamedly; and he has been read and studied almost as much as St. Augustine. All the principal forms of medieval devotion bear the mark of his influence, in respect not only of their content, but also of their outward manifestation—Cathedral and Crusade. It was not simply by prayer, teaching, and personal example that the great abbot sought to achieve the glorification of mankind. We shall presently find him at work in every sphere of life, engaged in the most mundane of affairs. It is indeed

---

11. In the following passage he speaks of the mystical union with as much precision as it is possible to attain: "Bear for a moment with my folly. I wish to tell you, for I have promised to do so, of my own experience. It is really hopeless to talk about such things; but the Word has entered into me—He has, in fact done so more than once. He may have entered frequently; if so, I have not always been conscious of His coming. But I have felt His presence within me, and I remember it quite well.

   "I rose to the topmost part of myself, but still higher reigned the Word. Like some anxious explorer I descended to the very depths of my being, but found Him lower still. I looked outside myself and saw Him to be beyond all things. I looked within, and found Him more intimate than I am to myself.... When He enters into me, the Word betrays Himself by no movement or sensation; it is only the secret trembling of my heart which reveals His presence. My vices take wing, my carnal affections are mastered; my soul is refreshed; I am inwardly renewed as it were with the mere shadow of His glory."

of no small significance in the history of religion that one cold monastic cell became the centre of the Western world. As for Bernard, even amid those strenuous duties which, as the conscience of his age, he was obliged to undertake, he never forgot that the one true source of all his strength was supernatural. "I light my fire," he used to say, "at the flame of meditation."

5. ST. BERNARD, THE CONSCIENCE OF HIS AGE

AND what a fire! One cannot think of this man's life without recalling our Lord's words: "I came to bring fire on earth, and what would I but that it be kindled?" Nothing so exasperates a zealous Christian as to see the flame of Christ burn feebly, a pile of smouldering ashes where there should be a furnace of love. "God's affairs are mine," he once exclaimed; "nothing that concerns Him is alien to me." He felt himself responsible for the truth which he possessed, and desired that all should recognize it. He longed that his Mother the Church might be faithful in all things to her divine Spouse.

So, when "God's affairs" were imperilled, Bernard was immediately aroused. He cared for nothing and spared no one when God's interests were at stake. At such times he was outspoken to a degree, and his mordant irony was directed at all alike. He once told an archbishop: "Your conduct is odious; you are so intractable that I am resolved to have no more to do with you. You prevent the good will of your friends and invite the hostility of others. You know no law but your own whims, and behave like a despot, regardless of Almighty God...." The following admonition was addressed to the Sovereign Pontiff: "I might as well shut myself away in silence and retreat; for the whole Church will clamour no less against the court of Rome, so long as it pursues its present course...."

The greatness of the Middle Ages is surely apparent in this fact, that the great ones of the earth were prepared to tolerate such language, and usually submitted to the saint's injunctions. It is difficult to imagine one of our modern rulers hearing himself thus denounced without taking immediate steps to silence the offending voice in some secret prison cell.

The Abbot of Clairvaux viewed "God's affairs" from a twofold standpoint. Those interests were at stake whenever God's law was violated or
His precepts ignored. Bernard was at the very heart of that great reforming movement which had been, and would continue to be throughout the
Middle Ages, a reviving element in the Church's life. But God's interests
were no less imperilled when His Church was threatened in her liberty, her
sovereignty, or the reverence due to her. On all such occasions St. Bernard
intervened.

Count Thibaut II of Champagne was Bernard's immediate overlord,
for Clairvaux lay within his territory. He was among the greatest of French
nobles, and his estates exceeded the royal domain of France. Although pious
and generous, he was sometimes proud and brutal, and Bernard never failed
to rebuke him. Thibaut once refused to do homage to the Bishop of Langres, of whom, under the peculiar anomalies of the feudal system, he held
some land in fief. This was an infringement of ecclesiastical law. St. Bernard
at once sat down and wrote so stern a reprimand that the Count submitted.
In another case the principles of charity were involved. After a trial by battle,
the loser had had his eyes put out, and Thibaut's officers had confiscated his
goods. Bernard protested against this barbarism and obtained reparation
for the unhappy victim's children.

Remarkable episodes of the same kind are found in his relations with
the King of France. Bernard had experience of two Capetian monarchs,
whose characters were very different. Louis VI, the Fat, was a wise sovereign
whom the saint loved and esteemed; but he tended to use the Church as an
instrument of government, and on that account was called to order by the
Abbot of Clairvaux. Again, in 1127, the king named as his seneschal (com-
mander-in-chief) a prelate, Stephen de Garlande, archdeacon of Notre-
Dame. Bernard denounced in scathing terms this confusion of dignities,
which might be harmful to the Church, and scourged the new seneschal
with bitter irony: would he say Mass in armour, or perhaps lead his troops in
alb and stole? So terrible, indeed, was his onslaught, that Louis revoked the
nomination. The same intolerance of abuse appeared soon afterwards in the
matter of a dispute between the king and Stephen of Senlis, Bishop of Paris.

118 Stephen had undertaken the reform of his chapter; but Louis, apprehensive lest he should find the canons less amenable to his wishes, counter-attacked by confiscating the diocesan estates. Stephen promptly laid them under an interdict and fled to Sens. He notified St. Bernard of his predicament, and in due course the sovereign received a letter from Clairvaux: "The Church has been driven to lodge a complaint against you with her Lord. She finds her old friend changed into a tyrant..." and so on through four long pages.

In another instance he went so far (perhaps a little too far) as to address Louis VI as "a second Herod"! The most extraordinary fact is that the king never ventured to rid himself of so troublesome a prophet. As for Louis VII, a second-rate monarch, whose divorce from Eleanor of Aquitaine was to prove so detrimental to the kingdom, Bernard had to remonstrate with him ten or fifteen times. His asperity on these occasions was, if possible, even sharper than that used toward his predecessor; for he had known his sovereign as a boy, had loved him, and been sadly disappointed.[12]

---

12. The following passage gives an exact idea of this quiet severity with its undertone of regret for misplaced affection. "Since I had the honour to know your Highness, I can vouch for my unfailing devotion to your welfare. During the past year you cannot have been unaware of my repeated efforts, in concert with your ministers, to re-establish peace in the kingdom. But I fear you render my labours ineffective. It seems that you are going light-heartedly to cast aside your present advantages, that the Devil has inspired some counsellor to urge upon you the renewal of those disastrous ills of which you had repented.... Maybe the inscrutable decrees of Providence have so arranged that Your Highness should view the world from upside-down. You count the dishonourable as matter for self-satisfaction, and you believe that to be honourable which should cover you with shame.... For my part, whatever resolution you may take against the welfare of your kingdom, your own salvation, and the glory of your name, I cannot disguise the outrage and the desolation which afflicts Holy Mother Church. I am determined to persevere and, if need be, to combat unto death. In default of shield and sword, I shall employ the arms of my state, which are my prayers and tears.

"I call heaven to witness that I have never ceased to implore God for the peace of your kingdom and the prosperity of your person; and I have used my good offices with the Pope on your behalf. I begin to regret having so far excused you on the grounds of youth. Henceforward I shall take a more realistic view. Sire, if you will not amend, I venture to predict that your sin will not go long unpunished. With all the zeal of a faithful and loving servant, I exhort you to lay aside your malice. I pray you earnestly, remember the Wise Man's saying: 'Wounding words from a friend are better than the kisses of an enemy.'"

If St. Bernard was the Church's advocate against the secular power, he was no less God's advocate against the Church. The question was, whether the principles governing a monastic order differed in kind from those which all Christians were obliged to follow. Bernard thought not; at the very most, he allowed a difference in the degree of effort required of a monk and of a layman, and in the heights of perfection to which he hoped they might attain. He wished to make the whole Church hear that call to sanctity which he himself had heard.

He appealed first to the head, the Pope; and nothing is more characteristic of Bernard than his attitude towards the papacy, which was one of admiration and respect. He agreed with Gregory VII that the Sovereign Pontiff "is the only man whose foot all nations should kiss." But he considered that the holder of so exalted a position should match the dignity of his office with the purity of his life; and no one has better described the duties of a pastor than this austere monk whose humility led him to refuse the tiara. In 1145 he had an opportunity to speak his mind; for one of his monks, Bernard of Pisa, was elected Pope and took the name of Eugenius III. The Abbot of Clairvaux lost no time in addressing to the Holy Father, between 1145 and 1152, five noble letters which now form his celebrated treatise *De Consideratione*, a magnificent work which may be truly described as the Charter of the Papacy. Bernard loved this man, and wrote to him in terms of exquisite grace: "What matter that you have been raised to the Chair of Peter? Walk on the wings of the wind, if you will; you can never escape from mine affection. Love will recognize a son crowned even with the tiara." At the same time, however, he reminds the new Pope in solemn phrases of the awful dignity of the title which he bears.

> You are the bishop of bishops; the Apostles, your forbears, were instructed to lay the world at the feet of Jesus Christ. You have inherited that duty; the whole world is your legacy. Pastor of all the sheep, Pastor of all their pastors! In case of necessity, and if the fault deserves, you can bar heaven to a bishop, depose him, cast him out to Satan. You are in very truth the Vicar of Christ.

What is this your power? An estate to be exploited? Nay: a burden to take up. Be not proud on Peter's throne; it is but an observation post, a high place from which, like a sentry, you may cast your glance over the world beneath. You are not the owner of that world; you are no more than a trustee. The world belongs to Christ.

Do I, then, say you rule the world, but not as task-master? Indeed I do; for to rule well is to rule with love. You are the servant of Christ's flock; it is not your slave. Yea, and I will add this: there is no iron or poison that I fear so much for you as I fear the pride of power.

In the event, Eugenius III obeyed these warnings, notwithstanding the magnificence that surrounded him as Pope. He continued to lead the austere life of a Cistercian monk, "esteeming money no better than a wisp of straw," and showed himself in very truth one of the "reformed."

But that was only a start. Bernard knew that principles which do not pass beyond the realm of ideas are worthless, and so he turned his eye to details. The Pope's entourage was utterly corrupt; the Roman Curia was full of careerists, soft and worldly clerics—it was fast becoming, said the saint, a "robbers' cave." Hear with what stinging words he describes these birds of prey. The legates themselves, he cries, are worthless men; "they will sacrifice the people's salvation for the gold of Spain." All that must be changed. "The Pope must choose experienced and disinterested men. Nor must he limit the choice of his entourage to Rome, where corruption reigns; he must select from the whole wide world those who are destined to judge the world."

His strictures were not confined to the Eternal City, but were heard wherever he thought fit. One of St. Bernard's most remarkable achievements was the "conversion" of Suger, abbot of St. Denis, where the pomp of a royal court was more in evidence than the austerity of a religious house. Suger, the powerful minister of Louis VI, was told by St. Bernard that his luxurious living was a disgrace, that a servant of God should be ashamed to be attended on his journeys by a troop of more than sixty horse; and an astonished court beheld the unwonted spectacle of a prime minister exchanging worldly pomp for monastic observance. The royal policy, which had tended to ignore religious claims, was suddenly reversed; and Suger attained real greatness because Bernard had persuaded him to live as a monk serving God as minister of his king, rather than as a minister who, by chance, happened to be a Benedictine.

Bernard was prominent at every stage of the twelfth-century reform. His notorious dispute with Cluny may be held to have exceeded the strict limits of fair play; for in spite of his criticism, it cannot be denied that the great Order of Black Monks was by no means as lax as he suggested. He was in close touch with the Grande Chartreuse, whose prior, Guigo, was so much attached to him that William of Saint-Thierry assures us that they "formed but a single heart, a single soul." He also took part in the reorganization of the canons regular, and remained on the most friendly terms with St. Norbert and the Premonstratensians.

The secular clergy were no less an object of Bernard's constant solicitude, and the picture which he draws of them makes sombre reading. From one end of Christendom to the other "the goods of the Church are dissipated in vanity and extravagance." The bishops themselves were setting a bad example, at which the Abbot of Clairvaux did not hesitate to point his accusing finger. There was, for instance, Simon, the pluralist of Noyon and Tournai, who grew fat on the revenues of two dioceses; and Henry, Bishop of Verdun, who had secured his appointment by bribery. Bernard's reforming zeal went further still in his treatise on the *Manners and Duties of Bishops*, which was compiled at the request of Archbishop Henri le Sanglier of Sens. "Why do you get yourselves up like women, if you do not wish to be criticized like women? Be known for your works, not for your fur capes and embroideries! You think to shut my mouth by observing that a monk should not criticize a bishop? Would to heaven you might shut mine eyes also! But were I to remain silent, others would speak—the poor, the naked, and the starving. They would rise up and cry: 'Your luxury devours our lives! Your vanity steals our necessities.'"

That is the voice of a prophet; and the most surprising thing is that it was heard. Bernard was invited to decide contested episcopal elections at Tours, Langres, Rennes, and York; this simple monk became, in fact, the

conscience of the higher clergy. On the other hand, when he praised St.
Malachy, the great Irish bishop who died at Clairvaux, it was not long before
the object of his admiration was canonized.

In Bernard's eyes the Church was more than the clergy; it consisted of
the whole army of baptized, a fact which he never overlooked. The flaming
zeal of God's advocate could not ignore the needs of secular society. Institutions appeared to him deserving of respect in so far as they conformed with
the Christian ideal. Princes hold their power from God; they must govern
according to His law, protecting the good, punishing evildoers, and securing
justice to the oppressed. To the Queen of Jerusalem, for example, he wrote
these splendid words: "Learn from Jesus how to reign"; but toward those
who betrayed this ideal he showed no clemency.

Men of the world, too, came under his lash. Here is a knight, mounted
on a horse with gold and silken trappings, his helmet bright with precious
stones, the skirts of his finely woven surcoat reaching to his feet. Is that a suitable array for a soldier of Christ? Here are women, tripping along, adorned
like some pagan temple, with their heavy trains of sumptuous material, their
wimples held in place by golden diadems. Is that a seemly dress for Christian women? The occupations of lax Christians were equally reprehensible.
Men, he says, rush headlong into a fight, goaded by love of violence and of
danger. They never stop to inquire "whether the cause is just and the intention right." They fight innumerable private wars in the shape of tourneys,
forgetting that "the noblest occupation is to render oneself pleasing in God's
sight." As for the ways of women, the least said, the better!

It should not, however, be imagined that Bernard reserved his criticism
for the rich. He minced no words when addressing humbler folk, peasant or
middle class, and did not hesitate to show them up as greedy, egotistical, or
lacking in conjugal fidelity! Nor were these indictments heard as the lofty
exhortations of a fashionable preacher; for at the sound of Bernard's voice
men were inwardly transformed, and the light of Christ penetrated to their
inmost souls. The Abbot of Clairvaux was in truth the conscience of his age,
and as such he played no small part in rescuing Earth's salt from insipidity.

6. DEFENDER OF THE FAITH

It was not only in the sphere of moral conduct that St. Bernard bore witness to the law of Christ; the same energy is apparent also on the doctrinal plane. His attitude in this respect has been often misrepresented as that of an unbridled fanatic, hot on the scent of imaginary errors, and pitiless toward whomsoever he suspected of upholding them. His detractors, however, are themselves suspect. Berengar of Poitiers, for example, described Bernard's soul as "filled with rancour"; but Berengar was a disciple of Abélard, and more than prone to rancour.

He has even been called "torturer," devotee of the stake, predecessor of Torquemada. True, he maintained that heretics should be delivered to the civil arm and burned, as did most of his contemporaries; but he left no doubt as to what he considered the right procedure of the Church when confronted with unorthodoxy. She ought not, he says, to take up arms before she has tried by every means at her disposal to recall those who have gone astray. If they persist in error, and thereby show themselves a public menace, then let "those die who prefer to die rather than return to God."

Later on[13] we shall examine in some detail those Manichaean tendencies which gave rise, especially in Languedoc, to the heresy known as Albigensianism. In 1143 St. Bernard received warning from his friend Evervin, provost of Stanfeld, and launched a vigorous attack on the partisans of these wild doctrines, chief of whom were Pierre de Bruys and Henry of Lausanne. Two years later he accompanied the legate Alberic to the south of France, where his preaching was largely successful. He obliged Henry to withdraw, and made a deep impression on the masses by his example and his miracles; but he took no part in those senseless acts of violence which broke out some time before the spread of heresy called forth a deplorable expedition known as the "Albigensian Crusade."[14]

---

13. Volume 2, Chapter XIII.
14. St. Bernard also disputed with Arnold of Brescia, a Christian democratic leader and apostle of absolute poverty, who held that the clergy had no right to private property, and preached a kind of anticlerical Communism. When Arnold fled to Paris in the

So far was Bernard from fanaticism that he demonstrated on one typical occasion that the defence of Christian truth cannot be divorced from that of charity. On the eve of the second crusade, an anti-Jewish pogrom broke out at Cologne, Mainz, Worms, Spire, and Strasbourg. It was fomented by a Cistercian monk named Rudolph, encouraged by a party of nobles. Immediately he learned of these events, Bernard left Flanders where he was preaching the crusade, and hurried to the Rhineland in order to stop the massacre of Jews.

There is, however, one case, that of his famous duel with Abélard, in which the term "fanatic" might appear more justifiable, in which he might seem the very type of an "obscurantist" monk, the enemy of all progress. But it is absurd to call a man ignorant when his writings bear the stamp of erudition, when he enjoys the luxury of a digression to quote Statius, Ovid, and Lucan. Étienne Gilson well remarks that St. Bernard "renounced everything but the art of writing well." His literary output is surprising both in quantity and in quality. It includes no less than three hundred thirty-two sermons and fourteen treatises, not to mention a correspondence of which we still possess more than five hundred letters. It is marked also by wonderful variety and sometimes by an almost subtle elegance. There is the *Life of St. Malachy*, which provides much curious information about Ireland in the twelfth century; the enormous *Commentary on the Canticle of Canticles* in ninety-six sermons of inexhaustible richness; two powerful dogmatic treatises *On the Knowledge of God* and *On Grace and Free Will*; scathing polemics; and his "spiritual testament" the *De Consideratione*, from which we have quoted some passages on the duties of a pope. All these diverse elements proclaim him an orator and man of letters. Lastly, he was far from despising the human intellect and its activity, as witness his delightful remark: "It ill becomes a spouse of the Word to be stupid."

train of Abélard, St. Bernard persuaded Louis VII not to have him arrested, but to forbid the continuance of his subversive propaganda in France. Arnold of Brescia, as is well known, plunged deeper into heresy and died by decapitation after the defeat of the anti-papal Commune at Rome (1155). On Arnold of Brescia see Chapter V, section 6, and Volume 2, Chapter XIII, section 2.

But he ranked intellectual activity second among the ways of knowledge, convinced that neither by dialectic nor by science can man reach to that which alone is worthy of attainment. Like his friend William of Saint-Thierry, he maintained that "the humble love of a pure heart is worth more than reason and subtle disquisition"; that in order to understand and expound dogma, one should first live it. Such, indeed, is the sole conclusion of his treatise *On the Knowledge of God.*

He adhered firmly to the belief that faith is superior by far to every intellectual process. And it was in order to defend this principle that he engaged in conflict with Abélard, one of the most impressive figures in the history of medieval thought, of whom we shall have more to say.[15] But from the hermitage at Nogent-sur-Seine, where Abélard dwelt with a handful of disciples, there emerged ideas which were hardly compatible with Bernard's view. Not that the great dialectician was an unbeliever, a freethinker; at that period such words would have been meaningless. He had a lively faith, and spoke of Christ with a tenderness that Bernard himself would not have disavowed. Nevertheless, Abélard was consumed with the desire for speculation as other men are with carnal appetites. He himself used to say that he could not remain inactive in face of a problem, but must needs solve it at any cost. This craving, when applied to the mysteries of faith, invited catastrophe. If Abélard, champion of reason and the critical spirit, had prevailed, the clear-cut affirmations of dogma, the very principles of faith, would have become no more than academic theses, to be accepted or rejected at the discretion of individuals. The result would have been a process that ended, as did rationalism, by suppressing the distinction between the legitimate object of reason and that which transcends it, between human knowledge and divine revelation.

We have only to recognize the goal to which Abélard's steps were more or less consciously directed, in order to appreciate St. Bernard's motive in joining issue with him. Warned by his friend William of Saint-Thierry, who had sent him Abélard's *Christian Theology* with the simple observation,

---

15. Volume 2, Chapter VIII, section 6.

"Your silence is dangerous," the Abbot of Clairvaux tried in the first place to avoid so formidable a task. He questioned his ability to cross swords with so great a master of dialectic; but in 1140, among a crowd of students whom his reputation had attracted to Clairvaux, he met a pupil of Abélard, and forthwith understood the peril. He then made overtures to the philosopher in person; but his appeal was rejected point-blank. Abélard, as if to cut the rods that were to beat his own back, demanded the assembly of a council before which he would defend his thesis. The council met at Sens in 1141, and St. Bernard was present.

The two adversaries were far removed in outlook. One was an intellectual, sure alike of himself, of his position, and of his dialectical method; he would immediately pulverize this monk from Burgundy. The other was a mystic whose soul was filled with God, who sought not his own glory, and desired only to bear witness to the word of God. Abélard viewed the council as a debating society where he might indulge his passion for the scrutiny of ideas. Bernard considered it as a tribunal which was to pass judgment on one whose faith was suspect. Nor would he allow his opponent the choice of stations, but came straightway to the point by affirming that the very topics which Abélard proposed to discuss were not open to discussion. The faith must be accepted or rejected; dogma is a whole which cannot be pulled in pieces to suit private whims. Surprised by this attack, disconcerted, crushed at the outset by a torrent of quotation from scripture, compared in turn with Arius, Nestorius, and Pelagius, Abélard saw the ground open at his feet. He could not reply.

In this duel, it was unquestionably St. Bernard who represented his age and stood forth as the typical medieval Christian, holding the past exemplary and sufficient unto itself, the faith alone as *alpha* and *omega*. His adversary was the incarnation of a progressive movement whose intellectual courage bordered on audacity. True, Abélard's ideas subsequently played a useful part in the evolution of Christian thought; but in the middle of the twelfth century they constituted a real threat to society, whose cornerstone was unwavering faith. It is not always good to be too far in advance of one's time.

After this defeat, Abélard decided to lodge an appeal from the council
to the Holy See; but he was unable to make the journey. On arrival at Cluny
he was overtaken by sickness; the Pope approved the decision of the council,
and his humiliation was complete. Informed of this, St. Bernard hurried to
his bedside, in order that his adversary might not carry to the grave the sear-
ing agony of those wounds he had felt it his duty to inflict. Peter the Venerable watched the two men exchange the kiss of peace; and soon afterwards,
at the priory of Saint-Marcel near Châlon-sur-Sâone, the former master of
the Latin Quarter was surprised "by the angelic visitor in holy prayer and
the fear of the Lord."[16]

7. THE MAN OF AFFAIRS

ST. Bernard felt in duty bound to leave his cell and join in the battles of his
fellow men, simply that Christ might lack nothing of his testimony. "I never
regret," he once wrote, "having interrupted a peaceful meditation, if I see
God's word take root in a soul." This explains the paradox of a contemplative
who, from 1127 until his death, wandered over mountain and valley, like "a
fledgling exiled from its nest," and played a leading part in all the principal
events of that time.

It was not that he enjoyed doing so, not that he sought out the occasion
for a quarrel. On the contrary, whenever he was called upon to act, he resisted, hesitated, waited, reflected, and carefully inquired why he had been
approached. And if he at length consented, he did so in obedience to the
orders of a superior, through charity towards his brethren and the Church,
or through loyalty to truth and justice. No doubt he was torn between the

---

16. St. Bernard also engaged in a violent dispute with Gilbert of La Porrée, the learned
    Bishop of Poitiers, who had put forward unorthodox views when treating of the dis-
    tinction between God and divinity. Though denounced to St. Bernard by two of his
    own priests, Gilbert enjoyed the influential friendship of several cardinals, and there-
    by escaped the thunderbolts of his adversary. But he agreed to alter certain passages in
    his writing under the direction of Gottschalk, provost of the Premonstratensians.

128   monastic ideal and the overwhelming load of secular business in which he found himself involved; but he was sure that while thus engaged he was doing what God expected of him without betraying his vocation. It was precisely because he was a mystic that St. Bernard was also a man of action.

It might be said in our modern jargon that the great abbot was a "man of affairs," in the sense that he took risks and plunged into the most dangerous conflicts. But this busy life, wherewith so many men attempt to disguise the void in their own souls, was for Bernard nothing but the logical outcome of another and more exacting duty undertaken when, at the age of twenty-one, he knocked at the gate of Citeaux. Although he has been officially described as a statesman,[17] or politician, his labours in the temporal sphere had no other purpose than to secure the victory of Truth and Justice.

It is impossible to enumerate the many instances in which St. Bernard's intervention proved decisive. The events which called for his mediation were both great and small, for nothing could be a waste of time when his Lord's teaching was at stake. Whenever he took a hand, he was always the man of God, free of resentment and personal ambition. Thus he defended Thibaut of Champagne (of whose conduct he had had several times to complain) against King Louis VII; he protested with the utmost vigour at the devastation of Champagne by royal troops, and brought about a permanent settlement resulting in a marriage from which Philip Augustus was to spring.

Two outstanding events of this period reveal the saint's authority. First there was the Schism of Anacletus, which St. Bernard handled in a way so characteristic of his methods and of his influence, that the story deserves to be told in full.

While Honorius II lay on his death-bed, the families of Pierleone and Frangipani set to work on the College of Cardinals. They had the dying man carried to the abbey of St. Gregory, and showed him to a restive mob. He died on the night of February 13, 1130, and six cardinals in residence

---

17. At Dijon there is a commemorative plaque to "St. Bernard, Statesman." Though secular in outlook, the words form a splendid act of homage.

at the monastery elected Gregory of Sant' Angelo, a partisan of the Frangipani, who took the name of Innocent II. Their choice was confirmed by
other members of the College. But Cardinal Peter Pierleone, a well-known
and popular figure in Roman society, forthwith denounced this hasty procedure; he rallied his supporters, and was elected Pope under the name of
Anacletus II. The two pontiffs were crowned on February 23, one at Santa
Maria Novella, the other at St. Peter's. But Anacletus, an astute politician
who knew how to distribute gold to good purpose, forced his rival to leave
Rome. Innocent took refuge in France.

There were now two "heads" of Christendom; nor could their respective claims be settled on canonical grounds, for both elections had been
invalidated by irregularities. The nations took sides according to their interests. Louis VI convoked a council at Étampes in order to examine the merits
of the two claimants, and the Abbot of Clairvaux was requested to attend.
Bernard was reluctant; but a vision from God decided him to obey the sum-
mons. He found himself arbiter of the universal Church, and put forward
a threefold argument in favour of Innocent II: (1) he was morally the most
worthy; (2) he had been designated by "the most reliable" part of the Sacred
College, i.e., by the majority of cardinal-bishops, upon whom a decree of
Nicholas II in 1059 had conferred pre-eminence in the matter of papal elections; and (3) he had been consecrated by the Bishop of Ostia according to
tradition. The council accepted this ruling, and Louis VI proclaimed his
loyalty to Innocent.

The decision, however, could be of no avail if Christendom were divided; and Bernard sought to rally the other Christian states. He saw Henry I
of England, and overcame his reluctance; while in Germany, St. Norbert,
who was then Archbishop of Magdeburg, won over Lothair to the good
cause. The Pope and the German king met in March 1131 at Liége, where
the monarch held Innocent's bridle and showed him every mark of respect.
The gesture was no doubt intended to pave the way for demands of a merely political nature; but Bernard, says his biographer, "opposed them like
a wall," and Lothair promised to conduct the Pope back to Rome. Meanwhile, Innocent paid a visit to Clairvaux and was entertained by the monks

at their frugal board. At Rheims, Bernard stood beside the Pope while His Holiness received the submission of Aragon and Castile. Next, he intervened in Aquitaine, where Duke William, prompted by Bishop Gerard of Angoulême, had recognized Anacletus. But his success was not long-lived; for Gerard regained the upper hand, and obtained the see of Bordeaux. Bernard flayed him with merciless irony, and persuaded his suffragans to excommunicate him.

By this time Innocent had arrived in Italy, where Lothair was engaged in military operations. He sent for Bernard in 1133 to reconcile Genoa and Pisa, whose accord was necessary to oppose Roger II of Sicily, an opportunist who had declared for Anacletus with a view to increasing his own power. The Cistercian became a diplomat; he arranged a peace, and the people of Genoa gave him a triumphal welcome. Lothair, however, on reaching a point not far from Rome, found himself short of money. Bernard asked for and obtained subsidies from the King of England. Finally, on April 30, Innocent entered the Eternal City and crowned Lothair on June 4. Bernard returned in haste to his beloved monastery, hoping that his task was ended.

But in September, Innocent was again forced to leave Rome, being now deprived of the support of an imperial army, and harried by the troops of Anacletus, who had occupied the Castle of Sant' Angelo. Bernard set out once more. On his way through Nantes he won over the subjects of William of Aquitaine, whom he reminded that "there is only one Church, the Ark in which lies the salvation of the world; without it, by the just judgment of God, everything is doomed to perish as at the time of the Flood." After hearing Mass (during which he was obliged to stand outside the church, since he was excommunicated), William was reconciled to Innocent. So far as concerned France, the schism was at an end.

The situation, however, remained grave, for Anacletus was supported by Roger II, who had recently been crowned by the antipope. At the same time Lothair, who was at war with the Hohenstaufen, was prevented from undertaking an expedition south of the Alps; so it was for Bernard to effect the pacification of Germany, and he started without delay. At the beginning of 1135 he crossed the Rhine and arrived at Bamberg, where the Emperor

received the submission of his enemies. Then, passing the Alps in midwin-
ter, Bernard descended upon Italy, and in due course reached Pisa, where
Innocent II had summoned a council to discover who were his allies. "St.
Bernard" says an historian of that period, "was the soul of the council."

Anacletus was excommunicated, and the domains of Roger II laid under
an interdict. The delegates from Milan promised the adherence of that great
metropolis provided the deposition of their arrogant archbishop, Anselm,
were confirmed. The council agreed, and dispatched St. Bernard to Lombardy to forestall trouble. On the way he was jostled by huge crowds anxious to
see and hear him, to touch his cowl, and even cut bits from it. He was offered,
but refused, the archbishopric; and travelling by mountain passes, along
which he was escorted by herdsmen, he at length returned to Clairvaux.

His labour was not yet finished; for while working at his sermons on
the Canticle he received another urgent appeal from the Pope, and for the
third time turned his steps to Italy. Lothair's army had overrun most of the
peninsula; but Anacletus was firmly established in certain parts of Rome,
and Roger was invincible in Sicily. Disputes arose between the Emperor and
the Pope on the subject of Apulia and with regard to the abbacy of Monte
Cassino. Bernard smoothed out these differences, and was even for a short
time superior of that famous abbey; then in October 1137, while Lothair,
a sick and disappointed man, was journeying northward, he undertook to
negotiate directly with Roger. He was in extremely bad health, and likened
himself to "the pale spectre of death"; nevertheless, he hurried on to Salerno
to meet the King of Sicily and the canonist Peter of Pisa, who was to present
Anacletus's case. His exhortations to re-establish the unity of the Church
did not convince Roger; but so great an impression did they make upon
Peter that he went and prostrated himself at Innocent's feet.

The end was now in sight. Lothair died on December 4, Anacletus on
January 25, 1138. A few obstinate spirits, including Roger, set up a new
antipope, Victor IV, who, in horror at his own sacrilege, fled one night from
the palace, joined St. Bernard, and appealed to Innocent for mercy. Thus all
for which Bernard had striven had been saved. It mattered little to him that
Roger II, who had defeated the papal forces and now held the Pope at his

mercy, extorted from the latter sacramental absolution and the recognition of his crown. Desiring only that the victor should not abuse his triumph, he urged moderation; but he was unable to prevent those reprisals which overtook the partisans of Anacletus and even Peter of Pisa.

Throughout this struggle, which lasted for eight years, the issue was nothing less than the unity of the Church. Bernard was the great captain and the real victor; but raised as he was upon the pinnacle of honour and success, closeted with kings, and master in so many assemblies, what had been his ambition? To regain the austere tranquillity of his cell. "Soon, soon I shall be home," he wrote to the prior of Clairvaux; "I bring back a reward, the victory of Christ and the peace of the Church."

Victory for Christ was likewise his sole ambition in the matter of the second crusade. It was at Easter in the year 1146 that St. Bernard's preaching rekindled the sacred flame, and launched Christendom upon the second stage of its battle for the Holy Sepulchre.

Almost half a century before, after endless suffering and at the cost of untold heroism, the barons of Godfrey de Bouillon had stormed Jerusalem. But after that triumph, on July 14, 1099, the instability of their conquest had become plain for all to see. The feudal nobility had taken with them to the Holy Land their customary lack of discipline, and, late in 1144, Zengi, the Turkish governor of Mosul, having made himself master of Aleppo, took Edessa from the Christians. Edessa was an outpost controlling the road to Mesopotamia; it was recaptured and held for a very short interval, but fell once more in 1145 to the arms of Zengi's son Nureddin, who massacred the inhabitants. Their cry of anguish reached the West, and Christendom was thunderstruck.

It happened at this juncture that Louis VII was dreaming of some mighty enterprise which should cover him with glory. A first meeting at Bourges showed clearly that the enthusiasm of his barons was not what it had been: they were more chary of the risks entailed, knowing how much a crusade cost in blood and gold. But if Louis VII sometimes lacked wisdom, he was never wanting in courage: he appointed an assembly on the hillside at Vézelay, and invited St. Bernard to attend.

Now the Abbot of Clairvaux, with his vast spiritual horizons, had good cause to favour such an expedition; but he was too level-headed to ignore the difficulties involved, and asked for papal sanction. Eugenius III was endeavouring to suppress rebellion and intrigue at Rome, and some time elapsed before he signed the Bull and Bernard could begin his work. We may guess the nature of the saint's appeal from its results: so deeply did he move his audience, that crowds were anxious for the privilege of immediate enlistment; and since there was not enough material for the crosses which so many sought then and there to sew upon their clothing, Bernard had even to divide his tunic among them. Next, he took the road from Vézelay and travelled through Burgundy, Lorraine, and Flanders, to swell the ranks of the crusaders. "Come," he urged the Count of Brittany, "come, my brave soldier! Gird up your loins, do not fail your king, the King of France. Nay, do not fail the King of Heaven, on whose behalf your sovereign undertakes so perilous a journey."

He then went to the Rhineland to protest against a massacre of Jews, and invited Conrad III to join the crusade. On December 27, 1147, he obtained that monarch's consent to lead the German corps, and solemnly delivered to him the blessed standard; while at St. Denis Louis VII received the pilgrim's staff from Pope Eugenius.

No one denies that the second crusade was hopelessly mismanaged and ended in miserable failure.[18] St. Bernard, however, was not to blame for the incompetence of Louis VII and Conrad III. He suffered much in consequence, and felt obliged, in the *De Consideratione*, to justify his conduct. Having explained that the set-back was in no way attributable to Providence, but to the follies of the Christians themselves, he concluded with these noble words: "I welcome the blows of calumny, the poisoned shafts of blasphemy, so that they may not reach Almighty God. I am glad to lose my honour, provided His glory is untouched." As evidence that his personal prestige remained unaffected, we may recall that Suger, at the moment

---

18. See Volume 2, Chapter X, section 5.

when death found him out, was meditating a further expedition with whose effective command he proposed to entrust the Cistercian!

The extent of St. Bernard's activity is amazing, especially when we take account of the material handicaps under which he laboured. Travel in those days was arduous and uncertain; and yet this frail figure, emaciated by fasting, journeyed on and on from Paris to Sicily, from Rome to Flanders, from Languedoc to the Rhine, and even crossed the Alps on horseback in midwinter. His health was always failing; he slept badly; his stomach was so disordered that he was obliged "to sustain it at frequent intervals with a little liquid, for it invariably rejected all solid food"; while his hands and feet swelled for no apparent reason. Nor did the moral atmosphere of the age simplify his task. Remember, this holy man, before whom difficulties seemed to melt away, lived in a society where violence, intrigue, and the lust for power or profit were no less in evidence than they are today. No obstacle, however, was too great for him; he never failed to reach his goal.

All this goes to prove that St. Bernard was not only a saint, but a genius. No one of mere average ability could have assessed his contemporaries and the passing scene as did the Abbot of Clairvaux. No ordinary man could have shouldered so many tasks at once, keeping in touch with the whole vast network of his Order and making sure that his instructions were carried out. None but a saint and a genius could have maintained a huge correspondence with everyone of importance in Western Christendom, and still remain a man of thought, of prayer, of contemplation. "His greatness," says Pascal, "lies not in his being at the far end of the scale; he is at both ends and fills the interval between."

It need scarcely be added that some of the admiration bestowed upon the leader is reflected in that society which submitted to his guidance. Just because Bernard was a superman it seemed natural to take orders from him in the political, diplomatic, and even economic sphere, which would today be strictly reserved for "experts." Just because he was a saint, whose only weapon was his word, and whom the least petty princeling could have placed under arrest, the greatest sovereigns bowed to his decisions. The

twentieth century, in which force is, more than ever before, recognized as
the *ultima ratio*, would do well to ponder on these things.

8. ST. BERNARD AND THE ARTS

WE have seen the great Cistercian put forth his influence in many different fields; but there is another in which that influence has been much discussed and adversely criticized. I mean the realm of art.

It has been forcibly argued that he was blind to beauty, and that during the new "quarrel of images" his part was that of a philistine hostile to all aesthetic achievement. Put like that, the thesis must be rejected. Bernard's attitude towards art cannot be understood except as the outcome of his profound spirituality, of his longing to be of service in God's cause.

When he first appeared on the stage of history, the prevailing force in Western Christendom was Cluny, whose builder-monks were busy throughout Europe. According to their tradition, external beauty was an aid to prayer and, in its several forms, gave praise to God; so that wherever the Cluniacs built, there was a wealth of ornament. Cunning geometrical patterns followed the line of the arcades; arch and cornice were a riot of exquisite detail; capitals became regular menageries; while the lintels and tympana of porches were peopled with kings and saints. Even the interior was rich with frescoes; the cross ornamented with enamel, chased gold, and precious stones. The masterpiece was Cluny itself, an enormous basilica erected by St. Hugh. It had seven towers, two transepts, and eight columns of rare marble to uphold the sanctuary. It contained also many priceless treasures, such as the famous candelabrum of Queen Matilda of England, which was eight feet tall and illuminated the high altar.

Against this unheard-of luxury St. Bernard protested in his *Apology*. He thought it unfitting that men who had renounced worldly display, who had sacrificed all that delights the senses in order to possess Christ, should be surrounded with a magnificence that could not but lead them into temptation. He therefore condemned "the enormous height of the churches, their extraordinary length, the useless width of their naves, the richness of polished stone, the paintings which distract attention. Vanity of vanities! nay, worse than vain. The Church's walls may shine, but her poor go naked; she covers her stones with gold, but leaves her children unclothed."

St. Bernard, however, was not the only one to criticize Cluniac ostentation. Peter the Cantor stigmatized excesses in construction, the poet Ruteboeuf cried out against the luxury of cloisters, and Suger, himself a Benedictine, adopted the same views after his "conversion" in 1127. That their words had some effect is clear from the remark of an abbot who, while visiting Suger in his cell at St. Denis, exclaimed: "This man puts us all to shame; he builds not as we do, for ourselves, but for God."

Did spiritual asceticism, transferred to the aesthetic plane, give birth to ugliness? The answer is found in those magnificent Cistercian abbeys which rose throughout the Western world, whose very ruins are overwhelming in their solemn beauty. Look, for example, at Fontenay, Pontigny, Fontfroide, Silvacane, Sénanque, and Alcobaça. Only the cellar at Clairvaux has been preserved from senseless vandalism; but Bouquen, with the noble façade of its chapter-house, is rising once more from the ruins. Gentle restraint, outward austerity, and that "sober intoxication" which St. Bernard desired in the interior life, are noticeable at every turn: in the naves with their perfect lines, in mouldings whose sole ornament is their purity of form, in rays of pearly light that fall through grisaille glass, unmixed with foreign elements, and bring with them a strangely fluid, almost secret quality that speaks to the soul more intimately than does colour. Cistercian art represents an aesthetic far removed from that of the cathedrals with all their wealth of detail; and its refusal to conform with the prevailing ostentation may well have delayed the fall of gothic down that slope of excess and superfluity which was later to become "flamboyant."

It should also be remembered that St. Bernard's view applied only to the building of religious houses. He never disputed that "episcopal," as opposed to monastic, art should "speak to the ignorant"; and he agreed with the use of such ornament as could stir devotion in carnal men, for whom things spiritual have little meaning. So far from contemning sculpture and stained

glass, he encouraged its development, except among those who have abandoned all things for God, and in whose minds a more spiritual outlook
should predominate.

St. Bernard's views on art spread throughout the West, helped by the
elevation of many Cistercian monks to the episcopal dignity, and by the
example of Cistercian monasteries which rose in every land.[19] Experts
like the monk Theophilus, author of an *Essay on the Several Arts*, were so
inspired by his teaching, that parts of this work have been found to correspond exactly with passages from the great abbot's writings.

It has even been suggested that Bernard's impact upon the history of art
was more profound than hitherto imagined. The revival of techniques which
helped the transition from romanesque to gothic during the thirteenth century was probably due to the influence of Clairvaux. Achard, novice-master
in that house, was architect-superintendent of the Order; while the celebrated builder Geoffrey of Ainay was a veteran of the same monastery. Furthermore, several primary features of gothic architecture can be traced to
St. Bernard. The prolongation of the cathedral choir to form a Lady chapel,
more imposing than any of those situated in the apse, would never have tak-
en place had not the White Monk laboured so hard to spread devotion to
Mary. The great symbolist's influence, more direct and more pronounced
than that even of Suger or Honorius of Autun, is discernible in sculpture
and stained glass. His mark is apparent in every detail. For example, a window at St. Denis, dating from the time of Suger, shows the chariot of Ami-
nadab surmounted with a green cross and drawn by the evangelists, exactly
as St. Bernard describes it. And some writers have maintained that the well-
known image of God the Father holding the crucifix in outstretched arms
is derived from the Cistercian's famous discourse on *Jesus Crucified Beneath
the Father*. Nor is it unlikely that his *Discovery at Easter* gave rise to that
custom of depicting the minutiae of the Resurrection (the open tomb, the
folded shroud, the angel lifting the stone) which originated in the twelfth

---

19. See the album of photographs *Abbayes Cisterciennes*, published by the Marquise de
    Maillé and Henry de Ségogne (Paris, 1943).

138   century. So far from being hostile to the arts, Bernard helped to give them life; his personality is engraved thereon as upon much else besides.

9. BERNARD THE KNIGHT

ST. Bernard's one and only purpose in the temporal sphere was to promote Christianity. His monks were to form a spiritual advance-guard leading society to the light of Christ. But, realist as he was, he understood clearly that this work required co-operation from the laity, who must therefore be inspired with the same ideal if it was to succeed.

When considering the life and labours of St. Bernard, one is struck by his resemblance to those great figures who embody the highest medieval ideal in the domain of action. The White Monk, who had "no weapon but his tears and prayers," belongs to the same family as Godfrey de Bouillon and St. Louis. The son of the lord of Fontaines never lost sight of the ideal inherited from his ancestors: and his contemporaries recognized beneath the Cistercian cowl the invisible armour of a knight.

Numerous instances in his life reveal this peculiar affinity. We have seen that Suger thought of entrusting him with the effective command of an army; and no one at that time was in the least surprised. In the strategic planning of the second crusade he was asked for and tendered his advice, though it was ignored by Louis VII and Conrad III. He too showed the German princes how necessary it was for Christendom to smash the pagan Wends.[20] The Christian spirit which he advocated was energetic, militant, one might almost say military. His very habit of addressing Mary by the charming title of "our Lady" was derived from the language of feudalism; he considered himself the Blessed Virgin's liegeman, and served her as a vassal would his sovereign.

Seeking to give this manly form of Christianity a concrete shape, St. Bernard dreamed of an institution which should embody it for all to see. Such was the Order of the Temple. In 1128, at the Council of Troyes, which

---

20. See Volume 2, Chapter XII, section 3.

he attended at the invitation of Pope Honorius II, he was requested to provide a rule for this military organization whose duty it would be to defend the Holy Land against renewed attack by the infidel. Accordingly, he drew up the statutes and wrote his *Praise of the New Chivalry*, in which he spoke with unveiled enthusiasm of the ideal which should inspire the soldiers of Christ. The white habit of the Templars (to which the red cross was a later addition) indicated their spiritual relationship with Citeaux; and the warrior-monks, unlike the worldly knights despised by Bernard, would pass their lives as "poor soldiers of Christ" in self-sacrifice and the practice of asceticism. The ancient seal of the Templars, in fact, showed two knights riding on one horse, reminding them of holy poverty.

Thus, according to St. Bernard, knighthood would find its most perfect expression in a body of men who represented both the loftiest temporal ideal of the age (that of the fearless soldier ever ready to die for his cause) and the noblest conception of a Christian soul. The "new militia" was the most perfect and most active element in society, for it achieved a union of the sacred and profane; it proved extraordinarily effective in the service of the Church generally, but more particularly in carrying out the grandiose designs of the Holy See.

The fate of the Order is well known. It became a great banking house with strong rooms in every commandery. It lent money to kings, and its commercial honesty was not always above suspicion. Thus do human institutions decline from their first fervour. The tragedy which engulfed the Templars is wrapped in such mystery that we cannot deliver an impartial judgment. One thing, however, may be said. It was Philip the Fair who, in the shocking "Outrage of Anagni," gave the signal for rebellion by the secular powers against the spiritual supremacy; and it was Philip the Fair who broke the "militia of Christ," which, though fallen from its high estate, was still the living symbol of force subjected to the spirit.[21] Times had changed; Bernard's two predominant ideas now lay in ruins, and through the mist of centuries to come the modern epoch might already be discerned.

---

21. See Volume 2, Chapter XIV, section 7.

This episode in the saint's life is not one upon which historians have laid much stress; but there is reason to look upon it as of first importance. At all events, it features prominently in the legend which grew up around this great figure as soon as he was dead. The main themes of the "Grail" cycle are probably connected with the tradition of the Templars. The Knight of the Holy Grail, pure, unselfish, heroic, is no doubt the literary symbol of the "new militia" founded by St. Bernard; and in that part of Wolfram von Eschenbach's poem which links up with the work of the French poet Guyot, Parsifal becomes king of the Templars. The author continually praises the Temple. "Happy the mother," he exclaims in the person of Trevrizent the hermit, "happy the mother who brings into the world a son destined for such service!" And many commentators are inclined to think that the prototype of Galahad, the ideal knight, the *preux sans tâche*, was none other than St. Bernard.

It has also been noted that, in the thirty-first canto of the *Paradiso*, Beatrice leaves the guidance of Dante's steps, on the last stages of his journey towards the region of eternal bliss, to "an old man dressed as the glorious family." What does this mean? Some authorities suggest that it is a reference to the Cistercian cowl or to the white mantle of the Templars. Others think that Dante belonged to one of the secret sects which are supposed to have lingered on after the disappearance of the Templars. In any case, the guide of whom he speaks is Bernard of Clairvaux.

"That thou mayest consummate thy journey perfectly," says the old man, "whereto prayer and holy love dispatched me—fly with thine eyes throughout this garden; for gazing on it will equip thy glance better to mount through the divine ray. And the Queen of heaven, for whom I am all burning with love, will grant us every grace, because I am her faithful Bernard."

10. NUPTIALS

SUCH was Bernard, Frenchman and Burgundian, son of the Church and saint of God. At intervals in the long course of history there appear these radiant and significant personalities, representing the essential features of the age in which they live and impressing on it the mark of their own genius. Observing the mysterious accord between the White Monk and the aspirations of the Middle Ages, and remembering the numerous occasions upon which his action proved decisive, we may call the twelfth century "the age of St. Bernard," even more legitimately than we speak of the age of Augustus or the age of Louis XIV. But if we consider the spiritual heights to which he attained, the impulse which he gave to Christianity and which has lasted until our own day, it must certainly be admitted that his greatness on the historical plane is as nothing compared with the glory that is his in that domain where the uncreated light shines forth alone, and where every figure is but the reflection of God. Following St. Paul and St. Augustine, a little though not much inferior to them, side by side with his two successors upon earth, St. Francis of Assisi and St. Dominic, Bernard ranks as one of the major heroes, one of the high peaks of Christianity.

His contemporaries of long ago honoured him as we honour him today. Glory, as it were, shone round about him, though he esteemed it but as dust. His biographer does not exaggerate in calling him the "darling of his age," for he was loved and fêted everywhere he went. At Milan he was almost crushed to death by cheering crowds, and the students of the Latin Quarter in Paris accorded him a boisterous welcome. When he visited Metz shortly before his death, the multitude was so enormous that he was obliged to take refuge in a boat on the Moselle. A blind man standing on the bank cried out, asking that he might be taken to Bernard; whereupon a fisherman in another boat threw him the end of his cloak, and hauled him to the saint's vessel. When at last the great abbot died, it was thought necessary to keep secret the hour of his funeral lest an excited crowd of relic-hunters should carry off his body.

Such popularity was bound to incur envy and resentment. Nathan stands at his peril before David, Elijah before Ahab. It is always dangerous to insist on the principles of truth and justice. "I know," said Bernard, "that by making war on abuses I earn the hatred of evildoers." He was even denounced to the Sacred College, and received from Cardinal Haimeric an unfriendly letter on the subject of "these monks who leave their cloister to pester the Holy See and the cardinals." But he was unmoved by such complaints, no matter from whom they came, and he replied, in terms of respectful irony, that the raucous voices which disturbed the Church's peace were rather those of the noisy frogs which filled the cardinalatial and pontifical palaces.

Nor could he be silenced even by death, before whom his friends and relations had gone down one by one—Malachy the great Irishman; Suger, the minister whom he had reconciled with Christ; Thibaut Count of Champagne, with whom he had more than once crossed swords, but whom he loved as the first protector of his work; and Eugenius III, his spiritual son, the beloved Pope. While his health steadily declined, he continued to observe the Holy Rule in all its rigour, and would accept no relaxation. Whether in the monastery or on the road, he lived like the humblest of his brethren. Though in the grip of fever, he travelled to Lorraine on one last mission, to arbitrate between the duke and the people of Metz; but when he returned to Clairvaux his strength was at an end.

With a full heart he watched the slow approach of death. His body was exhausted by suffering, but his spirit seemed to take on new life, his soul to burn with a yet brighter flame. He had looked forward to this crisis as the hour of ultimate illumination; and as he felt his physical powers ebb away, his spirit scaled the final pitch, a supreme effort of which the last sermons on the Canticle of Canticles remain as an imperishable monument. He was about to consummate the mystical marriage, and could not but overflow with gladness as he lay on his truckle-bed in that humble cell, waiting peacefully for the coming of the Spouse.

At nine o'clock on the morning of August, 20 1153, Bernard slept in Christ. He was sixty-three. "At the moment when he expired," says the chronicler, "the merciful Mother of God, his special patroness, was seen at his bedside; she had come to fetch his soul." Before committing his body to the earth, the monks took a cast of his features, a cast from which all later images of St. Bernard are derived: the sunken cheeks are deeply lined, but the high forehead reveals a mighty intelligence, and the whole face radiates a marvellous purity of soul.

It is stated in the *Great Exordium* that immediately after death he worked more miracles than in his lifetime. An epileptic approached the corpse, and was cured of his disease. A young mother laid her paralysed infant on the saint's body, and saw the child leap with joy. These prodigies continued after his burial, and such crowds flocked to the Val d'Absinthe that monastic peace was seriously disturbed. The Abbot of Citeaux therefore travelled to Clairvaux and, standing by the tomb, forbade the saint in virtue of holy obedience to work another miracle. The humble monk submitted from beyond the frontiers of the grave; a charming story which shows that Bernard was scarcely dead before he passed into legend.

But there was nothing legendary about the work he left behind. The life which he had breathed into his Order continued to flourish long after his death, and Cistercian houses sprang up everywhere. Clairvaux alone gave the Church a Pope, fifteen cardinals, and innumerable bishops. Many a great mystic, followed in Bernard's wake: William of Saint-Thierry, Guerric of Igny, Gilbert of Hoy, Alan of Lille, Beatrice of Tirelemont, Mechtild of Hackeborn, and Gertrude, to name but a few. Before the end of the twelfth century four *Lives* of the saint had been written. The *Vita Prima*, edited by his immediate friends William of Saint-Thierry, Ernaud of Bonneval, and Geoffrey of Auxerre,[22] is a mine of carefully selected information; while the *Liber Miraculorum* abounds in marvels which prove at least how greatly St. Bernard was admired by his contemporaries.

The Church was very soon obliged to confirm the judgment of the masses. Nor was he unworthy to be numbered in the calendar of saints, he whom Innocent II described as "the impregnable bastion of the Church." On January 18, 1174, less than twenty-one years after his death, Bernard was canonized by Pope Alexander III. Anticipating the decision of the nineteenth century, it was decreed that the Gospel for the Mass of the new saint should be that used in the Common of Doctors, *Vos estis sal terrae*; and

---

22. Geoffrey, once a pupil of Abélard, succumbed to Bernard's fascination and became his secretary.

shortly afterwards, in 1201, Pope Innocent III himself composed a collect in which he spoke of him as "Doctor Egregius."

That St. Bernard's writings were an object of constant study and meditation until the seventeenth century is clear from the words of Mabillon, who calls him "the last of the Fathers." *The Imitation of Christ* owes much to him, and Pope Nicholas V, a great patron of the arts, whose name is linked with those of Piero della Francesca and Fra Angelico, ordered a splendid manuscript of the *De Consideratione*. Bossuet, Pascal, Fénelon, all drank deep at the wells of his doctrine; but thereafter his glory suffered an eclipse. It may be that, like St. Augustine, who also fell into disfavour for a time, he was found "too Jansenistic," as Mme. de Sévigné remarked. Like the Bishop of Hippo, and indeed St. Paul himself, he was unlucky in his admirers, among whom were Luther and Calvin! Did not the dictator of Geneva say of the *De Consideratione*: "Truth herself speaks by the mouth of St. Bernard"?

It was reserved for Pope Pius VIII, the man who said he knew no policy "but that of the Gospel," to proclaim St. Bernard a Doctor of the Universal Church, in the Brief *Quod Unum* (July 23, 1830). Since that date his reputation has revived. Unfamiliar he may still be to the average schoolboy, who cannot be expected to appreciate his tremendous historical importance from a few scattered allusions. Nevertheless, he has been restored to his rightful place; he is the subject of innumerable books and enjoys a boundless veneration.

In the history of Christ's Church he is the most perfect figure of manhood as conceived by the Middle Ages, one of the supreme guides of Christendom on the road of light, the witness of his age before Almighty God.

CHAPTER IV

The Leaven in the Lump

1. RELAPSE

NOT all members of the Church were like St. Bernard, not all were saints. It was in the Middle Ages as it is today; and he who is surprised or scandalized thereat shows that he has failed to grasp the nature and mystery of the Church.

It is, of course, pitiable and depressing to see Christians fall back time after time into the same old rut. The process may be observed by each one of us as it unrolls against the familiar background of our guilty hearts. But the Church is not only a supernatural reality, the Mystical Body of Christ, associating man with God on the eternal plane through the mystery of Redemption. She is also the lowly mass consisting of all those for whom Christ shed His Blood on Calvary; and that is why a permanent contradiction is apparent between the grandeur of her ideal and the weakness of her members, between "the dignity of Christianity and the unworthiness of Christians."[1] We must accept this unhappy paradox: by her condemnation of the heresiarchs Montanus, Novatian, Donatus, and, later on, of the Cathars, Holy Church proclaims that she is formed not only of the just and the predestined, but also of those miserable sinners who are lured to the abyss and stand ever ready to plunge over the edge.

Within this "assembly" of the baptized, however, some men carry a special responsibility as witnesses of God. They are the appointed guardians

---

1. Nicolas Berdyaev.

of an institution which holds the deposit of faith, the apostolic privileges, and the right to confer the sacraments. The word "Church," indeed, is often used to describe those who are invested with such charges and enjoy such powers. Their fundamental role is that of the leaven in a loaf, to give it life and to prevent its collapse. "A holy clergy makes a virtuous people," says Blanc de Saint-Bonnet; and that was truer in the Middle Ages than at any other period. For the medieval Church, as an institution, was, so to speak, the framework of society; and any weakness on her part reacted upon the whole complex system.

Weak points were inevitable. A cleric is still a man, notwithstanding ordination; he bears within himself the same taint of original sin as the remainder of the flock. The invasions, together with the upheavals which followed in their wake, had resulted in a veritable "barbarization" of society. For six long centuries the West had been wrapped in darkness, nor had the clergy escaped the general contamination. It is true that throughout those six hundred years the struggle had been maintained by relays of holy men and women who had fought against evil both by word and by example; but the barbarian epoch had been ridden by fornicating priests, by prelates who were soldiers rather than men of God, and by brigand-clerks who traded in ecclesiastical benefices. At the turn of the year 1000 victory was not yet in sight; despite notable improvement, too many of those whose duty it was to direct the Church proved themselves unfitted to exercise responsibility, and the situation remained more or less stationary during the next three hundred years. Progress there certainly was, sometimes heroic and decisive. But the contradiction remained, the cruel paradox was still there: although the Church was governed by a long line of splendid leaders, there was not wanting base material even in high places.

It is neither pleasant to dwell upon these shortcomings, nor profitable to multiply examples. A study of the most reliable witnesses provides us with a shameful picture of ignorant, avaricious, lustful, and even criminal ecclesiastics. Few were above criticism. The diatribes of St. Bernard, and of others equally severe, were directed against the Roman Curia, which Jacques de Vitry described as "so busy with temporal and mundane affairs that it had

no time for spiritual interests."[2] They were directed likewise against those
parish priests whom St. Bernard himself described as "slaves of avarice, governed by pride, and smearing even the Holy Place with their abominations."
The visitation-book of Eudes Rigaud, Archbishop of Rouen and friend of
St. Louis, affords an outspoken comment upon clerics who boozed in taverns, kept concubines and children in their homes, and even frequented
houses of which morality could not but disapprove.[3] So much for Rouen;
but the Normans enjoyed no monopoly of such conduct.

A remarkable anthology, illustrating these undesirable practices, might
likewise be formed from the archives of the Church. They reveal that the
majority of clergymen were negligent as regards the divine office. Many
were unacquainted with the words and made a mockery of their recitation,
gabbling the sacred liturgy at top speed. Some took part in orgies, others
turned their houses into brothels; and there were even cases of erotic songs
in church. The very fact that popes and councils thought it necessary to
condemn such behaviour proves that it existed.

The root cause of these deplorable abuses was undoubtedly the poor
quality of those who offered themselves for ordination. Ignorance was rife
among the parochial clergy, which was drawn from the lower levels of society. Many parish priests knew no more than the mere outlines or most striking episodes of the Gospel, and even these they mixed with legend. There
was no question at all of moral theology. Clerics lived on a level with their
flocks; for, despite the efforts of certain bishops,[4] they had never been properly trained. Nor was there much improvement until the advent of drastic
reforms, when diocesan seminaries came into being.

An ill-trained clergy, its lower ranks devoid of solid principles and its
leaders contaminated by secular influences, could not defend itself against
the twofold temptation of the flesh and money. Celibacy of the priesthood,
though not originally of obligation, had been proposed as an ideal state

---

2.   Patriarch of Jerusalem and later Cardinal. In 1216 he visited the papal court which
     was then in residence at Perugia, and was absolutely scandalized.
3.   In one such place a certain reverend gentleman forgot his clothes!
4.   See Chapter VI, section 6.

since the fourth century. But there had been considerable laxity throughout the barbarian epoch. Married deacons, priests, and bishops were numerous, a fact which could not be disguised by the pretence of chastity; and the general laxity of the ninth and tenth centuries had resulted in a serious increase of such abuses. "Nicolaism," as it was called, was named after a heretical sect in the early Church. It is mentioned in Revelation (2:6–15) as well as by St. Irenaeus, and was one of the cardinal points of later ecclesiastical reform. But although official statistics showed a considerable decrease in the number of married clergy, the abuse continued. From the thirteenth century alone at least one hundred unedifying documents have survived, covering a period of less than twenty years. There were married priests at Norwich; others, at Tournai, kept concubines; others again, at Ratisbon, had large families. Nor is it without significance that the Council of Pau (1212) imposed heavy penalties for "unnatural sins of the flesh" committed by clerics.

Money was a still more dangerous stumbling-block. Simony, so called after Simon Magus who, according to the Acts, offered St. Peter money in exchange for the power to communicate the Holy Spirit, is the crime of purchasing an ecclesiastical benefice with temporal goods. Against this disgraceful practice too the Church directed her reforming zeal. A substantial improvement was effected, but the sin was never wholly rooted out. Temporal interests still dictated the appointment of bishops and abbots, and the Church was never able to free herself entirely from this servitude. Generally speaking, avarice, luxury, and dishonesty in certain members of the clergy were denounced, not only by pamphleteers such as Étienne de Fougères and the author of the *Bible de Guyot*, not only by fabulists and popular writers, but also by papal Bulls and conciliar decrees.

It is, indeed, depressing to observe this relapse, to watch the leaven become unfitted to fulfil its purpose. Pope Clement V, William le Maire of Angers, and the Dominican Alvarez Pelajo drew attention at the beginning of the fourteenth century to the same errors as had been deplored in the twelfth by St. Bernard, and in the thirteenth by St. Dominic and Innocent III. We need but to peruse Dante in order to find this mass of criticism

recapitulated. The *Divine Comedy* peoples Hell and Purgatory with cardinals "so heavy that they must be carried," with "ravening wolves in shep-
herds' guise," and with shameless priests. "Cephas and Paul, the Vessel of
Election," the poet indignantly exclaims, "went barefoot and ate when they
were able."[5] There is, however, something noble and encouraging in these
strictures: they were thoroughly deserved, but it is to the Church's credit
that she was never indifferent to her defilement. Time after time she found
new leaven that would cause the lump to rise again.

2. REFORM

IF the human lump has a regrettable tendency to fall flat, Christianity contains within itself an indestructible element which periodically supplies the
remedy. I mean the spirit of reform. In the darkest night of the barbarian age
it was manifested in St. Benedict, St. Columba, and St. Benedict of Aniane;
later, in the monks of Cluny, in St. Romuald, and in St. Peter Damian. All
these fiercely and fearlessly set their faces against evils which disgraced the
Spouse of Christ; nor did the following centuries look in vain for men to
carry on the struggle with like determination.

In what does the spirit of reform consist? First, in a clear view of those
dangers with which the Christian soul is menaced—the danger of routine,
of internal disintegration, and of compromise with the world. Second, in an
heroic effort to break with the forces of death, and so recover intact the first
fervour of freedom and holiness. The spirit of reform is for the Church, on
the spiritual plane, what it is for political parties seeking a radical transformation of society. When a revolutionary minority obtains power, it soon
finds itself bogged down by self-interest, undermined by indifference and
complacency, fixed in the groove of habit. It becomes "bourgeois," and must
strive to regain its original condition, to recover its early determination and
purity of intention, to break with the perilous advantages of victory. This

---

5.   See Volume 2, Chapter XIV, section 12.

is what Trotsky, in Marxist language, called the "permanent revolution." Reform is the permanent revolution of Christianity.

By what characteristics, then, may we distinguish the genuine reform, so necessary for the historical development of Christianity, from one of those anarchical movements which break out in the Church from time to time only to cause trouble and lose themselves in heresy and schism? The demands of a reformer are admissible only upon certain conditions: they must rest upon an exact appreciation of the errors calling for correction, and upon the true interests of the Gospel rather than on prejudice; they must be conceived within the framework of charity and Christian fellowship. The reformer must not seek innovation, but rather a return to the sources of that institution whose interests he claims to have at heart. He should take his stand upon "tradition" in the sense of that which best enables a society to progress while remaining true to the fountain-head of its ideal. Finally, he must not yield to pride; he must preserve humility of heart, submissive always to authority in the persons of the hierarchy, who are responsible before God, who alone may take the initiative, and who alone can bring it to fruition.

Fortunately for the Middle Ages, these conditions were fulfilled on more than one occasion. Heroic souls stood forth from the ranks of Christendom, filled with the love of Christ and respect for the Church, desiring only the kingdom of God and His justice, visibly united with the Apostles and early martyrs, never dreaming of rebellion. Such were Gregory VII, St. Bernard, St. Bruno, St. Norbert, St. Francis of Assisi, St. Dominic, and Innocent III. Through them the "permanent revolution" was achieved without dissolving in mere anarchy.

Two circumstances in particular aided the reform. First, the extraordinary latitude permitted, even within the Church herself, to criticism or, to use a political expression, to "self-criticism." We have noticed St. Bernard's independence in addressing himself to bishops and even to the popes. But he does not stand alone; St. Bridget was no less outspoken, as were the Poverello of Assisi and many others. Canon Thomas de Chantimpré's curious symbolic work *The Bees* (1248) relates how the Devil visited a certain preacher who was about to address a council, and said to him: "Don't you

know what to say? Just tell them this, that the Powers of Darkness salute the 151
Princes of the Church." The good canon was *not* arrested and condemned!
Grave as were ecclesiastical abuses, independence of this kind made it possible to combat them, and in such a way that criticism of individuals did
not lessen men's esteem for the Church and the function of her ministers.
These angry prophets had too deep a faith to identify the institution with
its faithless servants.

The second favourable circumstance was the hierarchy's ability to see
how far criticism was justified, and to act accordingly. Those in authority
were free from an all too human weakness which bids them remain silent
before such as might take umbrage at their words; and, if a few of them did
feel so inclined, they were sufficiently strong-minded to resist the temptation. Herein lay the strength of several great popes: Gregory VII, Paschal II,
Innocent III, and Honorius III saw and proclaimed the truth. The reforming movement, in fact, became the very life-blood of the Church, because
these popes realized its importance and shouldered their responsibility.

3. GREGORY VII, THE REFORMER

POPE Alexander II died on April 21, 1073, and Cardinal Hildebrand, the
most influential figure in the Roman Curia, ordered public prayers for God's
blessing on the forthcoming conclave. Next day, however, the crowd attending Alexander's funeral began to shout: "Hildebrand Pope! Hildebrand
Bishop!" and so overwhelming was their enthusiasm that the cardinals, to
whom, since 1059, had belonged the duty of nominating St. Peter's successor, hastened to confirm this popular election. The new Pope took no pleasure in his promotion: "The terrible weight of the Church," he wrote, "is laid
upon reluctant shoulders." But since God had spoken, he could not refuse,
and Hildebrand took the regnal name Gregory in memory of a beloved
master. This humble religious, elevated to the highest of all earthly thrones,
was still a deacon. He was therefore ordained priest on May 22, and on June
29, the feast of Sts. Peter and Paul, was consecrated Bishop of Rome.

He was now a man of fifty-three, and in the prime of life. Corpulent, short-legged, and small of stature, his appearance was not particularly attractive; but immense spiritual power radiated from him. A massive and penetrating intellect, a will of iron, ceaseless energy, and unshakable determination in adversity; such were Gregory's outstanding characteristics. His enemies have represented him as ambitious and unscrupulous, as a politician for whom all means to an end were justified, a violent and, indeed, a wicked man. Nothing is farther from the truth; we have numerous examples of his charity, of his refinement, and of his moderation. "Love men even while you detest their vices," he used often to say. He was one of those for whom love of God is the ultimate end of life, for whom "the whole law is summed up in two words: humility and charity." Throughout his pontificate he bore in mind that he must render an account of it to the supreme Judge, and he viewed the splendour of his crown as the symbol of terrible responsibility. Few popes have had so exalted a conception of the Church, whose faith he defended by the condemnation of Berengar; whose members, East and West, he longed to reconcile after a separation that had lasted twenty years; whom in his dreams he had already launched on the crusade; whom, above all, he passionately desired to see pure and holy, worthy of her Master.

Legend has represented Hildebrand as having in effect ruled the Church since about 1050, and as having inspired the movement for reform which spread throughout Christendom during the years prior to his pontificate. That is hardly true. But if his friends and enemies alike, though for different purposes, have exaggerated his influence, we cannot but wonder at the meteoric career marked out by Providence for this son of a Tuscan labourer, whose merit alone had made him supreme in the Roman Curia. Born at Sonno c. 1023, he was placed, while still a child, as an oblate in the monastery of St. Mary on the Aventine, a daughter-house of Cluny. Becoming secretary to Pope Gregory VI (1045–1046), he remained faithful to that pontiff in disgrace, and did much to promote the election of his friend Bruno, Bishop of Toul. It was thus, at the age of less than thirty years, that he came to play an all-important part at the side of St. Leo IX (1049–1054) who, to make clear his purpose of reform, had entered Rome barefooted on the morning of his coronation. Hildebrand was next entrusted with various missions by Victor II (1055–1057) and Stephen IX (1057–1058); he manoeuvred the election of Nicholas II (1059–1061) to the see of Peter, and was the "right hand" of Alexander II (1061–1073), who desired him as his successor. Charged, one after another, with embassies or visitations, adviser to the Pope, and a member of several councils, he had acquired an extensive knowledge of the whole of Christendom; and his influence had more than once proved decisive. It was Hildebrand, for example, who pledged the Church's support of William, Duke of Normandy, in his expedition against England. But above all, his contacts, his observation, and his private meditation had convinced him that reform was of paramount importance.

But the reforms accomplished by Gregory VII had their root in a much earlier movement, initiated more than a century before his birth by Gerard of Brogne, John of Gorze, Erluin of Gembloux, Bruno of Cologne, and others. More than a century had elapsed also since the foundation of Cluny, which became the headquarters of reform and which, during a period of one hundred fifty years, played an important part in this connection under its saintly abbots Odo, Maïeul, Odilon, and Hugh. The desire to live wholly in God had already produced the hermits of St. Romuald at Camaldoli, St. John Gualbert's monks at Vallombrosa, and the enthusiastic crowds of the Patarines who launched a furious attack upon the luxury of clerical life. Exactly contemporary with Hildebrand, there had grown up St. Peter Damian, that hirsute and formidable prophet who had been created cardinal by Stephen IX. The reforming spirit, issuing from the cloister and entering into the hearts of the people, had been welcomed by a succession of popes, who followed a road mapped out by Cardinal Humbert in his treatise *Against Simony* (1057). Clement II, Damasus II, Leo IX, Victor II, Clement V, Nicholas II, and Alexander II had openly embraced the principles of reform. Papal and conciliar decrees had condemned error and denounced abuses; while many a devout soul, urged by the longing for a better way of life, dreamed of restoring the Church to her pristine purity.

Gregory VII, therefore, must not be separated from his age; his merits should not be exaggerated at the expense of his predecessors and contemporaries. The fact remains, however, that his pontificate was of the utmost significance. In him the movement was consolidated; thanks to him, the interdependence of two problems was made clear, and the doctrine formulated which made it possible to solve them both.

When Alexander II first advanced Hildebrand to authority, two, or perhaps three, aspects were discernible in the attitude towards reform. Every right-minded person saw the necessity thereof, but there was some difference of opinion as to the best means of achieving it. Some, especially in Italy, stood for the direct, apostolic, and moral method: to preach against prevalent abuses, above all by example, and to impose heavy penalties upon the guilty. Chief among the representatives of this view was Peter Damian. Others maintained that the real cause of the trouble lay in the poor quality of the clergy, which they attributed in turn to secular interference; and they recommended an institutional and political method which, they argued, would free the Church from the tutelage of kings and barons. Such was the theory of several eminent clerics in Lorraine, good canonists and wise politicians, notably of Cardinal Humbert. But these differences were not irreconcilable, for both sides were agreed as to the essential purpose. Finally, it is not impossible that a kind of nostalgia for the past, especially for the splendid age of Charlemagne, convinced others that it was necessary to restore the Christian order which had suffered during the Carolingian decadence. They felt this to be the surest means of recalling the clergy to their duty and of restraining the power of princes. The great merit of Gregory VII was that he understood, at the cost of bitter experience, that history would reduce these three viewpoints to a single consideration.

At the beginning of his pontificate he tried the first method, and sought to enlist the co-operation of temporal sovereigns. He even attempted reconciliation with such avowed simoniacs and adulterers as the German Emperor Henry IV and Philip I of France, believing that no stone should be left unturned in God's service. A council met at Rome in March 1074, and issued four decrees: (1) Anyone who had obtained ordination or a spiritual benefice by simony was excluded from the ecclesiastical hierarchy. (2) Anyone in possession of a church or an abbey as the result of purchase was *ipso facto* dispossessed. (3) No cleric who was guilty of fornication might celebrate Mass or minister in any way at the altar. (4) In the event of a cleric publicly disobeying the three preceding ordinances, the faithful were forbidden to attend any service conducted by him, and were to do their best to make him submit.

The decrees of 1074 embodied the principles of a necessary reform, and Gregory VII forthwith sent legates to see that they were given effect. But these prelates met with general opposition in one shape or another. Simoniacs were supported by their respective sovereigns in employing every device to frustrate the Holy Father's wishes, and some rebelled outright. In Germany, for example, Hermann of Bamberg and Lieman of Bremen put themselves at the head of several thousand priests who treated the Pope as little better than a heretic. One meeting of German clergy declared that "if he won't assure that the divine offices are celebrated by the clergy, he had better apply to the angels!" The saintly Bishop Altmann of Passau was almost lynched for upholding the pontifical instructions. Otto of Constance, on the other hand, encouraged the priests of his diocese to marry, and the legates were stoned by fornicators. In France, Hugh of Die failed to make the least impression. The Council of Paris was dissolved, and Abbot Walter of Pontoise was assaulted for having argued in favour of reform; while the Council of Poitiers ended in uproar under the supercilious gaze of Philip I, who, not content with putting up bishoprics and abbeys for auction, organized raids on pilgrims within his territory! It was not easy to serve God.

Nevertheless, in spite of—one might say because of—this set-back, Gregory's action was to prove of lasting value. It was now perfectly clear that moral reform was not enough, that the axe must be laid to the root. Early in February 1075, therefore, he tackled the question of lay influence in ecclesiastical affairs, and set out to achieve a twofold programme of moral improvement and political measures. The latter, it was hoped, would free the Church from secular interference. His legislation, which may be studied in the celebrated *Dictatus Papae*, did no more than re-enact the four decrees of 1074. But this time Gregory found himself in direct conflict with rulers who benefited by the very state of affairs which he condemned; this time he had raised the issue of relations between the Church and the civil power. The battle for reform had passed from the moral to the institutional and political plane. It was the bitter "Quarrel of Investitures," which soon became a "struggle between the Priesthood and the Empire."[6]

In 1085 Gregory VII was a refugee at Salerno; and it is said that, feeling the approach of death, he cried out in the anguish of apparent failure: "I have loved justice and hated iniquity; therefore I die in exile." The story may be an invention, but the words are true enough. For a time, evil seemed victorious; but the great Pope left a mark on history which could never be effaced. Simony had received a mortal wound; the celibacy of priests had been revived; and this effort to give back to the Church her ancient purity, in spite of the difficult circumstances in which the Holy See was placed, had bestowed incomparable prestige upon the papacy.

4. RETURN TO THE SOURCES: THE NEW ORDERS

THE primary end of monastic reform was not the abolition of simony and of fornication among the clergy. It went much deeper, and sought to remedy abuses by a return to the sources of inspiration.

We cannot deny that many religious houses were the scene of grave disorders. Cluny herself, the great Cluny who once led the vanguard of reform, had merited reproach. Abbot Peter the Venerable admitted that "but for a handful of monks the community is no more than a synagogue of Satan, whose name and habit are their only title to the appellation of 'religious.'" Even in those monasteries, however, where abuses were not flagrant, there was a more fundamental and no less urgent need for reform. In the course of centuries monachism had deviated from the narrow path appointed by the Rule; its very success had caused it to compromise more or less with temporal institutions. Too much wealth, too much property to administer, perhaps also too much study and even too many hours spent in choir, had

---

6. See Chapter V.

acted to the detriment of manual labour and the practice of asceticism. Cluny had taken this direction. Rigorists might therefore claim that the true spirit of the Rule had been lost and must be recovered. Moral reform was involved in this "journey upstream," this return to what was then described as the "apostolic life."

A reaction against the evil habits of the time had already set in, and was still more strongly emphasized by the spread of eremitical life. Many conceived the idea of fleeing not only from the world, but even from the cloister, which they considered as too easy-going; of seeking uninterrupted solitude as did the anchorites of old. A direct link with the Fathers of the Eastern desert had been forged by St. Nilus, the great Basilian monk whose austere life had astonished Italy about the year 1000, and whose memory was preserved in the monastery of Grotta-ferrata. His example had been quickly followed by St. Romuald who founded the Camaldolese in 1012, and by St. John Gualbert who established Vallombrosa some twelve months later. These men it should be remembered, had originally no intention of creating new congregations. "Fools of God," their one dream had been of total solitude, a face-to-face communion with the One Unchanging; and it was almost in spite of themselves that they were obliged by the number of their disciples to establish collective discipline.

The same phenomenon was repeated several times in the course of the eleventh and twelfth centuries. When Stephen of Muret, son of a nobleman in Auvergne, erected his hut in the lonely forest of Limousin (1077), he little thought that his initiative would give rise to a new order[7] which soon numbered two thousand monks and seventy houses. The same applied to Blessed Robert of Arbrissel, a zealous Breton. Dissatisfied with his life as a canon, he took the road as an "apostolic missionary," denouncing clerical vices. But his rugged appearance attracted such enormous crowds that, in order to accommodate them, he founded Fontevrault (1096), a curious "double abbey" in Anjou, where men and women were received in twin houses. Such was the origin (1116) of a congregation which included three

---

7.   Grandmont, 1124.

thousand souls in France, England, and Spain. Stephen and Robert effected genuine improvements in religious life. The Rule in each case was that of St. Benedict with additional austerities; Stephen, in fact, forbade the ownership of land outside the monastic enclosure, and imposed regulations involving extreme self-sacrifice.

It was the same state of mind, the same longing for a return to eremitical life, which inspired the Carthusians, an Order founded in 1084 and still recognized as the pattern of monastic solitude. St. Bruno was a noble Rhinelander, a former student at Cologne and Paris, professor of theology and chancellor of Rheims. Declining to serve under an unworthy bishop, he resigned his offices and sought a place of absolute silence where he might have leisure to pray alone. On the advice of his former pupil, Hugh, Bishop of Grenoble, he established himself with six companions in the wild forest that he was to render famous. Summoned to Rome in 1100 by another ex-pupil, Pope Urban II, he could not endure life in that noisy city, and fled once more into solitude. This time he chose Calabria, where he founded another house of the Order. His work in Dauphiné survived and prospered; the constitutions were drafted by Prior Guigo in 1127.

The most remarkable characteristic of the Charterhouse is its combination of eremitical and cenobitical life. In the little three-roomed house allotted to him, each religious is a hermit; but in choir at matins, lauds, and vespers, as also in the refectory on Sundays and major festivals, he feels himself a member of the community. Perpetual silence is broken only by short periods of recreation and during the weekly walk. Fasting is obligatory from September 14 until Easter, and likewise on all Fridays and vigils; meat is absolutely forbidden. It is, in fact, an existence very similar to that of the hermits proper, but modified and rendered more adaptable to human nature by the nearness of one's brethren. That the ideal was well suited to the age is proved by its success. The first daughter-house was erected at Porres-en-Bugey in 1115; and by the end of the twelfth century there were thirty-seven Charterhouses.[8] The hard way drew men's hearts.

---

8.   Two were houses of nuns; the Calabrian monasteries had adopted the rule of Citeaux.

Camaldolese, Vallombrosians, monks of Grandmont or Fontevrault, and Carthusians, all looked to the eremitical ideal. That they played a vital part in the current of monastic reform was almost accidental; their achievement in this respect was due rather to the goal towards which they aspired than to what may be described as "structural alterations." Quite different was the history of Citeaux, which began in a modest way and encountered difficulties that came near to proving fatal.

About 1075, a few monks had withdrawn to the forest of Collon near Tonnerre, and Gregory VII had appointed Robert of Champagne, prior of Montier-la-Celle, as their Superior. Robert was a strange personality. Despite his great reputation for sanctity, some have charged him with cowardice. Be that as it may, he was a sensitive, retiring character, often capable of sudden boldness followed as quickly by withdrawal; a contemplative unfitted to deal with the contingencies of daily life. The new house, Molesmes, soon became famous. It was nominally a "reformed" abbey; but strict Benedictine observance was marred by "Cluniac customs," so called in spite of the fact that Cluny was in no way responsible for them. Gifts flowed in; Robert weakly accepted them, and soon had cause to ask himself in what respect Molesmes differed from other Cluniac abbeys. There was no laxity in the strict sense; but too many small concessions, too many practices undreamed of by St. Benedict, made it difficult to observe the Holy Rule in its original spirit and simplicity.

A group of religious, led by Alberic and Stephen Harding, planned, with Robert's approval, to reform Molesmes. Their attempt was strenuously opposed by the rest of the community, whose indignation was such that the abbot was obliged to leave the monastery for a time, and Alberic was violently assaulted. The reformers at length determined to secede. On March 21, 1098, Robert, Alberic, and Stephen Harding, with about twenty monks, founded a new abbey called Citeaux in the valley of the Saône.

The beginnings of this house were beset with difficulties. At the end of a year Robert returned to Molesmes on the papal legate's advice and Alberic took charge. The young community had to endure hunger and destitution while they cleared the wilderness and built their monastery. They lived, however, exactly as they had desired, in absolute poverty, refusing every comfort, devoting themselves to manual labour, fasting, penance, and obedience. The Holy See was informed, and extended its protection to "the poor monks of the new monastery." Recruits, however, were few and far between. Citeaux's austerity caused would-be members to fight shy; nor did the situation greatly improve when Alberic was succeeded by Stephen Harding in 1108.

We have seen[9] how the arrival of St. Bernard and his thirty companions in the spring of 1112 altered the situation and began a splendid chapter of monastic history. Citeaux became so famous that twelve months later the community had outgrown its accommodation and was obliged to found another house. La Ferté, Pontigny, Clairvaux, and Morimond, the four "elder daughters" of Citeaux, arose within the space of as many years; and the new congregation, under Bernard's foresight and unflagging energy, set out to conquer the whole world. On Stephen Harding's death in 1134, the Order possessed eighty-four houses; one hundred fifty when St. Bernard died twenty years later; five hundred thirty in 1199; and seven hundred in the following century. After 1125 there were almost as many houses of women as of men; and the general chapter prohibited further establishment, fearing it might become impossible to provide for the nuns' spiritual direction. In order to assure unity within the Order Stephen Harding had published a constitution known as the *Charter of Charity* (1119), which embodied two fundamental rules: new monasteries were to be subject to the control of their "mother houses," and the Order was to be governed by a "general chapter," a periodical assembly of abbots and delegates from every monastery.[10]

What exactly was the Cistercian reform? Nothing more or less than a return to the Rule of St. Benedict, excluding those elements which had

---

9. Chapter III.

10. The custom of holding general chapters was soon afterwards adopted by other orders, e.g., the Carthusians, Templars, Premonstratensians, Canons of St. Victor, and later by the Franciscans and Dominicans. The Lateran Council of 1215 made it obligatory for all congregations; the Benedictine abbots and priors were to hold national chapters every month.

been added in the course of centuries. Everything was forbidden that was not explicitly authorized by the Holy Rule. Built by preference in marshy valleys, not on those towering heights favoured by the Cluniacs, the Cistercian abbeys were intended as homes of total renunciation. The habit of these monks consisted of a plain woollen tunic with scapular and cowl of the same material. Their diet admitted of no meat, fish, cooking fats, milk-products, or eggs. They ate nothing except boiled vegetables; and from September 14 until Easter only one meal a day was allowed. They slept fully clothed on straw mattresses without covering. At midnight, roused by the monastery's one bell, the community rose for prayer and matins in a church that was of the utmost simplicity, without ornament of any kind. Above all, no monastery might accept gifts or tithes, and possessed no lands other than what was necessary to supply the monks with their food. Such austerity was unheard of; but still more wonderful was its success. The white habit[11] of the Cistercians was looked upon by the whole Church as symbolic of the perfect life; and the example of this Order born among the marshes of Saône, no less than the labour of her sons, made a deep impression on the Middle Ages.

One of the most curious features of the Cistercian movement was its effect upon the Cluniacs, who regarded the new observance as a reflection on themselves. The ensuing conflict was dignified at the highest level by an exchange of some magnificent letters between Peter the Venerable, abbot of Cluny, and St. Bernard; but among the rank and file, it must be confessed, Charity took many a hard knock. By and large, however, this rivalry was not unprofitable, as is shown by subsequent events at Cluny. The great Burgundian abbey had declined since the death of St. Hugh (1109), who had been succeeded by an incompetent abbot, Pons de Melgueil. The Order had ten thousand monks housed in one thousand four hundred fifty beautiful monasteries, but she was on the downward path; enormous wealth had inevitably reduced her first fervour to mere routine.

---

11. The white habit was also adopted by the Premonstratensians, Carthusians, the monks of Hirschau, and other congregations.

The current of reform, however, had not ceased to flow in Cluny's soul; it had reappeared towards the end of the eleventh century at Rüggisberg near Freiburg, at St. Alban at Basel, and at Siegbourg. The torrent was still further increased when Abbot William of Hirschau, instigated by Gregory VII's legate Bernard of Marseilles, decided to transform his community. The primitive observance of Cluny was revived in a spirit of almost combative zeal; and the monks of Hirschau, distinguished by their white habit, sent preachers all over Germany. One hundred fifty communities affiliated with them to form a congregation which was numbered among the staunchest allies of the papacy during the Quarrel of Investitures.

Peter the Venerable was abbot of Cluny from 1122 to 1156. Apart from his sanctity, he possessed a first-class intellect, and was both a mystic and a man of action worthy of his most illustrious predecessors. In 1132 he tightened up the rules of fasting and silence, re-established the "ancient and holy practice of manual labour," and reorganized recruitment. But he took care not to belittle scholarship, the arts, or the splendour of the divine office, three most characteristic and valuable features of Cluniac life. His example was infectious, and many houses of the Order adopted these reforms. The most remarkable instance was that of St. Denis, the famous royal abbey outside Paris, which had been inundated by an unhealthy tide of luxury. In 1127, as we have seen, it was reformed by Abbot Suger, who breathed into his sons the new spirit which, through the operation of grace, he himself had learned from the emphatic but affectionate admonitions of his friend St. Bernard.

Nor must we overlook the part played by canons regular in this laborious task of reform. An important element of religious life in the Carolingian era were those colleges of priests, who lived near the bishop, saw that the choral services were maintained, and formed, as it were, his general staff. But serious abuses had crept in: many canons were preoccupied with tapping the revenues of the chapter rather than with singing matins; many of them, too, were no better than gyrovagues, constantly absent from their stalls. Some were guilty of even more deplorable vices—violence and sexual immorality.

Here again, all that was necessary to terminate a sorry state of affairs
was the renewal of first fervour. At Tagaste, and later during his thirty years
as Bishop of Hippo, St. Augustine had lived in community with a group of
friends and collaborators. Whether or not he actually drew up the so-called
Rule of St. Augustine is open to dispute; but its principles are certainly
discoverable in his works. The proper course, then, was a return to those
principles: the secular clergy must be "monachized" and rendered worthy of
their mission. The plan, suggested long ago by St. Chrodegang,[12] was now
revived. The reformers aimed at persuading canons to live in community, to
renounce individual property, and to practise mortification; for it is obvious
that life in community precludes concubinage and general dissipation. The
flexibility of St. Augustine's "Rule" was well suited to those groups which
had to adapt themselves to circumstances, and they multiplied with wonderful variety.

The movement took several forms. Some chapters were led by grace to
reorganize themselves and adopt the Rule. The whole chapter of St. Martin
of Tours, for example, renounced their goods and went to live in poverty
on the island of St. Cosmas; while at Rome, Pope Gregory VII praised the
canons for having "embraced the communal life after the model of the primitive Church." In other cases, bishops imposed reform from without. Thus
at Cambrai the entire secular chapter was evicted and regulars installed in
their place. Arnulf, Patriarch of Jerusalem, desired his canons to "lead the
same life as the apostles." Elsewhere, a monastic community might choose
to become canons regular, thinking in that way to lead more useful lives, as
did the monks of La Trinité in Vendôme. New centres also were established
for bodies of secular clergy who wished to lead the perfect life: Mortain,
St. Quentin at Beauvais, St. Jean-de-Vigne at Soissons, St. Victor at Paris,
and St. Ruf at Avignon. Lastly, a few saints, with an eye to the more distant
future, united several of these collegiate groups into congregations. Such
was the origin of the canons at Murbach in Alsace, founded by Manegold of
Lautenbach, and those of Arrouaise and Artois established by St. Gervase.

---

12.   He was Bishop of Metz from 746 until 766.

Three of these congregations—St. Ruf, St. Victor, and Prémontré—had distinguished histories. The first two are now almost forgotten, but their influence was far from negligible. Founded at Avignon in 1039, the canons regular of St. Ruf moved in 1158 to Valence, where they continued until the French Revolution. There is no doubt that they were the first in order of time. Pope Urban II congratulated them in 1095 upon having "revived the primitive life of clerics," and Blessed Pons, a Carthusian who became Bishop of Grenoble, told them, in 1129, that they "had served as a model and norm for all, even the most distant, monasteries of canons." More than eight hundred chapters from Norway to Portugal, from Greece to Iceland, were affiliated to this congregation. Three popes came from their ranks; and without in any way neglecting the things of the spirit, they did much for the arts throughout Provence, as also in Catalonia, and even at Chartres. They were likewise an important influence in the framing of the Carthusian constitutions, and served as a model for the famous congregation of St. Victor.

The latter was founded by William of Champeaux and named after the nearby hermitage on Mont Saint-Geneviève whither it moved in 1108. Raised to the status of a congregation by Gildwin, Bishop of Châlons, and protected by Stephen of Senlis, Bishop of Paris, St. Victor was a regular monastic university. It revived the traditional austerity of religious life with a fervour that attracted thousands; and its glory was enhanced by the fact that reform had as yet made small headway in the neighbourhood of Paris. An attempt was made to rally the chapter of Notre-Dame; but so furious was the opposition that the prior of St. Victor was murdered by the archdeacon's nephews; while the secular canons of St. Geneviève only agreed to the presence of regulars in their midst when Suger, that determined statesman, threatened to "cut off their hands and put out their eyes."

The most outstanding figure in the reform of the canons regular was St. Norbert (1085–1134), founder of the Premonstratensians. The story of this young German nobleman is characteristic of his age. Refined and sensitive, he was more concerned with rich furs and hunting than with the Gospel; but having wasted his energies for thirty years, he was suddenly called by God to the accompaniment of a flash of lightning which killed his horse. As

a canon of Xanten, in Prussia, he had preferred the archbishop's palace at   165
Cologne or the court of Henry V to his own chapter; but immediately after
his conversion he began to denounce abuses with holy vehemence, implor-
ing his colleagues to reform their lives, and attempting to enforce regular
observance. All in vain: his good intentions earned him nothing but ill will.
One disgruntled cleric spat in his face, and a charge was laid against him in
the Council of Fritzlar. Turning his back on Xanten and his property, he
travelled the roads of Germany, Belgium, and France, preaching a return to
holy living and the necessity of penance, as Robert of Arbrissel was doing at
about the same time.

Norbert had begun to make a name for himself. We find him acting as
arbitrator in more than one feudal dispute, and his contemporaries compared him with Bernard of Clairvaux—sometimes even to the latter's disadvantage. In 1119 he met Calixtus II, who advised him to settle down.
It was a timely warning; for at this period, when the abbey was still the
true centre of religious life, the most effective means of action was to establish a permanent monastic base. The day of itinerant preachers had not yet
dawned. And so a new house of canons subject to the Augustinian Rule
was established in 1121 at Prémontré in the forest of St. Gobain. Norbert,
however, was in the grip of apostolic fever. He set out once more, and continued preaching until called to the archbishopric of Magdeburg, in which
capacity he strove to foster the ideals of reform, and crossed swords with
the antipope Anacletus II.

His friend and collaborator, Hugh de Fosses, was left behind to draft
the Order's constitutions, which included the Cistercian system of general chapters and regular visitations. It was Hugh also who conceived the
brilliant idea of employing the canons regular as an instrument of reform.
The Premonstratensians were to live in community, exactly like monks,
singing the divine office and practising mortification. But they would not
remain permanently in the cloister; they would devote themselves to parochial work, and their priories would thus serve as power-houses of Christian endeavour. The Premonstratensian, in other words, was to combine
the duties of a monk with those of a parish priest. The wisdom, and indeed

the necessity, of this plan was proved by its success; for in 1350 the Order counted one thousand three hundred houses, devoted principally to evangelizing the German countryside.

5. PASCHAL II

THE spirit of reform had come to stay; it could no longer be disowned. None of Gregory VII's successors ventured to turn back; the majority of them were zealous reformers, and even Victor III (1086–1087), an undistinguished pontiff, renewed his great predecessor's legislation. When Urban II (1088–1099) succeeded to the throne of Peter, he made this appeal: "Have confidence in me as you had formerly in Pope Gregory of blessed memory. I mean to follow faithfully in his footsteps: I condemn whatever he condemned; I love what found favour in his sight; I approve all that he considered right and Catholic." Certain popes have been accused of "anti-Gregorian reaction." The phrase is inaccurate—except on the political plane, where some of them felt the papacy had gone too far; but in essentials, i.e., with regard to the necessity for reform, not one of them is found to have advocated a different course. Calixtus II (1119–1124), Innocent II (1130–1143), Eugenius III (1145–1153), and Celestine III (1191–1198), all remained faithful to the ideals of St. Gregory VII.

The determination of these popes is even more admirable when we recall their circumstances. Throughout the twelfth century Peter's barque was in distress. Five pontificates in succession were disturbed by conflict with the empire on this very subject of reform. Antipopes sprang up at the nod of ambitious rivals, but no St. Bernard was at hand to meet the threat of schism that weighed so heavily upon the Church.[13] Rome was a prey to the factions of Pope, Emperor, and a demagogic senate of great feudal lords. Lucius II (1144–1145) died of wounds received during an assault on the

---

13. The schism of Anacletus has been considered in the previous chapter on St. Bernard section 7.

senatorial palace. A social revolution tinged with heresy broke out in the
Eternal City itself, and Arnold of Brescia proclaimed his republic.[14]

It is indeed astonishing that, in spite of these obstacles, the Church managed to hold a straight course. The decisive moment of her voyage was the ninth ecumenical council, which met at the Lateran in 1123. The question of secular influence upon ecclesiastical appointments having been settled, Pope Calixtus II determined to consolidate his advantages in a general assembly, the first of its kind to be held in the West. It was attended by three hundred bishops and other prelates. No new dogma was proclaimed, no disciplinary laws were enacted; but the council solemnly defined the principles of reform in such forcible terms that they could no longer be called in question.

Among these reforming popes there was one who deserves our special notice. Not that he achieved more than others, for in a sense his accomplishment was less than theirs; but his project, though so far in advance of his time as to seem chimerical, was in fact sublime. He was a monk (whether of Vallombrosa or of Cluny is not quite certain), a contemplative soul, somewhat narrow-minded, and ill equipped for the practical affairs of life. He took the name of Paschal II, and reigned from 1099 until 1118. Considering the perilous situation of the Church at that time, with Rome threatened by the armies of Henry V, his qualifications were inadequate; a statesman might have been preferable.

Paschal believed that if the Church was to be rescued from the servitude of politics, she must take her stand exclusively upon spiritual ground; and for that purpose, he considered, only one means would suffice—total renunciation of all her territory, of all those titles which bound her hand and foot within the feudal system. A poor Church, with no resources other than offerings made by the faithful, would surely enjoy greater freedom of action. The Pope, in fact, proposed to solve political problems by moral reforms. He believed that measures suited to personal improvement would be found no less efficacious when applied to the Christian body as a whole.

---

14. See the following chapter, section 6.

It was an audacious, if not a fantastic scheme; at all events, it met with scant approval. This dream of a golden age in which bishops and abbots, relieved of all temporal responsibility, would have only the care of souls, seemed to those dignitaries less attractive than their revenues. His generous proposals were answered with rebellion, an opportunity of which the Emperor at once took advantage. The Pope was seized and obliged to capitulate.[15]

The majority of Church historians have judged Paschal II unfairly. True, his action retarded rather than advanced the solution of a knotty problem; for to have repudiated temporal power at that date would surely have been to weaken the papacy. But who can say what would have been the future of the Church if his noble dream had materialized? How many compromises, errors, and even tragedies might have been avoided?

6. ANCIENT ERRORS AND NEW PROBLEMS

RELENTLESS effort backed by stern resolve could not, alas, eradicate the evil. Papal instructions and conciliar decrees met with strong resistance from private interest and personal prejudice. By the beginning of the thirteenth century simony and the marriage of priests were almost universally condemned, at least in theory; and that was all to the good, but in practice things did not work quite so smoothly.

The moral situation, of course, was in no way comparable with what it had been at the commencement of the eleventh century, or with that miserable state of affairs which had led to the Gregorian reform. But the old errors, the old temptations, were always there; and time had done its customary work. Those who once led the vanguard had since betrayed the ideal of Christ. The great Cluniac abbey at Vézelay was ruled by a simoniacal and incontinent superior who squandered the goods of his monastery to pension off his son and daughter! Nor were the Cistercians much better. We possess a document written in 1202 by Innocent III, addressed to the

---

15. See Chapter V, section 4.

abbots of Clairvaux, Morimond, Pontigny, and La Ferté, in which the Sovereign Pontiff makes reference to some shameful rumours. At Grandmont, there was brawling during the divine office, and a similar outburst among the Premonstratensians of Saint-Martin at Laon ended in bloodshed. The secular clergy presented much the same kind of picture, especially in remote dioceses where the reforming influence had been weak.

The situation was even more disquieting than in the eleventh century. It must not be forgotten that at the end of the twelfth society was undergoing a radical transformation; new customs were imported from the East by crusaders and travellers, and an enormous increase of trade was causing money to flow more freely. The feudal system was beginning to break up; the serfs were in process of emancipation; towns were developing; and fresh interests brought in their train an altered outlook upon life. The foundations of Europe were crumbling to dust.

It was virtually impossible that the clergy should remain unaffected by this atmosphere of general unrest. Innocent III regretted that "the shepherd had become a hireling, leaving his flock to the mercy of wolves. The evil which he should destroy, he protects by his treason. Nearly all clerics have deserted the cause of God; and of those who have remained faithful, too many are inept." Such lamentations speak for themselves.

What would the Church do to meet these new influences? Could she free herself from the many ties that linked her with the feudal regime? It certainly appears that she had allowed the gap to widen between herself and the deepest aspirations of the age. During the barbarian epoch she had assumed the terrible responsibility of preventing chaos, and had taken a leading place in the resulting "feudal" order. She had made the abbey a replica of the castle; she had sacramentalized the oath, the bond of warrior society; she had blessed the arms of knighthood, instituted works of charity, and created in the shelter of her convents a remarkable system of education. How many men, though dedicated to God's service, could have learned within the space of a few decades to regard as outworn a worldwide organization so clearly blessed by Heaven and guaranteeing them so many concrete advantages? Gregory VII had not attempted to break this link between the Church and the contemporary world; his reform had been erected on moral and spiritual bases, by strengthening the Church's power and by the exercise of her universal authority in every sphere. Paschal II had been looked upon as a fanatic for proposing such a rupture, and it is most unlikely that an exclusively moral reform could have helped the Church in the unsettled climate of that age.

For the tide of intellectual ferment was beginning to invade even the spiritual life. Prophets of both sexes denounced scandals and foretold chastisement. "Woe betide all nations!" cried St. Elizabeth of Schönau, "for the world is naught but darkness. The Lord's vine has perished; the head of the Church is sick, her members dead!" To which St. Hildegarde added: "The justice of God is about to strike, and His decrees will be your executioners; the papacy and the empire, fellows in corruption, will together fall." But she went on to say more optimistically: "From their ruins the Holy Spirit will cause a new people to arise; conversion will be general, and the angels will return to dwell confidently among the sons of men." The most famous of all these visionaries was Joachim of Flora (1145–1202). Abbot of a Cistercian monastery in Calabria, he was a saintly soul, a mystic whose heart was full of gentleness and poetry. A keen student of the Apocalypse, he had arrived at the idea of a new division of world history. After the reign of God the Father, corresponding to the Old Testament, there was the reign of the Son, intermediate between servitude and full liberty. Soon, however, there would begin the reign of the Holy Spirit, under which men would live according to the "eternal gospel," a gospel differing from that of Christ inasmuch as it would proceed not from a written book, but from direct spiritual comprehension of truth. The Church would then be finally regenerated, and would put an end to scandal. She would be pure and holy; the city of men would become the City of God.

So long as these prophecies did no more than encourage pious folk on the road to heaven, they were harmless enough, except perhaps in so far as they ran the risk of unsettling weak minds, as happened later on. But other voices made themselves heard, voices incompatible with Christian doctrine. Criticism was directed against the Church by certain heretics,

whose number and influence were on the increase. The Waldenses had been
followed by the Cathars,[16] whose leaders, styling themselves "the Perfect,"
had taught a stern lesson to many ecclesiastical dignitaries by the example
of their lives. In 1184 Pope Lucius III had condemned the Waldenses, and
there was now talk of resolving the Albigensian crisis by force of arms. But
to what purpose, if the Church would not put her own house in order? The
fight against moral degeneracy could not be left, for instance, to the Patarines; nor could clerical ignorance be allowed to continue amid the growing intellectual restiveness. The Church, despite her worldwide authority,
might at any moment witness the whole vast mass of her adherents slide
from the firm ground of grace and truth.

A new and quite different kind of reform was therefore indispensable. It
would naturally have to aim at the restoration of moral values, at the rean-
imation of the Christian lump with a leaven of enthusiasm and faith; but
it would also have to meet new requirements. Once again, Christendom
produced men who, understanding contemporary needs, strengthened the
Church's authority by adapting her characteristically feudal outlook to a
more popular and more universalist conception of society. This work was
performed chiefly by a great pope and two saints.

7. INNOCENT III

POPE Celestine III died on January 8, 1198. That same evening the cardinals met, and unanimously chose the youngest of their colleagues to succeed him. It was clear to all that a most important pontificate had begun.
Lothair of Segni, who took the name Innocent III, was tall and thin, a fine
figure of a man. His countenance radiated intelligence and determination,
suggesting at the same time a thoughtfulness that seemed almost to indi-
cate a troubled mind. A former student at Paris, then at Bologna, where he
had attended the lectures of Uguccio da Pisa, Innocent had received a solid

---

16. See Volume 2, Chapter XIII.

intellectual grounding both in the classics and in jurisprudence. At the age of thirty he was created cardinal-deacon by his uncle Clement III, and eight years later he succeeded to the Apostolic See, which he was to occupy for eighteen years.

He has been much maligned; and St. Lutgard claimed to have seen him, during one of her visions, doing penance in Purgatory until the Day of Judgment! His grand political designs may have overshadowed his truly Christian purpose, but it cannot be denied that his pontificate is one of the most remarkable in the history of the Church. He drove the Emperor from Italy; he appointed himself guardian of Sicily and suzerain of England; he disposed of the German crown; he controlled Hungary, Aragon, and Castile; he revived the crusade; he beat down heresy by armed force. In a word, his manifold activity reveals an exceptionally powerful character. On the other hand, it is no less certain that all his gigantic expenditure of temporal means had in view a single end—the glory of God's Church, whose grandeur was graven deep upon his mind.

He has been called "proud" and "brutal." His style was certainly vigorous, and there was a sharp edge to his tongue. When the interests of the Church were at stake, he would sometimes describe his opponent as a "conceited ass," or a "hog wallowing in muck"; which is not the pontifical phraseology of today. But few great administrators are without a tinge of asperity; and a glance at Innocent's correspondence will reveal a man far different from the image presented by historians. His charity was boundless, prompt to bind up wounds inflicted by the inevitable blows of Justice. Apart from deep humility, he had a sincere love of the poor, of captives, and of the sick, together with an almost mystical piety that had been nourished on the works of St. Bernard, of Hugh of St. Victor, and of St. Peter Damian. These qualities mark the finer shades in a portrait of one whom circumstance, as well as his own genius, had raised to the summit of the medieval Church. Innocent III was sometimes mistaken, but he acted in all things for God's glory.

He knew too well the plight of Christendom not to be zealous for reform. As a young priest, and later as a young cardinal, he had travelled much, and had more than once been angered by bishops who dared not proclaim the Gospel truth, and of whom he spoke as "dumb dogs who can no longer bark." So deeply had he pondered St. Bernard's *De Consideratione*, that its phrases flowed spontaneously from his pen. Moreover, from the very beginning of his pontificate, his Bulls made clear an inexorable resolve to combat the old abuses of simony and Nicolaism. In one of the earliest he insisted upon a seemly garb for clerics, forbidding them to dress like dandies, and threatened the visitation of his wrath upon those who indulged in drunkenness. He flayed those who so far forgot their vocation as to carry arms, and took immediate steps to reduce the size of the pontifical court.

Innocent III energetically applied those principles which he had laid down immediately after his election, and his "reforming" Bulls are legion. The Curia was reorganized by the elimination of noble careerists, forgers of false Bulls, and officials who were suspected of venality. The appointment of bishops was subjected to stricter control, and those who did not fulfil the canonical requirements as to age and learning were rejected. The Pope maintained close contact with the more worthy members of the episcopate, reminding them of their duties, and insisting, as he once wrote to the Bishop of Liége, that "he who has undertaken the care of souls must bear the torch of learning and example." Whenever he found that some abuse had crept into a diocese, he notified the bishop, ordered him to take appropriate steps, and, if that prelate proved reluctant, had him reprimanded by trustworthy persons. He railed against incontinent clergy at Norwich in England, at Gniezno in Poland, and in Denmark; he denounced the accumulation of benefices and the love of money wherever it appeared; nor did the regular clergy escape his stern solicitude. Innocent never acted without the fullest information; but once having obtained it, he went straight to the point. His personal intervention lent weight to the authority of those national and provincial councils whose duty it was to adapt his decisions to local circumstances.

The crowning event of Innocent's pontificate was the fourth Lateran (twelfth ecumenical) Council in 1215, an imposing assembly of four hundred twelve bishops, eight hundred abbots and priors, together with ambassadors from every nation.[17] Questions of reform occupied first place in its deliberations, and the conduct of the clergy was dealt with in a series of more than twenty canons, one of which enacted that every diocese should have a "master of theology" to instruct those seeking ordination.

The whole of Innocent's teaching on clerical reform was summed up in these canons, which were couched in the most solemn terms. But his legislation, notwithstanding its undoubted value, could have achieved little or nothing by itself; it was simply the re-enactment on a larger scale of principles which had been universally accepted since the time of Gregory VII. Innocent, however, had an intuitive sense of the changes that were taking place around him; he understood that any return to the Gospel must be accomplished by new means.

Characteristic of the pontiff's method was his attitude towards the religious Orders. He relied upon them to preserve vital contact between the Church and the common people, whose future was already in the crucible; he supported the Premonstratensians, who sought personal sanctification through the exercise of parochial duties; and he encouraged those religious who devoted themselves to charitable work outside the cloister. Such was the Order of the Holy Ghost, which received its rule in 1213, and, from quite modest beginnings, grew into an international body with many branches. In 1198, thanks again to Innocent III, St. John of Matha was enabled to found the Trinitarian Order whose vocation was to rescue Christian captives from the Muslims.[18] In Lombardy a group of priests, religious, laymen, shopkeepers, and businessmen formed themselves into a charitable organization bound by vows of chastity and poverty. These "Humiliati" were mistrusted by the authorities, who considered them more or less as heretics; but Innocent III understood their pious intention and gave them his approval in 1201.

There were also sections of the Waldenses and Cathars who desired to return to the Church, but hoped that, having submitted, they might be

---

17. See Chapter VI, section 4.
18. These two Orders will be studied later on (Chapter VI) in connection with the charitable works of the Church.

allowed to live as heretofore, preaching the moral regeneration of society, subject to episcopal jurisdiction. Innocent III was sympathetic; he welcomed them, and, to the horrified amazement of his court, gladly presented a statute to the "Poor Catholics" and their superior, Durand of Huesca. Such was the origin of what we call "the lay apostolate."

Looking, however, into a more distant future, the Pope realized that old methods would no longer suffice to combat heresy and re-mix the leaven with the Christian lump. He decided, therefore, to institute a new form of the apostolate, closer to the people and better equipped for its task. Innocent saw in his mind's eye a body of men inspired with burning faith and the evangelical ideal, unencumbered by worldly goods, and thus able to approach the poor with open arms, proclaiming once again the words of love and truth.

He thought at first that Citeaux might adapt itself and provide such men; after all, St. Bernard, great contemplative though he was, had proved himself a no less able preacher. Accordingly, he chose two Cistercians, Brothers Regnier and Guy, to whom he addressed the celebrated Bull of November 19, 1206, calling upon them to select a number of "trustworthy religious who would imitate the poverty of Christ and go forth boldly, in humble guise but with zealous hearts, to seek out and recall heretics from the darkness of their ways with God's help, by their own example, and by the persuasiveness of their words." But Citeaux was no longer the Citeaux of St. Bernard. The traditions of the Order had degenerated into mere routine; the Cistercian ideal of poverty was not what it had been a century ago, and Innocent's appeal, with few exceptions, fell upon deaf ears.

Notwithstanding this set-back, the Pope had issued a tremendous challenge, which Providence was soon to answer. It is perhaps, under God, the supreme merit of Innocent III that he understood and encouraged two saints from whom the Church was to relearn the lesson of self-sacrifice—St. Francis of Assisi and St. Dominic.

8. ST. FRANCIS, THE "PERFECT IMAGE OF CHRIST"

During the summer of 1210 Innocent III received in audience at the Lateran a frail young man with eyes of flame, clothed in the coarse tunic and hood of a peasant. He wore a girdle round his waist, and sandals on his otherwise bare feet. Francis Bernardone had come from Assisi, the chief town of Umbria, with twelve companions poorly clad like himself—twelve disciples like the twelve Apostles. He had come, the Pope was told, to lay before the Holy See his observations on the state of the Church, and his views concerning the apostolate. "Another of them!" the Pope no doubt exclaimed; indeed, he might never have consented to receive this vagabond, if Bishop Guido of Assisi and Cardinal John Colonna had not recommended him. No, the little Umbrian had nothing in common with those wandering prophets who crowded the roads at that period, brandishing the Gospels in the face of Holy Church, upsetting whole dioceses under the pretence of living an "integral Christianity," and of whom one could never be quite certain that they were not Waldenses or Patarines.

Francis began to speak in vehement but respectful tones, with no affectation, but with the serenity and persuasive force of those who have devoted themselves heart and soul to a lofty ideal. He expressed himself with a kind of eloquent simplicity, full of poetic imagery that came straight from his heart like an echo of the words of Christ. Listening in silence, the Pope felt himself carried away on a flood of strange anguish, and yet of joy; for on the previous night he had dreamed a dream in harmony with his most dismal thoughts. The Lateran basilica, mother church of Christendom, was tottering to its fall; but there came a man sent by Jesus Christ, who leaned against the crumbling walls and prevented their collapse; a little emaciated fellow, quite young, with ascetic face and eyes of fire, clothed in rough homespun—the exact image, in fact, of the one who now stood before him.

Innocent III was a good judge of men; he sized up Francis in a moment. There was no trace of pride, no grandiose ideas which would probably do more harm than good; he had no wish to found a new Order, and he made no attempt to expound the merits of a homemade Rule. When questioned

as to his principles, he replied in three verses of Scripture: Matthew 19:21,
where it is said that to follow Christ one must abandon all that one has;
Luke 9:3, where the disciples are ordered to set out on the road without
money or change of clothing, without scrip or staff; and Matthew 16:24,
which lays down that unique but all-embracing law—"If any man will come
after me, let him deny himself and take up his cross." Moved by such wonderful simplicity, astonished at the submissiveness apparent in every word
that fell from the mouth of his unwonted visitor, Innocent III felt sure that
Providence had heard his prayer. Here was one after Christ's own heart, such
as he had desired. After a long pause the Pope exclaimed: "For sure, this
holy man will re-establish the Church of God on her foundations!" Then,
coming down from his throne, he embraced the Poverello, and addressed
the little group: "Go with God, my brethren; preach penance according as
the Lord inspires you. And when the Almighty has caused you to increase
and multiply, come back to me, and I will grant you still more than I have
done today."

It was thus that Francis, who had come to Rome for no other purpose
than to tell the common father of his hopes and his resolve found himself,
and his brethren with him, invited to regenerate Christendom. These few
"Penitents of Assisi" had become an Order, the Order of Friars Minor, as the
founder was to name them six years later. A splendid page had been opened
in the annals of the Church.

Francis was then a young man of scarcely twenty-eight years, short of
stature, thin, but of distinguished appearance. All the known portraits of
him agree in showing us a small narrow face terminating in a scanty beard.
The features are regular and refined, with great black shining eyes, and lips
slightly parted in a smile; but the most striking of all these portraits, that by
Cimabue in the church at Assisi, reveals also a contemplative and exacting
soul, an iron will scarcely hidden by a veil of gentleness.

All his biographers who knew him personally describe a character in
harmony with these externals. From youth upwards his noble qualities combined with human shortcomings to render him impulsive in the extreme,
and yet of exquisite sensibility. He was generous almost to a fault, prompt

to volunteer his services, and always courteous; one, in fact, whose charm the most surly customer could not resist. These graces, however, concealed immeasurable reserves of strength, unbending determination, and a temperament which, as his biographers admit, would have led him to all manner of excesses, but for his power of self-control.

In this admixture of restraint and audacity lay the secret of his fascination. Though invariably polite, he never hesitated to proclaim what he believed true and just. He was never known to commit the slightest meanness, nor to betray that code of delicate refinement which governed all his actions as a knight of Christ.

This extraordinary man was also a poet. Like the troubadours from France, whose name he bore and whose language he loved to speak, those troubadours who sang love's joy and the beauty of this world, Francis heard within himself the fraternal voice of creation. It re-echoed in his heart. His soul lay wide open to the pure and unspoiled impulses of nature, like Adam in the first springtime. The faith, which others had reduced to narrow formulae, was not for him dry dogma or stern law, but joyous fervour, mystic gratitude. The created world stretched before him in its primeval innocence; therefore he looked upon wind, fire, water, and even death itself, as brothers; therefore too larks obeyed his word, and fierce wolves were ready to shake hands with him. Through him a new tone was introduced into the Christian symphony, a tone of ineffable purity and depth. He was the very model of those whom Jesus loved.

When Francis knelt before the Pope in 1210, some years had elapsed since he discovered his vocation and set out on the heavenly adventure. Nevertheless, God had been obliged to knock loud and call several times before the son of Bernardone, a wealthy wool merchant, became "Il Poverello." It had taken many a dream, the miracle of the talking crucifix, and even the less spectacular experience of imprisonment and sickness, in order that this handsome, hot-blooded young man, whom the wild youth of Assisi had acclaimed as one of its leaders, should be transformed into a humble penitent, clothed in homespun and on his knees before the Sovereign Pontiff to receive the tonsure.

Born in 1182 in Umbria which seems to consist, as it were, of red ochre
and light, in that Italian Galilee where nobility strikes the eye from near and
far, and in the city of Assisi which stands so proudly on its hill, perched on
the tawny flanks of Monte Subasio, Francis had lived hitherto as do most
boys of his class. Although a Christian by baptism and faith, he cared less for
prayer than for singing and dancing, earning money, and fighting in those
petty but ferocious wars in which the towns of Italy at that period were constantly engaged. It was, in fact, one such quarrel that gave him his first taste
of enforced inactivity. While a prisoner of war at Perugia, Francis began
to consider his own heart. After a year in jail he returned home, but in so
precarious a state of health that he was obliged to take to his bed. There
followed long hours of silence, which are more favourable to the Lord's
approach than is the dissipation of an active life. It was then, at the age of
about twenty-one, that he heard the call of God.

Francis remained henceforth and for ever a captive in the Master's
hands. He made up his mind to join the crusade, hoping thereby to win
knighthood; but on two occasions Christ warned him against such a course.
Torn between past pleasure and present duty, he was wandering one day
in the Umbrian plain along a hillside planted thick with cypress. Suddenly, and with overwhelming certitude, he realized that our Lord was there
beside him, in him, bowed down with sorrow and humiliation, pierced with
five wounds. The die was cast.

When God speaks, says the prophet, who can turn away? Yes, it was the
Lord whom Francis recognized in that putrid leper, whom he met by the way-
side and kissed upon the mouth. It was the Lord whose ineffable presence he
felt during those hours of solitary prayer spent in the mountain caves. It was
the Lord whom, while on a pilgrimage to Rome, he longed to serve, hum-
bling himself to beg among the beggars. Above all, there was that wonderful
and mystic day when, praying before an old Byzantine crucifix in the dilap-
idated chapel of San Damiano, he had heard the Lord say to him in a gentle
but irresistible voice: "Francis, go and rebuild my house; it is tumbling down."

Too modest to believe that Christ would ask him to rebuild a Church
whose walls are not of stone but of immortal souls, he spent some time

restoring with his own hands a number of chapels, oratories and other sacred buildings that had fallen into disrepair. His destiny, however, lay elsewhere; and God, who uses all things to fulfil His purpose, employed other means to make him understand. The elder Bernardone, furious at the sight of his boy now aged twenty-five neglecting his plain duty to sell woollen goods and earn a living, intervened. The chaplain of San Damiano, a good old priest who had treated the young devotee as his own son, heard himself abused for a thousand imaginary offences, and particularly for having fostered the credulity of a half-wit! Summoned to return home, and even hailed by his own father before the magistrates, Francis remained adamant. At last he understood the Lord's command: he must abandon everything, even his own property, and follow Him. He now took that decision once for all, and the population of Assisi beheld with deep emotion an extraordinary scene in the piazza. Francis, the one-time dandy, appeared almost naked before Bishop Guido, who had been invited to pass judgment on the case. Flinging his garments and what little money he had left at Bernardone's feet, he cried out that from now on he would recognize no father but the Father who reigns in heaven. The bishop, covering the young man with his cloak, welcomed him on behalf of Holy Church.

There are certain steps in a man's life which, no matter what befalls, can never be retraced. Sacrifice of self and of one's earthly goods, in obedience to that command heard but rejected by the rich young man, is the only means of becoming a disciple of Him who desired to be, on earth, as the least of men, a traveller without possessions, having nowhere even to lay His head. From the age of twenty-five Francis never forgot that his vocation was to be poor with the poorest of the poor; he was indissolubly wed to holy poverty.

This was his constant theme during the remainder of his life. Poverty, the absolute refusal to possess worldly goods of any kind whatsoever, was the kernel of his teaching. Insistence on this precept, the most difficult of all Gospel precepts, was his unique contribution to the reform of a Church threatened by her wealth with utter ruin. Poverty meant more to him than it had done, for example, to St. Bernard, more than it would do later to his great contemporary St. Dominic. They looked upon it as the means of liberating Christian men from all external cares that they might better serve the Lord. For Francis, on the other hand, total renunciation, utter destitution, was the supreme goal, not only the means to but the very end of sanctity. "Seek ye first the kingdom of God and His justice, and all things else shall be added unto you."

But that was not sufficient. The life of solitude and contemplation chosen by the son of Bernardone was no doubt of great merit in God's sight. But it lacked, so to speak, the power of radiation; and the Church at that date had need of more than the hermit or recluse. One day in February 1209, Francis was hearing Mass alone in the chapel of San Damiano, which his own hands had rebuilt, when a verse from the Gospel swept him off his feet: "Go ye forth and preach, saying: 'The kingdom of heaven is nigh....'" Go! Preach! He must leave this blessed solitude where God had sought him out amid the peace of meadows and the song of birds. He must wander far and wide, crying the Good News. So, wearing the grey tunic of a peasant, his loins girded with a cord, Francis climbed the hill leading to Assisi, and there, in the piazza of his home-town, began to speak. His vocation to poverty was enlarged by a call to the apostolate, and the twin foundation stones of the Franciscan Order were thus laid.

Those were mysterious and splendid times. Morality was no higher than it is today; but there was something spontaneous, something instinctive, in the spiritual atmosphere. Francis began his mission with a French song in order to attract the crowd; then he began to tell of God and His justice, of the necessity for repentance and self-denial. Many a heart was stirred, and there were not wanting men to follow in his footsteps: Bernard of Quintavalle, Peter of Catana, Giles, Sylvester, Morico, Barbaro, Labbatino, Bernard of Viridante, John of San Costanzo, Angelo Tancredi, Philip the Tall, and even John of Capella, who was to prove himself the Judas of this new "apostolic college." Their number included rich bourgeois and peasants, a knight, a labourer, and two priests who enjoyed no special privilege. With twelve disciples at his side, Francis resolved to submit himself to the judgment of the Pope and seek his approval of their undertaking.

Innocent III's encouragement gave them vital energy. Once the Pope had authorized them to preach, the Grey Friars were able to approach parish priests and obtain leave to instruct their flocks. From the humble monastery at Rivo Torto under the hill of Assisi, where they had built their own huts, the friars went in pairs through the whole countryside, to Spoleto, Perugia, Gubbio, Montefalco, and even farther afield towards Arezzo and Siena. A new aura of fraternal charity spread around them wherever they appeared. At Assisi, the factions were reconciled by the young saint's voice, and put an end to their quarrels. Vocations were so numerous that Rivo Torto was quickly followed by the establishment of another house, St. Mary of the Angels, which was to become famous through the "Portiuncula" indulgence. Before long the whole of central Italy had grown used to seeing these Grey Friars on the highway, begging their daily bread with no fixed dwelling place, but singing well of Christ in joyous fervent voices.

Among the most remarkable of Francis's adherents was Clare, a girl of exquisite form and feature, whose very name seemed to spread light around her, and whose portrait on the walls of the basilica at Assisi still moves us with its mysterious and penetrating charm. Rich, beautiful, and of noble lineage, she too might have embraced the gentle life marked out for her. But hearing Francis, in the cathedral at Assisi, speak of God and His love in words that were not of this world, she resolved to abandon all things and follow him. On Palm Sunday, 1212, she left home, confided her vocation to Bishop Guido, and set off in the radiant brightness of an Umbrian spring to dwell alone in a forest of holm-oak not far from Rivo Torto. Such was the origin of the Poor Ladies, or Poor Clares as they are known today. The first community was established soon afterwards at San Damiano, an Order which the poet in Francis had called "my little plant," but which was to increase rapidly and put forth many shoots.

When the Lateran Council met in 1215, Francis revisited the Eternal City in obedience to the Pope's injunction of five years ago. Innocent was delighted; and when the Council, alarmed by the mushroom growth of new religious Orders, decreed that all such associations must adopt an existing Rule, he declared that the Penitents of Assisi had already been approved.

This official act of recognition marks the third important stage in the history of the Friars Minor. At first there was no need for elaborate organization; Francis admitted anyone who desired to serve God and proclaim Him before the world, and clerics ranked no higher than laymen. It was an Order of religious, unencumbered with rich abbeys, travelling the world in that freedom wherewith Christ had made them free. Vocations continued to pour in, not excluding many learned men who gladly humbled themselves with the humblest, and sacrificed the pride of intellect as all their brethren had sacrificed the pride of fortune. Soon the Friars Minor, as they were now called, became so numerous that Francis was able to send them still farther afield. The first mission to France, Germany, Spain, and the East was a failure; they were not discouraged, but tried again, and with such determination that the grain at last took root. By 1221 the Order had spread throughout Christendom.

Meanwhile, another shoot had begun to flourish on the parent stock. This was the "third Order," which enabled persons of both sexes, whose duties kept them in the world, to observe a Rule similar to that of the friars. Many laymen desired a life of self-sacrifice; but their craving had fallen into disrepute as suggesting kinship with the Waldenses and Cathars, while the Humiliati of Lombardy and the Poor Catholics provided no satisfactory framework. Now that craving found an outlet within the great Franciscan Order. Important consequences flowed from the institution of this "lay militia." The Franciscan ideal spread deep among the masses, increasing the effect of the new leaven and raising up sublime figures such as St. Elizabeth of Thuringia and St. Louis, who were both members of the Third Order of St. Francis.

Nevertheless, the extraordinary achievement of the Poverello was offset by many trials. Success is an obstacle not easily surmounted. What had been suited to the first community of friars, whose only governor was God, and even to the conventual groups at Rivo Torto and the Portiuncula, was hardly sufficient for the direction of an Order which had assumed gigantic proportions, which had branches in every land, and to which thousands of souls looked for spiritual guidance. Some system of regular administration was clearly indispensable; but herein lay a difficulty. How could the work be organized without losing its essential freedom?

The freelance preacher is all very well when he happens also to be a saint; but it was doubtful whether such work could be safely entrusted to all and sundry who were attracted by the new Order's splendid reputation. Francis had long since realized the necessity of being able to rely on some-one with administrative experience, and in 1218 the saintly Cardinal Hugo-lin (afterwards Gregory IX) had become Protector of the Order. Again, in 1220, he had agreed that all who wished to join the Friars Minor should undergo a year's novitiate. Notwithstanding his dislike of innovation, which was apparent in his refusal to appoint only clerics to positions of authority, or to accept several offers of exemption from episcopal and other jurisdic-tion, he was obliged to allow some modification. This process may be seen by comparing the Rule of 1221 with that of 1223. The latter version laid smaller emphasis on manual labour, forbade secession from the Order, and insisted more firmly on the duty of obedience. As a precaution against vaga-bondage, all friars were to have fixed residence when not actually engaged upon the mission. Each house was subject to a "guardian"; all houses with-in a given area were placed under the authority of a "custos"; several "cus-todiae" constituted a province governed by a "provincial minister"; while the provinces together formed the Order of Friars Minor under a "minister general." The arrangement proved satisfactory. Later, as more priests joined the Order, clerical duties became prominent, and from 1223 the Francis-cans were obliged "each day to celebrate the divine office according to the Roman rite."

These changes, however, troubled the saintly founder's soul, causing him profound unhappiness. Was this, he asked, the will of Christ; had not his ideal been betrayed? "Who are these men who have dared to separate my brethren from me?" he would murmur in his sorrow, torn between the poles of inspiration and efficiency. Weary, and in broken health, he had handed over the government of his Order to Peter of Catana as minister general; but Peter soon gave place to Brother Elias, whose genius for organization was not always in accord with the simple and unsullied promptings of grace.

Francis himself returned as it were to his origins. He lived more and more 185 in God, sometimes on an island in Lake Trasimene, sometimes in the cave at Subiaco where St. Benedict had once dwelt as a hermit, sometimes on the glowering summit of Monte Alverno, which a friend had given him for his meditation. He desired as never before to live in Christ and to resemble Him. Beside that, what mattered the vitality and success of his Order?

At long last God gave him the mystic answer. In September 1224 he climbed Alverno, amid the glory of sunlight and birdsong. On the morning of the seventeenth, after days of burning prayer that was a veritable anguish of love, suddenly, in that blinding ecstasy, he beheld a seraph flying with six wings and bearing in its supernatural form the image of the Crucified. How long did the vision last? What was the visionary's experience? We do not know. But on returning to his senses, he found himself bathed in agony—pain terrible yet exquisite; for imprinted in his hands and feet and side were the wounds of our Lord's sacred Passion, bleeding. The witness of Jesus Christ now bore in his own flesh the stigmata of his God.

Upon this ineffable privilege the soul of Francis fed throughout his closing years. Onward from that tremendous hour he seemed to live only that he might sing of God and praise Him in a thousand ways. As if inspired, there flowed from his lips poems that spoke of God's glory manifested in creation, poems like the *Canticle of the Sun*, which is one of the most beautiful hymns uttered by the mouth of man. Sick, exhausted, almost blind, and tormented by barbarous physicians who pretended to cure ophthalmia by the application of red-hot irons to his temples, Francis still maintained his joyful serenity and sublime peace of soul, praising God for his tribulations. Having dictated his last will and testament, in which he recalled the substance of his message to the Church, his tenderness increased until he seemed transmuted into love.

As the final agony drew near, he asked to be carried to St. Mary of the Angels, which reminded him of his youth. In sight of the convent he made his bearers halt, and for the last time blessed Assisi. Then he asked Brother Angelo and Brother Leo to sing for him once more his *Canticle*, to which he had added a verse in praise of "our sister death." On Saturday, October

3, 1226, being now almost speechless, he managed to intone the Psalmist's words: "I have cried to the Lord with all my voice." He died immediately afterwards; and it is said that a great flight of larks rose into the sky, bearing his soul company.

So fruitful was his labour that Pope Benedict XV described him as "the most perfect image of our Lord that ever lived." He had supplied the Church with a new fighting force, adapted to contemporary needs. To the powers of disintegration he had opposed the irresistible might of the Gospel in its original simplicity. He had offered Christendom a form of piety more human than that even of St. Bernard, more closely linked with the marvels of creation, a piety full of enthusiasm and gratitude. Francis was canonized two years after his death, in 1228. Innumerable books and works of art have been devoted to his memory; but it is perhaps to an apostate from the faith that we must go for an all-embracing tribute. No man, says Renan, has been more acutely conscious than was Francis of Assisi that he was the son of his Eternal Father.

9. ST. DOMINIC: GOD'S ATHLETE AND BUILDER

WHILE the Poverello fought his heroic fight against the love of money, another man faced up to the second danger that beset the Church, the peril of complacency, of intellectual routine, of ignorance which opens wide the door to doctrinal error. His work resulted in an Order capable of disputing on equal terms with the adversaries of truth. But this Order was not based upon any preconceived plan or abstract ideal; it arose, as do most of the Church's institutions, from necessity and the dispositions of Providence.

One day in the summer of 1205, Innocent III was visited by Dom Diego de Azevedo, Bishop of Osma, a humble and little-known diocese of Spain. Two years previously he had been sent to Denmark by Alfonso VIII of Castile to bring back a bride for the Infante; but the young princess had died, and Diego was unwilling to return home without having prayed at the Apostle's tomb. He was a holy man, an excellent priest, who hoped to do

still more for God. The little diocese had been "reformed" by his predecessor, Martin de Bazan, and the canons of his chapter followed the usages of
Prémontré. Now Dom Diego was not satisfied with merely doing his best
in the peaceful occupation of a bishop. He dreamed of those millions of
souls wandering in darkness, souls whom his Lord desired should see the
light. He had heard tell of the Cumans, a barbarian tribe encamped on the
borders of Hungary, who were said to be particularly ferocious; and he now
sought the Pope's leave to resign his episcopal charge in order to visit and
baptize these savages. One of the principal members of his suite was Dominic of Calahorra, the young sub-prior of his chapter, whom Dom Diego
loved as his own son.

The Pope's conversation with his visitors has not been recorded; but we
may guess its tenor from subsequent events: "Why travel that distance to
evangelize the pagan when so many precious souls are being lost to Christ
right on your own doorstep, just across the Pyrenees? The formidable mission you desire to undertake awaits you in Christian Languedoc, which is
prey to heresy!" Innocent III was already concerned at the progress of Albigensianism; he had determined to recruit an army of preachers who would
fight the Cathars on their own ground, and had recently approached the
Order of Citeaux. Diego saw the point of this argument. He returned to
Spain, but made a detour through Burgundy in order to visit the great Cistercian abbey and don the white cowl of St. Bernard's sons. Later, he was to
rank, with his disciple Dominic, among the forty or so papal missionaries
who worked in Languedoc.

The situation throughout southern France was one of immense difficulty for the Church; and the struggle upon which he now entered at the
Pope's request proved for Dominic, youthful and enthusiastic as he was, a
wonderful experience, a time of trial and formation. The Catharist leaders, who called themselves "the Perfect," were challenging the Catholics to
public disputations, for which the latter were not always well qualified. The
simple and coherent fashion in which the heretics presented their dogmas
made a deep impression on the masses, as did the austere simplicity of their
lives and their undoubted charity. The papal emissaries, Regnier and Guy of

188 Citeaux, Peter of Castelnau (Archdeacon of Maguelone), and even Abbot Arnaud-Amalric of Citeaux, had despaired of success.

Our two Spaniards quickly sized up the difficulties involved; for they appreciated the dialectical skill of their opponents, who were more than a match for the arguments brought against them. But Diego and Dominic reached a still more important conclusion, though it is uncertain which of them first put it into words. At any rate, while attending a chapter of Cistercian abbots and other dignitaries of that Order at Castelnau near Montpellier, in the summer of 1206, they gave free vent to their view. The papal legates, they said, travelled in comfort with a retinue of horses, carriages, baggage, servants, and all the paraphernalia deemed necessary for persons of their rank. "The Perfect," on the other hand, lived poorly and journeyed on foot, as befitted those who moved in humble society. Which of these two groups, the Spaniards asked, would strike the people as more representative of the Gospel teaching? There was no need to look elsewhere for the cause of failure. Such too was the conclusion reached by Innocent III a few weeks later in his famous Bull of November 19. Diego and Dominic were indeed "tried men determined to imitate the poverty of Christ." They practised what they preached, sent their attendants back to Osma, and gave out that in future they would travel the roads unaccompanied and on foot, after the manner of our Lord's apostles. Dominic had learned a twofold lesson from this initial experience: he was clear as to his life's purpose—the establishment of a firmly grounded intellectual system to support the truth of Christ—and saw that he must bear witness to that truth by the example of renunciation and holy poverty.

He was now a man of about thirty-five years, calm and yet passionate, like all the best of his countrymen. Most of those who have left their mark upon the pages of Spanish history have sprung from Old Castile, a sublime but ruthless territory, the highest point in all that lofty plateau. Castile is a province of intense vitality and tragic violence. The deep blue dome of sky seems to press down with all its weight upon the desert floor; dark shadow contrasts with dazzling light; and night, twinkling with millions of stars, alternates with blinding noon. It is a province that hardens the body and

forges character. Cid Campeador, Guzman the Brave, and the Conquista-   189
dores, as well as St. Teresa and St. John of the Cross, were all Castilians.

Dominic, third son of Felix and Juana Guzman, was born in the Douro
valley about 1171. His birthplace, Calahorra, could offer little in the way
of education; so Dominic was sent first to reside with his uncle, the archpriest of Gumiel, and later to the University of Palencia, in Leon, where he
remained for about ten years. His parents could not fail to notice his keen
intelligence, which clearly deserved an opportunity for higher studies. It
was also related that, during her pregnancy, Doña Juana had dreamed a prophetic dream like that of St. Bernard's mother. She saw issue from her womb
a young hound carrying in its jaws a blazing torch which set fire to the whole
countryside. The prophecy appears to have been fulfilled in Dominic from
youth upwards; for he joined the canons regular at Osma, and soon dominated the cathedral chapter. When less than thirty years of age he was elected sub-prior, and took his seat as a member of the bishop's council.

All Dominic's biographers agree with his spiritual daughter, Blessed
Cecilia Cesarini, that he was a fine-looking man, well built, of no more than
medium height, but perfectly proportioned. His manly countenance was
rendered even more striking by the lustre of his eyes; his hands were long
and thin. His dignified bearing was enhanced by a certain radiant tranquillity that emanated from his person, inspiring both affection and respect
in all who met him. Never refusing a challenge, anxious to come to grips
with his opponent, he was a spiritual athlete, the athlete of Christ crucified.
Admired for his extreme simplicity, for his compassion towards the unfortunate, for his delicate and generous sensibility, and for his abiding charity,
his character was no less persuasive than his dialectic.

His genius, quite different from that of St. Francis of Assisi, lay not in
lightning intuition backed by gentle obstinacy, but in the lucid study of facts
and their assessment. Once the end was clearly defined he devoted himself
with unhurried energy to its attainment. Dominic has been called a "builder"[19]; his flair for organization and creative method, combined with fearless

---

19. By Mgr. Gillet, formerly Master-General of the Dominicans.

energy, were the marks of a singularly productive intellect. Moreover, he possessed the art of expressing his ideas, his plans, and the stages of an argument with remarkable eloquence. His biographers agree likewise in telling us that when he spoke, in a voice that was by turns affectionate and menacing, none could resist the beauty of his language, the force of his logic, or his infectious enthusiasm.

It was not without reason that Dominic came to be regarded as the very mouthpiece of God. A man of action, a thinker, and an able administrator, he was an even greater mystic, a soul devoted to Christ, upon whom he desired above all things to model himself; and his thought was steeped in the Bible, particularly in the Gospels, which he always carried with him. He possessed the faith of those to whom it has been promised that they shall move mountains; and it is therefore not surprising to learn that he worked numerous miracles and even raised four persons from the dead. St. Dominic was at once a man of affairs, a mystic, and an intellectual, according to a pattern of which the Middle Ages produced so many examples from St. Bernard to St. Louis. Together, those three characteristics make the perfect man.

After Dom Diego's return to Osma, where he died in December 1207, Dominic, helped no doubt by a few companions, assumed sole responsibility for the apostolate. These strange missionaries visited the towns and villages of Languedoc, where their self-denial, modesty, and charity rivalled the corresponding virtues of "the Perfect." We find them at Caraman near Toulouse, at Carcassonne, at Verfeil, and at Fanjeaux not far from Pamiers. Public disputation with the heretics became more frequent, turning more often to the profit of the Christian faith; and God Himself bore witness to His faithful servants. One day, by way of experiment, a treatise written by the saint was thrown into the fire together with a heretical book. Dominic's was rejected unharmed by the flames; the other was burned to ashes, and conversions began to multiply.

Shortly before Diego returned to Spain, but no doubt on his own initiative, Dominic made his first religious foundation. At Prouille, a small town situated at the foot of the Pyrenees between Montréal and Fanjeaux, there was a shrine of our Lady, a place of pilgrimage, where Dominic had often prayed. Here he conceived the idea of establishing a convent for women and girls who had abjured their heresy but who wished to continue living the same chaste and austere life that they had known among "the Perfect." It was an excellent plan; for these religious exercised a powerful influence upon women of the upper classes, and were later entrusted with the education of children. The convent also provided the itinerant missionaries with a centre from which they could reach the heretics in country places and still remain in contact with Toulouse.

On January 15, 1208, soon after the foundation of Prouille, the papal legate Peter of Castelnau was assassinated. The result was the Albigensian crusade.[20] Horror swept down upon Languedoc with the armies of the North; but in this terrible war—which he might justify in principle, but of whose inhuman cruelty he could never have approved—Dominic took no part. He may, in the course of his duty, have taken a hand in the "conviction" of certain heretics, that is to say in discriminating between them and the faithful. But this was part of his vocation; there is no proof that he ever sat on a criminal trial, and it is quite certain that he never participated in an act of war.[21]

Leaving Prouille, where he fulfilled the office of "nuns' prior," Dominic resumed his work as an itinerant preacher. He was virtually alone, for most of the Cistercians had departed. People were amazed at his energy, and impressed by his resolve to keep open the gate of the fold for those sheep who had gone astray. The newly appointed Bishop of Toulouse, a Cistercian named Foulques, appealed to Dominic and his companions. A wealthy citizen of that place gave them a house near the church of St. Romanus, and another milestone had been reached. Dominic now governed a community of diocesan missionaries subject to episcopal jurisdiction. This arrangement agreed well with papal policy; it was also the seed of a new Order which the

---

20. See Volume 2, Chapter XIII.
21. During the battle of Muret, at which the crusaders routed the King of Aragon, Dominic remained in church upon his knees.

saint already had in mind. His community numbered only seven, but they knew God had called them to a formidable task. Bishop Foulques called them "Friars Preachers," a name which was afterwards ratified together with their Order by Pope Honorius III.

By the time the ecumenical council met at Rome on November 1, 1215, Foulques and Dominic had decided that they ought to enlarge the sphere of their activity. Innocent III had prayed for just such an apostolate, as they were about to propose, but there was a difficulty. The council had decreed that all who wished to serve God in the religious life must adopt one or other of the already sanctioned Rules; Dominic and his friends received a good deal of encouragement, but nothing more substantial. It was necessary, then, to choose an existing Rule. That of St. Augustine was familiar to the canon of Osma, and its flexibility allowed of its adaptation to altered circumstances. The Friars Preachers accordingly embraced a constitution very similar to that of Prémontré. They were to be canons regular in virtue of their Rule, monks in spirit, and missionaries in their mode of life. Such were the fundamentals of the Order which now awaited canonical recognition.

On July 12, 1216, Innocent III died at Perugia, where the conclave met without delay and chose Cardinal Savelli to succeed him. This astonishing old man took the name of Honorius III, and died in 1227 at the age of more than one hundred years. At the time of his election Honorius was active both in mind and body. He recognized the Cathars as a most dangerous sect, and had learned of the part played in Languedoc by the little community of St. Romanus. On December 22 he sent them his warm approval, and wrote to Dominic that his brethren would become "champions of the faith and true lights of the world." The Pope formally "confirmed the Order, taking it under his protection"; and this act, repeated in January 1217, marks the institution of the Friars Preachers, who thereby reached the third and most important stage of their development.

They were as yet a mere handful, sixteen to be exact: half a dozen Spaniards together with recruits from Normandy, England, France, Provence, Navarre, and Languedoc. The international outlook of the Dominicans was thus clear from the very start. Their habit—the white woollen robe of

canons regular and the large black travelling-cloak of Spanish priests—was
suggested by the circumstances of their origin and institution.

The principal characteristics of the new Order were now firmly established: it was to consist of preachers and scholars, of men devoted to poverty and the spoken word. First and foremost they were preachers, spokesmen
of Jesus Christ, and soldiers of the Holy Spirit. They would go forth and
teach not only in those churches to whose clergy the diocesan authorities
recommended them, but wheresoever occasion offered, in the universities
and schools, and even in the public squares. The Order had scarcely been
ratified before Dominic dispersed his brethren to the four corners of Christendom. He had his eye principally on the great intellectual centres, where
the conflict of ideas, if more prolonged, would be more fruitful.

Now victory in this struggle required the necessary weapons. St. Dominic, recognizing the value of his own theological training at the University
of Palencia, had determined that the brethren must improve their education
preparatory to embarking on their mission. Before leaving for Rome in September 1216 he had asked the master of theology at Toulouse to undertake
the instruction of his subjects; but as soon as the Pope's approbation had
been obtained, the Order turned to the great universities for the training of
its members, many of whom attained professorial rank.

The Friars Preachers owed their third outstanding characteristic to
St. Dominic in person. During his struggle with the Cathars, he had realized the need of poverty and self-sacrifice; but there was danger that, as
the Order grew, its work might be hindered by endowments, or by the gift
of churches which it would then have to administer. In other words, their
functions as canons regular might interrupt their freedom of movement.
At Toulouse, as early as 1216, Dominic had sought to impose the principle of absolute poverty; but he had been prevented by the opposition of
Foulques, who foresaw "his" missionaries scattered beyond the confines of
his diocese. In Rome, however, Dominic met St. Francis of Assisi, probably
at the house of Cardinal Hugolin. Though different in so many respects,
the two men understood one another's point of view completely; and it is
said that at the second Franciscan chapter in 1217 a solitary white-robed

figure was present among the grey Franciscan ranks. A painting by Andrea della Robbia, in the Loggia of San Paolo at Florence, shows St. Dominic at the moment of parting from Il Poverello, asking the latter for his hempen girdle to commemorate their friendship. Confirmed by the example of St. Francis in his ideal of poverty, St. Dominic raised the question once again with his Order, and in a general chapter held at Bologna at Pentecost, 1220, it was resolved that the Friars Preachers should own no churches, convents, or landed property; they too would live as mendicants, and thus be free to wander in God's service.

Such, then, were the essential marks of the new Order in 1220. The Dominican Rule had not as yet been codified, and would not be until 1228; but the founder saw clearly what was indispensable if the tiny seed were to become a tree. That he did so is enough to prove his genius. Organization preceded expansion; and his successors had only to follow his design in order to avoid those tragic disputes which troubled the Franciscans. His broad views, his realism, his understanding of contemporary needs, and his determination to make straight for his goal, reveal St. Dominic as one of the ablest of all religious founders.

The Order, as conceived by him, was really a synthesis inspired by, but more highly developed than, the hierarchy of Citeaux. It was a synthesis of personal authority and dependence upon subordinates; for it had points in common both with monarchy and with the commune, two political institutions which were evolving at that time. The government of each house was vested in a prior elected by the whole community for a given period. When his term of office had expired, he became once more a simple religious; meanwhile, the conventual chapter acted as a brake upon abuse of power. One stage higher, the provincial chapter confirmed the election of priors and itself elected the prior provincial, whose chief task was to make the visitation of all his subject houses. This provincial chapter consisted of conventual priors, each of whom was assisted by an elected "definitor" and a number of "preachers general," friars who had been licensed to preach in all dioceses. The part played by these "definitors," reliable men chosen by their communities, was of great importance, for they were counsellors of

the priors provincial, between whom and their own brethren they served
as intermediaries. Finally, there was the master-general, elected by a general chapter composed of priors provincial and definitors. In order to assure
constant vigilance from above, and to provide as it were a safety-valve for
discontent, the general chapter consisted of two groups: the priors provincial assembled once every three years, the other two were reserved for meetings of the definitors, who investigated such complaints as had been laid
before them. The Dominican constitutions were so flexible that they were
easily adapted to new requirements, yet so secure that they have never been
revised; and there is no stronger testimony to the founder's inspiration and
foresight than the fact that his institution has remained practically unal-
tered since the thirteenth century.

St. Dominic was also responsible for what is known as "individual dispensation," a system which was to prove of great value to the Order. The
Dominicans sprang, as we have seen, from the canons regular, and were
therefore bound by the traditional duties of choral office and other monastic
observances; but it was not easy to reconcile such duties with the demands
of an active life. Suppose, for example, that a friar was so far distant from
his convent that he could not be present at sung prime or terce; what was
he to do? The nature and duties of his vocation necessitated some kind of
compromise, and this took the form of "individual dispensation," whereby
the superior had power to exempt a religious from the obligations of the
Rule, and thus make it easier for him to carry out his mission as a preacher.

Side by side with the Order of Friars Preachers, there grew up a number of kindred organizations. The female community at Notre-Dame de
Prouille developed into a contemplative Order, whose reputation was still
further enhanced when the nuns of Santa Maria in Trastevere at Rome
placed themselves under Dominican jurisdiction. This contemplative Order
was later supplemented by "*regular* third Orders" devoted to teaching and
care of the sick. The influence of Dominican ideals was strengthened by the
creation of another kind of third Order, whose original purpose was rather
different from that of the corresponding Franciscan institution. At first it
was described as an "Army of Jesus Christ" charged with the defence of Holy

Church, then as a "Fraternity of Penance." But its aim was before long indistinguishable from that proposed by St. Francis to his lay disciples: it sought to apply the Order's religious principles in secular life, and the Dominican scapular was worn alike by warriors and kings.

Papal approbation was the signal for a decisive thrust. Vocations became more numerous, and included a high percentage of scholars and intellectuals. Four years later there were several hundred Black Friars on the road; but even more striking than this numerical increase is the accuracy with which the first Dominicans summed up the current situation and appraised its need. Here again, we cannot help but see the founder's penetration. His Order established itself at those very points where lay the destiny of Christendom: Rome and Paris and Bologna. At Rome, under the Sovereign Pontiff's eye, there was the priory of St. Sixtus, followed soon afterwards by that of Santa Sabina on the Aventine. At Paris, the theological capital of Europe, and at the great legal centre of Bologna, Black Friars attended lectures by the most eminent teachers and soon reached professorial status. That Dominican learning was so soon qualified to rescue the beleaguered fortress of the intellect, that it was able to incorporate with Christian doctrine those yearnings which could otherwise have led only to rebellion and heresy, was due in no small measure to the fact that Dominic himself had placed his sons at these strategic points. Without him the Church would never have produced St. Thomas Aquinas.

Success had crowned his labour, and he was ready to resume the life marked out by his vocation. Simple as ever, with the same humility as of old, he set out once again upon his mission. The Plain of Lombardy, the Tyrol, the valleys of Switzerland, and the highways of France saw him come and go. Then, as though urged by a presentiment of death, he determined to revisit the land of his childhood, Spain, which he had quitted fifteen years ago. Reaching Segovia at the foot of the Sierra Guadarrama, not far from Osma and the castle of the Guzmans, he took up his abode in a cave. The good folk of the neighbourhood flocked to him in hundreds, and he made his first Spanish foundation, Santa Cruz. Leaving the new convent under the direction of Corbolan (who was afterwards beatified), he pushed on to

Madrid, always preaching, travelling almost without rest, in spite of failing health.

On his return to Bologna, Dominic was exhausted. He might indeed have contemplated his work with pride, had his humility allowed him to glory in aught else but Christ; for there were now eight Dominican provinces—Spain, Provence, Lombardy, Rome, Germany, England,[22] and Hungary.[23] But the servant of God had been warned by an angel that he must soon depart out of this life. He foretold that his death would occur before the feast of our Lady's Assumption, and set out on a final journey, this time to visit Hugolin at Venice. Having commended the affairs of his Order to the cardinal's benevolence, he returned to the priory of St. Nicholas at Bologna towards the end of July 1221. By this time he had fallen victim to incurable headache and the ravages of dysentery.

Dominic's end had all that calm and simple dignity which had accompanied him through life. He delivered a parting discourse to the young novices, and called twelve senior brethren to his bedside. Having given them his final directions with a view to the Order's prosperity, he made public confession before them all. His biographer, Blessed Jordan of Saxony, who describes the scene, gives us a striking picture of Dominic's grave visage as he spoke these words: "Divine goodness has preserved me from all stain until this hour; but I must admit that I have not escaped the weakness of discovering more pleasure in the conversation of young women than in that of aged crones." On Friday, August 6, shortly before noon, he bade the community range themselves on each side of his couch as if they were in choir. As the supreme moment drew near, he had the strength to bid them start the prayers for those *in extremis*; and at the words, "Come to his assistance, O ye saints of God," he rendered up his soul. At that same hour, according to tradition, the saintly Prior Guala of Brescia was wrapped in ecstasy. Like Jacob, he saw heaven open, while angels ascended a ladder to the throne of Christ carrying

---

22. Brother Gilbert of Fraxineto had recently arrived in England, and a Dominican priory had been established at Oxford.
23. The Hungarian foundation had been made by Brother Paul.

198   a man clothed in the Dominican habit, but whom he could not identify because the hood was drawn down over his face as is done for a dead friar.[24]

10. THE NEW LEAVEN

THE appearance of the mendicant Orders was the most significant event of the Church's interior life during the thirteenth century. Not from the seclusion of their cloister, nor even through the lecture-room, would this new class of monks influence the mass of Christians. Their approach was more direct; their method a form of preaching better suited to the aspirations of mankind at large. The extraordinary success of the mendicants goes to prove that they satisfied an urgent need. The stream of vocations soon became a torrent: in the second half of the thirteenth century, for example, the Franciscans had twenty-five thousand religious and one thousand one hundred houses; by 1316 there were thirty thousand friars in one thousand four hundred convents. The growth of the Dominican Order was not quite so rapid. Its emphasis upon intellectual attainments and its relative indifference to popular forms of devotion tended to limit the number of vocations. Nevertheless, it counted seven thousand members in 1256, ten thousand friars with six hundred priories in 1303, and twelve thousand friars in 1337.

These facts, however, are not meant to suggest that the two Orders suffered no growing pains. First, there were internal problems arising from an inevitable clash between pure ideal and practical exigencies. It seems that absolute renunciation of all worldly goods is incompatible with the efficient working of a great institution; and there is constant danger that intellectual labour, necessary though it be, may finish as an end in itself, rather than as a means to the knowledge and love of God. Personal ambition and mutual jealousy took advantage of this tension; nor indeed could it be hoped that among so many thousands all would prove exempt from human weakness simply because of their profession.

---

24. St. Dominic was canonized in 1234.

So far as the Dominicans were concerned, such crises had no grave
repercussions. To begin with, their organization was such as to prevent disagreement on many points. Again, St. Dominic had shown both firmness
and sagacity in his attitude towards two basic principles of religious life.
When St. Thomas Aquinas remarks that poverty is a means to but not the
essence of perfection, he shows himself a true disciple of the founder who,
while directing his sons to the universities, made it clear that the sole end of
study is knowledge of God and the victory of the Cross. Finally, as an Order
of clerics, the Dominicans were not confronted with the delicate problem
of relations between priests and laymen in the same community. It must
not be imagined, however, that they enjoyed continual fair weather. Faults
against poverty and obedience were not infrequent, and the deposition of a
master-general by the Holy See in 1291 caused a good deal of trouble.

But these squalls were as nothing to the storms through which the Grey
Friars passed. Here conflict was inevitable from the outset. The sublime
folly of the Poverello, already manifest in his early years, was repeated in
his Testament: "I expressly forbid any brother to accept money in any way
whatsoever, whether in person or through a third party.... He who is not
learned must not try to learn." An arrangement of that kind was scarcely
suited to a worldwide organization.

The first Franciscan crisis, however, was not provoked by differences of
principle; it was the result of a defective constitution. Brother Elias of Cor-
tona, appointed minister-general in 1232, behaved so autocratically that he
was deposed in 1239 by the general chapter, which took this opportunity
to reshape the Order and place it on a more democratic basis. The general
chapter would henceforth meet every three years, and provincials were to
be elected by provincial chapters. The same period witnessed a further modification, which brought the Order of St. Francis into closer line with the
Dominicans by reducing the status of its lay members. It was not long before
these were disqualified from acting as superiors,[25] and in course of time lay
membership was virtually prohibited.

---

25. Elias was the last minister-general who was not a priest.

There was also an acute divergence of opinion on the subject of poverty. Those who advocated the primitive austerity of the Rule met with violent opposition, both in theory and practice, on the part of those who stood for evolution. A marble offertory-box which had been placed on the site of the new basilica at Assisi was smashed to pieces by one of the Poverello's dearest friends, Brother Leo, who thereby earned himself a public whipping. In Germany, Brother Caesar's devotion to the saint's ideal cost him his life. But the force of circumstance was irresistible, and there were further mitigations. In 1230 the Bull *Quo elongati* lent authority to a juridical fiction according to which "no one is considered to *own* what he merely *possesses*, so long as he does not in conscience *consider* himself as owner, so long as he does not *refuse to give it up* or *lay claim to it*." The Friars Minor remained "poor" in principle, while a number of "spiritual friends" or "nuntii" were *considered as* owners and administrators of their property, and accepted money on their behalf. In 1245 Innocent IV tried to resolve the problem by declaring all property held by the mendicants to be vested in the Holy See. St. Bonaventure, who was minister-general from 1257 until 1273, came nearest to finding a solution. He endeavoured to save the vestiges of poverty by interpreting it as the "indispensable measure of control over indispensable goods."

From the second half of the thirteenth century Dominicans and Franciscans were both clerical Orders. They had now abandoned their hermitages and taken up residence in the towns, where they combined parochial work with the task of itinerant preachers—a form of activity which contributed much to their practical efficiency and immediate success. It is not improbable, on the other hand, that they would have achieved still more by adhering to the letter of their Rule, leaving the secular clergy to exercise its customary duties and learn from them the lesson of asceticism. Such a course would certainly have avoided other difficulties which the mendicant Orders were destined to encounter.

For it cannot be denied that they were not always well received. Not every parish priest was prepared to welcome these religious among the flock which had been committed to his care, and upon which he depended for his livelihood. An anonymous treatise, probably the work of a Picard priest, gives vent to this complaint: "Here are men who seek to forestall the clergy in their ecclesiastical functions. They claim to administer the sacraments of baptism, penance, and extreme unction of the sick, and also to bury the dead in their own churchyards. Worse still, in order to bring us into disrepute and keep the faithful from our pious reunions, they have created two new confraternities, which are joined by men and women in such numbers that nowadays one can scarcely find a single Christian whose name does not appear in one or other register." Nor were the friars regarded with much greater favour by the monks. The bishops frankly mistrusted men whom they suspected as agents, if not as spies, of the Holy See, and whose centralized organization was exempt from episcopal control. The Archbishop of Sens, for example, long refused them admission to his diocese.

In spite of these difficulties, the numbers and power of the mendicants grew steadily throughout two centuries. The Picard's lament, indeed, describes both the extent and the cause of their success. Many a "Rue Cordelier," "Marché des Capucins," and "Place des Jacobins" bears witness to their influence. Encouraged by the Holy See, popular with the middle and lower classes (who found them more approachable than the monks in their fine abbeys), they were able to establish one house after another. Within a quarter of a century, twenty-five Franciscan and twelve Dominican convents were founded in Belgium and northern France. The Dominican priory of St. Jacques at Paris, the Sacro Convento or "Great Convent" of the Franciscans at Assisi, Santa Sabina of the Black Friars, and Ara Coeli of the Minors at Rome together sheltered hundreds of religious; while Padua, Bologna, Lyons, Oxford, and Genoa were scarcely less important. Before long, the Church began looking to the new Orders for her senior officials. No less than four hundred fifty bishops, twelve cardinals, and two popes were to issue from the ranks of St. Dominic; and if the Franciscans produced only two hundred bishops and eight cardinals, this smaller proportion may be attributed to the tradition of humility bequeathed to his Order by St. Francis, and also no doubt to its having contained fewer men of learning.

Further evidence of the friars' impact upon ecclesiastical life may be seen in the fact that their organization and methods of training were copied by more ancient congregations. The canons regular, especially those of Prémontré, were influenced in matters of theology and pastoral work by the Dominicans, who were their offspring. The example of both Black Friars and Franciscans attracted Cluniacs, Benedictines, Cistercians, Premonstratensians, and Trinitarians to the universities; while the secular clergy were shamed into a more diligent exercise of their sacerdotal functions. Monastic life in general was stimulated by this form of apostolate; and despite the famous thirteenth canon of the Lateran Council, which forbade the introduction of new Rules, the first half of the thirteenth century reaped a veritable harvest of religious Orders.

In Palestine, a number of crusaders had determined to live as hermits in the celebrated caverns of Mount Carmel. About the year 1156, under the direction of St. Berthold of Malifay, they had founded a small association which prided itself upon having thereby revived a tradition of immense antiquity, dating from the prophets Elijah and Elisha. In 1209 the patriarch Albert of Jerusalem gave these "Hermits of Carmel" or Carmelites, a permanent Rule which was approved by Pope Gregory IX in 1228. It was an austere code, enjoining solitude and penance of the utmost rigour. Within twelve months, however, the Turks had rendered life on Carmel quite impossible; the Order therefore removed to Europe (1229), built a number of convents, and devoted itself to missionary work. In 1248 Innocent IV recognized it as the third mendicant congregation, named after "Our Lady of Mount Carmel."

A fourth mendicant Order, which came into being at about this time, was known as the "Hermits of St. Augustine." The Rule of St. Augustine had been adopted not only by the canons regular, but also by small eremitical communities such as the Guillelmites, founded before 1157 by St. William of Maleval; the Jeanbonites, instituted about 1229 by Blessed John Bon of Mantua; and the Brittinians who dwelt near Fans with the hermitage of St. Blaise of Brittino as their centre. In 1256 Pope Alexander IV united these three groups under the title of "Augustinians." Though described as hermits, they resided in towns and became almost as numerous as the Dominicans. It has been said that in the year 1300 the Order had some thirty thousand members. This is probably an exaggeration; but many a street-name, such as the "Quai des Grands-Augustins" or "Rue des Petits Pères," still preserves their memory. They too found their way into the universities, which they supplied with several distinguished teachers, among whom was Blessed Augustine Trionfo. So great indeed was their influence that in 1319 they held the offices of Sacristan, Librarian, and Confessor to the Pope.

These Orders of men had their female counterparts, with whom they formed the rallying point of the third Orders; but there were many more such congregations. One of the most interesting, as showing the effect of the new leaven among simple layfolk, was that of the "Servants of the Blessed Virgin," or Servites, instituted on August 15, 1223, by Blessed Bonfiglio Monaldi, a Florentine merchant to whom our Lady appeared while he was singing lauds. Six of his friends believed the vision, and these "Seven Founders" withdrew to Monte Senario. They too were recognized as a mendicant Order in 1255, and soon afterwards took up residence in the towns; they too held more than one chair in the universities; they too gave rise to an Order of nuns and a third Order; and it was they who spread devotion to our Lady of Seven Dolours. But if the Franciscans and Dominicans had competitors in the work of reform, which was in a special sense their own, we must not forget that its success was mainly due to them, not only because they were pioneers in the field, but also because of their numerical superiority.

No one can fail to recognize the influence, direct or indirect, of this new leaven upon the clergy. Its effect upon the Christian masses, however, was still more remarkable. The Benedictine chronicler Matthew Paris and the miniaturists of that period give us a picture of the mendicants, travelling barefoot, with no baggage other than a kind of cylindrical pouch slung from the shoulder and containing a manual of piety, a book of sermons, a *summa auctoritatis* (i.e., selected passages from the Fathers), and a volume of those *exempla* or anecdotes which were so prominent in their teaching. They halted everywhere—at churches, convents, castles, and tournaments, as well as in the public squares and harvest fields. Simple, austere, and poor, living on such alms as they received, they made a deep impression on the common people. They spoke the truth as they saw it, without fear or favour; and some

of them, e.g., the Portuguese Saint Anthony of Padua and Berthold of Ratisbon, acquired extraordinary fame. Their rough and ready speech together
with their penitential lives made a powerful appeal to those who heard them.

It is difficult to say just how far their ideal of poverty influenced society.
Gustave Schnürer affirms that it "checked the undue growth of a materialistic
civilization" and that "the Church in the thirteenth century received from
them a timely warning not to concern herself with temporal questions to
the point of forgetting her divine mission." The work of the mendicants was
no less fruitful in the field of charity. The "Great Devotion" of 1233, when
Dominicans and Franciscans made a concerted effort on an international
scale, brought about spectacular results in the way of reconciliation between
families, clans, and cities. At Paquara especially, the Dominican John of
Vicenza spoke so beautifully on the subject of fraternal love that hundreds
made their peace then and there. The mission of 1233 survived in those "associations of peace" which are often confused with the two third Orders whereby the Dominicans and Grey Friars maintained their hold upon society.

The activity of the mendicants took numerous forms. One of the most
curious was the promotion of certain friars to what can only be described
as theocratic dictatorships. Thus John of Vicenza, following his phenomenal success in 1233, was appointed Podestà, then Rector, and finally Duke
of Verona and Vicenza with plenary powers; an innovation which, repeated elsewhere, foreshadowed the rule of Savonarola at Florence. These were
exceptional cases, but innumerable friars undertook court duties which gave
them a hand in politics. Many, for example, acted as confessors to princes and
their families; and when St. Louis, resolving to base his administration on
the principles of charity and justice, revived the Carolingian "Missi Dominici" in the form of "Grand Inquisitors," it was the mendicant friars whom
he invited to undertake these delicate functions. While providing spiritual
directors and advisers to temporal sovereigns, they showed themselves no
less friendly towards the free towns; and their convents—built not upon
the Cluniac hill-tops or the solitary marshes of Citeaux, but in the heart of
cities—became centres of intellectual, spiritual, and even political life. Their
"democratic" regime, which enabled every religious to exercise a measure

of responsibility in his conventual chapter, was not unlike the communal
system; for the mendicants not only rejected the paternal jurisdiction of the
abbots at a time when the cities were repudiating feudal autocracy, but they
represented a new concept of the common good.

St. Dominic had realized his vocation in the struggle against heresy;
and it was to the friars that the Church continually appealed to defend the
purity of her doctrine. Thus, the mendicants found themselves engaged in
the unpleasant duties of the Inquisition[26]; especially the Dominicans, upon
whom fell most of the odium roused by that tribunal. Moreover, when
Christendom became aware that Islam could not be subdued by force of
arms, it was the mendicants who led the great missionary crusade, going
among the infidels whom they hoped to win for Christ by love.[27]

Finally, their exertions were of capital importance on the intellectual
plane. At a time of intense spiritual ferment, the new Orders were found
more capable than were the secular clergy or the old monastic congregations of identifying themselves with and giving direction to the interests of
their contemporaries. Their entry into the great seats of learning, however,
was not effected without opposition; and the annals of that period tell of
ceaseless conflict in the University of Paris. The triumph of the Dominicans
Roland of Cremona and John of St. Gilles, and that of the Franciscan Alexander of Hales, as teachers of theology, let loose a storm of protest. A pamphlet entitled *Perils of the Present Time* (1256), by William of Saint-Amour,
denounced the teaching of the mendicants with impassioned vehemence. It
was not merely a question of jealousy or profit; a new way of thinking and
of reasoning, a new approach to theology, was in process of formation. The
contest centred upon Aristotle, whose most illustrious and ultimately victorious champion was St. Thomas Aquinas.[28]

In short, it was to the mendicant Orders that the sixteenth-century
reform owed both its origin and its success. It is not difficult to see that the

---

26. See Volume 2, Chapter XIII, section 8.
27. See Volume 2, Chapter XII.
28. See Volume 2, Chapter IX, section 8.

"return to the Gospel," for which they strove, exercised no less profound an influence upon canon law, upon the notion of criminal justice, and upon social life, than upon devotional practices. True to that lasting and mysterious paradox that is the Church, the mendicants laboured not only to re-establish the pristine purity of Christian morals, but also to breathe the Gospel spirit into the new framework of life. We owe it to them that the necessary transformation was accomplished not outside and in opposition to the Church, but deep within her womb.

We come now to the part played by the Holy See in this colossal undertaking. During the twelfth century reform had been *attempted* side by side with, but independently of, Rome; in the thirteenth it was *accomplished* in close collaboration with the Sovereign Pontiffs and under their direction. Franciscans and Dominicans had, from the very first, placed themselves unreservedly at the disposition of the Holy See; and St. Francis once beheld a vision of his Order (represented by a brood of chicks) defended by the Roman eagle against attack by sparrow-hawks. Neither St. Francis nor St. Dominic asked for "exemption," but a succession of Bulls regulating the affairs of the two Orders made them exempt *de facto*; they were answerable to none but their own Generals, who worked in strict harmony with the Lateran.

We may also observe that every thirteenth-century pope favoured the mendicant Orders. The kindly eye of Innocent III presided over their birth. Honorius III (1216–1227) gave them canonical status. Gregory IX (1227–1241) showed himself, on Peter's throne, no less well-disposed than he had been as Cardinal Hugolin; and his successors, whether Italian, French, English, or Portuguese, manifested the same interest and goodwill. Even those who cared less for the Church's well-being—e.g., Innocent IV who, notwithstanding the blamelessness of his private life, was dominated by unworthy counsellors—continued to protect the advocates of an indispensable reform.[29]

---

29. It was two mendicants, the Franciscan St. Bonaventure and the Dominican St. Thomas Aquinas, whom Urban IV (1261–1264), "political" Pope though he was, instructed to compose the office of Corpus Christi.

Two outstanding events of this period were the Councils of Lyons in 1245 and 1274.[30] They concerned themselves with the reorganization of the new Orders in view of their encroachment on the rights of secular priests, but did not impede their work. A union of interests between the mendicant Orders and the papacy was sealed once and for all[31] in 1276 by the election of a Dominican, Peter of Tarentaise, as Pope Innocent V.

The mendicants thus formed an army devoted to the Sovereign Pontiff, a useful instrument for the dissemination of his views, and a diplomatic corps which might safely be entrusted with the most difficult and dangerous embassies. We find them, for instance, under orders from the Pope to support Charles of Anjou in Sicily, to arrange the peace between St. Louis and the English king, and to subvert the power of Frederick II. This latter achievement incurred savage reprisals; for in 1249 the Emperor actually decreed the penalty of death by burning for the Dominicans and Franciscans who, "under the cloak of religion, play the game of Lucifer!"

The coming of the friars, therefore, was a landmark not only in the field of moral reform. They upheld the cause of successive popes in their struggle with the temporal power. But they also represented a new conception of the Church and of her function in the world: a Church in whom the brilliance of feudal power would give place to interior prestige; the Church of the missions, and of the universities wherein human thought was to make notable advances; a Church in closer sympathy with the aims of an enlarged society. Thus, once again, as has happened so often in the course of history, the permanent message of Christ was embodied in a particular form of Christianity; once again the leaven had done its work.

---

30. The second of these Councils was summoned by the reforming Pope St. Gregory X (1271–1276).

31. Except towards the end of the pontificate of Innocent IV, who appeared for a time to be influenced by his entourage and to fear that the success of the mendicants would overshadow the prestige of the papacy. His alarm, however, was short-lived, and he later paid splendid homage to the new Orders by describing them as "Sons of Obedience ready to brave all perils in defence of justice."

CHAPTER V

The Church and the Powers

1. IN THE WORLD BUT NOT OF THE WORLD

THE spiritual and moral problem which the Church endeavoured so courageously to solve was not the only one with which she was confronted; for in order to accomplish her supernatural mission, it was necessary that she should clarify her relations with the civil power. The two realms of authority appear at first sight to be unconnected; actually they are inseparable. Christ Himself emphasized that the Church is "not *of* this world"; her essential purity tends to raise her above the things of earth. Nevertheless, her work lies *in* this world, among men, within the framework of their interests and institutions. She can no more be indifferent to the laws upon which her freedom depends than to those material resources which enable her ministers to carry out their supernatural function. She is a spiritual society, foreshadowing the City of God; but she is obliged to maintain close contact with the City of the World, and that is no easy task.

The problem is everlasting. It is the most difficult of all those which Christendom has been called upon to solve; and if no satisfactory solution has yet been found, it is surely because none exists, because it is in the nature of things that there should be continual tension between the spiritual and the temporal order. Three situations are possible. The secular power may be opposed to the Church upon ideological or political grounds, which means persecution; or the State may ignore religious activity and treat the spiritual society as nonexistent, which means neutrality. But persecution had ended in the fourth century, and neutrality was quite unthinkable in the Middle Ages; so there remained a third possibility, collaboration.

The pre-eminence of the Church throughout the Dark Ages, the universality of the faith, and the submission of temporal leaders to the Christian creed, had resulted in an unhealthy influence of the secular on the spiritual domain. The Church had set her seal upon the brow of emperors and kings; she had provided them with agents and administrators; she had received from them lands and other material benefits; and she had enjoyed their protection at a time when it had been of considerable value. By the same token, however, she had largely curtailed her freedom, until at last she found herself subject to those with whom she had meant only to walk hand in hand. During the barbarian epoch she had scored a notable success; but that same victory now threatened her with ruin. The moment had come when she must awake and act.

It should not, on the other hand, be thought that there was permanent antagonism between the medieval Church and State. Many a page of history is occupied with the Quarrel of Investitures and with the struggle between Priesthood and Empire, regrettable conflicts in the course of which St. Thomas à Becket suffered martyrdom and a French envoy insulted the Pope. But such was not the normal state of affairs. A vast majority of people thought with St. Bernard: "I am not one of those who say that the peace and freedom of the Church is harmful to the Empire, or that the Empire's prosperity is harmful to the Church. On the contrary, God, who is the author of both, has linked them in a common destiny on earth, not for the sake of internecine strife but that they may strengthen one another." For the most part there was concord between the spiritual and temporal powers; disagreement, no matter how violent a form it might assume, was the exception.

The gravity and the ferocity of these disputes must be sought in the fact that they involved the entire historico-social complex. To call in question the Church's ownership of material goods was to deny fundamental principles, and perhaps to overthrow the established order. Excessive zeal on behalf of temporal concerns was not hard to justify in the name of supreme spiritual interests. We may deplore clerical participation in the feudal regime; but in the circumstances which then prevailed, a Church without lands, a papacy without territorial sovereignty, would have been bound hand and foot at the mercy of rival factions. Moral, economic, and political considerations all played their part in the conflict between Church and State, not to mention the egotism, self-esteem, and other passions of antagonists in either camp.

It is therefore a false view to see the conflict simply as an affair of politics, as a struggle between powers equally determined to subdue the world. Political ambition was never the prime motive, even of the most theocratic popes. The true origin of that strife, which continued at intervals for a period of almost three centuries, was the deep-rooted longing of the Church to stand fast by her vocation. She resolved to put an end to secular interference, which was an obstacle in her path; and once having joined issue with her opponents, she was led to ask herself whether the divine law might not be more perfectly observed on earth through the predominance of spiritual over temporal authority. The question was not one of politics, national or international. The contest may appear to us marred by violence and by sordid intrigue; but what was at stake? The unity of Christendom, the primacy of the spirit, and freedom of the human conscience.

2. THE PROBLEM OF INVESTITURES

IN the early Middle Ages relations between Church and State were founded on a spirit of co-operation. Three dates are of capital importance. In 380 Theodosius decreed that all his subjects should embrace "the faith delivered to the Romans by the Apostle Peter"; in 490 the hierarchy of Gaul baptized Clovis, the young Frankish king, and thereby determined the fate of the barbarian world; while at Christmas in the year 800, Pope St. Leo III conferred the ancient crown of empire upon Charlemagne, a descendant of the invaders. Throughout six hundred years and more, by means of unending courage and endurance, the Church had kept a restraining hand upon those turbulent princes who dominated Europe, with the result that society had returned step by step to the light of civilization.

There was another side to this tremendous achievement. Though herself a spiritual power, the Church had worked well upon the temporal plane; but in doing so she had failed to put first things first. Her leaders had grown deaf to the Gospel precept; by mixing with the world they had lapsed into worldliness. The history of the barbarian epoch is that of continual co-operation between the spiritual and the temporal, a co-operation which Charlemagne treated as a principle of government.

Nor could the Church escape the rise of seignory and feudalism. By virtue of donations from the faithful, every bishop and every abbot became head of an enormous territorial domain. He was *ex officio* a rural landlord like other landlords, having his "reserve" and tenants, exacting labour, and dispensing justice. Moreover, an unavoidable system of "recommendations" involved him in that network of dependence and allegiance which was the feudal system. His lands were fiefs, held from an overlord to whom he owed the customary duties of a vassal—even that of military service, which he fulfilled through a lay deputy (the *vidame*) since divine law would not allow him to bear arms. The Carolingians had granted territorial rights to certain prelates, provided the latter agreed to exercise them as vassals; and it was not uncommon for laymen to obtain control of ecclesiastical domains. The result was that the Spouse of Christ lived on terms of intimacy with the established feudal order.

The union was not a happy one. The prelate bore a strange resemblance to his temporal neighbour. Like him, he had vast buildings, domestic officers, administrators for his estates, tax-gatherers for his revenue. One can hardly be surprised that his life was often "lordly," surrounded with pomp and far from the spirit of the Gospel. The moral problem was inextricably bound up with social and political factors.

The Church tried hard to free herself, not by withdrawing from the feudal system, but simply by attempting to gain a privileged position within it. Some clerical landowners were dispensed from homage, and thus avoided open recognition of an overlord. An abbey might enjoy "exemption," which

meant that it was dependent immediately upon the Holy See and therefore free from seignorial or even royal interference. But this privilege did
not remove the essentially feudal character of ecclesiastical principalities,
which continued to form part and parcel of the system, and from which
churchmen still collected "regalities." There was another so-called remedy known as "advocacy"; but it often proved more burdensome than the
evil it was supposed to remove. "Advocates," whose duty it was to protect a
clerical domain against attack by neighbours, gradually became permanent
and hereditary, and they frequently behaved as if they owned the property
entrusted to their care. Temporal rulers, however, united with the clergy to
abolish this institution.

Generally speaking, then, the medieval Church was engulfed by feudalism; consciously, or more often unconsciously, she had committed the
mistake of linking her fortunes too closely with prevailing sociological factors. This was the sole cause of the many crises which she survived and of the
disaster which finally overwhelmed her. Nevertheless, there was a point at
which collaboration became so dangerous that it could no longer be ignored,
for it affected the deepest loyalties of the Church, imperilling her very soul;
and it was on this point that there broke out the first great political conflict
of the Middle Ages, the Quarrel of Investitures. The problem may be formulated thus: was the Church to compromise so far as to entrust laymen with
the appointment of bishops? Surely the Church alone, as depositary of the
faith, should choose those who were to speak in God's name. To understand
the gravity of this question, we must go back and consider how the early
Church nominated those who were to govern her.

In Africa, for example, in St. Cyprian's day, the process of appointment
was twofold. The bishop was *elected* by the people, but he could not enter
upon his duties until he had been *consecrated* by another bishop. Divine
investiture, by virtue of uninterrupted tradition dating back to the Apostles,
made him the direct heir to powers conferred by Christ. Under the Christian
Empire, and before the barbarian invasions, the civil power had taken no
part in the appointment of bishops. Clovis was the first to do so. That cunning chieftain, newly elevated to the royal dignity, foresaw the advantages

214 of alliance with the hierarchy, and made sure that every diocese within his dominions was governed by a man whom he could trust. He exerted no pressure upon the clergy or the faithful; but he took care that no one should be ignorant of which candidate he preferred. His successors went still further. Notwithstanding the opposition of several councils, the Merovingians did not hesitate to control the elections in their own high-handed way, until it was agreed that no bishop should be chosen without the sovereign's consent. Charlemagne, that "pious guardian of the episcopate," regularly nominated them; and the fact that his choice was invariably good made the principle no less dangerous. From the ninth century bishops were to all intents and purposes chosen by the king, the clergy and people dutifully acclaiming the prelate thus appointed; so much so that we find instances of a temporal sovereign granting the clergy *permission* to elect!

This undesirable custom was so firmly established by the tenth century, when the feudal system began to take shape, that it became almost an integral part of the new regime. Bishops continued to be appointed by the emperor, the king, or some other temporal overlord; but there was worse to come. Of the two constitutional elements in the process of appointment, i.e., the choice of the new titular and his consecration, it was not merely the former which was usurped by laymen. In theory, the overlord delivered to the chosen candidate only the territorial possessions annexed to his title; in practice, however, it was not easy to distinguish the remission of temporalities from the spiritual election. There was a ceremony known as "investiture," during which the overlord handed the new bishop his crozier and ring with the words, "Receive the Church"; and one chronicler records Otto the Great as having delivered to a certain bishop the "pastoral charge," i.e., the right to guide souls, which only sacerdotal authority can confer. The result was intolerable confusion. In the middle of the eleventh century even those temporal overlords who were good Christians considered bishoprics and monasteries as fiefs analogous to other fiefs, the holders of which were exclusively bound to religious duties, but over which they claimed indisputable rights. They never suspected that spiritual interests were thereby placed in jeopardy.

Similar interference had been going on at the parochial level. The meth-
od was somewhat different, but its consequences were much the same. The
parish church had in many cases been built and endowed by the local landowner, whose descendants considered themselves its absolute master. They
expected, in particular, to enjoy part of its revenues, which consisted of
tithes, and taxes paid on the occasion of baptisms, weddings, and funerals.
The church, in fact, belonged to the lord as did the common bakehouse, mill,
and winepress; and he took care to put it in charge of a cleric chosen by himself, one who would take an oath of fealty to him and whom he would invest.

Nor did the papacy itself escape lay interference. Since the day when
Charlemagne's firm hand ceased to preserve order in the Eternal City, the
see of St. Peter had too often been the stake of warring factions; and the
majority of popes from the pontificate of Sergius III (904–911) until about
960 had been creatures of ambitious aristocrats or even of licentious females.
The restoration of the Empire by Otto the Great in 962 had put an end to
the tyranny of the Roman nobles, but it had not freed the papacy. Officially
indeed, by virtue of Otto's "declaration," the Sovereign Pontiff could not be
consecrated before he had sworn fealty to the emperor; and since that date
the German emperors, whether they were simply well-disposed like Otto
III, or saints like Henry II, had held the Holy See in a dependence that was
tantamount to subjection.

It is most remarkable that a great number, and even a majority, of these
popes, bishops, and parish priests chosen by emperors, kings, and local
landlords, remained true to their vocation and lived good priestly lives. But
there was always danger that unworthy men might be appointed to positions of authority. Simony and Nicolaism, two evils which afflicted the
medieval Church, had been due to secular influences; while the disposal of
the Apostolic See by a group of Roman nobles had resulted in the appointment of John XII, who, says the *Liber Pontificalis*, spent his life "in adultery and vanity." The emperors, in general, had acted for the best; but it had
only required a ruler such as Conrad II (1027–1039) to succeed St. Henry
for the appointment of bishops to become an object of disgraceful barter.
How were feudal chiefs to be prevented from selling investitures; and how

persuade their nominees to live worthy of their calling? As for parish priests, how were their moral qualities, or even the minimum of priestly learning, to be guaranteed, if the overlord who appointed them could secure their ordination by subservient bishops? It was precisely this moral and spiritual danger that roused the conscience of the Church.

The desire for reform, which had first appeared during the tenth century,[1] was at the root of a political crisis which brought the Church into collision with the civil powers; but many years elapsed before men perceived a connection between moral and spiritual problems on the one hand and political issues on the other. St. Peter Damian, for example, believed that royal support was indispensable to bring about the reform which he desired. Nor did those who, like St. Romuald and St. John Gualbert, preached the lesson of example imagine that a return to the practice of evangelical virtue must have repercussions in the political sphere. Others, however, saw more clearly. Long ago, in the tenth century, Rathier of Liége (afterwards Bishop of Verona) had proclaimed that the episcopate must be free from all secular influence and dependent upon none but the Holy See. A hundred years later, Wason, Bishop of Liége, defended the rights of the episcopate against temporal princes, and went so far as to rebuke the Emperor Henry III for having deposed Gregory VI; while Cardinal Humbert of Moyen-Moutier, in his book *Against Simony* (1057), wrote these words: "What right have laymen to dispose of ecclesiastical benefices and invest with the crozier and ring, a ceremony which is the climax of episcopal consecration?" The Quarrel of Investitures was implicit in the cardinal's forthright question, and events were soon to prove him right.

3. PAPAL ELECTIONS ENTRUSTED TO THE CARDINALS

THE first of a series of acts that were destined to liberate the Church was accomplished during the short pontificate of an energetic Burgundian,

---

1. See also Chapter IV.

Nicholas II (1059–1061). It deprived the Emperor of his right to nominate   217
the Pope. Circumstances were favourable; for on the death of Henry III, in
1056, his son Henry IV was no more than a child, whose guardian was the
Empress Agnes. When Leo IX died, in 1054, the clergy of the Eternal City
stole a march on the German court and the Roman aristocracy by electing
a pope of their own choice, Frederick, abbot of Monte Cassino, brother of
the Duke of Lorraine, friend of Cardinal Humbert, and a zealous advocate
of ecclesiastical independence. This pontiff, Stephen IX, reigned for only a
few months; but a precedent had been created—a Pope had been elected
without reference to the Emperor, who had simply been invited to approve
the choice.

On Stephen's death the factions combined to nominate one John, Bishop of Velletri, who took the name of Benedict X. The great Burgundian
monk Hildebrand, afterwards Gregory VII, was then in Germany. He made
contact with Agnes, who was indignant that the tyrannous Romans should
have dared to appoint a pope; and, assisted by the Marquis Godfrey of Lorraine, he secured the election of his compatriot Gerard, Bishop of Florence,
as Pope Nicholas II. A few weeks later, in order to prevent a repetition of
these intrigues, the new pontiff promulgated his famous decretal of April
13, 1059.

"We have decided," so ran this momentous document, "that on the
death of the Sovereign Pontiff of the Roman and universal Church, the cardinal-bishops shall take the utmost care for the appointment of his successor;
after which they shall invite the cardinal-priests together with the remainder
of the clergy and the people to confirm the new election.... They shall confine
their choice to the Roman Church provided they can find a suitable man;
otherwise they shall choose someone from elsewhere, saving the honour and
reverence due to Henry at present king and, God willing, future emperor."

It should be noticed that there are two parts to this decree. The first is
definitive and categorical; it withdraws the choice of the pope from laymen
and confides it to a group of dignitaries known as "cardinals" who, since
the tenth century, had occupied an increasingly important situation in the
Church. The second part consists of a respectful tribute to the Emperor.

No one could mistake the meaning or the import of this decision. The Roman nobility made a display of force, while the German court refused to entertain the legate sent to notify it of the decree. But Nicholas II was not to be caught napping. Reversing the whole policy of his predecessors, he made an alliance with the Normans who, though little more than bandits, had established themselves in the south of the Peninsula.[2] Seven years earlier, under the command of Robert Guiscard and Richard of Capua, they had defeated Leo IX and taken him prisoner. Later, fearing German ascendancy, they had agreed to negotiate, and had proclaimed themselves vassals of the Pope at the Council of Melfi in 1059. The oath taken by Guiscard to Nicholas II contained a clause expressly binding him, in the event of the Pope's death, to assist the cardinals in the election of his successor. Nicholas capped this manoeuvre with a French alliance, and the Roman nobility, on sight of the Norman troops, abandoned their antipope. The German court maintained an attitude of reserve, confining itself to the publication of a false decretal in which the rights of the Emperor were affirmed.

Encouraged by the effects of his diplomacy, Nicholas II confirmed it in August of the following year (1060); but this time there was no mention of "reverence due to Henry," nor even of popular consent. Henceforward the papal election belonged to the cardinals alone; and well-informed people studied the sixth canon of a council held in 1059. It ran as follows: "No priest or cleric shall in any wise receive a church from the hands of a layman, whether for payment or gratuitously."

Nicholas II died after a brief reign of thirty months; but his pontificate left its mark on history. Would his work survive? At one moment there was cause to doubt; for his successor, Alexander II (1061–1073), who was elected in accordance with the decree of 1059, met with violent resistance both from the Roman aristocracy and from the German court. Once more an antipope arose in the person of Cadalus, Bishop of Parma, and the future

---

2. The settlement of the Normans in southern Italy will be dealt with in Volume 2, Chapter X, which is devoted to Byzantium, since it was amid the ruins of the Byzantine Empire that they established their domain.

seemed wrapped in uncertainty. The new Pope, however, was no weakling.
He knew how to make numerous "concessions" while remaining firm in all
essentials. At his side Archdeacon Hildebrand stood fast by the principles of
reform, and he it was who was predestined to renew the struggle.

4. THE QUARREL OF INVESTITURES

AT the end of February 1075 the atmosphere in Rome was tense. A council, which had been in session for a week, had taken stern measures against
many persons of high rank: five members of the German king's council had
been excommunicated; and an archbishop, together with a dozen Italian
and German bishops, had been suspended "by reason of their stiff-necked
disobedience." Decisive events were in progress under the leadership of a
swarthy little man with a will of iron, who for ten years now had occupied
the Apostolic See. Momentous results were anticipated, and they were not
long delayed.

In the preceding year another synod had promulgated the famous
decrees for the moral reform of the Church, ordering the deposition of
simoniacal priests, and forbidding clerics guilty of fornication to approach
the altar. But these steps, as we have seen, had met with fierce resistance. In
Germany especially, and in France, the papal legates had been everywhere
rebuffed. This set-back at first caused the Pope "immense grief, boundless
sorrow"; but a man of his mettle could not yield to such emotions. Harsh
experience had taught him a lesson: it was not enough to inflict penalties,
to excommunicate or suspend recalcitrants; since his reforming policy had
proved inadequate, he must go farther and attack the root of evil. Gregory VII therefore changed his method and promulgated a fresh decree: "No
ecclesiastic shall in any wise receive a church from the hands of a layman
either gratuitously or by onerous title, under pain of excommunication both
for the giver and the receiver." This clause repeated almost word for word, but
with the addition of dire threats, the sixth canon of 1059, whose application
had been prevented by the untimely death of Nicholas II. Its terms, though

perfectly clear, involved some confusion. Its purpose was undoubted; but in forbidding every cleric "in any wise" to receive a church from the hands of a layman, the decree surely absorbed the temporal in the spiritual, and confused clerical functions with the temporalities attached to them. It is possible that Gregory was conscious of the mistake and foresaw the injustice to which it might give rise; but fifty years were to elapse before the distinction was properly understood. The situation, however, was extremely grave, and only drastic measures could provide a remedy. The decree of 1075, which condemned all lay investiture, was something quite new, and was to involve the Church in the most serious political conflict she had ever known.

For the issue was ultimately political. Temporal landlords would inevitably feel they had been robbed. To renounce the investiture of bishops, abbots, and parish priests was to give up rights which were considered at that time to be perfectly legitimate. For some it would have spelled ruin; for others (e.g., the German emperor), it meant the dismemberment of their States. Did Gregory VII take account of this? The decisions of 1075 admitted of no exception in principle, and he repeated them in 1078 and 1080, with even greater precision; but at first he was not invariably strict in their application. In countries such as England, which was ruled by his friend William the Conqueror, or in Spain, where simony was practically unknown, the decree was never promulgated; and even in France, where Philip I was not above criticism in this respect, he showed himself lenient. Outwardly his policy was dictated by the determination for reform; but so long as the sovereigns were not opposed in principle to this goal, they found the Pope ready to mitigate the full rigour of the sacred canons.

In Germany the situation was altogether different owing to the nature of its institutions and the character of its rulers. The great feudal clerics constituted a fundamental part of the imperial regime; for the bishops, who were responsible for much of the administration, were the mainstay of the central authority against the baronage. For the Emperor to renounce their investiture would have been to forgo the right to nominate his chief officials, to jeopardize the fulfilment of military duties by his vassals, and to imperil the financial resources of his government.

The young Franconian prince, Henry IV, who had worn the crown since   221
1056, was least of all prepared to make these sacrifices. Intelligent and tenacious, realistic and astute, he had derived from the spectacle of those disorders among which his youth had passed a consciousness of his imperial
rights and pride in his royal dignity. He had been engaged since the first
days of his reign in a hard struggle with the German nobility; he had come
near to defeat by the Duke of Saxony in 1073, and had been obliged to
flee at dead of night from his castle in the Hartz. But he had restored the
situation; and while Gregory VII was presiding over the famous council at
Rome, Henry IV was mopping up the rebel troops whom he had routed
on the banks of the Unstrutt. Such a man was unlikely to cede his rights.
His ancestors had appointed popes; what was all this talk about a campaign
against simony and fornicating priests? He had more important things in
hand. Thus the promulgation of this decree, which was otherwise quite
uneventful, was to bring about something like a state of war between Pope
and Emperor, Priesthood and Empire.

Since the conflict was in fact political, it is natural to inquire what forces the antagonists controlled. Those of the Empire were exclusively material,
and absolutely unreliable. The memory of Charlemagne persisted, though
somewhat vaguely. The Emperor might look to Germany for troops, to Italy
as a source of revenue; but along the highways leading from the Rhine to
Rome there were powerful men who sought an opportunity, as the saying
went, "to pluck the imperial eagle." His enormous territory, centred upon
the Alps, included Germans, Italians, and French; it was not easy to govern,
and suffered constant variations of frontier. Two institutions in particular
placed its holder in an unenviable situation; to become Emperor, the King
of Germany required to be anointed, which only the Pope could do; while
the three crowns of Germany, Italy, and the Empire were elective and made
the Emperor dependent upon those who raised him to that dignity.

In appearance, the papacy was weaker still. Its territory was minute,
smaller than the Duchy of Saxony or that of Normandy, consisting of the
Patrimony of St. Peter on the Tiber, the Romagna, and the March of Ancona. True, it was protected on the north by fiefs belonging to Matilda, widow

of Godfrey of Lorraine, who was devoted to the papal cause; and on the south, since the pontificate of Nicholas II, by the Normans, who had established themselves in Apulia about the year 1030 and had recently taken Sicily from the Muslims. But Robert Guiscard and his fellow brigands were uncertain allies, and, on the whole, a source of danger to the papal states. Tuscany and the March of Ancona, on twin routes to Sicily, lay open to the imperial armies; civil war was rife throughout the papal territory; while Rome itself was prey to the ambitions of the Senate, of the Commune, and of an aristocracy that would not be overshadowed. But to this unpromising material there were added the far more effective weapons of excommunication and interdict, and these were to prove decisive. The Pope's right to crown the Emperor showed on which side real power lay: there could be no emperor without the pope, whereas since 1059 there was no need of an emperor to make a pope. Besides, the idea of Christendom at that time was an infinitely stronger motive force than the nostalgic concept of imperial glory. The spiritual arm would prove more effective in the approaching conflict.

The decree of 1075 caused a great stir in the dominions of Henry IV. Hitherto relations between prince and pontiff had been cordial; annoyed, however, by the new measures, and urged no doubt by his entourage, which included a number of churchmen who had been excommunicated for simony, Henry flouted the papal decisions. He appointed one of his creatures to the vacant see of Milan, and subsequently repeated this gesture at Fermo, Spoleto, Spire, Bamberg, Liége, and Cologne. An angry letter from Gregory VII ordered him to desist. It reached Henry IV at Goslar on January 1, 1076; and before the month was out the indignant monarch replied in his own fashion.

On the twenty-fourth a synod of priests and prelates hostile to the Pope met at Worms. "The false monk Hildebrand" was loaded with insults, accused of having disturbed the peace of the Church, of usurping powers to which he had no right, of attempting to steal the crown of Italy, and even of immorality. He was declared deposed, and envoys were sent to Rome to invite the clergy and people to choose his successor. In the north of Italy a group of prelates, many of whom were simoniacs, assembled at Piacenza and confirmed their decision.

But Gregory VII was not the man to be upset by such insolent defiance. At a synod held in Rome on February 14, he stood up and spoke as follows: "King Henry has presumed with insensate vanity to defy the Church; wherefore I bar him from governing the kingdom of Germany and of Italy. I absolve all Christians from the oath which they have taken to him, and forbid anyone to recognize him as king."

This was an unheard of sentence: the Pope was deposing a sovereign prince! Its effect was astonishing. The partisans of reform took heart, and those who had hurried to obey the royal command at Worms began to think it imprudent to quarrel with so energetic a Pope. The earth seemed to open at Henry's feet, and his enemies once more raised their heads. An assembly of nobles and bishops met at Tribur, recognized the Pope as having justice on his side, and agreed that Henry IV should no longer reign. The German nobility was restive; some bishops set out for Rome; and at the beginning of 1077 there was question of holding an assembly to confirm the monarch's deposition and appoint his successor. Henry IV had learned his lesson.

There followed a prodigious scene which was to make a deep impression on the age, and whose memory still survives in a proverbial phrase after the passage of nine centuries. On January 25, 1077, Henry IV went to Canossa. He crossed the Alps and travelled through northern Italy with a small escort, turning a deaf ear to those few flatterers who would have encouraged him to remain firm, and letting it be known to all that he was now but a prodigal son returning to his Father's house. The Italian winter in that year was cold, and snow covered the Apennines where the Pope had taken refuge. The castle of Canossa, an eyrie in territory belonging to the Countess Matilda, might have withstood a siege. But he who now appeared before its walls was a penitent, stripped of the emblems of royalty, clothed in sackcloth, and barefoot.

The Pope himself tells us of what followed: the three days' wait outside the fortress, the supplication of the defeated king, the intervention of the Countess Matilda and various cardinals, and then the final scene when the heir of the Ottos, "of a stature and beauty worthy of an emperor," prostrated himself before the stocky little man in whom shone forth the power of the Apostle. Christendom stood amazed; but the vanquished monarch swore a vague oath in which the words "Henry, King" seemed to annul the political consequences of a year ago. The excommunication was lifted; and the crown, though shaken, seemed once again to sit securely on the Salian's head.

Many historians regard Henry as the true victor of Canossa; they maintain that the Pope, for all his strength, was worsted by the royal cunning, and that the pardon marked a political defeat. True, the absolution, couched as it was in equivocal terms, compromised Gregory's manoeuvre. But Gregory was a saint, and in his eyes the gesture had been no mere act of policy; it was an expression of God's infinite mercy, to which no sinner can appeal in vain. The pontiff was never more sublime than at that moment.

On the political plane, however, the results were disastrous. The German princes, shocked by a reconciliation which upset their plans, declined to recognize the penitent monarch, though he had been absolved. On March 13, they assembled at Forcheim, and there, in spite of the papal legates, proclaimed the deposition of Henry IV, who was to be succeeded by his brother-in-law, Rudolph of Rheinfelden, Duke of Swabia and Governor of Burgundy. Civil war broke out; and its fury was aggravated by Henry's renewed defiance of a Pope whom he now considered the ally of his enemies. Deposed once again in March 1080, the king replied with a decree of the Council of Brixen, deposing Gregory, "false monk, ravisher of churches, necromancer," and proclaiming in his stead Wibert, Archbishop of Ravenna, who took the name of Clement III.

For a moment it seemed that the issue must be determined by force of arms. Henry IV was defeated at Grona, between the Elster and the Saale; but Rudolph was left dead upon the field. Sweeping into Italy, the king seized the Iron Crown at Milan, and marched on Rome in company with his antipope. Gregory's situation was critical. Robert Guiscard had been excommunicated for his shameless looting, and would not stir; while in Tuscany the towns subject to Matilda sided with the German, who restored to them their privileges. Gregory VII hastened to negotiate with Guiscard,

and agreed to invest him with such lands as he had overrun; but all in vain.
The Norman was at war with the Byzantines, and would not intervene. Two years sufficed for Henry to establish his authority over the whole of northern Italy. After a prolonged struggle he entered Rome, and enthroned his Pope, who, in turn, crowned him Emperor on March 31, 1084.

The confusion may be imagined. The Emperor and the antipope occupied St. Peter's and the Lateran. Between those two points, Gregory VII held out in the Castle of Sant' Angelo, while two groups of his partisans defended the Capitol and the Palatine. There was some bargaining, in which farce was enacted side by side with tragedy. The Pope refused to leave his stronghold, but was prepared to lower the crown by rope on to Henry's brow! In the narrow streets of the city, however, both parties resorted to gang warfare. The Capitol was taken, and Gregory awaited a final assault upon his fortress, when Robert Guiscard, realizing at last that he had everything to lose by Henry's success, advanced in force. The king decamped; but the remedy proved far worse than the evil. Hordes of bandits (Muslims for the most part), of whom Guiscard's army was composed, gave themselves up to pillage, murder, sacrilege, and rape. The population retaliated under the leadership of Henry's supporters; but Robert Guiscard drowned the insurrection in blood, and thousands of innocent folk were massacred. Others, including women and children and a number of senatorial families, were sold into slavery. It is even said that a marabout recited Islamic prayers in the half-ruined basilica of St. Peter.

The Pope was overwhelmed with grief. He knew his principles to be sound; but his tender conscience was afflicted by the disasters brought about through their application in the political field. He could stay in Rome no longer, and allowed himself to be carried off to Salerno in Norman territory. When he died there soon afterwards, on May 25, 1085, it seemed that his efforts had entirely failed. But the bright light of his saintly soul preserved him from despair. His last encyclical had recalled his fundamental principles, and proclaimed in the nave of St. Peter's his indestructible belief that though the tempests of this world may shake the Church she can never be submerged.

It had now to be decided whether the struggle should be continued, or whether some basis for agreement should be sought. After the short pontificate of Victor III (1086–1087), which witnessed a clash between the moderates and intransigents, an energetic Frenchman, Eudes de Châtillon, was elected to the papal throne and took the name of Urban II (1088–1099). He declared himself a disciple of Pope Gregory, and thereby revealed his purpose; but the situation remained confused for years. Sometimes travelling the length and breadth of Italy to encourage his supporters, sometimes living at Rome in danger from the antipope's intrigue, Urban was the embodiment of loyalty to principle. Little by little fortune returned to the Church's camp, thanks to the subtle diplomacy of the Pope. Roger of Sicily, brother of Guiscard, who had just completed the conquest of that island, proclaimed himself, and was recognized as, papal legate within his dominions; so that Rome was no longer threatened from that quarter.

With Milan as their centre, the Italian towns in the north formed a league against Henry IV, in alliance with the Countess Matilda, who had recently been married to the Duke of Bavaria. Lorraine and Saxony rallied to Urban II, while the king's eldest son Conrad revolted against his father and submitted to the Pope. At the celebrated Council of Clermont, in 1095, it seemed that Urban II had restored to the papacy its ancient prestige. But the problem of investiture was far from settled. It had lately been revived in England, where William Rufus carried on open traffic in ecclesiastical benefices, and also in France, where Philip I, at loggerheads with the Church on account of his adulterous marriage, had resorted to the old practices of simony.

Paschal II (1099–1118), as we have seen,[3] was a holy monk, full of good intentions, but no statesman. From the moment of his accession he was confronted with a maze of difficulty. In England the way became easier on the death of Rufus. His successor, Henry I (1100–1135), guided by St. Anselm, adopted a policy of reconciliation with the Church, and the concordat of 1107 established an acceptable *modus vivendi*. France did likewise under

---

3. See Chapter IV, section 5.

the influence of Philip's son Louis (later Louis VI). In Germany, however, the situation deteriorated, although at first there were high hopes. Henry IV's second son, appointed heir in place of Conrad, rebelled in 1104; and Paschal II saw this as a means to break his adversary. The old Emperor died of disappointment and grief on April 7, 1106, but Henry V proved still more dangerous. Crafty and avaricious, so successfully had he posed as a devoted son of the Church that he had secured a promise of the imperial crown. Now, securely seated on the throne, he claimed the same rights as his father. In 1110, having quelled an Italian revolt, he entered Rome, full of honeyed words but with hatred of the Pope in his heart. Paschal was already dreaming of his mighty project, the Church's total separation from the feudal regime provided the sovereigns would renounce all claims to investiture. Their mutual antagonism flared up on the very day when the Pope was to crown Henry V as Emperor (February 12, 1111). The *casus belli* was an insurrection on the part of those who feared the damage they might suffer in consequence of Paschal's offer. Arrested and held captive for two months, the unfortunate Pope's nerve gave way; he capitulated, recognizing Henry's right to invest with ring and crozier. Nevertheless, as soon as he regained his liberty, Paschal revoked his concession and excommunicated the Emperor. From that time until his death he showed no more weakness; he refused to temporize, and would not lift the censure.

This troubled pontificate, in which so much goodwill did nothing but increase disorder, came no nearer to finding a solution. The world, however, was growing impatient; while diplomats argued and armies fought, philosophers took a hand. Chief among these was a Frenchman, Bishop Yves of Chartres, who died in 1116 without beholding the triumph of his theory. The solution he put forward was a simple one: it consisted in distinguishing the spiritual element of an ecclesiastical benefice from its concomitant temporal advantages. A bishop or an abbot was both a man of God, a depositary of powers handed down from the Apostles, and at the same time a tenant of lands, etc., granted by laymen. In any investiture, therefore, it was necessary to separate consecration, with delivery of the crozier and ring, from the remission of temporalities. *Spiritual* investiture could be performed by none but the religious authority; *temporal* investiture belonged of right to the overlord. This solution, so clear and so logical, obtained gradual recognition. It was favoured by Calixtus II (1119–1124), who, soon after his election, wrote to Henry V: "Let the Church hold what belongs to Christ, and let the Emperor have all that belongs to him."

Agreement was reached on this basis by the Concordat of Worms, September 23, 1122. The Emperor renounced all claim to invest with ring and crozier, which was reserved to the Pope or to the consecrating bishop, and also promised freedom of canonical elections. The Pope, in turn, recognized Henry's right to take part in the election of bishops and abbots, but without recourse to violence or to simony: "The prelate-elect shall receive his temporalities from the prince, and shall faithfully perform his duties as a vassal." In the following year these wise decisions were confirmed by a council held at Rome.

The Quarrel of Investitures was ended, and the Church free from lay tutelage. Not least of the benefits resulting from this settlement was the regular appointment of bishops who upheld the principles of reform. This did not mean that every problem had been resolved. The Church being still an integral part of the feudal system, there were repeated lapses in the moral sphere, while the political situation was doomed to end in a renewal of the conflict.

5. THE PRIMACY

THE battle revolved about this question: Where lies the primacy? Gregory VII had a very high notion of the papal authority, the highest that any pope had yet conceived. "The Pope," he wrote in all sincerity, "is the only man whose foot all peoples should kiss; provided he is canonically elected, he is rendered sacred by the merits of St. Peter." Anticipating by eight centuries the dogma of infallibility, he went so far as to affirm: "The Church can never err: Scripture bears witness she will never err." Whence he concluded that "he who wishes to obey the commandments of God must not despise *our* commands, where they interpret the decisions of the holy Fathers; he must receive them as if they came from the Apostle himself."

From such convictions it was natural to conclude that "kingly power was invented by human pride; the power of bishops is established by divine compassion." From this essential superiority of religious jurisdiction there followed consequences which Gregory VII did not hesitate to declare. At the beginning of his pontificate, early in 1075, he drew up a series of twenty-seven concise propositions, known as the *Dictatus Papae*, summarizing his intentions with a view to reform, and formulating the papal doctrine of Roman primacy. Since the Pope, as representative of Christ on earth, is the heir of powers given to the Apostles, no other power on earth can rival his. All are subordinate to him. The twelfth proposition expressly stated: "It is lawful for the Pope to depose emperors"; and by punishing Henry IV, Gregory was merely giving effect to this axiom. Papal theocracy, i.e., the government of men by God through a supreme hierarch, the Pope, was implicit in this formidable sheaf of propositions.

Contrary to general belief, these ideas did not originate with Gregory VII; they had been current in the Church for centuries. The theory, known as "Political Augustinianism" since it can be traced to St. Augustine, had been slowly and painfully evolved and given shape over a very long period. In the seventh century, St. Isidore of Seville had affirmed the subordination of the secular power to religious authority; and even at the height of Charlemagne's ascendancy, in 800, when Leo III was utterly dependent on the Frankish king, Alcuin, though devoted to his sovereign, had assured the Emperor that "the Holy See is subject to no one's judgment!" During the Carolingian decadence the Church had obtained control over the Emperor, affirming that the duty of princes is to "provide for the service of God." She had, in fact, established the imperial power in subjection to herself. Smaragdus, Hincmar, Agobard, and Jonas of Orleans had all upheld this theory, whose development had been made possible by the weakness of the emperors; and the *False Decretals* had formulated it so clearly that Gregory VII's *Dictatus* owed much to them. The great Pope, therefore, could claim to found his argument on venerable tradition.

But the Emperor too had considerable authority on his side. When Henry IV notified Gregory VII of his deposition in 1076, he wrote: "You have struck at me although I am, despite my unworthiness, among those who have received royal unction, and although, according to the tradition of the holy Fathers, I can be judged by none but God and cannot be deposed for any crime unless—which God forbid!—I have erred in matters of faith." This last reservation shows how lively a layman's faith could be, even when he opposed the Church; but the Emperor's words allowed of no misunderstanding. As the Lord's anointed he was subject to the judgment of God alone; the Pope had no power to depose him. Theocracy was face to face with imperial absolutism, and the Church's claim was answered in these words uttered by one of Barbarossa's henchmen: "What pleases the prince has the force of law."

Hence, during the Quarrel of Investitures, far-sighted ecclesiastics realized that it was necessary to insist upon the superiority of spiritual jurisdiction. Admittedly, the spiritual and the temporal power were essentially different and operated in different spheres; but this surely could not mean that the Church had no right to intervene in matters of state. The reasoning was perfectly logical: a government's first duty is to labour for the world's salvation, and in that respect it is clearly subject to the Church. Now it cannot be denied that in human affairs spiritual principles are sometimes violated, that politicians commit sin; and therefore, *ratione peccati*, the Church may justly claim to exercise control. True enough; but in politics it is hard to distinguish what constitutes moral guilt from what pertains to the defence of legitimate interests.

This doctrine found expression in a famous theory known as the "Two Swords" which attained its full significance under the auspices of St. Bernard. The two swords mentioned in St. Luke's Gospel (22:38) represent, so he maintained, the spiritual and the temporal power. "Both belong to Peter: one of them he actually wields, the other is at his disposal as and when circumstances require. Referring to the latter, our Lord told His Apostle: 'Put up thy sword in its scabbard.' It was Peter's sure enough, but not to draw with his own hand." These scriptural arguments seem to us mere

hair-splitting; but in the Middle Ages they carried a good deal of weight. St.
Bernard was expounding the one and only theory which his contemporaries
believed valid. On the spiritual plane, the Church, in the person of her head,
the Sovereign Pontiff, enjoyed a plenitude of power, and therefore the right
to judge all Christians (sovereign princes included) whenever they sinned.
But side by side with this *direct* right went an *indirect* right to compel the
obedience of lay rulers, in order that earthly institutions might conform
with divine principles.

Such was the attitude of every pope during the twelfth and thirteenth
centuries. As years passed, their situation became increasingly uncertain, and
they felt obliged to lay more and more stress upon this doctrine. If Gregory
VII claimed right of control over the civil power, Innocent III (1198–1216)
went so far as practically to usurp the imperial dignity. Because he "represented Him to whom belongs the earth and all that is or dwells therein";
because he was "the ambassador of Him by whom kings reign and princes govern, of Him who dispenses kingdoms to whom He will"; the Pope
claimed "power to overthrow and destroy, to disperse and scatter, to build
and plant." He was "above all princes, since it belongs to him to judge them."
The *spiritual* primacy claimed by Gregory VII tended later to become *total*
primacy—in the Empire as in the Church, where the Vicar of Christ would
share his power with none.

Moreover, the theory of two powers, each with its exclusive sphere of
jurisdiction, was nullified by the Church's view of her superior dignity and
importance: "The royal power borrows its splendour from the papal authority in the same way that the moon reflects the brightness of the sun." Here
we have a disastrous misunderstanding. To push the theory to its logical
conclusion would necessitate a vast governmental machine at once spiritual and temporal, with the Pope at its head and secular princes as no more
than his viceroys. This "theocratic Utopia," resulting from a distorted view
of political Augustinianism, would inevitably tend to absorb the whole of
secular society in the Church, so that the City of God would become identified with the City of men. No temporal sovereign could accept a proposition of that kind.

Around this doctrinal issue there were enacted a succession of dire events which brought the Church into renewed conflict with the civil authority. Right up to the terrible crisis at the beginning of the fourteenth century the popes held fast by their claims. Innocent IV (1243–1254) expressed them more categorically even than had Innocent III; and Boniface VIII in his famous Bull *Unam Sanctam* (1302) reaffirmed the Church's right to wield both swords.

The havoc caused by these contending ambitions may incline us to judge severely of the doctrine involved, to condemn the notion of a "theocratic Utopia" which is so repugnant to our psychology, and which the Church has now abandoned.[4] We must not forget, however, that the popes were activated by lofty intentions; they were not led on by vanity, but by a profound and lively faith in their supernatural mission, and by legitimate pride in bearing witness to the Holy Spirit.

The theory was acceptable to the medieval mind; it seemed to follow naturally upon a universal faith, and to crown the grand ideal of Christendom. "It corresponded to men's aspirations at the same time as it safeguarded Christian justice and created law in that society of Christian nations which formed medieval Christendom."[5] That it did not succeed was not due to lack of goodwill or of right intention; there was a much deeper cause. "We have been appointed prince over all the world," wrote Innocent III; but a more authoritative voice than his had long since murmured: "My kingdom is not of this world"—and thereby given him an answer.

6. FREDERICK BARBAROSSA

LESS than thirty years after the Concordat of Worms the question of primacy emerged from the realm of theoretical discussion into the harsh light

---

4. The present attitude of the Church is quite different. Leo XIII, in his encyclical *Immortale Dei* of November 1, 1885, expressly declared that the temporal and the spiritual power are sovereign, each in its own sphere which is bounded by clearly defined limits.
5. These words were written by Mgr. Arquillière, a leading authority on this problem.

of day. "Since by Divine Providence," wrote Frederick Barbarossa, "I call
myself and *am* Emperor of the Romans, I have but the shadow of power
unless I govern Rome." Was he going to revive the pretensions of Charlemagne and the Ottos? The popes could not agree to that.

Frederick had succeeded to the German throne in 1152, at the age of
thirty years. His sense of grandeur and his passion for glory were strengthened by remarkable gifts. Tall, upright, and slim, he was the very type of
those young Germans in whom moral instability combines with physical
fitness to further their ambition and combative instinct. There was nothing
about him to suggest the complex personalities of his son and grandson; he
was a soldier, a leader of men, a creature of boundless energy, though not
without intelligence and judgment. We cannot but admire his character,
in which cruelty could not overshadow an essential nobility, and in which
violence ran side by side with generosity. A firm believer, he was devout and
charitable; his faith was never in question, even at the height of his struggle
with the Holy See. He had a clear skin, keen blue eyes, well-formed red lips,
and fine teeth surrounded by a thick beard with glints of gold and flame.
"Barbarossa"—Red Beard—the Italians called him; the nickname passed
into history, and from 1152 until 1190 the political scene was dominated by the tall figure of Frederick I Barbarossa, the greatest of the German
emperors.

For thirty years the Germanic world had been in eclipse. Henry V's death
without issue in 1125 was followed by a period of confusion, during which
feudal ambition had enjoyed free rein. Three families had vied for supremacy: the house of *Saxony*, which had threatened the imperial government
since the minority of Henry IV; the house of *Welf*, which had held the hereditary dukedom of Bavaria since 1170, and whose power extended over a wide
area around Lake Constance; and finally the house of *Hohenstaufen*, which
was also known by its territorial name of *Weiblingen*. The rivalry between
"Guelfs" and "Ghibellines" (as the Italians pronounced "Welf" and "Weiblingen") had made way for the accession of Lothair (1125–1137); but on
the latter's death, a Ghibelline, Conrad III (1138–1152), had quickly overcome his adversaries, assumed the crown, and put down an insurrection of

the Guelfs. Conrad's victory was followed by a marriage between his brother and the widow of the vanquished leader. This union ended the struggle for the time being, and from it Frederick was born. Half Ghibelline and half Guelf, he seemed predestined to lead a reunited Germany in a career of magnificent achievement.

Meanwhile, the papacy also had lost something of its prestige. Rome, together with the whole Christian world, had passed through a period of storm and stress. On the death of Calixtus II an antipope had opposed Honorius II, upon whose death Innocent II had been confronted with another, Anacletus. The result had been more than ten years of schism, to heal which St. Bernard had laboured with all the might of his authority.[6] Two insignificant popes had followed, Celestine II and Lucius II. The Cistercian Eugenius III (1145–1153) had done much to rehabilitate the papacy, to strengthen the moral and intellectual life of Christendom, to revive enthusiasm for the crusade, and to bring about the submission of heretics. But after him the aged Anastasius IV (1153–1154) lacked strength to withstand the German king.

The Italian situation had been complicated by two new elements.

(1) Roger I was succeeded by his son Roger II (1101–1154), an able diplomat and warrior, a true descendant of Tancred de Hauteville. With him the Norman adventure reached its high-water mark: conqueror, then heir, of his cousin William, Roger II unified southern Italy regardless of papal protests. Honorius II intervened; but his army was beaten, and Roger was invested (1128) with the duchy of Apulia at Benevento amid barbaric splendour and the glare of torches. In spite of this success, he took advantage of difficulties created by the schism of Anacletus. Notwithstanding several appeals addressed to him at Salerno by St. Bernard, he continued to support the antipope, and was crowned king on December 23, 1130. On the death of Anacletus he raised up another antipope, Victor IV; but the latter quickly submitted to Innocent II. This pope, too, attempted to break his adversary by force of arms; but he was decisively beaten, and obliged to invest Roger

---

6. See Chapter III, section 7.

as King of Sicily, Duke of Apulia, and Prince of Capua. Henceforward the   235
Norman kingdom, which was subject to a discipline unusual at that time,
became an important factor in Italian politics.

(2) The beginning of the twelfth century witnessed a movement towards
communal independence. There was fierce hatred between neighbouring cities; Milan detested Pavia, while Venice, Genoa, and Pisa vowed one another
to destruction. Within the towns themselves, also, antagonism ran high; and
a bitter feud between the Montecchi and Cappelletti has been immortalized
in the legend of Romeo and Juliet. Both Church and Empire were hostile to
the growth of free towns, with whom they were constantly embroiled; and
the quarrel between Guelfs and Ghibellines was transferred to the peninsula,
where it came to represent the struggle of papal against anti-papal factions.

In Rome itself the communal movement issued in extremes of violence.
Until then the Pope alone had exercised authority, nominating the city prefect, directing the police, and trying criminal cases. The "Roman consuls,"
despite their grandiose title, were no more than his hirelings. But, powerful
though he was, the Sovereign Pontiff had numerous enemies, including the
Roman aristocracy who looked back with regret to the old days when they
made popes, and the common folk whom anything could rouse. In 1143
a mob stormed the Capitol and elected a Senate. Lucius II was mortally
wounded in a fruitless attempt to recapture this strong-point, and in 1145
Eugenius III agreed to recognize the Senate. The situation deteriorated still
further with the appearance in Rome of a brilliant demagogue. Arnold of
Brescia was an austere canon regular, obsessed with apocalyptic dreams. His
ideas were not unlike those which had inspired the generosity of Paschal
II; but they included social and political elements which made him heir
to the Patarines, a ferocious rabble of self-styled reformers who had caused
much trouble in Italy during the preceding century. Arnold insisted that
temporal power must be exercised by none but laymen; the clergy must surrender their wealth and landed property, and live henceforth exclusively on
tithes and public charity! Condemned by his bishop in 1139, he had gone
to France, where he was welcomed by his old friend Abélard. St. Bernard,
however, had secured his expulsion from that kingdom, and the champion

of revolution came to Rome at the very moment (1146) when Eugenius III was obliged to leave the Eternal City. His inflammatory tirades against ecclesiastical abuses made a deep impression. Most of the common people, and even a number of the clergy, rallied to his side. Arnold became a sort of dictator, and excited the mob with promises to restore the ancient glory of their city. The Republic of all-conquering Rome was to be revived along with the Senate, the equestrian order, and the tribunate; and even Eugenius III was obliged to compromise with the fiery tribune when he returned from exile. A third form of universal domination was thus conceived in opposition both to the papacy and to the Empire.

Immediately after his accession, Frederick Barbarossa, following the example of Charlemagne, turned his gaze towards Rome. His consuming ambition would not be satisfied by the unification of his German and Italian dominions; what he had in mind from start to finish was nothing less than to restore the worldwide authority of the Roman Empire. With this end in view he proclaimed himself *Romanorum imperator semper Augustus, divus, piissimus, imperator et gubernator urbi et orbi.* Charlemagne had never gone that far. In 1133 Frederick had inherited the kingdom of Arles, a remnant of ancient Lotharingia, to which there were added later not only Provence, but also Franche-Comté, Burgundy, the Lyonnais, Viennois, western Switzerland, Savoy, and Dauphiné. He did not simply annex these French territories; they came to him through marriage with the heiress of Upper Burgundy in 1156, when he assumed the crown of Burgundy at Arles. He regarded all sovereign princes simply as his lieutenants. Boleslav of Poland agreed to kneel before him; the rulers of Hungary and Denmark acknowledged themselves his vassals; and he himself created the kingdom of Bohemia by conferring on Duke Ladislaus a golden crown which had in it more of symbol than reality. Only the kings of France and England, Louis VII and Henry II, refused submission, though they displayed no small degree of respect towards this mighty prince. Frederick himself referred to them as "provincial governors" or "petty kings."

A man of Barbarossa's outlook necessarily viewed the Pope's claim to primacy as an obstacle to be removed at any cost. The government of Rome was indispensable to the accomplishment of his grandiose design; two years after his accession, therefore, he set to work. It seemed for a moment that he might reach agreement with the Roman demagogue; for Arnold of Brescia, together with the "Senate and People of Rome," recognized Frederick and offered him the crown of empire. Barbarossa's reply was contained in a celebrated letter: "Why vaunt the glory of your City, the wisdom of your Senate, the quality of your youth? Rome is no longer to be found in Rome. Would you see again her former greatness, the majesty of senatorial purple, the strength and discipline of an equestrian order? Behold our State. Those things belong to us already in virtue of our imperial dignity. We are your lawful master."

The Roman Commune could do little in face of the German army; the aged Pope Anastasius lay dying, and it appeared that Frederick must have his way. But at this critical juncture Providence sent one who would call a halt to his pretensions. Nicholas Breakspear was an Englishman, of rough exterior but keen intelligence, tenacious as a mastiff. His father, it was said, had been an ignorant peasant who ended his days as a lay-brother in some religious house; but he himself had grown up among clerics, and had become a canon regular of Saint-Ruf at Avignon. Eugenius III had created him cardinal and sent him as legate to Scandinavia.

Anastasius IV died on December 3, 1154. Forty-eight hours later a unanimous vote of the Sacred College elected Breakspear, who took the name of Adrian IV and reigned until 1159.

Frederick was at this time in northern Italy. He had assembled his vassals and representatives of the cities in the plain of Roncaglia near Piacenza, where he promised reforms and announced his intention of assuming the Iron Crown of Lombardy. After that, he would go to Rome. At present his interests coincided with those of the Pope; for Barbarossa had no love for Arnold, and Adrian IV had just laid the Eternal City under an interdict following the assassination of a cardinal. But their apparent friendship could not disguise mutual suspicion. At their first meeting, Frederick declined to perform the office of marshal by leading the Pope's horse and holding his stirrup, which for centuries had been a duty of strict etiquette; nor would he do so until it was explained to him that the tradition went back as far as Charlemagne.

Accompanied by the Pope, Frederick then set out for Rome. He captured the Leonine city by surprise, but the commune still occupied the remainder. The imperial coronation took place on June 18 behind locked doors in St. Peter's; and when the populace, warned by the soldiers' acclamation, rushed to the basilica, they were driven back before a murderous charge. "See," said one of the Emperor's suite, "you get iron instead of gold; that's the coin we Germans use." Not long afterwards, Arnold of Brescia was seized and hanged; his corpse was burned, and its ashes thrown into the Tiber. The Pope re-established his authority upon the ruins of the Republic, and Frederick departed, alarmed by the ravages of malaria among his troops; but his arrogance and cruelty had aroused general mistrust.

Relieved of his embarrassing associate, Adrian IV took stock of his position. He needed allies. Milan, the chief city of Lombardy, viewed the Emperor with feelings similar to those of the Pope. Moreover, William the Bad of Sicily (1154–1166),[7] who had been at loggerheads with the Holy See and had routed a joint force of papal and Byzantine troops under Manuel Comnenus, was alarmed by the German menace. Adrian IV gladly confirmed the titles and privileges inherited from his father, including an unusual degree of independence enjoyed by Sicily in ecclesiastical affairs. The imperial court looked with a jaundiced eye on a *rapprochement* whose significance was plain for all to see. After Barbarossa himself, the soul of antipapal policy was the chancellor, Rainald of Dassel, a diplomatic adventurer who had scant respect for promises; and tension between the two masters of Christendom rapidly increased.

The first clash arose from the Emperor's arrest of the Archbishop of Lund. Adrian wrote an outspoken letter, which was carried by two legates to Besançon. Frederick was holding a Diet there in the spring of 1157, and the assembly treated this epistle as an insult. In ambiguous terms, which were no doubt intentional, the Pope reminded Frederick of the benefits

---

7.   He was the son of Roger II, and merited his nickname.

(*beneficia*) which the latter owed to him, including the imperial crown
which he had conferred (*collata*). Rainald of Dassel protested at this outrage. *Beneficia!* That was the word used to describe fiefs granted by an
overlord to his vassal. The Diet re-echoed his indignation; but the legates
refused to be intimidated. "From whom," asked Cardinal Roland, "does the
Emperor hold his crown if not from the Pope?" Upon which, an equerry
rushed at him with drawn sword, and would certainly have killed him, had
not Frederick himself stepped between them. This outburst of wrath may
have suggested to Adrian that he had gone too far; or he may have thought
his gesture had achieved its end. At any rate, he made it clear that he had
used the word *beneficia* in the sense of benefits and not of fiefs (*beneficium
non feudum sed bonum factum*). The legates, however, were forbidden to
visit Germany, and Rainald set about the organization of antipapal propaganda. High words were exchanged with growing frequency, and war was
soon inevitable.

The issue at stake became apparent at the Diet of Roncaglia (1158).
Frederick engaged the four most celebrated jurists of his time to expound
the doctrine of imperial absolutism as conceived by Roman Law, which was
then on the flood-tide of its renascence.[8] By way of giving effect to his thesis, which was diametrically opposed to the papal view, the Emperor next
decreed that Italy was to be reorganized on the basis of Justinian's *Pandects*
and Byzantine methods. He insisted on the imperial authority, forbade the
federation of towns, and even provided for a common coinage. A grandiose
plan, indeed, but one which could not be applied except by force. Such were
the opening moves in this titanic struggle.

In order to subdue the Italian cities, Frederick placed them under the
rule of officials known as podestats. Genoa, Brescia, Cremona, and Piacenza
became restless. Milan openly revolted, and for two and a half years held
out against the imperial army. Supplies failed, and she was obliged to capitulate in the spring of 1162; not, however, before the Milanese had solemnly
destroyed the symbol of their freedom, the *carroccio*, a car drawn by four

---

8. See Volume 2, Chapter VIII, section 10.

oxen and carrying the communal standard. Frederick vented his cruel rage by delivering the whole city, with its churches, to the flames. The population was dispersed and condemned to forced labour, while German soldiers amused themselves playing bowls with the heads of slaughtered prisoners.

From Rome, Adrian IV had watched the conflict with grave anxiety. The Countess Matilda had died, and her estates had been seized by the Duke of Bavaria, notwithstanding her bequest to the Holy See. A number of important archbishoprics, including those of Cologne and Ravenna, were granted to imperial favourites; and when the Pope protested, Rainald answered that possession of Rome was necessary for the fulfilment of plans adopted at Roncaglia, and that the Emperor would soon take possession of the city. Adrian fled for refuge to Anagni, and was about to excommunicate Frederick when he died on September 1, 1159.

By an overwhelming majority, the conclave elected none other than Cardinal Roland, who had braved the German's wrath at Besançon. The new Pope, Alexander III (1159–1181), was gentle but firm, a leading jurist, and a brilliant diplomat such as Tuscany had frequently produced. The Emperor did not misjudge his adversary; but three dissenting cardinals had elected an antipope, Victor IV, who was recognized forthwith by Barbarossa.

In the long run, however, this attempt to create schism met with no success. Germany alone rallied to the antipope. As a refugee at Salerno, Alexander III was treated with the utmost respect by Louis VII; he was also recognized by Henry II of England, and, in fact, by almost the whole of Western Christendom. Frederick, though shocked by this display of unanimity, could not draw back. When Victor IV died he was replaced by Paschal III,[9] who was in turn succeeded by yet another antipope, Calixtus III.

These puppets, however, were of no avail, and Alexander now resolved to show his hand. Returning to Rome in November 1165, he was welcomed as a liberator; and before long his diplomacy made him the centre of

---

9. Paschal III decided to canonize Charlemagne, whose bones had recently been discovered at Aix-la-Chapelle. Frederick had them deposited in a golden barrel surmounted by a tabernacle crowned with lamps. Gigantic feasting took place on this occasion (December 29, 1165) at Aix, the magnificence of which astonished contemporaries.

resistance. Sicily confirmed its alliance, Venice asked for one. Several urban 241
leagues came into existence, one with Verona, another with Cremona as its
nucleus; and Milan, now rising from its ashes, joined the latter. Alexander
managed with great skill to form them into a single bloc with Venice, and
the alliance was governed by a council of Rectors drawn from sixteen towns.
The Pope had given his answer to the Diet of Roncaglia.

For the fourth time (1166) Frederick crossed the Alps and moved
through northern Italy. Entering Rome, he conceived the strange idea of
a second coronation, while Alexander fled, disguised as a pilgrim. But the
Emperor was overtaken by a catastrophe that seemed like a divine retribu-
tion; for a terrible epidemic carried off half his army and many of his close
associates, including Rainald. With great difficulty he made his way back to
Germany. Here the Empress assumed control, while he escaped into hiding
and thus saved his life (August–September 1167). In the following year an
attempt was made to bar future German invasions by the erection of a new
fortress at the confluence of the Tanaro and Dormida. It was called Alexandria after the Sovereign Pontiff. "A town of straw!" Barbarossa exclaimed
contemptuously; but all his fire could not subdue it.

For the next seven years Frederick nursed his wrath, but his third antipope did no more to secure for him the protection of Heaven than the
other two had done. In 1174 he undertook a final expedition which ended
in disaster. His subjects were tired of these costly descents upon Italy; he
scarcely managed to assemble eight thousand men, and they were defeated before Alexandria. He summoned reinforcements, but his new army
amounted to no more than six thousand. On May 29, 1176, at Legnano,
between Lake Maggiore and Milan, the city militia and papal forces, num-
bering ten thousand men, encountered Barbarossa's host. During an action
which lasted for several hours, Frederick was thrown from his horse, and
was only saved in the nick of time by one of his officers, who gave him his
own charger. The imperial standard-bearer lay dead upon the field, the standard fell into enemy hands, and the imperial troops disbanded.

Legnano is an important date in medieval history, for it confirmed the
primacy of the Holy See. After signing a treaty of peace, the Emperor assisted

242 Alexander to mount his horse, while the Pope, as a sign of forgiveness, gave him the kiss of peace. Never, perhaps, had a successor of St. Peter appeared so truly great; and the third Lateran (eleventh ecumenical) Council, which met in 1179, sealed his triumph.[10] But the troubles which disturbed Alexander's pontificate were not yet concluded. Barbarossa was meditating his revenge. He had prepared his way by the Peace of Constance, by exacting an oath from the Italian communes, by heaping favours upon the city of Milan, by defeating Henry the Lion in Germany, and by reaching an understanding with Sicily. Rome was once more on the verge of revolution when the Pope died in exile at Civitacastellana on August 30, 1181. But six years later Christendom was shocked by the fall of Jerusalem to the arms of Saladin; and Frederick Barbarossa, who was fundamentally a good Christian, set out on the crusade. It may be, also, that he hoped thereby to satisfy a thirst for power which he had failed to quench in Italy. He never returned.[11]

7. THE ZENITH OF THE PAPACY

THE dream of imperialism was not submerged with Barbarossa in the river Cydnus; his son and grandson both revived it, though in a different form. These two men, in whom there was a streak of genius, realized that so long as central Europe was a prey to anarchy it could no longer serve as the foundation of that colossal edifice which they intended to create. Moreover, in consequence of an economic revolution, the gateway to power was now in the Mediterranean and on the Channel coast. Henry VI, and after him Frederick II, conceived the idea of a Mediterranean empire. They were inspired not so much by the tradition of Charlemagne as by that of Trajan, Hadrian, and Constantine. Antagonism between the Holy See and the Empire assumed fresh significance: Italy was no longer the key to papal

---

10. It was the third Lateran Council that decreed, among other things, the necessity of a two-thirds majority at papal elections.
11. See Volume 2, Chapter XI, section 7.

independence. The papacy hoped to preserve the unity and orthodoxy of Christendom by increased centralization of power in its own hands; while the emperors sought to extend their authority over the whole Mediterranean area by reconciling a variety of religions and by establishing a civil authority independent of the Church.

As a matter of fact, the nucleus of this idea may well have been present to the mind of Barbarossa when, in 1184, he arranged a marriage between his eldest son Henry and Constance of Sicily. Ten years older than her husband, who never loved her, she was the posthumous daughter of Roger II and heiress to the Norman kingdom. Although she was under religious vows, Pope Lucius III (1181–1185) did not openly object; and when his successor, Urban III (1185–1187), a Crivelli who, like all Milanese, detested Frederick, ventured to protest, he was silenced by an invasion of the papal states. The popes had good cause to fear this policy of encirclement.

The situation became still more ominous when Henry VI succeeded his father in 1190, at the age of twenty-four. Ambitious, short of stature, pale, and with a lofty brow, he had inherited all his mother's Provençal refinement. He had scarcely mounted the throne when he descended upon Sicily in order to lay hands on the inheritance of his father-in-law, William II, which was disputed by Tancred, an illegitimate brother of William I. After an initial defeat, he was crowned Emperor by Celestine III, and returned to continue the struggle. But success was not easy; the Sicilians had no wish to be Germanized, while the Pope, who had begrudged him the imperial crown, secretly upheld the cause of Tancred. It was only when the latter died, in 1194, that Henry won the day. His enemies were burned in pitch, flayed alive, crushed between boards, or buried alive up to the neck and their heads shorn off like grass. The Empress Constance, a true Norman at heart, expressed her disgust at these abominations. She was promptly accused of adultery, and he who was supposed to be her lover suffered death with a circlet of red-hot iron fastened round his head. A centralized government, modelled upon that of the Capetians, made Sicily as it were the pattern of a modern monarchy; and the German emperor, in possession of rich territories, could set about the realization of his vast design, of which he made no secret. He married his brother, Philip of Swabia, to a daughter of the Basileus Isaac Angelus; and when the latter was dethroned in 1195, he gave out that he would be "revenged on these Byzantine traitors." Then he took the Cross, hoping that his army would return victorious from Jerusalem by way of Constantinople. Contrary to international law and without the slightest justification, he imprisoned Richard I of England on his way back from the crusade and forced him to do homage, tactics which gave Philip Augustus food for thought. Step by step, it seemed, Henry would become master of the whole white race; the popes at any rate could do nothing to stop him. Neither Gregory VIII, who occupied the chair of Peter for only two months, nor Clement III, who had to meet renewed troubles at Rome, nor the venerable Celestine III, who was elected at the age of eighty-five, left much evidence of their passage through the Lateran. Providence, however, intervened to snap the thread of Henry's dreams and destiny. A pernicious fever—aided, so rumour said, by poison from the hands of Constance— carried off the young Emperor on September 28, 1197. He was thirty-two. His fleet, which had gathered at Messina, never sailed for the conquest of the East.

A few weeks later, on January 8, 1198, there ascended Peter's throne one of the most powerful figures in the medieval Church, Lothair of Segni, Innocent III. His age, his nobility, his wide culture, all those many gifts which have been recognized by later historians no less than by his contemporaries,[12] enabled him at the most favourable juncture to play a vital part. Through eighteen years and with tireless energy he acted on the principle that the Holy See enjoys absolute supremacy.[13] Perhaps his knowledge of men was not his strongest point; perhaps, too, his feudal origins prevented him from seeing the real issue and sometimes caused his view to seem outmoded. This much, however, is quite certain: he had the interest of Christendom at heart; he was determined to make God victorious; and, even in the exercise of a theocratic policy, when pride might well have had its say, he

12. See Chapter IV, section 7 (*ad init.*).
13. See section 5 of the present chapter.

never forgot that he was simply an instrument of God, and showed himself a humble Christian.

Innocent III found Rome in the hands of an insolent commune, the papal states occupied by Germans, and Sicily administered by imperial officials. If Henry VI had been alive, it would have been impossible to remedy this perilous situation, but his death made all the difference. The Romans had no allies, and Innocent took advantage of this fact to destroy the Senate (which was reduced to two, and then to a single member), and to deprive the Prefect of his powers. The commune retained its autonomy, its assemblies on the Capitol, its army and finances, and even its right to coin money, which it exercised concurrently with the Pope; but so long as Innocent sat in Peter's chair, demagogy stood no chance in Rome.

The papal states were recovered; Spoleto, Ancona, and Ravenna were reoccupied; and Innocent was supported by the Tuscan cities in driving the Emperor's vassals from the former territories of Matilda. Having pacified the north, he accomplished a master-stroke of diplomacy in Sicily. In order to safeguard the rights of her young son Frederick Roger against the Germans, the Empress Constance offered to recognize the Pope as overlord. She died soon afterwards, bequeathing the guardianship of her child to Innocent III, whose legates henceforward administered on his behalf a splendid kingdom which in times past had caused the Holy See much anxiety.

Nor was the situation in Germany less favourable. Young Frederick Roger was styled "King of the Romans"; but the princes did not want a child as their sovereign. Some had already chosen Otto of Brunswick, others Philip of Swabia. Innocent III did not hesitate between the Ghibelline Philip, who was arrogant like all the Hohenstaufen, and Otto, a Guelf, who seemed accommodating and full of good intentions. Philip had been excommunicated; but in choosing Otto the Pope chose one who, though a brave soldier, was unreliable. Besides, Otto lacked the financial resources of his adversary, and was therefore a less valuable ally. He suffered one defeat after another; but Philip, who had begun overtures to the Holy See, was assassinated in a family quarrel. Whereupon Otto, recognized by the whole of Germany, asked for the imperial crown, which Innocent conferred upon him in 1209.

"Well beloved son," the Pope wrote to him, "behold us united in one heart and soul! Who can resist us, now that we bear the two swords which the Apostles once showed our Lord, saying: 'Behold two swords,' to which our Lord replied: 'It is enough!'" Applying a theory familiar to all, Innocent III undoubtedly intended to show that he was owner of the temporal sword and was merely entrusting it to Otto. But events soon gave the lie to these fair words. If Otto had seemed modest and conciliatory before his coronation, he now revealed himself as a worthy successor to Barbarossa. He occupied the Tuscan cities, placed his own vassals in charge of Ancona and Spoleto, and set his podestats over Vicenza, Ferrara, and Brescia. He also claimed homage from the Prefect of Rome, and even led an army as far south as Naples. Innocent III retaliated by excommunicating the Emperor in 1210, and recognizing as king his own ward Frederick Roger, who was then aged seventeen and took the style of Frederick II. Finally, the Pope took vigorous steps to counteract Otto's advantage by rousing Italian patriotism against German interference, but chiefly by siding with the French king Philip Augustus in his quarrel with Otto's ally, John of England. The French victory at Bouvines (July 27, 1214) was no less his own, and the fourth ecumenical council held at the Lateran in 1215 crowned this triumph.

The papacy was once again victorious, and Innocent stood forth, in accordance with his theocratic doctrine, as the first man of his age. But Otto's strength was as yet by no means exhausted, and continued to preoccupy his thoughts. Meanwhile, however, he laboured to reform the Church and launched Christendom against the Albigenses. He exercised sovereign rights in England, created the kingdom of Portugal, and imposed his authority on Aragon as also, to some extent, upon Leon and Castile. His influence was felt in Norway, in Sweden, on the Baltic shores, and in Poland, while Hungary became a papal fief. Innocent, in fact, was overlord of western Europe. It may be that Christendom could not otherwise have opposed the forces of disintegration, but how long could this situation last? Could the priesthood really govern the world? The answer was to come from Frederick II (1218–1250).

Otto IV was gathered to his fathers on May 19, 1218, two years after
the death of Innocent. Frederick was now master of Germany. Already king
of the Romans, and heir to Sicily, he held all the trump cards, and knew
how to play them. Hitherto he had shown himself so gentle, so polished,
always ready to obey the Holy Father. If there was talk of a crusade—why, of
course, he would join up at once. He had been told to create a diversion in
Germany on Otto's rear, and had carried out that task with undeniable courage. How, then, could Innocent have suspected on his deathbed that this
beloved youth would prove an even more dangerous enemy of the Church
than Barbarossa?

Frederick II in no way resembled his great Swabian ancestor. He was
so small, he looked so frail; even as a young man he stooped, and became
prematurely bald. An Arab chronicler, in fact, remarked that he would not
have been worth ten shillings as a slave; but his face revealed great strength
of character, and few could endure his piercing gaze. Highly strung, unstable, stubborn yet easily discouraged, his personality was a mass of contradictions. He delighted to recall his Norman-Sicilian ancestry, compounded
of high courage and strong passion. That was his mother's legacy; he was
the son of Constance, a Viking, who was said to have been revenged upon
her spouse by poison. Frederick's intelligence was of the highest order, but
he wanted restraint and, still more, the sense of personal guilt. He was too
prone to believe that cunning compensated for lack of principle. His energy
swept all before it; he was always ready to exert himself to the utmost, and
one of his contemporaries, torn between admiration and disgust, referred to
him as "the Wonder of the World." Frederick was a genius, but unbalanced.

The most surprising note in his character, one that became more apparent with age and experience, was his attitude towards religion. He is among
the very few medieval men in whom we can detect a strain of scepticism.
All religions were equal in his eyes—equal in their worthlessness. While
thirsting for knowledge, he would accept none but experimental and logical
demonstration. The Muslim scholars whom he invited to his court introduced him to the study of physics and chemistry, and thereby persuaded
him that Christian dogmas had no meaning. Among the numerous legends

which have gathered round his name, one tells how he shut up a man in a hermetically sealed barrel in order to prove that when it was opened no soul would fly up to heaven! It is not surprising that his contemporaries took him for antichrist, "the beast rising from the sea, its mouth full of blasphemy, with the claws of a bear, the body of a leopard, and the fury of a lion."

Nevertheless it is facile to regard him as a commonplace anti-Christian, or a mere fanatic. Though logical enough, he was extremely complex. He had been brought up under the Church's wing and never created an anti-pope, but he was excommunicated several times. He was pleasure-loving, but still admired St. Francis of Assisi. He was more or less an atheist, but made war on heretics. Though anathematized by the Holy See, he went on the crusade, even though, as a crusader, he had dealings with the Muslims and remained on friendly terms with them. Nor must it be forgotten that he died and was buried in the Cistercian cowl. No character of the Middle Ages is quite so enigmatic, and none, we must admit, has quite his fascination for those interested in psychology.

The Church would clearly have her work cut out to handle such a man. "The whole earth," he used to say, "looks forward to imperial domination." And again, "Is not the Emperor the embodiment of Law?" His chancellor, Pierre de la Vigne, later addressed him as "Caesar, bright Light of the World." Like his grandfather, he wished to be a second Charlemagne; like his father, he dreamed of reviving the ancient Mediterranean empire of Rome, "her victorious eagles, her fasces, and her triumphal wreaths." Conflict between him and the papacy was inevitable.

Frederick II was hardly seated on the throne when he began to prepare Sicily as the starting-point of his tremendous scheme. He was passionately fond of that island where natural beauty and historical tradition formed a perfect synthesis, where four civilizations one after another—Greek, Roman, Byzantine, and Muslim—had left their impress and were ultimately fused in the crucible of Norman culture. Palermo, his capital, became a glorious city with its crown of towers and domes, and with the fragrance of its gardens. The glow of golden mosaics mingled with delicate Arab lattice-work; in the basilicas, marble columns supported cupolas imitated from those of Byzantium; and gothic churches were enriched with Saracenic ornament. Frederick lived like a caliph, surrounded with Muslim sages and the mamelukes of his bodyguard. He even kept a harem full of oriental beauties. Within four or five years Sicily had become a centralized monarchy, where the least resistance met with massacre and deportation. The Constitution of Melfi formed a code inspired by Byzantium and rivalling the masterpieces of Roman Law, while the system of taxation was rigorously enforced.

Frederick turned next to Germany. Realizing that he could not annihilate the baronage, he sought to divide it. For this purpose he relied upon the Holy See, which had supported him in his contest with Otto, as also upon the Teutonic Order, which was then in its heyday and whose Grand Master, Hermann of Salza, was his willing agent. Apart from the short-lived revolt of his son Henry, his dominions in this part of the world caused him no anxiety. His marriage with Isabel of England enabled him to keep France at arm's length, while he employed Raymond IV of Toulouse as a further threat to the Capetian monarchy. He was virtually omnipotent; and when the newly formed Lombard League defied him in 1237, it was crushed by Swabian and Muslim cavalry at Cortenuova. The carroccio was captured and borne in triumph to the Capitol. And now, with Machiavellian cunning, Frederick strengthened his hold on Italy by quartering German veterans in the towns and using local collaborators, Ghibellines, to carry out his policy.

The papacy, meanwhile, had made no move. Honorius III (1216–1227), convinced that an understanding was possible with a ruler who was so emphatic as to the necessity of reform, who persecuted heresy, and who swore three times to take the Cross, had even crowned him Emperor (November 22, 1220). But it is not unlikely that, towards the end of his life, Honorius realized the truth. His successor, at any rate, was under no delusion; it was not the first time a militant and resolute Pope had followed a peaceful trimmer. Gregory IX (1227–1241) was none other than the great Cardinal Hugolin, whose vigour had not been impaired, let alone destroyed, by the advent of his eightieth year. This fiery old man could never have sat by and watched Frederick entangle the whole of Italy in his web.

The Emperor was vulnerable in that he had not kept his oath to take the Cross. Gregory therefore excommunicated him and, when Frederick at last set sail, followed him even to Jerusalem with maledictions because of his extraordinary behaviour in negotiating with instead of fighting Islam. In due time the Pope learned of Frederick's success in the Holy Land, and for a short period the two were reconciled. But their enmity quickly revived. Following the defeat of the Lombard League, Gregory allied himself with Genoa and Venice; he excommunicated his adversary a third time when the latter occupied papal territory in Sardinia, and finally absolved the Emperor's subjects from their allegiance.

But the days had gone when one word from the Pope could bring an emperor to Canossa. Frederick II was firmly in the saddle, and his excommunication proved of no effect. How, indeed, could it restrain the mamelukes whom Frederick had let loose upon the papal states? Driven from Rome, which was on the verge of revolution, Gregory trembled as he beheld the imperial armies sweep through Italy unchecked, and Frederick name his bastard Enzio governor of the peninsula.[14] In desperation, he offered the imperial crown to St. Louis for his brother; but the French king prudently declined to thrust himself into a hornets' nest. At this juncture, the Mongol invasion under Genghis Khan struck terror into Europe. The yellow cavalry, having annihilated the Russians, the Poles, and the Teutonic Knights, rode headlong for Vienna and the Adriatic. Rivalry between the two heads of Christendom looked very much like double suicide; but how to find a basis of agreement? Gregory resolved to break his adversary, and summoned a council. Most of the prelates who were to take part embarked at Genoa, but they were intercepted by the imperial navy; and the fathers of the council, instead of passing judgment on the rebel, were forced to kick their heels in prison until such time as he might choose to free them. The Pope died on August 22, 1241, at the age of almost one hundred, and it seemed the temporal power must triumph.

14. Frederick's eldest, and legitimate, son Henry had rebelled against his father, but in vain. He was now dying of grief, a prisoner in Apulia.

For two years Frederick II dominated the West. Gregory's successor, 251 Celestine IV, reigned for only fifteen days; and two years elapsed before the election of his successor, for the Sacred College was a prey to pestilence and harassed by imperial intrigue. Besides, the Emperor assumed full responsibility for the defence of Europe, and devised a strategy so remarkable that it exhausted the effort of the Mongols and obliged them to withdraw. At the same time, he strengthened his hold upon his dominions, purposely setting aside the feudal lords of Germany, and even the ecclesiastical princes, in favour of the towns whose fortunes he established. But the tireless adventurer was growing old. His hatred of the Church had become an obsession: he persecuted the mendicant Orders, bullied the Teutonic Knights, and boasted to the Egyptian ambassador that he had founded a caliphate in direct line from the Prophet, "far superior to the absurd Christian institution of electing anyone at random as their head."

The situation, however, altered unexpectedly. St. Louis would not stand idle and watch a man like Frederick II obtain control of Europe. He began by requesting him to release the French cardinals whom he had imprisoned. "Let not your imperial wisdom surrender to the intoxication of your own sweet will," wrote Louis to the despot of Palermo; "for the kingdom of France is not so weak that it cannot kick against the spur." He then called upon the Sacred College to proceed with the election of a Pope.

Innocent IV (1243–1254) was a lawyer, a Genoese aristocrat, and a man of unrelenting determination, who was destined to save the Church at a moment when her cause seemed hopeless. It was no mere chance that he had assumed the name of a great theocratic pope, and his encyclical *Aeger cui levia* formulated the doctrine of papal primacy in terms more definitive than those even of Innocent III. He was prepared for mortal combat with the Emperor.

Innocent took up residence at Genoa for greater security, and summoned a council to deal with Frederick II. In vain did Frederick plead the yellow peril which he must oppose, and the renewed Muslim threat which had culminated in the recent fall of Jerusalem to the Sultan of Egypt. The council met at Lyons in 1245; Frederick dared not retaliate for fear of

French intervention, although Lyons was an imperial city. The assembly would not even hear the message of this "Proteus," as the Pope described him. A lengthy indictment set forth his usurpations and his crimes. Convicted of perjury, sacrilege, and heresy, Frederick II was excommunicated and declared no longer emperor or king.

This sentence had profound repercussions. The Emperor was desperate, and tried to enlist the support of other rulers by pretending that their interests were identical with his own. Then he had recourse to social revolution in the name of evangelical principles, but failed completely. Together with his son Conrad IV, whose election he had secured, he managed to hold his own in Germany; but the patriotism of the Italian towns proved fatal to his cause. Parma revolted, and the disaffection spread to Florence, Milan, Ferrara, and Mantua. Frederick tried to recapture Parma, but his camp was surprised and he was obliged to flee. This spelled ruin. Enzio, his beloved Enzio, was taken prisoner, and all his friends began to fade away, even the chancellor Pierre de la Vigne, whom he blinded in revenge. At the height of his rage, the beaten monarch was gathering his forces for a final throw when he was carried off by dysentery on December 13, 1250, in the camp of his Moorish troops.

Innocent IV declared the race of Hohenstaufen accursed, and Heaven heard his imprecation. Conrad IV died prematurely four years later (May 21, 1254), followed soon afterwards, on December 7, by his redoubtable opponent. Southern Italy was drenched in fire and blood through the rebellion of Manfred, an illegitimate son of Frederick by an Italian woman. But he was already doomed, and met his death at Beneventum in 1266 at the hands of French troops under Charles of Anjou, brother of St. Louis. His naked body was paraded through the streets astride an ass; and the tragic story closed with the execution of Conrad's sixteen-year-old son Conradin in 1268.

8. A DANGEROUS VICTORY

THE Church's victory, won at so great a cost, brought with it serious disadvantages. Scarcely had the papacy attained its zenith in the temporal sphere

than it was stricken wellnigh as grievously as its rival. The struggle of the   253
Priesthood and the Empire proved fatal to both.

There could be no doubt as to the Empire; after the deposition of Frederick II, a succession of puppets wore that most illustrious of crowns. First there was one William of Holland, set up by a couple of archbishops. On his death in 1256, seven princes met to elect an Emperor; they were the origin of an electoral college to whom the right henceforward belonged. These rulers had an eye to business, and put up the imperial throne for auction. Alfonso of Castile and Richard of Cornwall pretended to have obtained it; but so little importance was attached to their respective claims that no Pope would crown either of them. This period (1250–1273), when the throne was, to all intents and purposes, without an occupant, is generally known as the Great Interregnum. And even the election of Rudolph of Hapsburg (1273–1291), who was preferred by the Electors to Philip the Hardy, if only by reason of his weakness, did not terminate the imperial decadence. Both Rudolph and his son Albert I (1291–1308) failed to make the throne hereditary in the house of Austria, as did Henry VII (1308–1313) in that of Luxembourg, and Louis IV (1313–1347) in that of Bavaria. Germany and Italy, in the throes of feudal anarchy and communal unrest, were to find the heritage of Barbarossa, Henry VI, and Frederick II a long and painful burden.

Nor did the Holy See fare much better. There was no immediate cause to suspect that the papacy would not continue to dominate Christendom; but among the twelve popes who succeeded Innocent IV, few were equal to their task. Some, like Alexander IV (1254–1261), were no more than the puppets of unworthy counsellors. Some, like Nicholas III (1277–1280), were guided by their nephews. Others, like Urban IV (1261–1264), Clement IV (1265–1268), and Martin IV (1281–1285), were not, to say the least, of consummate ability. Providence seemed to bear a grudge against the papacy. Three pontiffs died in less than a year (1276–1277): the Dominican Innocent V, a nephew of Innocent IV; Adrian V, who reigned for only thirty-six days; and the unfortunate Portuguese John XXI, who was killed after a pontificate of six days when the ceiling of his room collapsed. Honorius IV

(1285–1287) befriended the University of Paris, and Nicholas IV (1288–1292), a Franciscan, was likewise interested in the advancement of studies; but neither had means or time to change the course of Peter's barque.

Only St. Gregory X, who was elected in 1271, had the qualities of a leader and a large-scale plan. He meant to revive the crusade, to end the Greek schism, and to reconcile the Ghibellines and Guelfs; but he reigned for no more than five years. A two-year interregnum (1292–1294), when the cardinals split up into gangs and fought one another in the streets, was followed by the curious election of Celestine V in 1294[15]; and these two events are characteristic of the spiritual disorder prevailing at the end of a century during which the papacy had been so great.

Its political influence continued to decline. In Germany, the towns asserted their independence, while the feudal lords prepared to strike a blow which fell in 1356, when the Pope was excluded from all share in the appointment of an emperor, and confirmed this decision by the Golden Bull. The lawlessness prevailing in the towns of northern Italy had similar results. Obedience to the Holy See was the object of perpetual conflict between Ghibellines and Guelfs. At Rome, there were repeated outbreaks of violence. Sicily had been conferred upon Charles of Anjou by the Holy See, which soon repented of its choice. That scatter-brained but ambitious ruler publicly opposed his Angevin cardinals to those of Italy, while his manifold injustice exasperated the Sicilians. When, therefore, on March 31, 1282, the bells of Palermo sounded the "Sicilian Vespers," resulting in the massacre of all Frenchmen resident in the island, the French Pope Martin IV was unable, even by means of excommunication, to prevent Peter of Aragon, Manfred's father-in-law, from assuming the Norman crown. The papacy had lost its ancient fief.

The Church's struggle and her hard-won victory had consequences even more profound, one of which was not at first apparent. The Popes, in order to achieve their goal, had been obliged to concentrate power in their own hands. By doing so, however, they had altered the ancient structure of a

---

15. See Volume 2, Chapter XIV, section 1.

Church which, though it had for centuries recognized the Roman primacy, had never considered that primacy synonymous with centralization. "An
instrument of reform, though useful at a given time, may afterwards become
a fruitful source of evil," writes an eminent Jesuit historian; "and ecclesiastical centralization, which in the thirteenth century freed the Church from
the trammels of feudalism, opened the door at a somewhat later date to serious abuses."[16]

By their defence of an ideal, which was essentially feudal in that they
proclaimed themselves suzerain of all suzerains, the Popes had already
shown their failure to understand a process of evolution which had begun
during the twelfth century. The future of the Church lay with the mendicant Orders. The free towns and centralized monarchies stood outside the
theocratic sovereignty; while the insult hurled at Boniface VIII by a French
minister in 1303, together with the "Babylonian" exile at Avignon, may be
thought to have avenged the discomfiture of Henry IV, of Barbarossa, and
of Frederick II.

9. THE CHURCH AND THE COMMUNAL MOVEMENT

FROM about the year 1150 onwards urban civilization counted for more
and more in the destinies of Western Christendom. The towns were now
the centre of social life; they played a vital part in production and distribution, as well as in the intellectual domain. What attitude would the Church
adopt in face of this new movement?

She herself had contributed to the development of urban centres,[17]
many of which had grown up round a place of pilgrimage or an abbey. The

---

16. Fr. Joseph Leclerc, *Études*, September 1951.
17. The great historian Henri Pirenne denied that the abbeys (which were often situated
    miles away in the country) had anything to do with the growth of medieval towns.
    Mlle. Françoise Lehoux, in her work *Le Bourg Saint-Germain*, a masterpiece of erudi-
    tion, shows how the case of the abbey of Saint-Germain-des-Prés, cradle of the town
    of that name, disproves his thesis. Pirenne's view is far from general acceptance among
    historians, many of whom consider the abbeys to have been "seeds of the towns."

people were glad of clerical protection; they enjoyed the greater leniency of clerical courts, and need pay taxes to no one but the abbot. St. Denis, Vézelay, La Charité-sur-Loire, Conques, St. Sernin, and many other towns originated in this way; and by means of franchise or exemption the monasteries had given birth to many a "new town" where citizens and clergy benefited by mutual exchange of services. Urban institutions were, in principle, not unlike those of the Church. Like her, the townsfolk wanted peace, though chiefly for commercial reasons; the parochial militia, raised to defend the Truce and Peace of God, were the germ of communal associations; mass movements in the form of pilgrimages and crusades, though religious in origin, served as means of distribution, thereby furthering the development of urban trade; while the liberty afforded by the Church to those who dwelt within her shadow gave them both the longing for independence and the means wherewith to attain it.

Nevertheless, when the communal movement began, the clergy were hostile. For two reasons, one ideological and the other practical. A cleric, used to spiritual command, was unlikely to sympathize with this claim to freedom, which seemed to him nothing less than rebellion and a door to anarchy. Besides, the position of the Church within the feudal system caused her to mistrust these townsmen who would prey upon her goods. The mitred lords did not hesitate to oppose what they considered as unpardonable disobedience. Hence those brief but bloody convulsions which, first in Italy and then in France, marked the beginning of the communal movement, and in which the senior clergy behaved so high-handedly. Such episodes occurred at Cremona about 1030; at Parma, Milan, and Mantua shortly before 1050; at Cambrai in 1077; and at Beauvais in 1099. Most famous of all is the tragedy of Laon in 1112, a detailed account of which is given by Guibert of Nogent. It shows the harm suffered by the Church through her entanglement in the feudal system, and explains the opposition of the communes to ecclesiastical authority.

The city of Laon was subject to Bishop Gaudry, a perfect specimen of those mitred barons who were unworthy of their titles. Supported by his Negro steward, of whom the inhabitants were terrified, his conduct was

that of a petty tyrant. Not a week passed without some member of the
episcopal clique waylaying one or other of the citizens and holding him to
ransom; while the burden of fines, tithes, and taxes was intolerable. Profit-
ing by the absence of their master, the townsmen reached agreement with
the clergy and nobility, and purchased for hard cash the right to organize
themselves as a free town. Gaudry, on his return, was furious. The citizens
hoped to appease his rage with a donation. He pretended to accept it, but
took immediate steps to abolish their association. The king was called upon
for judgment. "Four hundred *livres* if you recognize the commune!" cried
the citizens. "Seven hundred if you suppress it," answered the bishop. Louis
VI took the last-named sum, but left the inhabitants to fight it out with
their tyrant. This they quickly did. A general strike was declared. Cobblers
and shoemakers shut up their shops, innkeepers and publicans refused to
sell; and when the bishop declared his intention of recovering in the shape
of taxes those seven hundred *livres* paid to the king, the population was
seized with murderous rage. Gaudry was warned, but only laughed at the
threat. "Well, well! So those people mean to kill me? Why, if my Negro
John tweaked the nose of the bravest man among them, the fellow would
not dare to make a sound!" Rioting broke out, and the avenging cry, "Commune! Commune!" was heard in the streets. Armed with swords and two-
edged axes, the townsfolk rushed into the episcopal palace. The terrified
Gaudry took refuge in his cellar and hid under a barrel. He was found, and
there ensued a lamentable and disgusting scene: the bishop was hacked to
pieces, while the mob set fire not only to his house but even to the cathedral.
Only the arrival of royal troops could bring back calm to Laon.

The communal movement as a whole, then, was looked upon with disfavour by the Church. Time and again the popes expressed their disapproval. Thus in 1139, Innocent II invited Louis VII to support him against the
citizens of Rheims, begging him to "dissolve the criminal associations of the
Rémois"; and Eugenius IV wrote to the same king, asking him to intervene
at Vézelay and oblige the citizens "to abjure the commune which they have
set up and return to the obedience of their abbot." Innocent III, though he
looked to the Italian cities for help in his struggle with the Emperor, indicted

penalties on the commune of St. Omer; and Gregory IX later described the townspeople of Rheims as "more savage than vipers." Preachers thundered from the pulpit against "these communities, or rather these conspiracies, like heaps of tangled thorn; these conceited people who, confident in their numbers, oppress their neighbours and subdue them by violence." Such too was the opinion of Abbot Guibert of Nogent, of Bishop Yves of Chartres, of the preacher Jacques de Vitry, and of St. Bernard himself—none of whom resembled Gaudry.

Antagonism between the Church and the cities continued throughout the thirteenth century.[18] The higher ranks of the clergy not seldom had good cause to charge the communes with extortion, with encroachment on ecclesiastical property, and with attempting to impose communal taxes upon the clergy. The townspeople, on their side, were conscious of their strength, and endured with dwindling patience what remained of episcopal or abbatial tutelage. They were also aware that they enjoyed the tacit approval of the Capetian monarchs, who, while restraining the communal movement within their own dominions, were not dissatisfied at its growth in the territory of their vassals, and who, from Philip Augustus onward, appointed burgesses to governmental posts. Hence those numerous incidents which foreshadowed the anti-clericalism of the French Revolution: monasteries were pillaged, bishops were insulted, and men took part in sacrilegious masquerades. Jacques de Vitry denounced the communes as "modern Babylons."

This antagonism was widespread in Germany, where the urban movement was a key-piece in the contest between Emperor and Pope. The towns

---

18. The parochial clergy often sided with the communes, an alliance which foreshadowed that of the clergy with the Third Estate in 1789. The same was true of many bishops, a fact which makes it possible for Petit-Dutaillis, the historian of the communal movement, to refute the opinion of Luchaire who, in a work entitled *Les Communes françaises*, exaggerated the hostility of the Church. Petit-Dutaillis hits the nail on the head when he explains that the clergy misunderstood the communal movement, "just as Renan misunderstood the Paris commune of 1871." At all events, there are cases in which a bishop fostered the growth of a commune in opposition to some local tyrant. Thus at Le Mans, in 1069, bishop was party to a conspiracy against Geoffrey of Mayenne. At Beauvais the bishop was supported by the commune; while the Bishop of Noyon prided himself upon having "made a commune."

were on the imperial side. Thus we find Henry IV and Henry V conferring many privileges on the citizens of Worms and Spire, while the "new
town" of Fribourg-im-Brisgau was granted so liberal a statute that many
cities—Frankfort, Munich, Vienna, Aix-la-Chapelle, Dortmund, and others—demanded equal rights. When Frederick II entered upon his decisive
combat with the Holy See, he was able to rely upon the towns; and even
the episcopal cities, which had been held in check so long as the Emper-
or was in alliance with the higher clergy, set out on the road to independence and soon became virtual republics. During the Great Interregnum
the emancipation of the towns made still further progress, urban leagues
proving the only real force that remained in Germany, which was otherwise
a prey to anarchy. Emancipation was often achieved in face of the Church
and at the cost of violence. At Cologne, for example, between 1263 and
1266, the rebellious townsfolk attacked the property and even the person
of their bishop, for which they were condemned by a council. At Liége the
population rose against Bishop Henry of Gueldre, a prelate so pitiable that
not even Rome would support him.

In Italy the situation was rather different. It was complicated by the
Pope's struggle with the Empire, an Empire that represented Germanism.
Here the Church was looked upon as the champion of patriotism or local
privilege; and that is why the communal movement, which had emerged
during the eleventh century in opposition to the bishops, now sided with
the Pope. But if the urban leagues were his allies, their relations were still
founded on mistrust. That much is clear from the history of the Roman
commune under Arnold of Brescia and later. Innocent III's control of the
Senate was not destined to survive him; and we shall find his successors
often obliged to leave the City when its one Senator spoke as master, in the
name of "the Roman people."

It would be wrong, however, to conclude that the communal movement
was anti-Christian. It may be that certain elements—for political reasons
rather than from conviction—used the Catharist heresy as a lever against
the Church; but a great majority of the urban population had no idea that
by resisting their bishops they were attacking the Church. Cologne, while

in rebellion against its bishop, still bore inscribed upon its seal: *Sancta Colonia Dei gratia Romanae Ecclesiae fidelis filia.* Men might mock the clergy, scorning their prerogatives; yet, as Henri Pirenne rightly observes, "this secular spirit was linked with a more intense religious fervour." Having bullied their bishop, townsmen continued to frequent pious confraternities and to multiply charitable foundations, while the most glorious testimony of their youthful vigour was seen in the cathedral.

As years went by their vast increase of wealth gave the cities a new outlook upon life. Business was often their main preoccupation, until materialism contended (sometimes victoriously) with the spirit. In the towns of Italy and Germany, on the eve of that golden age known as the "Quattrocento," materialism was much in evidence. The same was true of France, where the towns experienced a rapid decline due to bad management and lack of unity, to internal dissensions between the great burgesses and smaller craftsmen, and to the influence of an all-powerful monarchy. Contrary to what has sometimes been alleged, the Church was not hostile to trade, and the arguments of certain canonists, such as Pancapalea of Bologna, who condemned all commercial profit, were never taken literally. The trading class was unreservedly praised by men whose orthodoxy cannot be called in question, e.g., the hermit Honorius of Strasbourg and the preacher Berthold of Ratisbon. Excessive wealth, however, became a source of anxiety to those who proclaimed the Gospel message; and from the beginning of the thirteenth century money was one of the chief pulpit-themes. It was no mere coincidence that the Church's emphasis on poverty, as represented by St. Francis, and the establishment of the Friars Minor in the cities, was exactly contemporary with plutocratic expansion. But while the "new leaven" did much to reanimate religious fervour, it was unable to prevent the gradual ascendancy of riches and the consequent growth of materialism.[19]

About the year 1300 tension between the Church and the towns took on a new and graver significance. The bourgeois mind was at the root of that movement which pretended to emancipate the human conscience

19. See the final section of the previous chapter.

from faith. The great urban universities revived the study of Roman Law,   261
and thereby furnished arguments against the doctrine of papal sovereignty. They too produced a number of theorists, and even theologians, who
taught the independence of temporal affairs. Such were Marsilius of Padua, William of Occam, Peter of Ailly, and the celebrated John Wyclif, who
eventually lapsed into heresy.[20] Nor were politics the only subject of discussion in the towns. It is significant that in 1270 the Bishop of Paris was
obliged to condemn certain propositions embodying ideas current in his
diocese but incompatible with Christian doctrine upon such matters as
the creation of man, the immortality of the soul, free will, and the resurrection of the body. It was in the towns also that there took root a new spirit
from which the Church would one day have much to suffer.

10. MONARCHY AND THE CHURCH

AT the beginning of the fourteenth century the medieval equilibrium was
broken, the primacy of the Holy See was called in question, and the Church's
authority defied. The reason for this was not so much the social and psychological transformations of that time as the growth of nationalism, a phenomenon of great importance in the political field. Like all changes that
disturb society, it was slow to appear, and we can follow its development in
the relations of the Church with various monarchs over a period of three
hundred years.

Throughout the barbarian age the Church had been the auxiliary of
kings; and that is no less true of the troubled days when the Capetians
set out on the steep path to glory than of the momentous morning when
Clovis was baptized. The alliance of Church and monarchy in feudal times
is among the determining factors of history. Clerics appealed to the king
against baronial oppression, and the system of advocacy[21] gave place to royal

20. See Volume 2, Chapter XIV.
21. See section 2 of the present chapter.

patronage. It was common during the twelfth century for kings to issue letters, declaring that they took such and such a church or abbey under their protection. This privilege was extended to all churches during the thirteenth century, and was considered by the great Capetian monarchs as entailing the most solemn obligations on their part.

Protection of the Church, however, was only one aspect of a more general function—that of keeping peace. The Church desired peace, and did her best to secure it. Realizing that the organic weakness of the central power had been a constant source of disorder throughout the Carolingian decadence, she looked for a strong political regime, a single unit capable of guaranteeing peace. The kings thought likewise; and when, at a later date, St. Louis declared that his mission was to assure the "tranquillity of order," in fulfilment of the Beatitude "Blessed are the peacemakers," he was only formulating a rule of conduct which had been observed by all his ancestors. Philip Augustus added the "Quarantaine-le-roi" to the Church's two pacificatory institutions, "God's Truce" and "God's Peace."

This alliance between Church and monarchy is apparent in the rite of coronation, a ceremony which is said to date back to the kings of Israel, and which had been in use throughout most of Christendom since the eleventh century. Its three elements are all religious: the *oath*, whereby the prince swears to protect the Church and uphold justice; the *election*, proposed by the archbishop, ratified by the assembled prelates, and then by popular acclamation; and the *anointing*, which confers upon the sovereign his character as elect of God.

In England the royal coronation was even regarded as a sacrament, and one chronicler, known as Anonymous of York, goes so far as to suggest that the king is a member of the clergy! In France he was supposed to have supernatural powers of healing, especially in cases of scrofula. The Oriflamme, or royal banner, which appears in history as early as 1100, was an explicit symbol of the monarch's Christian faith; he bore it as "attorney of St. Denis," and tradition held that it originated either from a legacy of St. Peter or from St. Martin's cloak.

The French coronation was a magnificent rite to which the Church 263
brought all the pomp at her disposal, and an *Ordo* compiled at Rheims
during the reign of St. Louis describes the ceremony in detail. It took place
on a Sunday in Rheims Cathedral,[22] which was adorned with tapestries, and
where a lofty dais had been erected in the middle of the transept.

On Saturday evening the prince was solemnly received by the chapter,
and spent some hours in prayer. Next morning, at dawn, matins, lauds, and
prime were sung while the barons and other dignitaries assembled at the
main doors. Archbishops and bishops were grouped around the high altar.
The prince entered the cathedral at nine o'clock to the sound of pealing bells.
A long procession of monks from the abbey of St. Remi escorted a canopy
beneath which was carried the sacred ampulla said to have been brought
from heaven by an angel for the baptism of Clovis; the archbishop received
it at the great west door and laid it on the high altar. Mass then began and
was celebrated with full liturgical splendour. When the time came for him
to take the oath, the king laid his hand upon the Gospels and swore to
uphold the rights and observe the laws of Holy Church, to do justice, and to
combat heresy. Meanwhile, there had been laid upon the altar the sceptre,
the long slender rod of justice, the sword in its sheath, and finally the crown.
A little apart from these were laid the silken shoes embroidered with golden
fleurs-de-lis together with the violet tunic and cope brought by the Abbot
of St. Denis from his monastery, where they were carefully preserved. Piece
by piece the king was arrayed in his magnificence. The Great Chamberlain
tied the silver shoe-strings; the Duke of Burgundy attached the spurs; the
archbishop girded him with the sword, which the Constable immediately
took and carried unsheathed during the remainder of the ceremony, upright
before the king. And now came the most solemn moment. With the point
of a golden needle the archbishop took a little chrism from the ampulla,

---

22. Sens also claimed this honour, as did Orléans. When Louis VI decided to be crowned
    at Orléans, the Archbishop of Rheims protested, asserted that Rome had conferred
    upon him an exclusive right to crown the king; to which Yves of Chartres replied that
    the *efficacy of the sacrament* (note the expression: the rite is likened to a sacrament)
    cannot depend on those who administer it.

while the king knelt before the altar to receive might from Heaven through the holy oil applied to his forehead, breast, back, shoulders, and elbows. Meantime there was sung the anthem: "Thus was king Solomon anointed." Vested now in tunic and cope, almost like a priest, holding the sceptre in his right hand and the staff of justice in his left, he mounted the throne so that the whole people could see and acclaim him, while the archbishop and the peers of the realm together took the crown, and placed it slowly on his brow.

From this alliance with the Church, sealed with liturgical solemnity, the kings derived considerable advantages. The first of these was political: by agreeing to crown the heir during the lifetime of his father, as was done during the first two centuries of the Capetian dynasty, the Church established that house on foundations such as no feudal rebellion could undermine. There were also military benefits, for the kings enjoyed ecclesiastical support in their struggle with robber-barons or revolted princes. Thus in the famous episode of Castle Puiset the wicked baron Hugues was defeated by the troops of Louis VI assisted by the local peasantry under their parish priest. Finally, there were economic considerations: in return for their protection of the Church the kings obtained subsidies which, though at first occasional, became gradually more regular. And these were paid with the approval of the Holy See, which preferred to assist local monarchs rather than the Empire.

The Church expected those kings who enjoyed her patronage to live as good Christians, as representatives of God on earth. There was a celebrated formula which originated at the Council of Paris in 829 and was repeated on many subsequent occasions: "It is the duty of a king to govern and rule his people with equity and justice, and to see that they enjoy peace and concord." All Christian thinkers from St. Bernard to St. Thomas Aquinas lay it down that "the people does not exist for the prince, but the prince for the people." Later on the poet Eustache Deschamps (c. 1340–c. 1406) would enumerate the duties of a Christian king in these words:

First, he must love God and the Church;
Let him have a humble heart, pity, and compassion;

Above all things he must prefer the common good;
He must hold his people in great affection;
He must be wise and diligent.

Let him have truth, such must the ruler be.
Far from punishing the good, he must do them no harm;
But let him do justice on the wicked,
So that all goodness may be manifest in him.

Fine principles, indeed. What if a sovereign failed to abide by them? *Ratione peccati*, the Church claimed a right to censure monarchs in order to recall them to right ways. The theory of "Two Swords" applied to them no less than to the Emperor.

But where did royal wrongdoing begin and end? In some cases there could be no doubt, and when the king sinned in his private capacity he fell under canonical sanctions. Nor was that uncommon; for many princes treated matrimony in a far from Christian manner, repudiating their wives and remarrying, living in concubinage, or ignoring the canonical impediments. There was no royal family that did not provide examples of this kind, and the list is wellnigh interminable of those who were excommunicated upon such grounds. The principle was quite clear: the Church would punish king and commoner alike. In fact, however, a monarch's guilt involved questions of private morality and of politics that were inextricably interwoven. Excommunication for open adultery might drive a whole kingdom into the camp of those hostile to the Church, and it sometimes happened that the Pope had to close his eyes to scandal if he wished to avoid so disastrous a consequence. The case of Philip Augustus illustrates to perfection the link between private morality and political interest.

It was not only against the sixth and ninth commandments that royalty sinned. A king might be guilty of violence or injustice; what would the Church do then? To intervene might be to take sides in the political game. Here again the principle was never in doubt. It was expressed by Innocent III in unambiguous terms: "We, whom divine Providence has entrusted

266 with the government of the Church, are resolved that neither death nor life shall prevent us embracing and upholding justice." But when it came to dealing with hard facts, this doctrine raised a thousand difficulties. When, for example, the Pope tried to prevent war between France and England, he considered himself as acting not by virtue of a feudal right, to exercise which belonged to the king, but by virtue of a superior duty, that of preventing the misery and injustice which follow in the train of war. All the same, ecclesiastical intervention could have political consequences and provoke political retaliation. The Church was led almost inevitably to take a hand in the affairs of kings. Her quarrels with them, unlike her struggle with the Empire, were not concerned with universal primacy; but she often had cause to dispute claims which they believed legitimate.

Theoretically, the solution in such cases was the doctrine of "Two Swords": the Church enjoyed a twofold power, one direct over the souls of men, the other indirect over their bodies by reason of the sins which men commit and which the secular arm must punish when called upon by the spiritual authority. Many kings, in fact, submitted to ecclesiastical control in such matters as the fight against heresy. But their obedience was not so prompt when more mundane interests were at stake. Although disagreement with the various kingdoms in the matter of investiture was less acute than with the Empire, this fact did not eliminate tension between the papacy and certain monarchs; for the principles of reform were not welcomed by all rulers with the same degree of enthusiasm. During the twelfth and thirteenth centuries the papacy became aware of its own strength; it tended, therefore to exert direct pressure on the kings, treating them sometimes as little better than vassals. The Pope was virtual head of a federation of states, or League of Nations, upon which he endeavoured to impose the rule of Christ for the benefit of Christendom as a whole. This led in effect, to the absorption of the feudal system by the Church, culminating in that confusion of spiritual and temporal affairs the inherent dangers of which we have already seen. There were cases in which this theocratic ideal was actually applied. Kings who felt themselves imperilled by their neighbours' avarice, or who needed a trump card in the diplomatic game, were prepared to recognize the Pope as overlord and to pay him annual tribute, as also were those princes who wished for the royal title. The classic instance was that of Aragon, one of five small kingdoms manoeuvring for power in Spain.[23] In 1204 King Pedro II, who had come to Rome for his coronation by Innocent III, laid upon the Apostle's tomb in St. Peter's the crown and sceptre he had just received, and made what can only be described as a deed of gift to the Pope. "I declare this kingdom," he said, "tributary to Rome in the sum of two hundred fifty gold pieces payable each year from my treasury to the Apostolic See; and I swear on behalf of myself and of my successors that we shall remain your vassals and obedient subjects." Several kingdoms did homage in analogous terms, and we have already seen the Norman rulers of Sicily employ this means of assuring papal support against imperial ambitions. Hungary was almost a replica of Aragon, in its subjection to the Holy See, its first king, St. Stephen, having received his crown from Pope Sylvester. A papal legate had delivered the crown of Bohemia to Ottokar; and Portugal became a kingdom in 1179, when Alexander III conferred the royal dignity on Alfonso I, the Conqueror, in return for his victories over the Moors. John of England, at war with France and threatened with baronial unrest, declared that he meant thenceforward to hold his kingdom "as a vassal of the Pope and of the Roman Church," and offered to pay the Holy See an annual tribute of £1,000. The Latin Empire of Constantinople, the kingdoms of Jerusalem, Serbia, and Denmark, together with the dukedom of Poland and a number of lesser states did likewise; while the Pope enjoyed nominal suzerainty even over the distant kingdom of Kiev.

It is not difficult to understand how dangerous for the Church was this "League of Nations" with the papacy at its head. As temporal sovereigns, the popes were involved in all those financial and other entanglements which are the lot of rulers; even Sancho I and Alfonso II of Portugal were excommunicated for arrears of tribute. Nor could the Holy See stand aloof from the political differences of its vassals. In England, for example, King John,

---

23. Aragon, whose frontiers marched with those of Languedoc, was half Spanish and half French.

who had recognized the Sovereign Pontiff as his overlord, enjoyed the protection of Innocent III. Forced by his rebellious subjects to sign the Magna Carta in 1215, he was supported by Innocent, who condemned the proceedings and rebuked those prelates who had defied their king. Again, when the barons and clergy threw off their allegiance and proposed to crown the son of Philip Augustus, they were excommunicated by Innocent III, who solemnly forbade the King of France to launch an attack on England. Nor is it certain that the Pope was influenced in these matters by purely spiritual motives.

Papal authority was effective only in those states that were relatively weak or constrained by circumstances to obey. As soon as a monarch had learned how to keep a firm hold upon his subjects through strong central government, he thought no more of declaring himself a vassal of the Holy See. National consciousness began to develop as monarchy made headway, and did much to undermine the concept of Christendom as a single unit. The result was increasing tension between Rome and the leading monarchies, especially England and France.

The kingdom of England as established by William I had proclaimed its devotion to the see of Peter in thanksgiving for the moral assistance rendered by the Church through Hildebrand's good offices in 1066. But England had never acknowledged the Pope as overlord; and the Conqueror, while observing the formalities, had used a free hand in the appointment of bishops. When William II "Rufus" (1087–1100) succeeded his father, matters came to a head on the subject of investitures. The new monarch was "more ferocious and more wicked than any other man," and his unblushing simony merited a stern rebuke from Urban II, of whom he took no notice whatsoever. The champion of Christian principles in this crisis was St. Anselm (1033–1109), a nobleman from the Val d'Aosta. After thirty years as abbot of Bec in Normandy, he had won such renown by his theological writings as well as by his remarkable personality that he had been promoted to the archbishopric of Canterbury in 1093. Anselm withstood Rufus, who refused to apply the decrees against lay investitures and would not listen to those timid prelates who urged him to submit. He preferred exile to

surrender; and it was not until Henry I (1100–1135) showed better dispositions than his predecessor that the saintly archbishop consented to reoc-
cupy his see. The contest between the English monarchy and the Church
reached its climax in the death of St. Thomas à Becket, an event which made
so deep an impression on the contemporary mind that we find it depicted
by sculptors and glass-workers in the cathedrals of Coutances, Sens, Paris,
and elsewhere.

With the accession of Henry II in 1154 the Anglo-Norman monarchy
became the most powerful in Europe. Heir to England and Normandy, and,
through his father, to Anjou, he married Eleanor of Aquitaine, divorced
wife of Louis VII, who brought him the greater part of France. He was a
heavily built man, broad-shouldered, with a leonine head and powerful
limbs. Tireless, always in the saddle, he travelled the length and breadth of
his dominions. He was also a good Christian, heaping wealth and favours on
the Church. But he did not intend that his clergy should escape the policy
of absolutism upon which he had resolved; and being a foreigner who never
learned to speak the English language, it is hard to see how he could have
maintained a grasp on his enormous territories without some measure of
despotic rule. He subdued the baronage with the help of Thomas à Becket,
a man of culture, high intelligence, and subtle pride, a minister experienced
in business and of unlimited devotion to duty. Appointed Archbishop of
Canterbury by his devoted sovereign, in spite of ecclesiastical opposition,
Becket, the one-time politician, underwent a psychological transformation due to the promptings of divine grace. He was now a churchman, and
devoted himself body and soul to the interests of the Church; henceforward
the royal tyranny would have no more able or more zealous an opponent.
When the king determined to raise a tax on ecclesiastical lands, Becket protested. When he sought to reorganize the administration of criminal justice
so as to make the clergy answerable before secular tribunals, the archbishop
would not agree. Henry, enraged, instituted proceedings against him; but
Becket refused to appear, and was declared a felon for his contumacy. The
fearless prelate withdrew to Sens, from which city he directed the resistance,
devoting himself meanwhile to fasting and mortification, feeding his mind

upon Holy Scripture and theology. In 1170 he was given a safe-conduct and returned to England, only to protest once more. Henry II had had his eldest son crowned in defiance of ecclesiastical regulations and tradition. Becket now excommunicated those prelates who had taken part in the ceremony, and the royal anger knew no bounds. "What!" exclaimed Henry, "is there not one among all these cowards whom I support that will rid me of this wretched priest?" His words proved fatal; for on December 29 the archbishop was set upon in his cathedral by a band of ruffians and brutally murdered. Disgusted with himself, and conscious of the growing horror at his deed, the king hurried to meet the legates who were on their way to inform him of his excommunication. He met them at Avranches, humbled himself before them, and did public penance. The same day it was learned that his army had won a victory in Scotland, and men concluded that the martyr had forgiven him; but the Church had scored.[24]

She scored again fifty years later when King John attempted a policy of despotism which he had no means to support. He launched violent attacks upon the Church, forcing the Archbishop of York into exile for refusal to pay a subsidy, declining to recognize Stephen Langton who had been appointed to the see of Canterbury at Innocent III's request, and even confiscating the temporalities of the English clergy. But these measures ended in disaster; for the prelates, uniting with the barons in a revolt which ended at Runnymede, obliged him to give way. John planned to escape from his predicament by declaring himself a vassal of the Holy See; but this act of submission was short-lived, and the English never took it seriously. Henry III (1216–1272) maintained a close alliance with the Church as a counterpoise to baronial influence; but his successor, Edward I, would admit of no dependence upon Rome, and by 1300 the English monarchy had become no less secular than the French.

The Church had lent the full weight of her support to the Capetian kings, who, though they were not all of St. Louis's calibre, were without

---

24. We may compare the martyrdom of St. Thomas à Becket with that of St. Stanislaus of Cracow, who fell victim to Boleslav II of Poland in 1079.

exception convinced and practising Christians. Yet it was in France that
the problem of relations between Church and State was most acute. French
history is darkened by no tragic drama such as that of Becket. Nevertheless, it was in France that the monarchy became most keenly conscious of
its political independence. This is a remarkable fact when we consider the
importance of Capetian France in medieval Christendom; nor is it without
reason that we use the word "Gallicanism" to describe theories and practices
which tended to limit the papal authority in several countries.

France had shown herself friendly towards the popes, who had always
found a refuge in French territory when driven from Rome. Many French
theologians, from St. Bernard onwards, had upheld the papal primacy; and
this was unanimously recognized by the French prelates assembled in the
Council of Lyons (1274). The French people, too, had been most generous in their support of the crusades. On the other hand, as the Capetian
kings awoke to their increasing strength, they became progressively hostile
to papal interference.

Their desire for independence is shown by numerous events. The first
Capetian to become conscious of his power was Louis VI (1108–1137). He
was a good Christian, and heaped privileges upon the Church; but he kept
a close watch upon bishops and abbots, intervened in ecclesiastical appointments, and never lost an opportunity to prove himself master in his own
house. Thus, when his friend Suger was elected abbot by the community
of St. Denis without reference to himself, Louis imprisoned those monks
who brought him the news. When Calixtus II claimed that the Archbishop
of Lyons (which was at that time an imperial city) was primate of all Gaul
and had rights over the Church at Sens (to which Paris was subject), Louis
protested and gained his point. Strange as it may seem, we find the same
independent spirit in Louis IX, the holiest of kings. That great Christian
did not hesitate to speak his mind to the Curia upon excessive increases
of ecclesiastical taxation; he allowed his bishops to air similar grievances
against the papal exchequer, and would permit no interference from Rome
with his own policies. He withheld assistance from Innocent IV when the
latter joined issue with Frederick II; and although he pressed for the release

of some French cardinals who had fallen into Frederick's hands, he made no move to join in the celebration of that Emperor's defeat.

St. Louis, in fact, was a true scion of his grandfather, Philip Augustus (1180–1223), who, in the course of a long and acrimonious dispute, had clarified the principles governing relations between the French crown and the papacy. This man of steel, in whom a high sense of his royal duties was allied with somewhat unscrupulous ambition, had conceived a notion that was later formulated by French jurists: "The King of France is Emperor in his own dominions." Good Christian though he was, he would not be ruled by clergymen. The quarrel between Philip Augustus and Innocent III was further complicated by the monarch's private life, which fell under ecclesiastical censure. In 1193 Philip had married Ingeborg of Denmark, but quickly divorced her for reasons which did not entitle him to remarry. Immediately after the accession of Innocent III he received this stern note from the Lateran: "The royal dignity cannot take precedence of Christian duties, and in this matter it is impossible for us to distinguish between a prince and his subjects. If, contrary to our hopes, the King of France ignores our present warning, we shall be obliged, in spite of ourselves, to raise our apostolic hand." The Pope's position was unassailable. The king refused to put away his "second wife," and Innocent laid France under an interdict. But the extent to which the royal strength had developed is shown by the fact that a majority of bishops ventured to disobey the Pope and formed a solid bloc around the throne, while those who carried out the papal instructions suffered loss of property. Here, then, although the Pope was indubitably right, the king had scored a diplomatic victory.

The problem became still more involved when the issue was one of public morality. Following the capture of Jerusalem by Saladin, Clement III called for a crusade, and Philip seized this golden opportunity for an attack on England. The Pope intervened with threats of a new interdict, to which the French King replied: "The Roman Church has no business to impose censures when the king chastises a rebellious vassal. The legate no doubt smells English sterling.... I do not fear your sentence; it is unjust." And there for the time being matters were allowed to rest. But when, in 1203, Innocent resolved to terminate the Anglo-French affair at any cost, the royal answer was more forcible than ever: Philip required of all his barons an oath to support him, *even against the Pope*, and took his stand upon the principle that "in feudal matters, the king is not bound to take instructions from the Holy See; the Pope should not interfere in disputes between sovereign rulers." Innocent III forthwith replied that he had nothing to say from the feudal standpoint; but *ratione peccati* his jurisdiction was absolute, and he had a right to condemn war between Christians. Notwithstanding his strength, he could not bring his adversary to heel; and John "Lackland" was deprived of Normandy, Anjou, and Touraine. The claims of the monarch prevailed over those of the Pope, for spiritual and temporal interests were so closely linked that the former were at an inevitable disadvantage. Innocent III failed to overcome the French king's resistance: Ingeborg remained a prisoner, while Philip protested against the election of Otto IV, and accepted on his son's behalf the crown of England.

In this way the interests of Church and State drifted farther apart. The breach opened by Philip Augustus in the majestic edifice of the papacy grew ever wider until, in the next century, Philip the Fair tore down a whole wall. The irresistible current of history dissolved the feudal mass, transforming it into a number of centralized monarchies which could develop only by means of a proud self-assertion. Meanwhile, the secular ideal of Christendom as a theocratic Utopia had involved the popes so deeply in political disputes that the Holy See was correspondingly affected by this universal tide of change. In order to defeat the Emperors, Rome had had to rely upon the youthful vigour of new-born kingdoms; but these same kingdoms had rapidly become "as a reed that wounds the hand that grasps it." By confusing (though from the highest motives) its spiritual function with the exercise of earthly power, the papacy may be said to have betrayed its mission. Its future was undoubtedly compromised.

CHAPTER VI

A Society Within Society

1. A STATE WITHOUT FRONTIERS OR AN ARMY

WE have watched the Church engage in bitter struggles, waging war, sealing alliances, and taking her place at the head of a "League of Nations." It may therefore be asked, was she herself a State? By virtue of her territorial possessions, yes.[1] True, she was a State without frontiers, a State unarmed amid the most military of societies; but she could still command the obedience of warriors. The members of this State were not unlike the rest of men. They were of equal birth; and their dress at that period differed little from that of laymen, except during Mass and other liturgical ceremonies. The clergy, however, though part and parcel of medieval society, was clearly distinguishable therefrom.

It was distinguished in the first place by its sacred character and peculiar function. Next, it formed a learned hierarchy, firm but flexible, and governed by clearly defined principles. Again, it was international; "the class that prays" became a veritable super-State. Above all, its purpose was neither temporal dominion nor the securing of man's temporal happiness;

---

1. See the preceding chapter. The States of the Church involved her in many difficulties; but at that time temporal power was considered indispensable, and until the organization of their financial system in the thirteenth century, the popes derived therefrom the chief part of their revenue (see section 10). Innocent III tried to form this State into a single barrier stretching from the Tyrrhenian Sea to the Adriatic. Its elements were disparate: the Patrimony of St. Peter, the Plain of Perugia, the March of Ancona, and the Romagna, all given by the Carolingians; then there were Tuscany and territories north of the Apennines bequeathed by the Countess Matilda in 1155.

but because of the confidence it enjoyed, and because of its reasonable approach to human problems, it excelled in the art of government and made its authority not only acceptable to, but even loved by, mankind at large.

The medieval Church had many faults, but during the eleventh century she evolved that harmony and that enduring system of government which we admire in the thirteenth. Her methods and institutions came into being under pressure of events; but when compared with other political systems of that age, she appears always in advance of the time. Though guided by supernatural principles, her management of affairs was remarkably practical and realistic.

2. ENLISTMENT OF THE CLERGY

THE medieval clergy represented a far larger proportion of the total population than is now the case. They were perhaps ten times as numerous. This fact must be constantly borne in mind; it was partly due to unanimity of faith, but there were other causes. The Church attracted innumerable vocations because her function was so highly esteemed, apart from the fact that men in holy orders enjoyed many privileges. There was no problem of vocations. Candidates for the priesthood were plentiful; chapters were never below strength; and the smallest parish had its vicar, often assisted by several curates. This great stream of aspirants naturally contained elements of unequal value, but there was abundant material from which to choose. Those who could not hope for military command gravitated towards the Church.

The regular clergy were particularly numerous, and formed a *corps d'élite* upon whom the Church mainly relied. The growth of the monastic orders is wellnigh incredible. Thus, in the year 1100, Cluny, which had been founded in the tenth century, numbered ten thousand monks in one thousand four hundred fifty houses, most of them in France and the remainder scattered throughout western Europe. The Cistercians founded three hundred forty-eight monasteries within a period of fifty years; nor does St. Bernard's biographer exaggerate in describing the great abbot as "a terror to mothers and wives, for, wherever he spoke, husbands and sons embraced the religious life." When St. Francis and St. Dominic invited men to follow in Christ's footsteps, they were heard with no less enthusiasm. In 1316 the Franciscans had one thousand four hundred houses and more than thirty thousand religious; the Dominicans, in 1303, had six hundred houses and ten thousand friars. Other Orders were almost as flourishing. Furthermore, congregations which admitted lay brothers (lay monks not destined for the priesthood but bound by the threefold vow of chastity, obedience, and stability) received crowds of postulants. These *conversi*, or "bearded brethren," relieved the choir-monks of material duties and external business. Oblates, too, were numerous. They were semi-seculars, better educated than the lay brethren, living as it were on the outskirts of the community and taking part in the divine office. Religious houses, in fact, though sometimes below standard, were unfailing nurseries whence the Church drew many of her greatest rulers.

From what class of society did the clergy spring? From every class without exception. Intelligence, study, and practice of the virtues could lead anyone at all to the highest offices in the Church, thus ensuring the continuity of culture which is necessary for the life of any society but is seldom found in worn-out civilizations. The famous Carolingian Archbishop Adalberon had expressed the principle in these words: "Divine law admits of no distinction of rank or birth; before God, the son of a labourer is not inferior to a monarch's heir." True, the Church was an aristocratic society, a monarchical organization; but she recruited her clergy on a democratic basis, reviving herself unceasingly at the living springs of the people. Here are some examples. Suger, abbot of St. Denis, was the son of a serf; Maurice de Sully, the Bishop of Paris who built Notre-Dame, was the son of a beggar; St. Peter Damian, a future cardinal, had been a swineherd, as had Bishop Wazon of Liége. More remarkable still is the list of those who occupied the papal throne: Gregory VII, son of a carpenter; Benedict XII, son of a butcher; Urban IV, son of a cobbler; Benedict XI, son of a goatherd;

not to mention others such as Urban II and Adrian IV whose origin is most obscure.

The Church, therefore, enabled each and all of her sons to be revenged upon the accidents of birth and fortune, attracting to herself the finest elements in society. She was, indeed, no "closed shop"; but that does not mean to say that there were no ties of affection and mutual interest, no "class-spirit," among the clergy. All those ecclesiastical dignitaries who took part in political life, who built the cathedrals, who led the masses on pilgrimage or crusade, all were conscious of belonging to a ruling caste. They held together, forming within each State a spiritual unit isolated from, and not seldom opposed to, the feudal world. They also secured places for their friends; thus Eudes of Paris had Aubry de Humbert appointed to the see of Rheims, and Hervé to that of Troyes. The clerical vocation, too, sometimes ran in families; thus Peter of Nemours had three brothers who were respectively bishops of Meaux, Noyon, and Chalon.

The bishops and abbots, as leaders and administrators, were the main sources of ecclesiastical influence; but they were by no means the only workers in that field. Priests and monks occupied situations of every kind—as statesmen, civil servants, diplomats, professors, warrior chiefs when need arose, and spiritual advisers to the barons on crusade. Not even monks were wholly separated from the world. For monachism had roots throughout society, to which it rendered service in exchange for men; and when God's interest required, as in the case of St. Bernard, a monk might be granted leave of absence from his monastery.

The Church, then, was incarnate in society. We do not deny that "clericalism" of this sort had defects, that the counter-influence of laymen upon the clergy was detrimental to the latter. But the activity of the Church cannot be ignored if we would understand medieval institutions as a part of history, if we would explain the beneficent influence of Christian principles in every walk of life.

3. THE HEAD OF THE CHURCH

AT the head of the clergy stood the Pope, common Father of all the faithful. During the three great centuries of the Middle Ages the Church tended more and more to organize herself upon the pattern of a strongly centralized monarchy, with her own government, local executives, inspectors, and diplomats. The papacy, though criticized and abused in the game of politics, continued to increase in stature.

By whom was the Pope elected? After the decree of Nicholas II, in 1059, by the cardinals. This word "cardinal," already of great antiquity in the Church, was used at first somewhat vaguely to designate those clergy who were so to speak the hinge (*cardo*) of the Church. To "incardinate" a cleric to a church was to fix him to it like a hinge to a door. In the course of the tenth century the word took on the more general sense of "principal" or "very important," and was applied to ecclesiastics of high rank—archbishops or patriarchs of various sees. It was at Rome, however, that the "cardinal clergy" attained supreme importance and became associated with the ancient glory of Peter's city. The cardinal-bishops were the "suburbican" bishops of seven dioceses around the capital, of which the farthest, Palestrina, was less than fifty miles from the Lateran. The cardinal-priests were rectors of the chief parishes in Rome; they also served the basilicas of St. Peter, St. Paul outside the Walls, and St. Laurence. Finally, the cardinal-deacons claimed to represent the regional deacons who had once administered the seven wards of the City, but their number had already exceeded this traditional figure. Altogether, the College of Cardinals consisted in the thirteenth century of fifty-three members: seven bishops, twenty-eight priests, and eighteen deacons. Alexander III was the first to confer the title of cardinal upon foreigners, appointing them to real or fictitious duties in the Roman Church.

The importance of the cardinals gradually increased. Not only was it their duty to elect the Pope, but they formed a sort of Council, or Senate, of the Church. By the end of the eleventh century cardinal-bishops took precedence of all other bishops; and at the two Councils of Lyons, in 1245 and 1274, even cardinal-priests and deacons enjoyed this privilege. In 1245

Innocent IV conferred a red hat upon his legates, and this was slowly adopted by all cardinals.[2] "Pillars of the Church" and "Successors of the Apostles" became current terms denoting these high dignitaries.

Curious to relate, the solemnities of the Conclave have an almost comic origin. Though entrusted with the papal election, it sometimes happened that the cardinals could not make up their minds; and the decree of Alexander III (1179) requiring a two-thirds majority made their choice still more difficult. Between 1241 and 1305 the papal throne was vacant for a total period of ten years. After the death of Clement IV, in 1268, the Princes of the Church deliberated for seventeen months without result. They were then shut up in the palace at Viterbo, where their meetings were held; but as they were still undecided at the end of two years, the mob rushed the palace one pouring wet day, and tore off the roof in hopes that the rain might bring them to their senses. At the same time, a semi-ultimatum from St. Louis called upon them to make a choice. They elected St. Gregory X, who, in order to prevent a repetition of the scandal, caused the second Council of Lyons (1274) to make strict rules governing the election. It was decreed that within ten days of the Pope's death the cardinals should assemble at the papal palace, each accompanied by one servant only, and should not leave until they had given Peter a successor. Inside, there was to be a single "conclave" where all would live together. The door was to remain closed, and none might go out on pain of excommunication. If there were no election at the end of three days, the cardinals would be entitled to no more than one meal a day for five days, after which they were to subsist on bread and water! Except for the restrictions on food, and a somewhat longer period to allow for the arrival of foreign cardinals, this canon of 1274 is still in force.

These rules show to what humiliation the papacy at that time might be exposed, but in no way detract from its greatness. The popes were threatened, insulted, exiled, and even imprisoned; but they had so strong a sense

---

2. The red robes were not introduced before the pontificate of Paul II (1464–1471), nor the title "Eminence" before that of Urban VIII (1630). Cardinals belonging to religious orders continued to wear their habits, and it was only in the reign of Gregory XIII (1572–1585) that they were authorized to wear cardinalatial insignia.

of the dignity of their exalted position that even their enemies were conscious of it. We have heard Gregory VII assert that "the Pope is the only man
whose foot all peoples should kiss," and his statement was accepted more or
less throughout the Middle Ages.

A pontificate was certainly a splendid episode when he who sat upon
the throne of Peter was one such as Gregory VII or Innocent III. Ever anxious for God's glory and the good of souls, the Pope watched over the universal Church both as ruler and as father. He wished to see all, to know all,
and to do all. By summoning bishops and abbots to his presence, often from
far away, he kept himself informed upon men and affairs. An enormous
correspondence flowed from his chancellery, ranging from affairs of the
highest importance to the smallest details. His chosen legates made known
his views and saw that his instructions were carried out. Firm but cautious,
he knew how to restrain their ardour as well as how to fire their zeal. He
attended also to administrative, diplomatic, and even military business; he
was the life of the whole Church. Meanwhile, he renewed his strength at
the deep wells of prayer and contemplation, for the greatest of the medieval
popes were saints.

The authority of such a pope was almost unlimited. Subject to Holy
Scripture and conciliar decrees, he was absolute sovereign in the realm of
dogma and of discipline. Papal infallibility was not yet an article of faith,
but it was in fact admitted. "The Roman Church cannot err, and Scripture bears witness that it will never do so." This formula of Gregory VII, to
which we have already alluded, is precisely that of Pope Hormisdas in 516.
St. Thomas bases the infallibility on Luke 22:32, in which our Lord tells
Peter: "I have prayed for thee that thy faith fail not, and do thou in turn
strengthen the faith of thy brethren." He also quotes 1 Corinthians 1:10,
where St. Paul requires unity of faith, a unity of which the Pope is both
guardian and measure. To rebel against him, therefore, is to rebel against
God and deserve terrible chastisement. Thus, all those rulers, except Frederick II, who opposed the Pope, made clear that their action was directed not
against the papal authority as such, but against a man; they pretended to
show him up as a bad pope.

Let us now take a look at some of the main points in the growth of papal power. An oath of canonical obedience was exacted by Gregory VI from certain prelates with a view to the reform. It was imposed on all metropolitans by Gregory IX, and extended to all bishops by Martin IV. The right of confirming episcopal nominations, which was already reserved to metropolitans, belonged henceforward to the Pope, who often himself appointed *motu proprio* the titulars of dioceses and "exempt" abbeys. Canonization, which was formerly done by the bishops at their own discretion, was reserved to the Pope by Alexander III in 1170. Authentication of relics was also reserved to Rome. Absolution from certain grave sins, e.g., the sack of churches, fraternizing with excommunicated persons, and forgery of papal documents, belonged exclusively to the Pope. We shall have something to say later on about his right to hear appeals.

The Sovereign Pontiff's dignity was emphasized by numerous external signs. It is true that in official acts proceeding from his chancellery he took the lowly title "Servant of the servants of God"; but he often referred to himself more proudly as "Vicar of St. Peter" or "Vicar of Jesus Christ." The form of address "Holy Father" was common; likewise "Your Holiness" borrowed from the imperial liturgies of the East.

He did not yet wear the white soutane,[3] but he already had the *tiara*, a special kind of mitre which distinguished him from other bishops. It was probably Nicholas II who to the lower rim of the *frigium* or *camelaucum*, which he wore in common with all persons of high rank at Rome, added a golden crown as symbol of his sovereign power. At the beginning of the fourteenth century Boniface VIII added a second crown, and one of the Avignon Popes—Clement V or Benedict XII—a third. Thereafter it was claimed that these three crowns represent papal sovereignty over the Church militant, suffering, and triumphant. Besides the tiara, the Pope had various liturgical ornaments peculiar to himself. Such was the *subcingulum*, a kind of maniple marked with three crosses and suspended from the girdle.

---

3.   This dates from the pontificate of Pius V (1566–1572), who was a Dominican and retained the white robe of the Friars Preachers.

On his right hand he wore the Fisherman's Ring, the stone of which was
engraved with an image of St. Peter casting his nets. When he celebrated
pontifical High Mass, the ceremonial, though distinct and splendid, was
not so magnificent as that introduced during the Renaissance, and which is
still in use today. His audiences were already governed by strict etiquette: it
was customary for all visitors, even royalty, to kiss his hand or the hem of his
robe; and when he was on horseback the most exalted of the princes present
held his stirrup and led his mount.

The papal residence was worthy of its occupant. This was the Lateran,
where the popes had lived since the beginning of the fourth century. The
Emperor Constantine or his second wife Fausta presented them with the
ancient house of the Laterani, which had long since been taken from its
owners by Nero's exchequer; and the papacy had for so long been associated
with the place that its possession was looked upon as tangible proof of legitimate election. It was a splendid and well-planned group of buildings, comprising the palace, the basilica, and the baptistery with its enormous hall of
five apses where councils met. There was also a priceless collection of relics,
including memorials of the Old Testament, and the *Scala Sancta*, a staircase
which was claimed to be that of Pilate's praetorium, the very staircase which
Jesus had ascended to His trial.

Outside the city[4] stood St. Peter's, built over the tomb or "Confession"
of the Apostle, on the spot where he confessed his faith by martyrdom. St.
Peter's was also the basilica of Constantine, with its "quadri-portico" beneath
which lay so many popes, its glorious apsidal mosaic, and its twelve twisted
columns adorned with vines and supporting the *pergula* or rood loft. The
church was crowded with so many small sanctuaries, altars, and tombs that
the whole formed a picturesque medley quite unlike the orderliness of St.
Peter's today. Nearby, on the site of some modest houses erected by Pope
Symmachus about the year 500, and rebuilt in 800 for Charlemagne, Innocent III raised a palace standing amid gardens. This was the Vatican, where
his successors preferred to live until their departure for Avignon.

---

4.   The Lateran was within the Aurelian wall.

The government of the Church necessitated a great number of departments, for the weight of business steadily increased. There was the examination of candidates for ecclesiastical dignities, there were appeals to be heard, there was the drafting of Bulls and other papal documents, besides a host of miscellaneous matters in which the Pope's intervention had been requested. Together, these numerous departments formed the *Curia*. The consistories, which replaced annual synods formerly held in Rome at the beginning of Lent, consisted of cardinals, whose duty it was to keep the Pope informed and to assist him with their advice. In turn, he revealed his plans to the consistory, and notified them of his principal appointments, especially of nominations to the Sacred College.

The most important office in the Curia was the *chancellery*, which dealt with all the most vital affairs of Christendom. From the beginning of the thirteenth century it was directed by a chancellor and vice-chancellor, who were assisted by notaries charged with the drawing up of Acts, and by subordinate officials both clerical and lay. The chancellery was divided into four offices: (1) "Minutes," where the schema or draft of the Act was prepared; (2) "Engrossment," where the original document was written; (3) "Registers," where a copy was taken in order to keep a record of everything that went out; and lastly (4) "Bulls," where the seal (*bulla*) was affixed. This seal was a disk of lead marked on one side with the Pontiff's name between the arms of a cross, and on the other with images of St. Peter and St. Paul. Extraordinary care was taken to guarantee the authenticity of papal documents; their drafting and presentation was in itself an art and a tradition. The formulae varied according to the type and purpose of each; the style was metrical, rhythmic, sometimes almost poetic; and there were rules governing the manner of dating, of affixing the seal, and of choosing the ribbons to which it was attached. He was a devilish clever forger who could imitate such models, but it was quite often managed. The rules of the papal diplomatic service were copied by all the chancelleries of Europe. No state, except England, had such well-preserved archives, and none, of course, were of such universal application.

To provide for the execution of its orders and to control the bishops, Rome employed the services of legates. This idea, which was borrowed from the Carolingian *Missi Dominici*, had begun to take shape in the Gregorian period. St. Peter Damian, Cardinal Humbert, and Hildebrand had all sent out "legations" to settle particular affairs. After his election to the papacy, Hildebrand extended and improved the system. Hitherto the appointment of legates had been temporary, and the popes continued in certain cases to entrust a special envoy with the delivery of instructions. These *Legati Apostolicae Sedis* or *Legati Sanctae Romanae Ecclesiae* were vested with superior authority during their mission; their powers superseded all others; and they had the right of deposing bishops, even though they themselves were simple priests or monks.

Notwithstanding, however, the importance of their function, temporary legates could not achieve lasting results, for the very nature of their appointment made their presence in any one place short-lived. Gregory VII, therefore, decided to make some of them permanent; and in this way the legate became the Pope's personal representative or ambassador in a particular locality. Very often he took the archiepiscopal title of the country wherein his duties lay; and in many cases it was the result of this procedure that an archbishopric attained "primacy," an ancient dignity which had more or less fallen into disuse. Thus Gregory VII's Grand Legate became "Primate of the Gauls"; while Urban II conferred the primacy of Belgium on the Archbishop of Rheims, and that of Narbonnais on the titular of Narbonne. The Archbishop of Canterbury was created primate of England, and the Archbishop of Salerno primate of southern Italy. There was no question of a mere honorary title, but of real jurisdiction; and the Archbishop of Aix was sternly rebuked for having shown too little *obedience* and *reverence* towards his primate.

Naturally, the appointment of a permanent legate, especially if he became a primate also, was not to everybody's taste. Protests were frequent; and the letter sent in 1078 by the clergy of Cambrai to those of Rheims is nothing less than an indictment charging the legates with aiming at personal despotism, with tyrannical behaviour, with corruption, and with disrespect for venerable diocesan customs. But if centralization tended to destroy the fruitful variety of the Christian world, it enlarged the Pope's sphere of action and strengthened his authority.

Nor were the clergy alone in their experience of papal jurisdiction. Legates, like modern "nuncios," were sent to kings; papal ambassadors were attached to the imperial court, to those of England and of France, but above all to those realms which recognized the suzerainty of the Holy See. Here the legates exercised enormous power, claiming, and often obtaining, "Peter's Pence." No other sovereign at this period controlled such efficient means of government.

4. ECUMENICAL COUNCILS, THE ASSIZES OF CHRISTENDOM

WE may now ask whether the Pope's authority was restricted by those assemblies which formed the assizes of Christendom and which are known as ecumenical councils. No. Theories which were later described as "conciliar," and which maintained that councils are superior to the Pope, were first put forward by William of Occam at the beginning of the fourteenth century. From the eleventh to the thirteenth century there were isolated cases of resistance to papal authority, but these never amounted to doctrinal disputes.

An ecumenical council was always summoned by the Pope; and he did so only when he felt the need of support from the whole Church in determining some point of dogma or in taking some grave decision. The careful preparation of agenda, and not seldom the drafting of "canons" which the fathers of the council would have to approve, was done by the Curia. The Sovereign Pontiff presided over sessions with all the pomp of Roman ceremonial. The council appears to a large extent as a consultative chamber rather than as a parliament giving expression to its will. At the same time, there are no grounds for treating this fact as an instance of unjustifiable authoritarianism, for the council was almost always in full agreement with the Pope upon essentials, and no one disputed his *de facto* authority.

The traditional list of ecumenical councils includes no more than twenty since the foundation of the Church, and seven of these were held during

the Middle Ages. The Lateran Council convoked by Innocent III in 1215 is
considered as the twelfth. The first eight were common to the Eastern and
Western Churches, but after the ninth, in 1123, the Orientals ceased to take
part. Moreover, while these assemblies were "ecumenical" in principle, the
number of delegates who attended them varied enormously. In 1215 more
than three thousand clerics of all ranks and nationalities met at the Lateran, but at the Council of Lyons in 1245, which was part of the war against
Frederick II, there were only three patriarchs, one hundred forty bishops
(most of whom were French or English), and a few hundred priests and
monks. Any pope who summoned a council when in difficulty had far less
chance of welcoming large numbers than had a strong pope who was feared
and respected by all.

We may say, then, that the typical general council, the supreme assembly of the Middle Ages, was that of the Lateran in 1215, which marked the
zenith of Innocent's pontificate. On April 19, 1214, the Pope sent invi-
tations to all patriarchs, archbishops, bishops, abbots, princes, and kings
throughout the Christian world, asking them to meet at Rome on November 1, 1215. The delay of eighteen months allowed between the convocation
and the assembly is significant: no pains were spared in preparation, and no
one could excuse his absence. The Pope had also given strict orders regarding
attendance at the council: only two prelates in each province might remain
at home to deal with urgent business, and even they would have to send
representatives. The same applied to chapters and religious congregations.
Apart from these cases, no excuse would be accepted; and the Archbishop
of Lund in Denmark, who tried to evade his obligation, was quickly called
to order.

The early autumn of 1215, therefore, found all Christian Europe on the
road to Rome. Four hundred and twelve bishops answered the papal sum-
mons. Eight hundred abbots and priors were likewise on their way—the
whole of Western monachism. The secular powers were also present in this
assembly of Christendom, represented by ambassadors chosen from among
princes of the blood. The Latin Emperor of Constantinople, the Kings of
Germany, France, England, Jerusalem, Aragon, Portugal, and Hungary each

sent the highest member of his entourage. Many barons came in person. Among these was the Count of Toulouse, for the Albigensian affair was on the agenda. From the East, there were only three or four hundred Greek bishops, but the magnificent delegations from Poland and Dalmatia proclaimed the attachment of those countries to the Church. As for the clergy of subordinate rank, there were at least three thousand.

The opening session on November 11 may be imagined. The basilica of St. John Lateran proved too small to hold the crowd; and when Innocent III appeared he was greeted with a tremendous and prolonged ovation. In the presence of Christendom gathered in that place the great Pope seemed to embody the supremacy of Mother Church over all other powers. Business was concluded in three public sessions, on November 11, 20, and 30; for the debates had been so well prepared that there was no long-drawn-out discussion. The fathers voted with exemplary dispatch and in accordance with the Pope's wishes upon the liberation of the Holy Land, upon the reform of morals, upon the Albigensian affair, and upon many more thorny questions. Between times, a number of smaller groups were at work on the seventy canons for approval in solemn session. The twelfth ecumenical council, in fact, was a striking manifestation of the Church's unity, and set its seal upon the glory of the papacy.

5. BISHOPS AND DIOCESES

THE regional organization of the Church had rested from the very beginning upon a fundamental unit which was both spiritual and administrative. This was the church, a community of persons governed by a bishop and afterwards identified with a distinct geographical area. Long before the barbarian invasions, the bishop was a man consecrated to rule a given territory corresponding to the Roman *civitas*. In fact, the bishop's authority was almost always associated with a city or town behind whose ramparts he had his cathedral and his palace, the seat of his administration. But as Christianity penetrated the countryside, and rural parishes grew up, his authority became

more extensive by the addition of a country "suburb." During the tenth century the region included within a bishop's jurisdiction came to be known as
a "diocese," an imperial administrative term which has survived until today.

Dioceses varied greatly in importance, and first as to their dimensions.
That of Nantes, for example, covered three thousand eight hundred square
miles as against Laon with nine hundred sixty-five square miles in the same
province; nor can the diocese of Bourges with nine thousand two hundred
ninety square miles be compared with that of Orange, which included no
more than one hundred sixty-eight square miles.[5] Numbers also varied, not
only in relation to area, but also according to density of population. In Normandy there were about thirty people to a square mile, but at least sixty in
Flanders. Hence there were dioceses large and small, rich and poor; that
meant to say there were differences of "kudos" among the bishops, which
personal merits might lessen but never eliminate.[6]

But whether his diocese were large or small, rich or poor, the bishop
always enjoyed great prestige, and exerted considerable influence. He spoke
as an equal of the greatest barons, who generally respected him no less than
did the common people. His cathedral was the church of his "cathedra" or
chair; and as he mounted the steps of his throne, the crowd beheld a splendid figure. He wore an alb of fine linen, a stole fringed with gold, embroidered dalmatic and chasuble, and, on his head, the tall pointed mitre as seen
in the sculptures at Chartres. His left hand grasped the crozier, while the
right, adorned with a golden ring, was raised in benediction. If he were an
archbishop, or a bishop specially favoured by the Holy See, there hung on
his breast the pallium.

The bishop's powers were extensive, embracing those of order and of
jurisdiction. It was he who conferred major orders and the sacrament of

---

5. See the interesting paper read to the International Congress of Historical Sciences in
    1950 by J. de Font-Réaulx on the "Comparative Structure of a Diocese in the thir-
    teenth and fourteenth centuries" and published in the *Revue d'histoire de l'Eglise de
    France* (July–December, 1952).
6. Hence the curious proverb *Blé vaut mieux que sac* (Bayeux, Lisieux, and Évreux are
    worth more than Séez, Avranche, and Coutances).

290   confirmation. As a rule, it was he who consecrated every new bishop, who blessed new abbots and abbesses, who consecrated the oil and chrism, who blessed bells, sacred ornaments, new churches, and cemeteries. He possessed administrative and judicial powers over his clergy, and could even degrade them for serious faults. Directly or indirectly he supervised education; charitable works were subject to his control; and his was the last word in all matters concerning faith and morals.

Over the bishop there was generally a metropolitan archbishop (France had eighteen of them) who had jurisdiction over his "suffragans," i.e., the bishops in his province. Since the Carolingian epoch, however, the powers of metropolitans had steadily decreased, and they continued to do so until the sixteenth century, when the Council of Trent virtually abolished them. If they confirmed the appointment of and consecrated their suffragans, it was by virtue of ancient custom rather than by right; and their visitations of all dioceses in their province were, with certain exceptions,[7] chiefly a matter of etiquette. They continued to act as judges of second instance, before an appeal to Rome, and they retained the right to preside over provincial councils; but this did not amount to much. The pyramidal notion of the Church, so dear to Boniface VIII and some of his contemporaries, did not last. Notwithstanding the respect accorded to a bishop, he can hardly be said to have preserved the importance, the freedom, or the means of action that he once enjoyed. The formula *Ecclesia in episcopo* was certainly not as true in, say, 1200 as it had been in 400 or 600. The extension and centralization of papal government brought about the decline of episcopal authority; so that the bishops, even when they were not primates or legates, gradually became representatives of the Pope in their own dioceses. Rome's ascendancy over the episcopate is particularly noticeable with regard to the choice of bishops and the conferment of benefices attached to the see.

---

7.   See the observations of Cardinal Baudrillart in his Introduction to M. Andrieu-Guitrancourt's *L'archevêque Eudes Rigaud et la Vie de l'Église au XIII siècle*. Eudes Rigaud, archbishop of Rouen, made several visitations of every diocese in his province, and kept a close watch on the administration of his suffragans.

The whole purpose of the Church in her quarrel over investiture was
to deprive laymen of their right to nominate bishops. Would she return
to the ancient method of election in which the canons of the chapter, the
monks of the diocese, and the people all took part? The Council of Lyons
in 1245 entrusted elections to the chapters alone; but in point of fact the
canons were not always in a position to nominate their bishop, for the Pope
reserved the right to decide a candidate's merits and to regulate the election. Bishops were often elected "by the grace of God and of the Apostolic
See." When the chapter was unable to choose between several candidates,
the matter was settled by an appeal to Rome; and the Council of Lyons in
1274 stated that the number of these appeals was "inconceivable." Since a
bishop-elect frequently sought consecration not from his metropolitan but
from the Sovereign Pontiff,[8] it is not difficult to estimate the extent of papal
influence in the dioceses. Such influence reached its climax in Castile, where
Alfonso X recognized the Pope's exorbitant claim to depose and reinstate
bishops, and also to annul an election "even when the chosen candidate was
worthy."

Again, the ceaseless flow of events drove the papacy to claim (and not
seldom to obtain) the right to dispose of benefices at its sole discretion.
Either to reward some faithful servant, or to please a monarch, the Pope
would grant the revenues of an ecclesiastical charge by appointing the titular. This practice began on a modest scale with Innocent II; it was a good
deal more common under Alexander III and Innocent III, and many a clerk
of the chancellery or other Roman employee received benefices in various
parts of Christendom. In 1225 Honorius III decreed that "in every church
and every cathedral one prebend shall remain at the disposal of the Holy
See," and the Pope sometimes went so far as to promise a benefice during
the lifetime of its present holder! Urban IV extended this form of advow-
son, and Clement IV laid down the principle that "the free disposal of

---

8.   It was at this period that there grew up the custom of journeys *ad limina* by newly
elected bishops. The Pope wished to make his acquaintance in person; and if that
were not possible, he desired a representative to come and do him homage.

ecclesiastical charges, whether before or after the death of their holders, is an Apostolic prerogative." The importance of this fact is obvious: the immense wealth of the Church was in the papacy's control. Naturally, there were protests. Robert Grosstete, for example, is celebrated for his outspoken denunciation of this abuse at the Council of Lyons in 1245. He accused the Holy See of granting benefices to unworthy persons; and even allowing for the Bishop of Lincoln's irascible temperament, we may agree that his criticism was not wholly unjustified. For the most part, however, resistance proved ineffective; and in this respect the episcopate lost nearly all its privileges.

There was also opposition to the power of bishops, first from the cathedral chapters. The canons had a right to administer the diocese while the see was vacant, and the bishop was supposed not only to take their advice, but to allow them some share of his authority. Disputes were inevitable. The most famous of these occurred at Bordeaux, where Archbishop Geoffrey de Loroux was actually obliged to flee for his life. Generally speaking, however, the canons cared little for their rule; most of them lived alone and received a part of the chapter's revenue known as the "prebend." Sometimes, in order to increase the prebend, the chapter would reduce its own numbers, arranging for the divine offices to be sung by substitutes called "vicars"; and this was one of the abuses which the canons regular, especially those of Prémontré, strove to remedy.[9] Again, it was from among the canons that a bishop chose his officials—the cantor, the chancellor, the theologian, the inspector of schools, the penitentiary, and the custos or treasurer. It is not difficult to see that two neighbouring powers so closely associated might easily become rivals.[10]

During the barbarian age, bishops were assisted by archdeacons, who inspected, supervised, and presided at certain functions in their name.

---

9. See the paragraphs on the canons regular in Chapter IV, section 4.
10. There were also groups of canons unconnected with the cathedrals, serving a church and living on its temporalities. They were not obliged to observe a rule or to live in community. Such groups were described as "collegiate." Thus the canons of La Charité-sur-Loire were collegiate before becoming regular. The collegiate canons of Saint-Ours at Aosta were the true spiritual centre of that region.

But in course of time many of these dignitaries acquired benefices which   293
gave them independent rights and revenues. Having their own interests
and duties, they found it difficult to remain mere deputies of the bishops,
who accordingly had sometimes to complain of their abuse of power. Their
authority decreased, and the office was abolished by the Council of Trent.

Meanwhile, at the end of the twelfth century, a new figure made his
appearance in the diocese. This was the vicar-general. Originally he depu-
tized for the bishop when the latter was travelling or absent on crusade; but
from the pontificate of Gregory IX onwards he was entrusted with regular
duties, and served his chief more directly in administrative and judicial business. Finally, a bishop who was aged or sick was given a coadjutor who succeeded him at his death. The coadjutor often received the title of a bishopric
which had been created in the East during the crusades but had vanished
beneath the tide of Muslim conquest. Holders of these honorary and commemorative titles were known as bishops *in partibus infidelium*.

Lastly, the bishop had his *diocesan council* or *synod*, in which parish
priests and representatives of religious orders assembled at irregular intervals. Metropolitans were likewise entitled to summon *provincial councils*,
which had been of great importance during the preceding era. In Spain, for
example, the Council of Toledo had ranked almost as a national senate. But
the growing power of popes and kings left such institutions with little part
to play.

6. PRIESTS AND PARISHES

THE elementary division of Christian society was the *parish*. Like the diocese, it varied in extent: some parishes covered a very small area, others were
enormous. Historical circumstances, too, gave rise to different characteristics. Thus, in southern Italy, which was often ravaged by war and constantly
threatened by the Saracens, parishes were described by the significant word
castra (forts) and were closely concentrated. In northern Italy, on the other
hand, they were known as *plebes* (peoples), and had many chapels remote

from the centre. In peaceful Normandy they were subdivided into numerous self-contained units.

The parochial clergy were variously named. *"Presbyter"* and *"rector ecclesiae"* were terms of great antiquity. The latter still survives in Britain, where we speak of the "rector." During the thirteenth century "curate" was a more common designation. The curate (not to be confused with the modern English sense of the word) was a priest who had the cure or charge of souls—a *pastor.* But there were other terms in use, without necessarily implying any particular function or dignity; e.g., *dean, chaplain, prior,* and *vicar.*[11]

Generally speaking, the bishop was entitled to appoint these lower clergy, although landowners claimed the right of "patronage" and "presentation." A canon of the third Lateran Council had forbidden the erection of "cures" except with the bishop's approval; but there were many violations of this rule, and the parish priest was often little more than an employee of the castle.

Nevertheless, strenuous efforts were made to remedy abuses. Alexander III laid down that only the bishop could appoint a parish priest, though he agreed that the choice should be made from candidates nominated by the overlord. The fourth Lateran Council insisted that the parochial clergy must be sufficiently educated in matters pertaining to their duty; and it was decreed that the bishops were to provide for their instruction. The Council of Lyons (1274) went still farther, and wisely forbade the appointment of anyone below the age of twenty-five years. The one appointed must already be in priestly orders, or must seek ordination within a year. Anyone who obtained the appointment of an unworthy candidate was subject to heavy ecclesiastical sanctions. It cannot, however, be denied that these regulations were often treated as somewhat elastic.

The rural clergy were extremely poor. Most parishes had funds for the use of their clergy; but apart from the fact that such funds were often embezzled by some temporal overlord or prelate, they were in many cases

11. The *archpriest* (or dean) usually supervised a number of parishes; but this duty was somewhat vague. The same title was held by the parish priest of a cathedral.

quite insufficient. The study of royal taxation in France has revealed the existence of many parishes not subject to assessment because their annual income was less than ten and even than seven livres (scarcely one-third of a sou per day), though a labourer earned at least half a sou. There were numerous parishes of this kind in mountainous country and in the barren regions of Champagne. As for vicars, they frequently had nothing at all upon which to live, except the *droit d'étole*, i.e., freewill offerings.

We can hardly, therefore, be surprised that under such conditions the behaviour of the clergy sometimes left much to be desired. Even those who were not open to criticism on grounds of ignorance or immorality must often have been tempted to obtain a little money in exchange for their spiritual services. The Lateran Council of 1215 was hard put to it to discriminate between the necessity of free administration of the sacraments and the natural desire of clerics not to die of hunger. All the same, it is rather surprising to find a priest demanding the baptismal robes of new-born children in order to re-sell them, and even carrying off the bedclothes of a dying man to whom he had just given extreme unction! The bishops were obliged to lay down a regular scale of charges: the diocesan of Noyon, for example, allowed a parish priest to take three sous for a marriage, but twelve for a reconciliation!

This last item is an indication of the parish priest's authority and manifold activity. The parish was a far more closely knit unit than it is today. The clergy alone had the right to baptize, preside at marriages, and to conduct funerals. It was expressly forbidden to attend Sunday Mass in any but one's own parish church; and an Archbishop of Bordeaux threatened with excommunication any priest who received a parishioner not faithful to his or her own parish. In Brittany the offence was punished with a fine of twenty sous—a very large sum, equal to at least two months' salary. The priest was therefore in constant touch with his flock. He knew each one individually. He was the common receptacle of petitions and complaints. He had charge of the health as well as of the morals of his parish, keeping an eye on lepers, and acting as a sort of police-superintendent in the matter of lost property and day-to-day upsets. Above all, he kept the register of baptisms, marriages, and deaths. Since he came from the same social stratum as most of his parishioners, it is not surprising that he intervened on familiar terms in their personal affairs, and would even denounce a thief or an adulterer from the pulpit. Thus, in spite of obvious faults, the medieval clergy was the link of Christian society; it kept alive the faith of simple folk.

7. THE REGULARS

THE immediate task of the secular clergy, from archbishop to parish priest, was to lead the people to salvation; and for this purpose they lived "in the world" among their flocks. But there was another body of clerics who exercised no less important duties in the Church, and about whom we have already spoken.[12] They were distinguished by the fact that they lived according to a Rule (*regula*), and were therefore known as "regulars." The regular clergy numbered thousands of religious, who were governed by superiors entitled, according to circumstances, *abbots*, *priors*, or *provosts*. The twelfth and thirteenth centuries were the golden age of monachism, the summer-time of a tree whose countless blossom was of infinite variety. The number of religious; their influence upon the civil and ecclesiastical authority; their contribution to the secular hierarchy in the form of bishops, cardinals, and even popes; and, not least, their economic and social activity, made the regular clergy one of the foundation-stones of Christendom.

These numerous Orders are difficult to classify. We may distinguish the more ancient institutions, which followed the Rule of St. Benedict, from those observing one of more recent date, e.g., the Franciscans. But there were also much later foundations, such as the Premonstratensians and Dominicans, whose way of life was based upon the venerable Rule of St. Augustine. Even setting aside the Benedictines, Cistercians, Franciscans, and Dominicans, the whole complexus of "lesser" Orders was of great importance. A more logical basis of distinction is that of proximate ends—contemplation

---

12. See Chapter I, section 4.

or the active life. But while the Carthusians fell within the former category, 297 the Cistercians joined activity with the apostolate of prayer. Besides, the active life was of several kinds. The Premonstratensians and other canons regular, for instance, devoted themselves chiefly to the work of reform; the Antonine Hospitallers, the Brothers of the Holy Ghost, the Brothers of St. Lazarus, and the Croisiers to works of charity; the military associations of the Temple and Teutonic Knights to armed contest in the cause of Christ and Holy Church. And when St. Francis and St. Dominic instituted the two great mendicant Orders, they established an entirely new form of religious life.

Let us try to draw a picture of one of those great monasteries belonging to the most celebrated observance—that of St. Benedict—in its heyday: Cluny, say, or Saint Gall, or Fulda. It was a world within itself, a human society of which no modern religious house can give the least idea. The conventual buildings were surrounded by high walls and covered an enormous area. They were arranged according to a strict plan, and each one was suited to the purpose assigned to it by the requirements of community life: chapter-house, cloister, *scriptorium*, cells or dormitories, guest-house, and infirmary; not to mention storehouses and farm-buildings. The whole of this vast agglomeration was dominated by the abbey church, whose several towers thrust proudly towards heaven.

Around the monastery, with its hundred or two hundred monks, there lay a whole *familia*, a regular monastic city, where the dwellings of the *famuli* encircled the conventual buildings and were in many cases the origin of a town. There were agents, *vicarii, villici*, and stewards who managed the estates of the abbey; there were hereditary administrators of the kitchen, of the bakehouse, and of the tannery; there was a crowd of hired servants employed on the hardest work in place of the monks, who were now more concerned with the divine office and copying manuscripts than with ploughing and reaping; there were the oblates, who had pledged themselves and their goods to the abbey in return for the privilege of living in cloistered peace and wearing the habit of the Order; and finally, there were *voluntary serfs*, free men and women who had literally enslaved themselves to the community in order to satisfy their piety, and about whose necks, in the course of a symbolic rite, the abbot had passed the rope of the conventual bell. All together, these various categories included at least as many souls as the monastic population. They all worked in the immediate neighbourhood of the abbey, from which, however, they were separated by the "enclosure" so as not to disturb the recollection of the monks. Thus, at Corbie there was a cloister between the apartment where the domestics prepared the food and the kitchen where the religious cooked it according to prescribed regulations and to the accompaniment of psalms. That all these busy folk were content with their lot is indicated by the proverb: "It is good to live under the crozier."

So much for the *familia* proper. There was another and still larger *familia* which included those pious Christians who had been enrolled in confraternities of prayer or in charitable "societies" attached to the monastery. Membership of such groups authorized them to be present at the offices recited on their behalf, and to be buried in the holy ground of the monastery. Lists of these confraternities[13] have been preserved, and that of Saint-Gall contains more than one thousand seven hundred names. Nor must we forget the members of those numerous bodies which, though not so closely connected with the abbey, visited the hallowed spot on major festivals in tens of thousands.

The abbey was governed by an abbot who was elected for life and whose authority over his flock was in theory absolute. All those qualities demanded by St. Benedict, and described by Pope Gregory the Great in his life of the holy founder, made the abbot a leader in every sense, a true father, a spiritual guide, and an administrator. Assisted by two subordinate officers, the prior and novice-master, he was relieved of temporal cares by the cellarer or bursar, who, in turn, was assisted by the refectorian, cook, *custos panis*, *custos vini*, and guest-master. But in point of fact the whole weight of responsibility rested on the abbot's shoulders. The worth of his community depended on his own merits, and there lay the problem.

---

13. The list was usually entitled *Liber Vitae*.

In theory an abbot was elected by all the professed monks. The fourth 299
Lateran Council accepted this principle, specifying three methods of election: by "inspiration" in the case of unanimity, by conventual scrutiny,
or, finally, *via scrutinii mixti*, i.e., in two stages. This latter form meant
that the whole community appointed ten or twenty delegates by whom
the final choice was to be made. But in the election of abbots, as in that
of bishops, secular interference was a notorious evil. Princes would send
ambassadors to a community which had just lost its abbot, in order to
suggest the name of his successor, and in some cases even enthroned their
own candidate by force! Intervention of this kind was often nothing short
of scandalous.

Thus at Hautmont we find a monk named Guy, who had been installed
by the Countess of Blois, holding the monastery with a garrison of one hundred twenty-seven men and imprisoning such religious as opposed him.
Needless to say, no good could come of a contested election. It was fraught
with inextricable difficulties which could only be resolved by a costly appeal
to Rome, unless some neighbouring baron put paid to the quarrel by stronger methods.

Generally speaking, every great Benedictine monastery was autono-
mous; Cluniac centralization was on the decline. Autonomy, however, did
not mean isolation. Communities "fraternized" to the extent of exchanging spiritual and even material services, hospitality, and mutual assistance,
without question of the Order exercising control over each house. But the
reforming movement and the example of Citeaux[14] gave rise to a more
closely knit organization. The Benedictine abbots of the province of Rheims were the first to meet in plenary assemblies. This practice spread in
face of opposition, and Innocent III resolved to make it of universal obligation. In 1215 the Lateran Council ordered the establishment of provincial
chapters to be held every three years, but appointed no central authority
capable of exercising strict control. The Benedictines never adopted the
hierarchical system of Citeaux, and it is to this lack of centralization that

---

14. See Chapter IV, section 4.

300 we must attribute the decline of the Black Monks from the fourteenth century onwards.[15]

Meanwhile, however, the religious Orders served as a moral link between one diocese and another, until the thirteenth century when relations between the universities became a far more potent agency of intellectual exchange; and this is true alike of those Orders which were modelled on the pattern of Citeaux, of the Franciscans or Dominicans with their central government, and of the more independent Benedictines. Their influence may be traced in many lands: the Norman Benedictines had priories in England, the Cluniacs in Spain; and if we could draw a map of those regions which were affected by the Parisian abbey of St. Denis, it would cover an area equivalent to that of France. St. Norbert and La Cluze in Italy, St. Ours in the Val d'Aosta, and St. Maurice in Valois all remained in close touch with their daughter-houses and with laymen whom they counted among their friends, despite the fact that they were often separated by difficult mountain ranges. Later, in the thirteenth century, houses of the mendicant Orders served, one might almost say, as barracks where shock-troops awaited call-up for the Master's service; and having once established themselves in the towns, they formed a network of influence "more or less closely woven, but careful never to leave too many gaps."[16] Side by side, then, with the secular clergy who had charge of the Christian flock, the regulars were the motive force of medieval Christendom.

8. ECCLESIASTICAL JUSTICE AND CANON LAW

THE Church's elaborate organization and hierarchy of rulers made her a society within society, a state above other states. Her independence and authority were still further increased by the twofold fact that, as a state, she had her own courts of law and her own finances.

---

15. The mendicants were organized on lines different from those of the more ancient Orders; see the final section of Chapter IV.

16. J. de Font-Réaulx.

Ecclesiastical justice[17] is wellnigh as old as Christianity. The early Christians, under imperial persecution, could not submit their differences to
the tribunals of their executioners; disputes were therefore argued before
the religious authority. Judicial functions had also been assumed by bishops during the barbarian epoch, when they upheld the principles of equity against the rough and ready procedure of Germanic law. Charlemagne,
who combined religion with politics, followed the same practice and often
appointed clerics to act as judges. In the troublous days of the ninth and
tenth centuries the Church alone enjoyed sufficient prestige to command
that degree of respect which is necessary for the effective running of any
legal system. From the eleventh to the fourteenth century, therefore, we find
ecclesiastical tribunals which occupy a place proportionate to the Church's
role in medieval society.

What was the scope of ecclesiastical jurisdiction, and what the powers
of ecclesiastical courts? The principle was clear enough: the Church claimed
an exclusive right to try her own members. This was known as the *privilegium fori*, which removed from the competence of lay judges all who were
dedicated to God. It was a matter of jurisdiction *ratione personae* (by reason of the subject to be judged), to which the Church clung tenaciously.
In 1279 the Council of Avignon decreed excommunication against any lay
official who arrested a cleric, even *in flagrante delicto*, and refused to deliver
him to ecclesiastical judges. Moreover, the term "cleric" was given the widest

---

17. Ecclesiastical justice must not be confused with clerical justice which developed from
the feudal system. A bishop who was a lay overlord had legal rights over his territory, similar to those enjoyed by every overlord and quite independent of those which
belonged to him as a spiritual ruler. Such was the case, for example, with the bishops
of Metz, whose temporal domains included the city of Épinal, which lay outside their
diocese. Likewise, the archbishops of Rouen were Lords Chief Justices of Louviers,
which came under the spiritual jurisdiction of Évreux.

It sometimes happened that this justice, which, though essentially laic, was "clerical"
inasmuch as it was exercised by churchmen, came into conflict with that of the Church.
Thus, M. Maurice Veyrat, in his remarkable study *La Haute Justice des Archevêques de
Rouen, Comtes de Louviers* (Rouen, 1948), shows us the bishop of Évreux demanding
in vain the delivery of a cleric arrested at Louviers. In this town, the strongest evidence
of the archbishop's jurisdiction was a four-posted gallows capable of "holding a dozen
criminals at once." A realistic symbol of the Church's part in temporal affairs!

possible application. Slowly but surely the Church extended the privilege of her tribunals even to married and degraded clerics, leaving to the civil courts only those who were guilty of bigamy, forgery, or inveterate heresy. Others so entitled, on grounds of the "Church's interest" or the "charity of Christ," were widows, orphans, students, crusaders, and pilgrims. Now ecclesiastical justice was an improvement upon that of the civil courts: its procedure was more exact, more rapid, and also more humane, inasmuch as in criminal matters it recognized neither the "Judgment of God" nor "Trial by Ordeal." On that account, vast numbers posed as "clergy," and towards the end of the thirteenth century the competence of ecclesiastical courts was almost unlimited.

There was yet another cause which tended to increase this jurisdiction. The ecclesiastical courts enjoyed authority not only *ratione personae*, but also *ratione materiae*, i.e., by virtue of the object of an offence and of the matter at issue. This second basis of competence was less clearly defined than the *privilegium fori* which had been laid down in several Carolingian capitularies. In practice, however, it was made to cover a very wide field. The Church normally claimed jurisdiction in all cases where her interests were at stake (e.g., tithes, benefices, donations, and wills). Normally, too, she made it her business to pass judgment upon crimes that bore a religious character, such as sacrilege, blasphemy, and the practice of witchcraft, as well as all offences committed in holy places. Since her jurisdiction included all spiritual causes—both those related to vows and ecclesiastical discipline, and also those involving a sacrament or affecting her as guardian of oaths—and the right to sentence those guilty in any of these respects, there was scarcely a limit to her intervention; for in medieval society wellnigh everything was connected with a sacrament or depended upon an oath.

By the same token, there were strong protests and some open resistance; e.g., in England, where Henry II attempted to restrict the sphere of clerical privilege. In France, under Philip Augustus, it was the barons who leagued themselves against the tribunals of the Church and addressed a formal complaint to the king. St. Louis settled these differences by a series of concordats. In Germany, Frederick II could not resist so fair an opportunity of injuring the Church, and obtained from his jurists a solemn declaration of the State's superiority in legal matters. As the monarchies became stronger, the privileges of Church courts declined. Thus, in 1349, the famous assembly of Vincennes lodged sixty-six objections against them; and shortly afterwards, in the middle of the fourteenth century, the Parliament of Paris claimed the right to hear appeals against abuse of power by ecclesiastical tribunals. Custom, in fact, tended to limit the Church's competence to cases that were exclusively religious.

It may now be asked, who administered justice in the Church's name? We need scarcely remark that the increasing complexity of legal business prevented the bishop from hearing all cases in person as he had done until the beginning of the twelfth century, giving judgment "in his synod" or "in his court." The *official* (professional judge), acting on the bishop's behalf, made his first appearance during the pontificate of Alexander III; and before long a regular judicial system was evolved.[18] The judge sat with a number of assessors; the "keeper of the seal" acted as clerk of the court; the "promoter" was perhaps the origin of our public prosecutor; and there were also advocates and notaries. The arrangement was gradually improved as follows. Over the judges, whose jurisdiction was confined to limited areas, was the chief justice. His powers extended to the whole diocese, and he might hear appeals. In course of time heresy was removed from the competence of ordinary tribunals, and special courts were established "to seek out heretical perversity." These formed what is known as the "Inquisition," whose procedure helped to bring the Church's legal system into disrepute. Lastly, at the summit of the whole edifice, the papacy had its own courts to which every convicted Christian had the right of appeal; in principle at all events, for this right was for a long time somewhat vague. Under the stronger popes the number of appeals was enormous. Even in the twelfth century St. Bernard complained that the pontifical palace "re-echoed every day with the noise of Justinian's laws rather than with Christ's," and that there was heard "from morning to evening the shrill cry of pleaders." Innocent

---

18. After the fourteenth century the system was known in France as *officialité*.

III and Innocent IV eventually took steps to define the right of appeal and restrict its use.

This huge mass of judicial business had at least one fortunate result, which was also partly due to the Holy See's resolve to secure its own rights. The Church became the leading jurist of that age, and her law—the *Canon Law*—attained a degree of importance similar to that enjoyed by Roman Law in the ancient world. Theoretically, the "canons" were disciplinary regulations decreed by councils (κανών = rule or regulation). In practice, since nearly all private and secular affairs were dependent on religious principles, Canon Law enlarged its scope to include many precepts and prescriptions which we should now regard as having little or nothing to do with priests.

The golden age of Canon Law extended from the twelfth to the thirteenth century. The Church was for long without a code; but since the sixth century she had used a collection of canons compiled by a Scythian monk, Denys the Little, who also fixed the beginning of the Christian era. Later, Charlemagne had prescribed a more elaborate "corpus," called "Hispana" because it originated in Spain. Next, we have a celebrated forgery known as the "False Decretals," which attributed to former popes a number of decisions and decrees which in themselves reveal no small degree of wisdom. In the middle of the eleventh century the Church decided to systematize her legal text-books, and a start was made by French canonists, notably by Yves of Chartres. But their work was quickly superseded by that of Gratian, the great Master of Bologna University, who in 1152 published his *Concordia discordantium canonum*, a regular treatise of canonical lore which completed, corrected, and pruned the ancient corpus. Though not official in the strict sense of that word, Gratian's work became a classic in the Law schools, and was adopted by the courts. Innocent III brought the Canon Law under papal supervision by appointing a commission of notaries to revise Gratian. They added several more recent canons and decretals, and presented the result of their labours to Bologna University. The new publication, however, was both diffuse and defective; about 1230, therefore, Gregory IX requested his chaplain, the Dominican Raymond of Pennaforte, to draw up a systematic code of Canon Law. This epoch-making work, entitled *Quinque*

Libri Gregorii IX, was completed within four years; it was adopted by the
whole Church and received no additions until the Sixth Book of Boniface
VIII. The *Clementines* of Clement V were published by John XXII in 1317.
These three works, forming the *Corpus juris canonici*, continued to represent
the Church's law right down to the promulgation of the present *Codex* in
1917.

We must also say a few words about the human aspect of ecclesiastical
justice. It is true that the Church borrowed much from Roman Law, especially with regard to procedure[19]; it is also true that she was influenced to
some extent by Germanic custom. But if we consider her legal system as a
whole, we shall recognize it as an original creation. She was the successful
guardian of principles far more liberal than those of Roman or Germanic Law. It was she who fixed the limits of power, and who first laid down
the rules of war. It was she who first guaranteed the rights of the weak, of
widows, and of orphans. It was she who distinguished the sacramental and
contractual elements in marriage, and who admitted the equality of spouses without undermining the husband's headship. It was she who restricted parental authority; and it was she who enforced respect for a man's last
wishes as expressed in his will. Canon Law was the pioneer in many fields
of jurisprudence. We should not, for example, possess our modern ideas of
delinquency and punishment, were it not that the canonists studied the difference between *crimen* and *peccatum*, between felony and misdemeanour.

Modern society has in some respects moved far from the principles of
medieval jurisprudence, notably in regard to the right of asylum. If a malefactor, a political opponent, or a condemned criminal managed to reach

---

19. The Church's attitude to Roman Law was complex. The popes and the great (religious) universities, especially that of Bologna, encouraged its study; and St. Yvo, a
future judge of Trégniers, attended the school of Orléans. At the same time, however, there was a noticeable tendency to forbid clerics the study of Roman Law, on
the grounds that it inculcated non-Christian principles and favoured the power of
princes (Lateran Council, 1139). Later, Roger Bacon lampooned the clergy for their
preoccupation with Digests and Pandects. In the thirteenth century the renaissance
of Roman Law was encouraged by temporal sovereigns, and even used by them as a
weapon against the Church. See Volume 2, Chapter VIII, section 10, and Chapter
XIV, section 3.

"asylum," he was inviolable; and "asylum" included not only the fabric of a church or religious house, but any centre under ecclesiastical control, even the cross which marked its extreme limit.[20] This merciful provision might, of course, save some jail-bird from the gallows upon which he should rightly have been hanged; but it rendered justice less implacable, and safeguarded that last chance of repentance and forgiveness which the legal systems of our day are more than ever inclined to withhold from those within their clutches.

9. THE FINANCES OF THE CHURCH

As the Church administered her own justice, so she had her own finances. During the great centuries of the Middle Ages her wealth as a whole increased considerably, though somewhat irregularly.

The Holy See had its particular sources of revenue. These consisted, first, of income from the papal states, a detailed account of which was drawn up in the *Liber censuum* by Cencio Savelli, a Roman cleric and a good financier who later became Pope Honorius III. Next, there was *Peter's Pence*, contributed chiefly by those countries which acknowledged themselves vassals of the Holy See. Thus, in the reign of King John, England paid a tribute of £700 and Ireland £600; while Frederick II promised one thousand gold pieces on behalf of Sicily. The papal budget was further augmented by "fees for protection" paid by churches and religious houses which had applied for direct dependence upon Rome. There were also dues paid by high dignitaries for the confirmation of their appointments, and by archbishops on receipt of the pallium. Finally, there were payments for Bulls and other papal documents, as well as for various dispensations and indulgences, not to mention certain extraordinary clerical taxes levied on a variety of occasions. It must be admitted, finance was far too prominent

20. This is the origin of the calvaries often found at the entrance to continental villages and whose memory is preserved in the street-names of certain towns.

a feature in the history of the medieval papacy, especially from the middle
of the thirteenth century. Innocent IV's exchequer became notorious for its
repeated demands, for its skill in raising "voluntary donations," and for its
co-operation with Florentine bankers in fleecing archbishops on their visits
ad limina. These methods were continued by Innocent's successors, and the
amounts of "gratuitous offerings" were fixed with minute precision by the
Curia of Alexander IV, Urban IV, and Clement IV. At the end of our period
the popes at Avignon had developed an even more elaborate though not
altogether edifying system.

The remainder of the Church had four sources of revenue: *tithes, perquisites, donations,* and *benefices.*

The tithe, or gift of the faithful to their clergy, was an ecclesiastical
institution of great antiquity which had been codified by the capitularies
of Charlemagne and then by the Council of Paris in 870. Theoretically, it
was payable by all laymen from their revenues of whatsoever kind; and the
amount, as shown by its etymology (Latin, *decima*; French, *dime*) was one-
tenth. It was collected locally and brought to the tithe-barn. In practice,
however, things did not work so simply. Many of those from whom tithes
were due obtained dispensation by purchase or favour. Rates varied considerably; the tithe on corn, for example, was in some cases "one sheaf in ten,"
in other cases every eleventh, twelfth, or even thirteenth sheaf. As to the
duty of carriage, many peasants excused themselves, and the parish-priest
had to go and fetch what was owed to him.

Perquisites, known in some districts as "altar money," were an offshoot
of the *"droit d'étole."* In order to save priests from destitution, with which
many of them were threatened, the authorities had been obliged to allow
remuneration for pastoral duties which, in canonical theory, were gratuitous. Presents made to the parish-priest on the occasion of a wedding or
baptism became almost everywhere fixed charges.

The principal source of ecclesiastical revenue took the form of donations, some of which were imposed by Canon Law. Clerics were bound to
bequeath to the Church whatever they had managed to acquire through
their priestly functions; but this rule was less strictly observed as time

went on. Many laymen, on the other hand, made valuable bequests to the Church, sometimes from piety, sometimes out of gratitude, or in order to assure prayers for their souls.

Benefices were the revenues of property attached to an ecclesiastical office. Bishops and abbots frequently had at their disposal great wealth derived from land, farms, town-property, workshops, and other real estate belonging to the see or monastery. In principle, no one was allowed to "cumulate," i.e., to touch the revenues of an abbey or bishopric other than his own, and this rule was stressed over and over again by councils in the eleventh and twelfth centuries. But in the thirteenth century this wise regulation was relaxed, together with that of "residence" according to which a cleric was bound to reside in the see to which he had been appointed. Henceforth we find canons enjoying the benefit of cures in which they never set foot, and fulfilling their duties through poorly paid vicars, while many a high dignitary collected the profits from appointments in which he was not otherwise interested. The strictest theologians and canonists, especially those of the University of Paris, vehemently condemned such practices, but in vain.

We must not infer from this account of ecclesiastical revenues that all clerics lived in opulence. Disparities were often so great as to be nothing short of scandalous. The priest in charge of a parish whose beneficiary lived miles away had to make do on what was called "adequate emolument," which never represented half the benefice and often not so much as a third. That meant destitution. Between the income of a vicar and a wealthy bishop the proportion was in many cases as much as three hundred, and sometimes one thousand, to one.

Even if we consider them as a whole, the finances of the Church varied greatly from one region to another. Where it is possible to refer to documents of the French royal exchequer, we find that diocesan revenues varied from three to thirty-five livres per square mile. Yet, France was "the paradise of God"; in Italy or Spain the Church's income was far less.

Moreover, these resources were not without enemies or over-zealous friends, first among whom were the temporal sovereigns. The revenues of the clergy were theoretically exempt from taxation, but not in practice.

Kings who were proud to call themselves protectors of the Church did not
hesitate to ask her, in terms no less imperative than polite, for all kinds of
subsidies. In France alone we find heavy taxes laid upon the clergy, now for
the crusades, now to stamp out the Albigensian heresy, now to provide for
war in Aragon. Until the end of the thirteenth century these subsidies were
never raised without permission from the Pope; but after that date governments levied taxes on the clergy with unfailing regularity, and Philip the
Fair did so whenever he pleased. The practice soon became general everywhere. The Italian clergy were oppressed by the communes; but the popes
could do nothing about it, since they needed assistance from the urban
leagues against the Emperor.

Another ingenious method employed by secular princes to lay hands
on Church property was the so-called royal prerogative. This curious custom was a relic of secularization as practised by the Carolingians, a relic of
the privilege of investiture once claimed by temporal rulers. On the death
of a bishop or abbot the king took his place for as long as the see remained
vacant, and collected its revenues.[21] The practice was not universal, nor was
it employed in every province of a kingdom such as France; but those who
could hope to benefit thereby seized every chance to do so. It is not difficult
to imagine with what solicitude the holders of such privileges hurried, while
the see was vacant, to hew down forests, empty fishponds, sell the flocks and
harvests, so long as they formed no part of the deceased prelate's personal
estate. Official protests, such as were heard at the Council of Lyons in 1274,
fell for the most part on deaf ears.

This method of taking from the clergy part of their wealth was a recognized procedure. But many laymen succeeded in making handsome profits. Barons in search of money, especially during the eleventh and twelfth
centuries, preyed upon bishoprics and monasteries, nor was the communal

---

21. C. Laplatte, in his essay on "The Administration of Vacant Bishoprics" (*Revue d'Histoire de l'Église de France*, 1939), has shown that the temporal prerogative was not a
rich source of revenue for the kings; but it was accompanied by the "spiritual privilege" (i.e., the right of nominating to benefices normally enjoyed by the titular),
which enabled them to pension off many a favourite.

movement blind to its opportunity. Others acted in a more underhand fashion, embezzling tithes and even converting them into dowries for their daughters! With the collusion of civil governments and certain members of the clergy, this practice was so well established that Innocent III was obliged to tolerate "enfeoffed tithes." The tithe, in fact, became an article of trade.[22]

These losses were, after all, no more than occasional; but there was another, infinitely more far-reaching in its effects, and in certain cases much more severe, which the Church unwittingly incurred. The urban renaissance and the growth of trade gave rise, as we have seen, to ever-increasing monetary exchange, resulting in a general fall in the value of coinage. This phenomenon corresponded to what we should now call "inflation," and it is well known that during a period of inflation fixed incomes tend to fall. The fact made little or no difference to those ecclesiastical beneficiaries who had been wise enough to exact payment in kind; but those who had preferred money to goods suffered an inevitable loss of income, for it was, of course, practically impossible to persuade debtors to accept a higher scale of charges. The principal victims of this situation were the great Benedictine abbeys, and it was largely responsible for their decline towards the end of the thirteenth century.

The revenues of the Church, therefore, were not altogether secure. Considered as a whole, she was possessed of great wealth and must be recognized as the leading financial power; but against that must be set her enormous expenditure. The papacy had to meet the salaries of a host of officials, the upkeep of the pontifical palace, and that traditional splendour which the most saintly popes could not forgo. It had to subsidize crusades, missionary

---

22. This explains why the tithe, which was not in itself exorbitant (especially if we take account of the public services rendered by the Church), soon became unpopular. The common people were angered by this diversion of their pious offering from its lawful ends and by this misuse of the "goods of the Crucified." From about the year 1200 payment of tithes was stoutly resisted, complaints were made to the king, and organized strikes occurred. A judgment of the ecclesiastical court at Sens condemned certain persons who had not paid their tithes for four years, and the monks of St. Berlin wrote to the Pope asking him to apply ecclesiastical sanctions to those who would not pay. There is record of still more serious incidents: priests were beaten up when they came to collect tithes, and in 1226, at Dunkerque, some were actually murdered.

work, and religious building schemes. Gigantic sums of money were con- 311
sumed by such undertakings as the chimerical attempt to restore the Latin
empire of Constantinople, which was pursued by the Holy See from 1261
onwards.[23] The clergy were alone responsible for services which today are
provided by the State and for which the twentieth-century taxpayer has to
find sums he might well wish reduced to a tithe rent-charge. Education,
charitable institutions, hospices, parochial administration, and certain public works were among the numerous activities which fell to the clergy but
which we now regard as the province of lay officials. Ecclesiastical revenues
were by no means earmarked for the comfort and recreation of the clergy.[24]

10. THE CHURCH AS AN ECONOMIC POWER

THE Church was indeed a society within society; but she must not be
thought of as a foreign body, drawing upon the common stock of men and
money and giving nothing in return. She took a prominent share in the daily round of life; and no historian, however anti-clerical his bias, has ever
denied her civilizing influence. None has failed to recognize her vital part
in the work of production and exchange, or that her impact upon human
culture, vast and permanent as it has proved to be, was not intentional. The
Church's purpose was neither to increase production, nor to make profits,
nor to extend her commercial sphere. True, all these things were added unto
her, but only because she was concerned first and foremost with "the Kingdom of God and His justice."

---

23. See Volume 2, Chapter XIII.
24. It is worthwhile to notice the means whereby the papacy rewarded its servants. It was
    concerned with remunerating the more important among them by granting benefic-
    es, but left the salaries of inferior executives to these beneficiaries of apostolic favour.
    Again, until 1310 payment was in kind: officials of the Curia drew "ration" from the
    kitchen, while the Marshal's office issued hay and oats for horses which were indis-
    pensable in an age when the papal court was always on the move. Equerries received
    their liveries. In the fourteenth century money came into its own. Accounts show that
    wars fought in Italy represented the greater part of papal expenditure.

The economic doctrine of the medieval Church could not have been further removed from modern theory and practice. It was an economy devoid of avarice, in which wealth was never sought for its own sake, in which commercial transactions had no profiteering motive, in which production was proportionate to demand, and in which expenses (gratuitously incurred for God's sake) were always ahead of savings or capital deposits. It was, moreover, an economy close to those who laboured for it. A century ago Disraeli praised it in these words: "Today we deplore absentee owners. But the monks were always in residence; they spent their income among those who produced it by the labour of their hands." We might vary his observation and say that the Church had nothing in common with capitalist bosses, who are entirely cut off from the masses responsible for production. Ecclesiastical economy was at any rate man-sized.

We know what was the economic role of the monasteries in barbarian times. Whereas the barons and other temporal landowners only just managed to preserve the (mainly rural) centres of economic life in the Roman world, the monks undertook an immense task of colonization. The sons of St. Columban, followed by those of St. Benedict, completely altered the appearance of huge tracts of land, turning woods and swamps into arable and pasture. A religious house, established in the most impenetrable of German forests, became at once a nucleus of culture, of production, and of exchange; the whole countryside was transfigured.

Monks in the eleventh and twelfth centuries had, of course, less need than their predecessors to work as pioneers, except on the borders of Germany and Poland and Central Europe. The early economic stage was passed; but each abbey continued to exercise important economic functions, thanks to the Holy Rule of St. Benedict, which requires every monastery to be self-supporting.

Again, it must be remembered that monastic life itself was favourable to the growth of intense economic activity. The monks, especially the Benedictines, most of whose time was devoted to spiritual reading and the divine office, could not be "producers"; their manual labour, though ordained by the Rule, was fast falling into disuse and was quite inadequate to the needs

of a large community. A monastery was therefore a wage-paying corporation, distributing money in its neighbourhood.

What did these expenses cover? First the subsistence of the monks,
their food and clothing—often a considerable item when we consider the
size of communities. Next, there was the heavy cost of divine worship: material for vestments, wax for the candles, oil for the lamps. Far heavier was the
cost of building. One need only visit the ruins of a medieval monastery to
realize the sums necessary to erect and maintain it, more especially as the
monks built on the grand scale for God's glory and the benefit of future
generations. Without seeking comfort, they had an eye to hygiene and convenience, as may be seen from a glance at the latrines of Fontenay. A monastery in the twelfth century had a better supply of flowing water than has
the Palace of Versailles.

The expenses of building and upkeep were by no means the limit of
monastic economy. The monks' vocation included works of charity no less
than contemplation. We may be sure that the greater part of their revenues
was employed for purposes other than religious. For *what* purposes? Mainly
for charity in its several forms. We shall have more to say about the importance of this branch of monastic activity in the sphere to which it properly
belongs—that of human relationship; but it was clearly no less considerable
on the economic plane, and here the secular clergy vied with the regulars.
Think what the Church as a whole must have spent in works of charity at
a time when she alone was responsible for social security and public assistance, not to speak of education. Even the business of hotel-keeping, which
appears to us strictly commercial, was part of Christian charity; most places
of call on the roads were hospices, religious establishments for the convenience of travellers and pilgrims.

There were even cases in which the charitable funds of the Church were
strained to breaking point, e.g., in times of public calamity, plague, or famine. The civil authority was extremely short-sighted and held no reserves; so
that men looked to the Church, and especially to the religious houses, whose
granaries, fishponds, and resources of every kind were forthwith placed at
their disposal. There are numerous instances of dioceses and monasteries

selling their treasures, even the sacred vessels, in order to save the neighbouring people from starvation.

One of the most curious undertakings of the Church in the economic field was that of bridge-building. Here we have a surprising and little-known chapter of history, obscured by legend. It begins about 1084 in the south of France, where the confraternity of St. Sibert constructed a bridge at the place long known as Maupas but thereafter as Bonpas. Their example was followed elsewhere, and enterprising laymen undertook to bridge the Rhone. Thus in 1177, so it is said, there came to the city of Avignon a pious shepherd named Benézet, whom God had instructed to build a bridge at that point where the river is particularly wide and difficult to cross. St. Benézet and his "bridging brethren" worked at the job for seven years, and it was their hands that produced the famous bridge whose ruins may still be seen. In 1265 the Cluniac Benedictines decided to erect a bridge somewhat farther north. They probably called in the confraternity of the Holy Ghost, which originated at Nimes; whence, no doubt, the legend that the Third Person of the Trinity took a hand in the work.[25] At all events, the bridge took nearly a hundred years to build; it was called Pont-Saint-Esprit, and gave its name to that delightful town. Many more examples of this kind might be cited. At Lyons the wooden bridge collapsed and was rebuilt in stone by a religious confraternity; the same was done at Saumur by the monks of St. Florentin; while in Portugal, Blessed Princess Mafalda instituted an order of builders to bridge the Tagus. The whole Church became interested in these useful projects, and special indulgences were granted to

---

25. The bridge at Avignon was the first to be made of stone; its completion, therefore, marks an important date. The building of the bridge at Pont-Saint-Esprit is the object of a learned study, entitled *Un Pont au Moyen Age*, by M. Guy Dupré (1947). This work was undertaken by the prior and apparently entrusted to a confraternity. Some of the workmen were dedicated (*donati*) to the task by way of penance; they wore a white dress ornamented on the chest with a bridge in crimson material. About 1349, priests were allowed to take part in the work, thus foreshadowing the modern worker-priests. The labourers were often at loggerheads with the prior. Leopold Delisle, a great French scholar, doubted whether there was an Order of "Bridgers"; history has not yet spoken her last word upon this matter (*Académie des Inscriptions*, vol. 19 [1892], p. 540).

bridge-builders. When in 1275 the bridge at Maestricht gave way, carrying with it an entire procession, as many as forty days indulgence were promised to anyone who helped to reconstruct it. Nor, on such occasions, were the hierarchy slow to act. Thus, at Grenoble, in 1219, Bishop John himself raised the money to rebuild the bridge destroyed by the Isère, as was also done at various times and under other circumstances by the bishops of Rodez, Bourges, Metz, Basel, Minden, York, Durham, Orvieto, and many others. The most remarkable instance was that of Conrad von Scharfeneck, Bishop of Metz, who in 1233 ordered that the best suit of clothes belonging to each person who died in his diocese should be sold, and the proceeds used for building a bridge over the Moselle. This was the Bridge of the Dead, which is still standing. Those bridges which the Church helped to build were often sanctified by the erection either of a chapel at one end or midway, or of a cross, or even of a simple niche from which the figure of a saint might watch over the structure. The saint, of course, was invariably St. Christopher, a poor ferryman of whom the Golden Legend relates that he was once privileged to carry on his shoulders none other than Jesus Christ.

The Church's vital role as a medium of exchange was represented not only by building bridges and mountain-hospices, nor even by the construction of roads and river-embankments. The ordinary course of monastic life involved a number of activities which affected the neighbourhood, sometimes over a very wide area. For example, monastic workshops, mills, forges, saw-mills, etc., gave rise to large-scale industries in many places; and we have a striking instance of this in Dauphine, where the Carthusians were the first ironmasters. Certain abbeys had business interests far from their own walls: e.g., seaside fisheries, or the vineyards around Laon which belonged to the abbey of Lobbes in Hainaut.

Again, the crowds who flocked to a religious house, to a shrine, or to some place of pilgrimage, might begin a considerable flow of trade. Nearly all the great fairs were of ecclesiastical origin: Lendit, not far from the abbey of St. Denis, Tarascon-Beaucaire, Provins, Troyes, Frankfort, Cologne, even Wisby on the Baltic and Novgorod in Russia. Since all fairs were held on religious festivals, it is no mere accident that French peasants still speak of

St. Martin's or St. John's market; and that the same word (*Messe*) is used in German to signify both "Mass" and "fair."

To sum up, the economic activity of the Church throughout the eleventh and twelfth centuries was principally monastic. It coincided with the full flowering of religious life; and when, during the thirteenth century, the monastic edifice was undermined by causes that were at once moral and financial, there set in a twofold decline, not only of its spiritual vitality but also of its economic force, so that former opulence gave way sometimes to actual distress. At that juncture, however, there appeared another great economic phenomenon in the Church, side by side and largely connected with the growth of urban centres—I mean the building of cathedrals.[26] Although it was no longer the monks, but the bishops and Christian people generally, who were at the helm, the economic result was just the same. Year after year the building sites drew to themselves an endless stream of manpower, ensuring thousands upon thousands of working hours, and calling for the services of every guild. Imagine the quickening of economic life in France, say in 1250, when some fifty cathedrals or large churches were in course of construction. There again, as the monasteries had done in preceding centuries, it was the Church who took the lead in what we should now describe as an "extensive programme of public works."

11. THE CHARITY OF CHRIST AND SOCIAL SECURITY

IF we would estimate the benefits conferred by the medieval Church upon the society in which she lived, we must take into account her labour in a field which is now described by such phrases as "public assistance" and "social security." Here she stood practically alone. The State as such, whether described as empire, kingdom, or republic, did not consider itself bound by any duty towards its subjects even though they were helpless, destitute, or

---

26. For the present we need only refer to Volume 2, Chapter IX on the cathedrals, which deals at length with the causes and progress of this phenomenon in the twelfth and thirteenth centuries.

sick. By the end of the period in question only very few municipal or royal
hospitals had come into existence, and these were administered by religious.
The Church, however, taught her children that each one is answerable for
all.

There you have one of the paradoxes of the Middle Ages: a society which
was, on the whole, more violent and more indifferent to suffering than that
of western Europe in the twentieth century, could behave with extraordinary generosity and refinement, working the constant miracle of Christ's
charity. It is astonishing that, with no official organization and no help from
the Government, Christian generosity sufficed to run welfare institutions
upon a scale which would have done credit to ourselves. Private charity,
about which it is, of course, difficult to learn much, was both widespread
and open-handed. So much at any rate is clear from biographies, the heroes
of which make gifts to those in misfortune; from chronicles which refer to
"God's table," meals for the poor, and portions left over for any unfortunate
who happened to knock at the gate; and also from innumerable wills containing bequests in favour of the poor.[27]

This tide of charity continued to increase, reaching its high-water mark
in the time of St. Francis of Assisi and St. Louis. Encouraged by the concession of indulgences, and prompted by the mendicant Orders, it resulted in a
veritable flood of donations and in the founding of congregations dedicated
to the service of "our lords the poor."[28]

The Church, through the medium of her clergy, had opened up the way,
and she carried on the task with unfailing devotion. There had been an organized system of poor-relief in every parish at least since the eleventh century;

---

27. In Germany the word *Seelegerat* was used to designate gifts made by a Christian for
   the sake of his salvation. It occurs in many wills.

28. This observation was suggested by Dr. Fleurent's most interesting article "Une assur-
   ance-maladie à Colmar pendant le Moyen Age" in the *Annuaire de Colmar* (1950). It
   deals with the administration of a "sick fund" belonging to the journeyman tailors of
   Colmar. Members who fell sick had a room reserved for them in the hospital under an
   agreement between the latter and the confraternity. The head of the confraternity was
   bound to visit his sick at least once a day to "hear complaints, console, and encourage
   them."

and a register, known as *matricula*, was kept of all those who received help. The parish priest and his curates administered the fund, which, in accordance with an Act of 818, was supplied by one-fourth of the tithes and one-half of all donations made to the parish. But it was not easy to protect this budget against cupidity, and a rule was made that only those in genuine trouble might receive assistance, and then only on condition that they were local people. Each monastery had its own *matricula* in charge of an "almoner." In general, there were two classes of assisted persons: a body of poor folk (usually twelve in number) who were lodged, fed, and clothed within the convent walls, and a varying number of destitute men and women who were provided with the necessities of life. In some cases the number was very great. St. Riquier, for example, served more than five hundred meals each day; Corbie distributed fifty loaves; while Cluny kept an annual reserve of five hundred sides of salt pork for the use of the poor. The work of relieving poverty was so fundamental that St. Bernard never delegated it, even when burdened with those heavy cares which made him the arbiter of Europe.

In the eleventh century there sprang up simultaneously religious Orders expressly vowed to works of charity, and joint benevolent societies. The earliest and most widespread Order of hospitallers was that of the *Antonines*. It was founded in 1095 near Vienne (Dauphiné), in the parish of Mota, where relics of St. Anthony the Hermit were preserved. The district had recently suffered from an outbreak of that mysterious disease known as "burning sickness" which is thought to have been caused by the use of spurred rye.[29] Those affected turned black and died almost at once. Two noblemen, Gaston de Valloire and his son Guérin, were miraculously cured, and, as an act of thanksgiving, founded a congregation known as the Hospitallers of St. Anthony to nurse those afflicted with this disease. It was reorganized in 1297 by Boniface VIII as a congregation of canons regular. The Antonines were

---

29. Doctors nowadays call it ergotism. During the summer of 1950 in the neighbourhood of Pont-Saint-Esprit on the Rhone, cases of bread poisoning were attributed to ergotism. The *Burning Sickness* has been exhaustively studied by Dr. Henry Chaumartin (Paris, 1947). Grünewald's famous reredos at Colmar illustrates the work of the Antonines.

celebrated as far afield as Livonia and Transylvania. These begging brethren, with their black mantle marked with a Tau-cross (called St. Anthony's
cross) and their small hand-bells, were welcome everywhere. If they entered
a country that lay under interdict, the terrible sanction was suspended; and
if anyone gave them a pig, it was marked with St. Anthony's cross, a bell was
tied round its neck, and it was allowed to wander freely, eating whatever it
pleased.[30] The Antonines, however, were not alone in tending the sick. An
Order of the Holy Ghost, founded in 1178 by Guy of Montpellier, worked in
the hospitals and also took in foundlings. Though a religious institution, it
was governed by a lay grand master, and towards the end of the thirteenth
century possessed more than eight hundred houses. Two other "crutched"
orders vied with the Antonines, though on a more modest scale. These were
the *Cruciferi* instituted at Bologna about 1150 and approved by Alexander III in 1160, and the *Stelliferi* of Bohemia and Silesia. They were distinguished respectively by a red cross and a six-pointed star of the same colour.
In 1099, after the capture of Jerusalem by the crusaders, a group of nobles
founded the Order of St. Lazarus to care for lepers in the East. Louis VII,
who saw them at work, brought twelve brethren to France; and the Order
spread rapidly until it possessed, in Europe and Asia, no fewer than three
thousand lazar-houses. It was reorganized by Innocent IV, as the Order of
Knights of St. Lazarus, and survived into modern times. Finally, there was
a congregation of canons regular known as *Brethren of the Cross*, founded
about 1210 by Theodore de Celbes, a canon of Liége. Their duty was to visit
countries ravaged by heresy, especially Albigensianism, in order to nurse the
sick and thereby reveal the true charity of Christ.

Thus, by the conjoint efforts of the hierarchy, the new Orders, and
private generosity, there came into being a host of charitable institutions.
That is why, until quite recently, French hospitals were called *Maison-Dieu*,
or *Hôtel-Dieu*. Many of them were established by a bishop, a monastery, a

---

30. Such is the origin of St. Anthony's pig, which is still proverbial. Medieval artists often
depicted the great hermit accompanied by a porker; more recent theologians, in
search of a learned explanation, have claimed that this useful animal was symbolic of
the carnal temptations overcome by the saint!

religious Order, a rich layman (king or prince), or, later on, by a commune. But their character was always markedly religious; the staff consisted of men or women dedicated to God and styled "brothers" or "sisters" who, even if they belonged to no recognized congregation, followed a Rule inspired in most cases by that of the Hospital of St. John of Jerusalem, and were almost always governed by a cleric, priest or monk. The majority of hospitals were vast buildings—that of Milan was renowned for its beauty—where the sick, the infirm, and the aged alike were received and cared for. Treatment, however well-intentioned, might be far from scientific, but at least the destitute found shelter and consolation.

Among these hospitals, there were already some that specialized in particular diseases. That opened at Paris by St. Louis was intended for the blind; it took the still-famous name of *Quinze-Vingt* because it could provide for 15 x 20 = 300 cases. William the Conqueror had long ago established one in England, and about 1220 the Bishop of Chartres built the *Six-Vingts* for one hundred twenty patients in his cathedral city.[31] Abandoned children, according to ecclesiastical law, were to be laid at the door of a sanctuary or religious house as a precaution against their being killed. They had their own hospital, run by the Order of the Holy Ghost, or were sheltered by Hospitallers of Jerusalem who had left their normal duties in Palestine so as to carry on this holy work in Europe. Some of these children's hospices were enormous, and the inmates were looked after until they reached adult age, when work was found for the boys and a dowry provided for those girls who did not wish to take the veil.

Most impressive of the specialized hospitals were the lazar-houses. Leprosy, which was far more widespread than today, was the terror of the age; so much so that Joinville told St. Louis that he would rather commit thirty mortal sins than be afflicted with the dread disease! But Christianity had learned to respect the brethren of Christ in these hapless folk covered in revolting sores. St. Francis's kiss bestowed upon a leper, not to mention the

31. There appear to have been no mental hospitals before 1375, when the *Tollkiste* (madhouse) was opened at Hamburg.

solicitude for lepers shown by St. Louis, St. Elizabeth of Hungary, and St. Hedwige, is sufficient proof that in this domain also the saints preached by their example. The leper (Latin, *misellus*), that supreme example of misfortune, was likened to the unhappy Lazarus who, the parable assures us, will find joy in heaven. Hence the words *lazar* and *lazar-house*. We have all read some account of the heart-rending ceremony with which the leper was conducted to a house which he might henceforward never leave without his rattle and a distinctive mark sewn on to his clothes. The same methods have been used in modern times; and the story of Father Damien shows how inhuman the seclusion of lepers can be. In the Middle Ages they were at least accompanied with words of supernatural hope. Innumerable establishments were reserved for them; and in 1225 a census ordered by Louis VIII revealed that there were more than two thousand lazar-houses in France alone. The patron of this struggle against the frightful scourge was St. Roch (1295–1327), son of an illustrious and noble house at Montpellier, from whom the present family of Castries descends. He spent his whole life caring for lepers, so far forgetful of himself, says the legend, that his faithful dog had to beg bread for him. Roch himself died of the horrible disease. His radiant personality became one of the best known in medieval times, and remained so into a later age, if we may judge from the many pictures of him by Tintoretto, Carracci, Rubens, David, and others.[32]

It is impossible to enumerate all the forms assumed by Christian charity, or the institutions to which it gave rise. Some of the most curious were devoted to the *recovery of prostitutes*. This social sore existed throughout the Middle Ages, but increased during the thirteenth century with the growth of towns and universities. Prostitutes were found everywhere, even in the crusading armies! St. Louis took steps to regulate their trade, and an encyclical of Innocent III in 1198 promised total remission of his sins to any pious man who married a harlot with a view to her rehabilitation.

---

32. Cf. Prof. Jeanselme, "Comment l'Europe au Moyen Age se protégea contre la lèpre" in *Bull. Hist. de la Médecine*, 1931. For life in a lazar-house, see C. Schmidt, *Notice sur l'église rouge et la léproserie de Strasbourg* (Strasbourg, 1879).

In 1204, Fulk, parish priest of Neuilly who was afterwards celebrated as Peter the Hermit of the fourth crusade, began, with his curate Peter of Rossiac, haranguing fallen women in the public squares and in the streets. Later, he founded a congregation for the purpose of reclaiming them; and his devoted efforts soon brought into being an abbey which adopted the Cistercian Rule. Fulk was not alone in this work; in 1272, Bertrand, a citizen of Marseilles, established a similar community which was recognized as a monastic Order by Nicholas III. Their example was imitated at Rome, Bologna, Messina, Bourges, Dijon, and even at St. Jean d'Acre in Palestine. But the most interesting and most successful of these undertakings was that of Canon Rudolph of Hildesheim, who was asked by the Archbishop of Mayence to reclaim the *fahrende Weiber* (street-walkers). He founded the Order of Penitent Sisters of St. Magdalen, under whose austere rule these ladies might walk the road to heaven.

Not even so generous an outpouring could exhaust the fire of Christian love. If the sick and the infirm were dear to God, there was yet another class of men for whom our Lord demanded succour in the parable of the Good Samaritan. These were travellers, especially pilgrims, who journeyed in search of Christ, and for whose benefit several congregations were founded. In Italy, the Hospitallers of Altoparcio guided travellers through the dangerous marshes around Lucca; in Spain, the Knights of St. James protected pilgrims on the road to Compostella; and a like duty was performed by the Templars in Palestine. In the Alps, where the passes were especially difficult in winter, hospices were established by St. Bernard of Menthon (996–1081), a young nobleman from the Val d'Aosta, whose father resided on the lake of Annecy and who had already spent a long life in the apostolate. His memory is preserved by the Great and Little St. Bernard, whence (until 1953) the canons regular and their famous dogs guaranteed the safety of travellers in those parts. In the thirteenth century, when a new road was opened from Central Switzerland towards Italy, the monks of Disentis built a hospice and named it St. Gothard in memory of the holy bishop whose charity had shed light on Hildesheim. So hospices sprang up on all the highways of Christendom, centres of Christian welcome where travellers and pilgrims found food and lodging, where they could mend their clothes and shoes, get a shave and haircut, and confess their sins. 323

All this provides tangible proof that the idea of Christendom was no abstract notion, and that the Church imparted to secular society the very strength of Christ. If we desire one more proof of her boundless charity, we shall find it in the *Redemptive Orders*, whose founders were inspired by the most sublime of motives. In Africa and Asia the infidels treated their Christian captives as slaves, who were not seldom in peril of their lives. A number of heroic souls combined in an attempt to deliver these unfortunates: they begged money for ransom, and even visited Muslim territory, offering themselves as substitutes for any captives whose salvation was thought to be in danger. This extraordinary undertaking involved grave risks, as witness St. Raymond Nonnatus, who was martyred in 1240 by the Bey of Algiers on account of his unrelenting zeal. Two great Orders were vowed to this work. The *Trinitarians* were founded in 1198 by St. John of Matha and Felix of Valois with encouragement from Innocent III. Their white habit with its red and blue cross soon became famous. The chief house of the Order in France was the convent of St. Mathurin at Paris, where they became known as Mathurins, or "Donkey Brothers," because those of them who went on begging missions were content with this humble form of transport. The *Ransomers*, otherwise known as the Order of Our Lady of Ransom, was founded in 1223 by St. Peter Nolasco and St. Raymond of Pennaforte, who introduced into their Rule the vow of self-substitution for captives. Between the date of their foundation and the French Revolution, these two orders delivered more than six hundred thousand captives, among whom was Cervantes.

Such was the splendid service rendered by the Church in return for the privileges granted to her by medieval society. Nevertheless, we shall misunderstand her economic and institutional role unless we bear in mind that her charitable work was not the fruit of cold calculation on the part of statesmen anxious to maintain order and to avoid misery which begets trouble. Her work in this field had nothing in common with the regimentation of Social Security or with the anonymity of Public Assistance. The Rule of

324   the Paris hospitals in 1230 stated that they were to receive "the poor and wretched as our Lord Himself," that they must be "honoured and served as if they were God." Our lords the poor were loved indeed. For when the Church taught her children to be charitable, she was not taking her stand on the merely administrative plane; she was teaching them how to obey Christ's command.[33]

---

33. The Middle Ages had a mystic nostalgia for poverty, and came within an ace of treating it as a sacrament. In every medieval will made at Paris we find a bequest in favour of the Hôtel-Dieu. (See E. Coyecque, *L'Hôtel-Dieu de Paris au Moyen Age*.)

CHAPTER VII

Man Under the Eye of God

1. "WHEREVER THERE IS MAN, THERE IS HUMAN NATURE"

THE Church asked nothing more of her children than to be faithful to Christ's message; but at no time has it been easy to obtain this fidelity. "Wherever there is man, there is human nature," says Montaigne; and no matter how strong religious faith may be, it cannot avoid the fact that man is a creature of flesh and blood, full of sin and disobedience. Human nature was of no higher quality in the Middle Ages than it is today.

The barbarian epoch had witnessed an alarming decline of moral values and of civilization. Pillage, rape, and murder had long been fashionable occupations. The law of force, *Faustrecht*, prevailed; it was impossible, therefore, that violence and immorality should vanish from the earth within a few brief decades. Though profoundly Christian from many points of view, medieval society was none the less brutal, merciless towards children and defeated enemies, while its sexual life left much to be desired. In this atmosphere the Church strove untiringly to inculcate the civilizing principles of justice, human dignity, and peace.

Violence was the most striking feature, represented by the armed and armoured warrior galloping at the head of his men. When a creature of that kind is roused, men do better to avoid its path. Now fury was the only sentiment a true warrior thought worthy of himself; "to think is to make oneself ridiculous" was a common saying. To rush upon his neighbour, upon Church property, and upon helpless peasants was considered almost a professional duty, whereby the soldier trained his hand for operations on a larger scale. How else, indeed, could he avoid boredom in his thick-walled castle, half fortress and half barracks, when chase and tourney, both images of war, did not suffice to occupy his days?

"They preferred combat to fine gold and food," says the *Chanson d'An-tioche*; while a knight confesses outright: "If I had one foot in Paradise and the other in a castle, I would step down from above to go and fight." Read any of the *Gestes*, and you will at once smell fresh-spilled blood and "earth bestrewn with brains"; you will see widespread massacre on every page, dying men at their last gasp on the field, the wounded forcing back "their guts into their bellies." Family ties were no obstacle to such deeds, and it was often the warrior's own brother, his father, or his cousin whom he dispatched in this way. A man who clove his enemy in two, or opened his breast and tore out his heart; a hardened old soldier who dashed children against a wall, or boozed on the ruins of a convent whose nuns he had just slaughtered; neither of these types was looked upon as a savage brute, but rather as a hero who deserved pardon for his whims. Such are the chief characters, for example, in the lays of Raoul de Cambrai or in the Lorraine Cycle. There was little protest, unless a whole population was massacred, or the soldiers behaved with abnormal cruelty. The Sire de Coucy was a bestial figure, as was Bernard de Cahuzac, who put out the eyes of one hundred fifty prisoners at Sarlat while his wife amused herself by cutting off the breasts and tearing out the nails of a female prisoner.

Such practices were not confined to the feudal class; urban wars were every bit as frightful as those waged by the barons. Quarrels between the Italian cities were full of unimaginable violence. Whole provinces were laid waste and devoured by fire; the utmost refinement of torture was visited upon the losers[1]; and men were put to death in pitch, in boiling oil, and by still more hideous means.

It was often impossible to excuse these acts of violence on grounds of war, for many "soldiers" were no more than highway robbers. Suger says of

---

1.   For example, at Forli, where prisoners were shod like mules.

the Sire de Coucy that he "devoured like a ravening wolf." The monks of 327
St. Martin at Canigou used ten pages of a large folio volume to recite the
cruelties inflicted upon them by the lord Pons du Vernet. Many families of
noble extraction descended to the level of feudal brigands, taking up their
abode on some mountainside and lying in wait for travellers. The very name
of Hohenzollern (high customs-officers) is suggestive! These bandits, too,
were orthodox Christians. Abélard, speaking of the Count of Blois, says
with disillusioned irony: "Thibaut gives plenty of money to the religious
orders; the more he steals, the more he has to hand out. It would be better if
he stole nothing and gave nothing."

Violence and cruelty, then, were part of medieval life. Men were so
accustomed to it that their sense of indignation had become atrophied.
Nothing is more striking in this connection than their system of criminal
justice. For example, there was a feudal law which reserved the right of chase
to the landowner on his own property, and Enguerrand de Coucy once
applied this law by hanging three boys who had poached a rabbit. St. Louis
summoned him to court and punished him severely for this outrageous act
of cruelty. Whereupon several barons protested that there had been no mis-
carriage of justice. The use of torture after condemnation as an increase of
punishment, as well as beforehand in order to extract a confession, steadily
increased. The Germanic custom of trial by ordeal continued in use, whereby the accused had to plunge his hands into boiling water or walk barefooted on live coals. There was also the judicial duel, a strange method of settling
differences by allowing the parties to cut one another's throats and leaving
Providence to point out the winner.

We might at least expect to find that women behaved better. They may
not all have gone so far as the hideous torturess of Sarlat; but many of them,
living in their castles as in a guard-house, seem to have been formidable vira-
gos. We find them leading armies into battle, as did Blanche of Navarre,
Countess of Champagne, who burned Nancy. Aubrée d'Ivry built a stronghold during her husband's absence, and shut him out on his return; but a
dagger put an end to her pretensions.

It need scarcely be said that sexual morality fared little better. We have just been speaking of women, and it is an admitted fact that the women of any period are the true gauge of its moral standards. Judging by medieval literature (which, by the way, was often so outspoken and realistic as to take the heart out of any twentieth-century novelist), female manners seem to have been deplorable. We are assured that women spent so many hours at their toilet that they arrived for Mass "long after the consecration"; and as for their dress, a little poem by Robert of Blois describes a technique of coquetry that seems not yet to have grown old:

> *Aucune laisse desfermée*
> *Sa poitrine, pour ce qu'on voie*
> > *confaitement sa chair blanchoie.*
> *Une ses jambes trop descoeuvre...*
> *Prudhomme ne loue pas cette oeuvre.*

Nor was there only question of peccadilloes; the *fabliaux* and *gestes* make constant reference to adultery. Documentary evidence suggests that society as a whole showed scant respect for sexual morality. Preachers never ceased to inveigh against the corruption of manners; and even allowing for the professional character of their invective, we cannot suppose that it was all mere imagination. We must likewise assume that the detailed lists of carnal sins found in confessors' manuals were not dictated simply by a taste for classification.

It stands to reason that men were no better than women. If proof be needed of the moral chaos, there is plentiful evidence in the matrimonial fantasies of kings and emperors. Examples of divorce, remarriage, and public concubinage are numerous. Some of them have a certain quaintness, such as that of the Capetian Philip I deserting his wife Bertha of Frisia. Premature stoutness had diminished her charms, and the monarch, in his hurry to replace her, carried off Bertrade, Countess of Anjou, the wife of one of his chief vassals. Others kept a mistress—sometimes more than one; and the Emperor Henry IV was notorious for the indignities with which he loaded

two successive wives, Adela of Turin and Praxede. One of the counts of
Poitiers bundled his wife and children out of doors, and installed a younger
woman who was herself already married.

The kings of Sicily also distinguished themselves in this respect. No
son of Roger II made any secret of his harem, and we know that Frederick II imitated their example. Well-behaved sovereigns, such as William the
Conqueror in England, and St. Louis in France, were considered anomalies.
Noblemen, of course, followed in the footsteps of their rulers; and after the
capture of Barbastro, in Spain, the Muslim chroniclers were horrified at the
licentiousness of the French barons. In the East, the crusaders gave a shameful exhibition of Western morals. Incidentally, too, the crusades and wars
in general were often a severe test of conjugal fidelity, as were pilgrimages in
general. Absent husbands frequently returned to find themselves supplanted. Enguerrand de Coucy was renowned not only for his barbarous justice, but also for his rape of Sibyl, Countess of Namur, while the count was
fighting elsewhere. Nor were clerics themselves altogether free from guilt.
The satiric poet Mahieu assures us that the clergy of "St. Geneviève, Notre-
Dame des Champs, and St. Maur seduced the women of Paris." Nor was it
without reason that in 1231 the synod of Rouen forbade the keeping of vigils in churches, or that another assembly referred more explicitly to "wolves"
who profited by these occasions to "sollicit" the pious females of the flock.

It is foolish to generalize, for documentary evidence in any period is
more often concerned with evil than with good; and while History names
the profligates, she overlooks the mighty host of those who remained true
to the laws of chastity and to their marriage vows. Nevertheless, the upper
classes of medieval society as a whole impress us no more favourably than
do their counterparts of today. As for the lower orders, what little we know
of them through *fabliaux* or chronicles suggests a level of morality scarcely
higher than that of brute beasts.

The Church strove manfully to stem this degrading current, calling
her children to the practice of those Christian virtues which are depicted on the sculptured porches of cathedrals in the form of chaste, simple,
and heroic girlhood. Men did not reject her lesson outright; human nature

is weak in the presence of temptation rather than fundamentally bad. All the same, those who bore witness to the teaching of Christ often went in peril of their lives. Bishop Robert de Meung, for example, was assassinated in 1220 by a robber-baron whom he had recently excommunicated, and Bishop Robert of Clermont was thrice imprisoned by Guy II, Count of Auvergne, a notorious raider of abbeys. Seculars and regulars alike were hated by all the riff-raff of society. It would be impossible to set down the revolting details of cruelty and blasphemy to which so many churchmen were subjected by these brutes; yet, in spite of repeated set-backs, and at the cost of age-long effort, the Church persisted in her formidable task. Slowly she raised the moral standards of society, and put an end to numerous horrors and injustices, by forcing the animal in human nature to feel itself continually in God's sight.

2. RESPECT FOR THE HUMAN PERSON AND LIBERATION OF THE SERFS

AT the root of her endeavour lay one vital factor: respect for man, i.e., for the human person. Had not Christ said that God cares for each and every individual, that God, whose solicitude extends even to the humblest sparrow, is interested in each and every one of us? The idea that man's importance consists in his being a unique and personal entity was seen by the Church to derive support from the whole feudal regime, within which all social relationships were personal, as between man and man, and within which nothing counted apart from the individual (*nihil praeter individuum*). The terrible notion of mankind as an anonymous mass in which the individual is annihilated, or reduced to a mere number in the mechanism of administration and production, would have horrified medieval men, who were closer than we are to reality and to life.

Today we think of slavery in the ancient sense as the ultimate degradation of human personality. It was a system under which one man belonged to another, as does an animal or lifeless chattel. This melancholy institution

had not disappeared in the Middle Ages. The slave-traffic was a black spot on
the period; Saracens and Jews were the principal commodity. These human
cattle came chiefly from Illyria, Dalmatia, and the Slav countries. But German barons were not ashamed to deal in pagans from the Baltic; and when
Rome was taken by the Normans, all the efforts of Gregory VII failed to
prevent the sale at a low price of thousands of inhabitants to the Muslims.
There was still a slave-trade in England and Ireland in the twelfth century,
and also at Lyons, Florence, and even Rome itself; nor was it regarded as
unlawful, provided the individuals sold were not Christians at the time of
their capture.

The early Church, while reminding masters that their slaves were also
their brethren, had not condemned slavery, and Patristic writers followed
Plato and Aristotle in admitting that it was part of natural law. "The slave
should be resigned to his lot, in obeying his master he is obeying God,"
wrote St. John Chrysostom; and according to St. Augustine, "God introduced slavery into the world as punishment for sin." But in the fifth century churchmen began to protest against the iniquity of slave-owners, and
at least fifty regional councils between 451 and 700 enacted canons for the
protection of slaves. Many bishops refused to allow them on their estates,
and urged their masters to enfranchise them; while a council held at Toledo
was obliged to check the zeal of certain holy prelates who were on the way to
ruining their dioceses in order to meet the cost of manumission.

The anti-slavery movement increased from the twelfth century onwards;
and councils, such as that held at London in 1102, forbade "this ignoble
trade whereby men are sold like beasts." The popes also did their utmost, and
with some success, to ensure that slaves who embraced the Christian faith
were granted freedom. In France, under Philip Augustus, it was declared
that "any slave who passes within the frontiers of the kingdom and receives
baptism is free," and the same was done at Florence in 1289. There were, of
course, always a number of bishops who closed their eyes to this disgraceful
traffic; but Christendom as a whole tended to condemn slavery as immor-
al and to improve the lot of its victims, for whose deliverance the orders
founded by St. John of Matha and St. Peter Nolasco put no bounds to their

charity.[2] Side by side with the slaves properly so-called (and these were not very numerous) there existed a class of men known as serfs, who are often confused with them because their name is derived from Latin *servus* (slave). The serf was in no sense a slave; he was treated not as an animal but as a person; he possessed his own family, home, and plot of land, and he was quits with his master once he had paid his dues. He was not the property of a man, but was attached to a domain in accordance with the essentially medieval concept of an association between men and land, an association which, at the other end of the scale, forbade even a nobleman to alienate his domain. While the *villein*, or free peasant, had the right to "move out," i.e., to leave his land, the serf was tied to it. On the other hand, his land was not distrainable, and he owed no military service in the event of war. He was therefore proof against those vicissitudes which threatened his "free" neighbour. His position was, from many points of view, so advantageous that one collection of usages speaks of the "privilege enjoyed by serfs of being guaranteed against eviction from their land"; and there are numerous instances of free peasants making themselves serfs for the sake of peace and security. It has been held[3] that serfdom, by keeping families on the same parcel of land generation after generation, did much to create the sturdy French peasantry.

A serf's attachment to the soil, however, entailed certain restrictions. His lord had a "right of pursuit," i.e., he could bring him back by force if he absconded. He had also the "right of formariage" which originally enabled him to prevent a serf marrying outside the fief, but which was later reduced to monetary compensation for any loss the master might suffer in consequence.[4] Finally, when a serf died his lord possessed a "right of mortmain,"

---

2.   See the preceding chapter, section 11.

3.   By G. Roupnel in his excellent *Histoire de la Campagne française*. Some historians go even farther and maintain that the burdens of serfdom, viz. *formariage*, *mortmain*, and *chavage*, were common to serfs and to villeins holding land from an overlord. These charges were in origin purely domanial. It has even been denied that the serfs formed a distinct class. Thus in Champagne "all villeins were regarded as serfs." Whatever the truth may be, it appears that in the Middle Ages serfs were a small minority. (Cf. Jean Imbert, *Histoire du droit prive*, p. 42.)

4.   Hence the "right of thigh" about which so much nonsense has been spoken and written. The serf (male and female) required the lord's permission to marry; and since in

i.e., could sieze any goods acquired by the serf during his lifetime. In theory
this was an oppressive right, but in practice it was often mitigated by permission to make a will. Such permission was expressly granted, or was exercised by virtue of a custom which recognized the whole family as joint owners and therefore exempt from mortmain.

The Church was not slow to take an interest in serfs and their condition. The first bishop to promulgate a decree determining their rights was Burchard of Worms (d. 1025), who forbade the imposition of fresh burdens; and his example was followed in many dioceses. During the crusades, the Church recognized that every serf had a right to take the Cross, that his lord could not prevent him doing so, and that, having done so, he was *ipso facto* free. One matter in which she acted with the utmost vigour, in order to enforce respect for human dignity in the serf, was the question of his marriage. She opposed the separation of married couples by the sale of one spouse together with the land on which that spouse resided. The *Concordia* of Gratian declared that "the marriage of serfs cannot be dissolved, even when the two partners belong to two different masters"; and Pope Adrian IV, in a decretal of 1155 which was afterwards included in the *Corpus Juris Canonici*, went still further by declaring the indissolubility of marriage between serfs, even if it had been celebrated without the master's leave. Marriage between a serf and a freeman, to which landowners were evidently opposed, was authorized by the Church; it was even encouraged in many monastic and other ecclesiastical domains, and in 1135 Pope Urban III decreed that all children born of such unions were free.

The Church, then, laboured to ensure respect for the servile class; and there is a remarkable difference between the treatment of serfs in religious documents and in the *chansons de geste* or *chantefables* which speak for the governing classes. The story of Aucassin and Nicolette in *Garin de Lorrain* represents the serf as nothing better than a beast and utterly contemptible.

---

the Middle Ages everything took the form of symbolic gesture (e.g., delivery of a fief was effected by handing over a clod of earth), the lord, in order to signify his agreement, placed his hand on the serf's leg or on the marriage-bed. From that fact, much has been imagined.... (Cf. L. Venillot, *Le droit du seigneur*.)

But at the beginning of the eleventh century Archbishop Adalberon of Rheims, in his *Poème satirique*, speaks with tender feeling of these folk "without whom no free man could live, and of whom the very king and bishops are in a way servants, so much do they depend on them for everything." And what finer homage could the Church render to the serfs than to admit their sons into her ranks? She never barred them from the religious Orders, and many reached the summit of the hierarchy.[5]

The Church did more than this. She was not alone responsible for the great movement which, between the tenth and the thirteenth century, succeeded in abolishing serfdom in the West, but she is known to have given it a powerful impetus. Circumstances were favourable; for, as we have seen, the Middle Ages were a period rich in material achievement, and certain medieval inventions placed at man's disposal a store of accumulated energy. The hard horse-collar attached to the animal's body, instead of a soft collar around its neck, enabled it to draw loads weighing two or three tons as against a maximum of nine or ten hundredweights by the old method; while the introduction of horseshoes still further increased its hauling power. A new style of cart with independent front wheels made it possible for drivers to turn more easily, and helped to increase the volume of overland transport at the same time as carriage by water was facilitated by the invention of lock-gates. This increase of energy resulted in the use of animalpower instead of manpower in mills. At sea, the stern-rudder, which supplanted the steering-oar, permitted the construction of larger sailing-ships, and partly did away with the use of slaves as rowers. These technical advances had their repercussions upon social life. "After the tenth century, complete mastery of animal driving-power freed men from work in that capacity, caused great strides in land-travel, and favoured the use of water-power with all its mechanical possibilities.... The inspired invention of an unknown man (probably a Frenchman during the so-called darkness of the Middle Ages) was destined to change the face of the world..."[6] It was during this same

5. See Chapter VI, section 2.
6. Lefebvre des Noettes.

period that serfdom died out in the West; and if we add that the increased wealth of the towns worked in the same direction by encouraging the acquisition of money rather than of land, it is easy to recognize the disappearance of serfdom as a sign of the times.

Here, again, we have an illustration of the Church's insight, of her readiness to seize an opportunity, and of the vigour with which she employed circumstances in the interests of faith. Technical achievement had reached a point from which mankind could make decisive progress; the Church applied her basic principles to new historico-social conditions, and took a leading part in the liberation of the serfs.

The list of wide-scale enfranchisements carried out by the Church and affecting whole populations or estates is too long to set down in full. In France alone there were many such occurrences, which created a considerable stir. In 1197 the Abbot of St. Rémy at Sens liberated all his serfs at Vareilles and Liège; in 1200 the Abbot of Vézelay set free all those who lived on the estates of that great abbey; in 1225 the chapter of Sainte-Croix at Orléans emancipated five hundred serfs at Étampes; and in 1246 the monks of St. Denis accorded the same privilege to their serfs. Next, in 1249, the Abbot of Saint-Germain-des-Prés enfranchised all those at Ville-neuve-St.-Georges, and in 1250 those at Thiais. Finally, in 1290, the Abbot of St. Gildas at Châteauroux gave every serf at St.-Marcel-lès-Argenton his freedom. Enfranchisement on a smaller scale was still more frequent. The abbots of Saint-Fère at Chartres and Marmoutier each liberated more than one thousand serfs; while in Normandy all the great abbeys followed suit, so that by the end of the thirteenth century there was hardly a serf left on their estates.[7] If we allow personal freedom to be a recognized privilege in

---

7.   The Church has often been blamed for observing the custom of that time and requiring compensation from liberated serfs. But the practice is explained by the fact that enfranchisement involved her in a very heavy loss of revenue and the risk of labour-shortages. That is why, in many cases, manumitted serfs were required to put in so many days of work, on the "instalment plan." The amount of compensation has been greatly exaggerated; it was generally one sheaf of corn in every twelve and was known as the "*gerbe libératrice.*" Serfs very often resisted emancipation, but such cases were rare on ecclesiastical estates. Laymen, on the other hand, frequently demanded enormous sums by way of compensation and taxes.

336   any civilized society, we must likewise admit that the Church, together with the monarchy,[8] was a potent factor in the task of civilization.

3. THE HOLINESS AND DIGNITY OF LABOUR

WHILE the Church looked upon man as a free and responsible agent, she was far from teaching him individualism. It is undoubtedly to Christian influences, to the doctrine of fellowship as taught in the Gospel, that we must principally attribute what Père Mandonnet[9] has described as "the most characteristic phenomenon of European life in the twelfth and thirteenth centuries, the strength of fellow-feeling"; by which he means the remarkable aptitude in men to form themselves into groups and work together. Time and again we find in the charters of free towns and trade associations reference to the law of Christ's love.

Medieval man, aware of a higher law binding him to others, was fully conscious of his obligations to the community. He looked upon work, therefore, not merely as the means of earning his living, but as an activity worthwhile in itself and productive of virtue. In this matter, too, the Church was foremost in the field. She respected manual labour, which St. Benedict had enjoined upon his sons both for their personal sanctification and for the common good; she taught men to value it by pointing to the example of Joseph the carpenter, Crispin the shoemaker, Eloi the goldsmith, and many another working man whom she herself had canonized. Everyone was familiar with St. Paul's warning: "He who worketh not, neither let him eat." The labourer tilling his field, the craftsman producing wrought iron, dressing wood or leather, were each and all engaged in charitable work, preparing

---

8.   Louis VI was the first Capetian king to free serfs in his domain; Louis VII went so far as to declare that liberty was part of French law. St. Louis, in particular, enfranchised many serfs and encouraged his vassals to do likewise. These grants of freedom were almost always onerous, for the king and barons were in great need of money to resume the crusade. See G. Tenant de la Tour, *L'homme et la terre de Charlemagne a saint Louis* (Paris, 1942).

9.   In his *Saint Dominique*.

for themselves a place in heaven. Contempt for manual labour, which is felt by many intellectuals today, had no place in the age of the cathedrals; nor was it until the eighteenth century that men came to recognize a difference in meaning between the words "artist" and "artisan."[10] Now since labour was a form of Christian virtue, the very organization of the working-class was specifically Christian. Theoretically there were two kinds of association, the *confraternity* and the *guild*. In practice, however, there was not much difference between them. Confraternities were originally indistinguishable from those many devout societies which had sprung from the cult of a saint, from companionship on pilgrimage, or from the wish to benefit by prayers after death. They were sometimes known as "candles" or "clubs," after the candle offered by members to the church or the meal for which they "clubbed" together. When the confraternity united men who followed the same trade it had this twofold character of a religious brotherhood and mutual aid society. Members were required to attend certain offices, especially on the patronal feast-day; while pensions were paid from the common chest to those who were aged, sick, or unemployed. Moreover, these brotherhoods or confraternities gave rise to a system whereby travelling members might be lodged and fed by the local branch in almost every Christian country.

The guilds were organized on hierarchical lines, comprising masters, companions, and apprentices. Note, however, that this hierarchical system

---

10. It is important not to misunderstand the nature of the medieval working-class movement, which was often tinged with anti-clericalism. Banter and ridicule at the expense of monks and canons was only part of a small quiverful of arrows which the common folk loved to let fly against the clergy, simply because they were top-dogs and children have always enjoyed a joke against their elders. That it did not amount to much is shown by an amusing thirteenth-century poem entitled *Dit des fevres*:

    In my view the workers are
    The folk for whom one should pray more.
    Believe me, workers do not live
    To dawdle; that's the very truth.
    Their property is not let out at interest.
    Workers live honestly by honest toil;
    They give and spend more open-handedly
    Than usurers who do not a stroke of work—
    Canons, provosts, or monks.

338   did not become widespread until about the fourteenth century with the ascendancy of the middle class; in the twelfth and thirteenth it was easy to rise from the degree of apprentice to that of master. The guild was essentially a professional body, uniting all workers employed in a given trade and subject to no authority. When St. Louis instructed Étienne Boileau to draw up the *Livre des Métiers*, he intended no more than to codify established custom, not to make new regulations having royal authority.

For the most part, these associations of working men were fostered by the Church, who, it has been suggested, preferred that her children should emphasize their purely professional solidarity, since brotherhoods or confraternities tended to beget the Chapel spirit, and ran a risk of sowing tares in her midst. Christianity, then, kept a firm hold upon the guilds and other trade groups, many of whose statutes have a strong religious tone: "Brethren, we are images of God; that thought is the keynote of our association. With God's help we shall achieve our purpose, provided fraternal charity is found among us; for it is by love of our neighbour that we rise to love of God."

Actually, the guild modelled its pious customs, its liturgical traditions, and its charitable works upon those of the confraternity. In the stained-glass windows of our cathedrals we can still recognize both the collective labour and the faith of medieval workmen. Coopers, furriers, tanners, or bakers would subscribe to do honour to their patron saint, and present a window at the bottom of which was a panel showing them engaged in their particular occupations. In the reign of Philip Augustus, when Eudes de Sully presented Notre Dame with relics of his illustrious predecessor, St. Marcel, the goldsmiths of Paris presented a valuable casket for their reception, and this was the origin of a custom known as "may des orfèvres," which lasted until the Revolution.[11]

Work thus performed beneath the eye of God ennobled man, and satisfied his heart's desire by giving him that "pride in a job well done" which

---

11. Cf. P. M. Auzas, "La traditionelle offrande de la Corporation des orfèvres," *Ecclesia* (Paris), May 1951.

Péguy praised in ancient France, and of which there are many examples in
the stories of the guilds. We read, for instance, in Thomas Deloney's tales
of the weavers and shoemakers of London: "Every son of a shoemaker is a
prince by birth" and the art of mending shoes is called a "noble trade." The
guilds also made rules governing manufacture. It was important to avoid the
production of shoddy workmanship by unscrupulous individuals; and these
regulations (which prescribed, among other things, the number of threads
that should go to an ell of cloth, the thickness of stones used to build a
house, and even the wood from which coffins should be made) bore witness
to the dignity of labour.

The application of religious principles to labour organizations benefited the public by ensuring the production of sound commodities. It was
likewise advantageous to the workers themselves, providing for their spiritual and moral welfare but also improving their material circumstances
by forbidding unfair competition, preventing too low a level of wages, and
condemning undue extension of the working day.

All the main feasts of the Church were what we should now call
"bank holidays." Sunday (which included Saturday afternoon), together
with many liturgical feasts, each of which frequently took in two or three
days besides, were recognized holidays. The number of days thus set aside
for prayer and rest from work varied from one diocese to another; they
might be as few as thirty-three days (excluding Sundays) and as many as
fifty-three or even seventy-four. But this number was clearly excessive; in
the thirteenth century a reaction set in, and it was gradually reduced. Rules
concerning rest from work were obeyed to the letter. Woe betide anyone
who worked on Sunday or a feast day! Ecclesiastical penalties descended
on him like a ton of bricks. Exceptions were extremely rare: the goldsmiths
of Paris, for instance, were allowed to work during the morning on Sundays and feasts of the Apostles, but only in order to meet the expenses
of an enormous banquet which they provided for all the poor of Paris at
Eastertide.

A whole body of labour-laws thus came into being, not imposed by the
State but arising spontaneously from the collective soul of Christian people.

340   This code governing the production of goods was so effective that no one can confidently claim superiority for our modern regulations.

4. THE CHURCH AND MONEY

IT may be asked: What was the position of wealth and profit in a society which treated work both as a means to individual progress and as a service to the whole community? Here again, the fundamental idea entertained by medieval Christendom appears full of common sense: it respected the existing order of things, even though practice was often enough opposed to doctrine. It is one thing for society to stand by and watch certain of its members yield to the temptation of huge profits (more or less justly acquired), even while it condemns the abuse of money; but it is quite another thing for that society to prostrate itself before wealth and to recognize, in Péguy's terrible phrase, "money as master in the place of God." In the first case, man retains his dignity, his liberty in face of mammon; in the second, he is riding headlong towards servitude and degradation. The Middle Ages certainly had their quota of wicked millionaires; the economic principle, however, on which society rested was not the familiar cry, "Get rich!" but our Lord's saying, "Blessed are the poor in spirit."

Generally speaking, the notions of property, work, and profit were not so clearly defined as they are today, from a strict economic point of view, but in relation to services rendered. Landed property did not belong to a man simply because he had inherited or bought it, as is now the case. A modern owner of real property may be dispossessed in order to settle his debts, *but not because he misuses it or does not use it at all.* In the Middle Ages the exact opposite was true: a landowner, though up to the neck in debt, could never *on that account* be dispossessed of his estates, but he could be if he proved himself unequal to his responsibilities or broke his feudal oath. The moral principle took precedence of economic considerations.

The same thing applied in the case of work. Today, money is the measure of labour; transactions between one man and another are in essence monetary, i.e., a certain sum of money passes in exchange for a certain amount of service or merchandise. Medieval man based his dealings and justified his services on wholly different grounds—fidelity, devotion, protection, charity, and, above all, on the notion of the common good. Granted there were many exceptions; avarice was plentiful, but the principles of human relationship were moral and not economic.

Exactly what part the Church played in this respect may be seen in the famous question of *loans at interest*, or, as theologians and canonists described it, *usury*. This word did not refer merely to interest above a legal rate, but more generally to all interest obtained by lending money. Usury included a number of transactions which political economy distinguishes. There were loans at interest in the strict sense, coalitions or monopolies of production and sale, time bargains, and indeed every kind of speculation.

From her very inception, the Church had been opposed to usury. Lending at interest was quite common in the Roman world, and Cicero tells us that in his day the rate was as high as twelve percent. But it seemed intolerable that a man should profit by lending money to his brother in time of need. The Fathers of the Church had answered transactions of this sort in our Lord's own words: "Give to one another without expecting a return" (Luke 6:34); and in the fourth century many councils had forbidden usury on the part of clerics. At the end of the eighth century and the beginning of the ninth this prohibition had been gradually extended to laymen; clerical usurers were even threatened with dismissal, and all (both clergy and laity) with excommunication. But the fact that these measures were repeated time and again throughout the medieval period suggests that they were not altogether effective. In 1049 the Council of Rheims, presided over by Pope Leo IX, included in one censure both usury and fornication. Later, in 1139, the Lateran Council declared usurers "infamous." This severe canon was repeated at the Lateran Council in 1179, at the Council of Lyons in 1214, and in 1311 at the Council of Vienne, which condemned as heresy the doctrine that usury is permissible. Names of usurers were posted on church doors, and the third Lateran Council excommunicated any Christian who did business with them. Innocent III favoured punishment of those who lent money at interest on a large scale, hoping that by these few well-chosen examples others might be brought to think again.

All our evidence points to the Church having had principally in mind those material abuses which were the more intolerable because they involved (at least at the beginning of the period) poor people who found themselves obliged by some misfortune to seek cash loans. The financial or speculative loan hardly as yet existed. Besides, the Church herself lent money: her treasures formed a rich storehouse; she had only to melt down a few pieces of plate, and there was money to lend to the unfortunate. But these were loans *without interest*—if not in effect free gifts, for there could be little hope in such cases of getting anything back. Such loans could not encumber the borrower. As Henri Pirenne[12] remarks: "By forbidding usury upon religious grounds, the Church rendered signal service to the farming community during the early Middle Ages. She spared it the crushing burden of increasing debt which had so grievously afflicted the ancient world. Here Christian charity managed to apply in its full rigour the precept of lending without interest; and the saying '*mutuum date nihil vice sperantes*' was well suited to the character of a period when money had not yet become an instrument of wealth, so that all remuneration for its use must necessarily have seemed extortion."[13]

---

12. *Histoire économique de l'Occident médiéval.* The Church's economic role has been closely studied by R. Genestal, *Rôle des monastères comme établissements de crédit* (Paris, 1901). He has shown clearly that the Norman monasteries had become veritable farming banks advancing money to smallholders. Their work in this respect was of considerable importance.

13. In fact, the prohibition of loans at interest and speculative practices gave rise to semi-clandestine, or at least officially unrecognized, groups of people who devoted themselves entirely to these forbidden trades. Such were the Northern Italians or "Lombards" and, to a less extent, the Jews. These did not become really important until about the twelfth century when big business began to spread its tentacles, and with it the bank. The natural ill-feeling of debtors towards their creditors was visited upon the Lombards and the Jews, especially upon the Jews, who were held at arm's length like criminals, and more or less confined within their Ghettos. Such is the origin of "pogroms" to which Jews have so often and in so many lands fallen victim, and which constitute one of the least lovely pages in the history of medieval Christendom. But as a whole the Church, through the voices of her rulers, opposed these outbreaks of popular fury. We have already seen St. Bernard going to the rescue of persecuted

The Church condemned not only lending at interest, but all excessive   343
profit from business. On the other hand, the Lateran Council of 1123 threatened with excommunication those who oppressed merchants with excessive
tolls and taxes, a decree which passed into Canon Law. The Church was
also first to condemn the universally accepted law of piracy. She intended
to set a limit to commercial ambitions. A sixth-century document, included
by Gratian among his canons, expressly stated: "Whoever buys a thing in
order to re-sell it intact, no matter what it is, is like the merchant driven
from the Temple." Literally interpreted, this sentence would have prevented
trade altogether. The Canonists, and especially Rufinus, who studied the
question in his *Summa Decretarum*, wisely decided that what was forbidden
was purchase and sale *without work or risk*. Commerce was licit so long as
it required some financial outlay or personal labour. But there is no doubt
that the general tendency at that period was to bring buyer and seller into
direct contact without a middleman, and also to keep an eye on merchants
so as to deter them from trickery, fraud, and misrepresentation. The Church
considered every commodity as having a *just price* based on the work necessary to produce it, an indubitably better idea than that which leaves prices
dependent on capital and advertising.

This doctrine was evolved during the Middle Ages under pressure of
circumstances. Big business had never ceased to operate, even in the worst
days of the barbarian epoch. Towards the beginning of the eleventh century
we discover tycoons like the famous St. Godric (or Goodrich) of Finchale.
He made a fortune in the coasting trade along the shores of England, Flanders, and Denmark, as well as by lucky speculation, but was then touched
by grace, gave his goods to the poor, and became a hermit. It was chiefly in

---

Jews in the Rhineland; the Popes often took Jews under their protection; and when
Duke Henry of Brabant ordered in his will (1261) that all Jews should be expelled
from his domains, St. Thomas Aquinas told his widow to do nothing of the kind. For
the discussions that raged around the prohibition of usury, and the casuistry to which
it gave rise, see an article by M. Louis Vereecke entitled "Licéité du *cambium bursae*
chez Jean Mair," in *Revue historique de droit français et étranger*, 1952 (p. 124). He
prints the text of an opinion given by the Faculty of Theology at Paris in answer to a
question as to the lawfulness of engaging in the money-trade.

the twelfth century, however, that commercial undertakings assumed really gigantic proportions. The millionaire type began to multiply, producing men like the Venetian Romano Mairano, who invested the equivalent of twenty or thirty million francs (1928 standard) in naval armaments, and profited to the tune of fifty percent. Widespread commercial networks such as those operated by Rhenish or Flemish weavers, who dealt in bales of wool by the hundred, could no longer be run on a cash basis; so that commercial credit, i.e., banker's loans, by means of drafts, discount, and bills of exchange, became necessary.

The Church adapted her principles to the new situation by deepening their foundations. What was it she meant to condemn? Mere speculation, money gained without work or risk. Surely it was no more than fair that a lender who risked eventual loss or obvious failure should have a right to be indemnified; and likewise if his debtor purposely delayed repayment. Canonists of the thirteenth century recognized this fact and distinguished the *titulus morae* (right in case of delay), the *titulus poenae* (right in case of loss), the *titulus periculi* (right in case of certain danger to the capital), and the *titulus lucri cessantis* (right in case of failure to succeed). At the beginning of the fourteenth century a theologian named Alvarez Pelayo declared that the prohibition of usury could not extend to these cases.

The fact remains, however, that the Church upheld her principles. All profit derived from moneys lent without work or risk was unlawful; nor did she hesitate to free debtors from liabilities which seemed excessive, and we know of contracts in which borrowers engaged not to use this cunning method of escape. It cannot be denied that in some cases the Church closed her eyes to abuses, that the popes were sometimes obliged to seek aid from financiers and allowed them to handle the papal revenues in a manner far from consistent with morality. But those cases were exceptions which prove the rule. The Church did her best to destroy the primacy of gold, or at any rate to bring it within the principles of divine law. And it was at that very time when she upheld those principles and when her greatest saints preached the ideal of poverty that she reached the zenith of her glory.

5. THE CHURCH OPPOSED TO VIOLENCE

WE come now to a more fundamental, more elementary, and far worse danger threatening the human person, that of unrestrained violence issuing in massacre and assassination. It is to the Church's honour that she headed a movement that was gradually to elevate the conscience of mankind until public order was restored. Amid the chaos of the ninth and tenth centuries, when Norman and Saracen spread terror far and wide, and when feudalism was becoming more or less a hierarchy, the Church had both the courage and the perseverance to instruct man once more in the principles of peace. The worst menace at that time was, and continued for another century to be, the private war, which respected neither place nor age nor person, and often resulted in those deeds of almost inconceivable horror to which we have referred. The principal victims of these conflicts were, of course, the weak and innocent, defenceless villeins and serfs, priests and monks whose resources covered the cost of such enterprises. It was against these repeated acts of private war that the Church launched her campaign for the "Peace of God."

The movement began unpretentiously towards the end of the tenth century when the Councils of Charroux in Poitou (989) and Narbonne (990) re-enacted the prohibition against armed attack and pillage. In this latter year also the Council of Puy founded a "league of the friends of peace" which was supported by both clergy and laity. The Church had early recognized an oath taken upon relics or the Gospels as a means of restraining violence. Faith was so firmly rooted in the souls of men that she was able to assume that most warriors who took such an oath would observe it; in any case, it brought the offender within the Church's jurisdiction, for she was the guardian of oaths. The Council of Verdun-sur-Saône (1016) had been the first to apply this method. It had been followed by a number of others, at which supporters of the Peace of God had undertaken "not to attack the clergy; not to seize the peasant's ox, cow, etc. (a long list of animals follows); not to kill; not to attack travellers; and not to encourage any kind of brigandage or violence." The Council provided for sanctions, and after 1031 any district in which the Peace had been violated was laid under interdict.

The movement, once initiated, swept away all resistance. Opposition, however, was sometimes keen, and came from unexpected quarters; for certain bishops frowned upon the Peace of God, arguing that, whatever happened, they could not excommunicate every baron in their dioceses! The idea, however, caught on in Italy, Spain, and the Germanic lands. In 1081 the Bishop of Liége obliged all those in his diocese to swear to observe the Peace of God, and almost all his colleagues in the Empire quickly followed suit. In Italy, the synods of Melfi (1089) and Troîa (1093) applied it to Apulia and Calabria. In Spain, it was promulgated by a council held at Gerona in 1068. The great territorial princes had too much interest in the maintenance of order within their domains not to side with the Church. As long ago as 1021 Robert the Pious and Henry II of Germany, who dreamed of universal peace, had taken steps to give the institution official status. All the Capetians, too, were zealous supporters of the Peace of God. Thus, in 1155, Louis VII proclaimed a general and absolute peace of ten years, and he discussed it at an interview with Frederick Barbarossa in 1164.

The Church went still farther and recruited volunteers for the defence of peace. These formed a militia whose duty it was to punish offenders and enforce their submission. "War upon those who cherish war!" was the watchword to which thousands from every class of society answered with enthusiasm. The experiment seems not to have been at first an unqualified success. These champions of peace, ill trained in the art of war, were often badly mauled by the veterans whom they sought to convert. In 1038, for example, on the banks of the Cher, the warrior-bandit Eudes of Déols easily annihilated the holy militia sent against him by Aimon, Archbishop of Bourges. But the system was gradually improved; peace associations hired professional soldiers, who formed a kind of Territorial army paid from the proceeds of a special tax known as the *paxagium*. The volunteer militiamen were often commanded by royal officers, and we know what help they gave the Capetian kings, particularly Louis VI the Fat, against the robber-barons.

The institution of a militia in defence of peace shows that the Church recognized that war might be justified in principle. She was far from professing what today we should call "pacifism," and Pope Gregory VII himself

declared: "Cursed be the man who will not dip his sword in blood." What   347
she did do was to introduce the notion of justice into warfare. The *Liber feudorum*, a code of Christian chivalry, expressly states that a vassal is not a felon, i.e., does not violate his feudal oath, if he refuses to assist his overlord in an unjust war. If the Church not only permitted but even encouraged the use of arms, she did so in the name of higher principles: the principle of justice which defined the aggressor and obliged him to keep the peace, and the principle of charity which requires us to help the weak against unjust aggression. Such were the ideas expressed in many councils and papal documents, studied and sifted by jurists and canonists from Manegold of Lautenbach to Yves of Chartres.

In virtue of this second principle, that of charity, the Church instituted another movement, more or less connected with the first and called the "Truce of God." Her purpose was to suspend fighting altogether for a certain time without inquiring whether a particular war was in itself legitimate. The idea had been mooted in 950, though without success, by Pope John XV at the time of a quarrel between the Duke of Normandy and an English king. A synod held at Elme, near Perpignan, in 1017 had decided that all military operations must cease "from the ninth hour on Saturday until the first on Monday"; while the synod of Nice in 1041 had prescribed a truce from Wednesday evening to Monday morning, since Thursday was the day of our Lord's Ascension, Friday of His Passion, Saturday of His Burial, and Sunday of His Resurrection. The Truce had been gradually extended to two whole periods of the liturgical cycle, Lent and Advent; then to certain feasts of our Lady, St. John the Baptist, and the Apostles; and lastly to vigils and ember days. In 1054 the Council of Narbonne embodied this regulation in the splendid formula that "a Christian who slays another Christian sheds the Blood of Christ."

The "Truce of God" became increasingly popular. It penetrated into northern France and the Rhineland, then into England, Italy, and Spain. It was adopted by the papacy in the second half of the eleventh century; and at the celebrated Council of Clermont, in 1095, Urban II called for a general truce. "You have seen," he said, "that the world has long been troubled

348 by these injustices, so much so that in certain parts it is impossible to travel safely on the roads. By day there is little or no security against brigands, or at night against thieves who lie in wait for you both within doors and without. That is why the so-called *treuga*, instituted long ago by the holy Fathers, needs tightening up. Each one of you must enforce it in his diocese; and if anyone, urged by cupidity or rashness, should violate the Truce, let him be punished with the appointed penalty of excommunication through the authority entrusted to you by God and on the strength of decisions reached in this council...." In 1123, 1139, and 1179 the first three Lateran councils prescribed the Truce of God for the whole Church, and their resolutions became part of Canon Law.

The question was, whether these lofty ideals would prove effective. It is certainly true that they often did so, that many great lords overcame the temptation to violence and submitted to rules of conduct which a purely moral authority claimed to impose on them.[14] The problem became infinitely more complicated when there was no question of private wars or of relatively unimportant differences between nobles, but of clashes between kings or national interests. Even in these difficult cases the Church did not hesitate to intervene.

At such times the cause of peace was upheld chiefly by the papacy. The papacy by definition, at least in theory, transcended political strife and party quarrels, because its authority was of divine origin, and because it enjoyed universal prestige. It was therefore eminently fitted to act as arbitrator, inasmuch as one man could hear and decide the case. If we would understand the attitude of those who admitted the papal claim to judge between belligerents, and that of the popes to whom it belonged, we must bear in mind all that has been said in a previous chapter concerning the doctrine of Two Swords, which gave the Holy See both a direct and an indirect right to intervene in temporal affairs. But the popes were not the only ones who acted in

---

14. Even before the kings approved these measures, as did Philip Augustus and his successors by introducing the *Quarantaine le Roi*, a truce which suspended hostilities and thereby gave their own forces time to take a hand.

this way. Several men, notably St. Bernard and St. Louis, were accepted as political arbitrators merely because they were saints: their judgments were considered as proceeding from the Almighty Himself.

Much has been written concerning the Church's function as peacemaker.[15] "To mention only a few of the cases summoned before the court of Rome," says Drouard:

> there was the affair of William the Conqueror and Harold of England, followed by the Quarrel of Investitures. There was the intervention of Clement III between the kings of France and England; of Innocent III between Philip Augustus and Richard Coeur de Lion, to whom threats and exhortations were alternately addressed; and between John Lackland and Philip Augustus. The Emperor Frederick was condemned by Gregory IX in 1236, and deposed by Innocent IV in 1245. Boniface VIII endeavoured to make Philip the Fair observe his truce with England; while John XXII sided with Ludwig of Bavaria against Frederick of Austria, and spoke in a letter to Philip V of "exercising the right of imposing truce which belongs to the Apostolic See." Next, there was the general intervention of Nicholas V, who, in order to provide for large-scale recruitment against the Turkish invaders, proclaimed peace throughout the Christian world, conferred authority on ecclesiastical dignitaries to negotiate the same, and required at least that armistices should be concluded and observed.

Drouard's list of papal arbitrations in the strict sense is no less impressive. He cites "that of Gregory VII between Philip I of France and William the Conqueror, of Innocent III between England and Scotland, and the mediation of Clement III and Celestine III between France and England. Innocent III likewise intervened in the affairs of Italy, Portugal, Serbia, Armenia, and Bulgaria."

---

15. See especially the essays by Père Delos in *La Société internationale* (1928), and G. Drouard, "La Paix médiévale," in *Cahiers du Monde Nouveau*, 1, 2, and 4, 1945.

All these efforts, it need hardly be said, failed to establish an indefinite reign of universal peace. But they did enforce the recognition of a Christian Peace similar to the *Pax Romana*, preferable to armed conflict, and which so impressed the minds of men that we are justified in claiming that, by and large, the great medieval centuries enjoyed a season of international tranquillity far superior to anything known in the barbarian epoch or during the succeeding period. Thanks to papal Bulls and conciliar decrees, there grew up slowly but surely a framework of International Law embedded in those canonical treatises which alone could give it universal application.

The Church's activity was not confined to the realms of public and private law. She attempted, in a more general way, to train the conscience of mankind away from cruelty and violence. The majority were in favour of and anxious for peace, and the collective conscience was both formed and directed by the Church. Insisting on the Gospel precepts, "Love one another," "My peace I leave unto you," she created a body of opinion the strength of which was eventually recognized by the warrior class. If there had been no such thing as public opinion, or if the collective conscience had not been Christian, it is unlikely that the spiritual weapons would have been so effective, or that so many excommunicated rulers would have submitted to an unarmed clergy.

This endeavour to stem the tide of violence and atrocity is immediately discernible in two particular instances. First there was the matter of ordeal and judicial duel, methods of trial which were so much part of an accepted system that the Church could not at once abolish them. They were even recognized by some provincial synods, though the papacy always disapproved of them both in theory and in practice. They were never employed by ecclesiastical tribunals, and the Lateran Council of 1215 expressly forbade priests to bless those who had recourse to them. The judicial duel had long since been condemned as a monstrosity. Archbishop Agobard of Lyons (779–840) declared it to be "no law, but murder"—*non lex sed nex*; and Pope Nicholas I (858–867) added that it was equivalent to tempting God. In 1216 Honorius III prohibited its use, and St. Raymond of Pennaforte's great juridical compendium contains these words: "The duel and every

other form of ordeal are forbidden, because they lead to the condemnation
of innocent persons; to have recourse to them is to tempt God."

The second instance was the tourney, an often bloody sport in which the nobility indulged with unbelievable brutality. It was originally fought with blunted arms, but early in the thirteenth century the use of sharp weapons was introduced, and every meeting became a sort of miniature battle in which the two sides confronted one another before a bevy of fair ladies who would be their reward. Combatants were often wounded, and sometimes killed. The Church took a firm stand against this form of entertainment,[16] which, as the Council of Clermont said in 1130, "endangered both body and soul." The Lateran Council in 1179 forbade these "detestable festivities," and instructed priests to refuse Christian burial to those killed in a tourney. It must, however, be conceded that in this matter the Church's denunciation fell mostly on deaf ears. Those taking part cared little for excommunication, for this mock warfare was already too much part and parcel of contemporary life. No matter with what energy and patience the Church might set to work, violence was so deep-rooted in the medieval mind that any attempt to eradicate it altogether was bound to meet with failure. Therefore, with characteristic common sense, the Church, having done all she could to loosen the stranglehold of brutality, adopted another method intended to Christianize force and its employment. This method was twofold. First she offered her warlike sons the crusade as an outlet for their passions. "Now," cried Urban II at the end of his great sermon at Clermont, "all those who have abused their right of challenge against the faithful must embark on a worthy undertaking that will end in victory. All those who have lived as brigands must become soldiers of Christ. Henceforth they will fight the good fight against barbarians, and those who have been in one another's pay for the sake of a few pence will reap an everlasting reward." If "to kill a Christian" was "to shed the blood of Christ," to slay an

---

16. There were rare exceptions to this rule; in 1200, for example, the great tourney at Ecry-sur-Aisne was blessed by the episcopate because the victors had promised to join the fourth crusade.

infidel now became a sacred duty, a work deserving of salvation. Here was a splendid opportunity for hot-heads itching to use their swords.

As regards the other means adopted by the Church with a view to hallowing the arms of war, it occupies so prominent a place in Christian society that we must consider it at some length. I refer to the institution of Chivalry.

6. CHIVALRY: A CHRISTIAN IDEAL

OF all familiar types representative of the Middle Ages, none is more likely to captivate our imagination or to move our hearts than is the knight. All the animal passions in man, all his will to power, all that issues from the dark regions of his soul, driving him to violence and destruction, is satisfied and transcended in this noble image of the just and upright warrior, haloed with virgin purity; whose aim is rather sacrifice than victory, blood offered than blood shed.

Chivalry was not born on Christian soil. It sprang from the traditions of Germanic tribes in which no young man bore arms until he received them (helmet, buckler, javelin) from the hand of his father or his chieftain[17]; and the Church laboured with undying patience to endow this military investiture with the quasi-sacramental character of knighthood. Centuries were needed in order to effect a complete merger of the two traditions, that of the savage north with that of the Roman and Christian south, a synthesis of which knighthood was the perfect symbol. It was in the middle of the barbarian epoch that the Church began to accomplish this union, by blessing the weapons of those who went to war and by giving them appropriate battle-cries. About the year 1000 priests used to say the following prayer over youths who were ready to take arms: "Hear, O Lord, our petitions and bless with Thy majestic hand this sword wherewith Thy servant desireth to be girt, so that he may be enabled both to defend churches, widows, orphans, and all servants of God against the cruelty

17. See Tacitus, *Germania*, Chapter XIII.

of pagans, and also to strike fear into the hearts of traitors!" From about
1050 this ideal grew still deeper and more Christian. By the beginning of
the twelfth century the institution had come to stay, and in fully civilized
countries was recognized and respected by all.

What was a knight? What qualities and virtues were demanded of one
who bore this title? He was a soldier—a cavalryman (*chevalier*), for to fight
on horseback was a privilege. He was a warrior, whose primary vocation was
armed combat; but he was also expected to live up to certain moral principles, and bound himself by oath to do so. He was a man who believed that
over and above force there existed values to which he dedicated himself. In
this way, the commandments which regulated his conduct bore a military
and a Christian character indissolubly linked. As a soldier, he must above all
be brave, never give ground, and meet the enemy wherever his leader bade.
Such were the duties of his state. And in order that he might fulfil them to
the letter, he was required to possess physical strength, perfect health, and
skill; no dwarf or bandy-legs might be a knight. These qualities were indispensable; but they were not enough, and there was an old saying: "Tant
est prudhomme si comme semble qui a ces deux choses ensemble valeur de
corps et bonté d'âme."[18]

"Goodness of soul" meant the whole scale of virtues, religious as well
as secular and social. At the summit was faith, which gave the others meaning and importance. Because he was a believer, the knight was obliged to
respect the Church and to defend her at all times; but he was assured that
whatsoever he accomplished in the rough school of arms, he did it for God.
If ever a man was conscious of living in the presence of God, it was the perfect knight. Such were Godfrey de Bouillon, Baldwin the Leper, and St.
Louis, soldiers whose life and death were committed from the outset into
God's hand.

The qualities demanded of a knight were really the fulfilment of a
Christian's obligation. He was faithful, devoted to his leaders, strict in the

---

18. He, it seems, alone is worthy who has these two things together, strength of body and
goodness of soul.

354 observance of his feudal oath. He was loyal, hated deceit, and faced up to the truth as he faced up to the enemy. He was loyal, nay more, an unflinching servant of the ideal of justice, "in order," says William Durand's *Pontifical* (a code of chivalric liturgy), "that Justice may find a champion here below." He was also charitable, vowed to defend the weak, the clergy, widows, and children; generous to his subordinates and even to the enemy. Chivalry was a sublime ideal which no civilization has managed to surpass. True, it was seldom realized, and frequently obscured by human covetousness; even so, there is merit in the fact that a whole society acknowledged the worth of that ideal and strove, in the persons of its noblest representatives, to spread it far and wide.[19]

Entry into the ranks of Chivalry was effected by means of an elaborate and spectacular ceremony known as *dubbing* (*adoubement*).[20] Its fundamentally religious character shows the institution to have been a true Order; it was, as we have seen, in the nature of a sacramental. In the eleventh century this rite, which might almost be described as a liturgy, was quite simple, but it was gradually improved and enriched with symbolism. The ancient Germanic elements, e.g., the purifying bath and delivery of the sword, were retained; but they became part of a mystical ceremony calculated to impress upon the candidate his future responsibility before God.

It is night, a holy night—the vigil of Easter, say, or some other great festival. Locked in the silent church, alone with a few candles to accompany

---

19. Gustave Schnürer has some penetrating remarks on the history of the word "honour." "Knightly honour," he concludes, "was attended by particular prestige. A great moral advance was involved in the Church's development of this concept, an advance not only upon the immediate past but also upon antiquity. In pagan antiquity the word signified no more than the rendering of external honours. This idea was subsequently elaborated: external honour was due only to one who was interiorly worthy, i.e., the man of honour whose worthiness resided in himself. The essence of the new conception of honour, then, was the link established between exterior honour and interior worthiness. For the knight, honour of rank was only a particular form of Christian honour. His honour must consist in rendering the honour due to Jesus Christ and to God; for Them he was bound to fight, suffer, and die. The knight remained faithful unto death to the cause of Christ; and thus fidelity, which was a particular obligation of knighthood, became a Christian obligation."

20. From Old German *dubban* to strike.

his prayer, the young squire keeps watch and meditates. He is twenty years of age, strong and courageous. For some time past he has resided in his overlord's household, learning to ride, to handle a sword, and to tilt at the "quintain." Earlier this evening he has confessed and taken a ceremonial bath, so as to be pure in soul and body; he has also donned a long white tunic as if for second baptism. A new life is now opening before him.

At length the great day dawns, and hour by hour the long ceremony will unfold its pomp. Witnesses are there, usually twelve distinguished knights, together with his family and neighbours. Mass is celebrated by some high dignitary of the Church surrounded by a vast assembly of clergy; and when Holy Communion has confirmed him in the pious resolutions taken during his vigil, the ceremony of admission begins. Facing his sponsor, the candidate "lays claim to knighthood." Next, the witnesses clothe him in his new attire: two of them help him on with the heavy linen acton, each one lacing a sleeve; another with the coat of mail; two more with iron hose; and the last buckles on his spurs. As he receives each of these insignia he is reminded that this arming should "righteously serve justice," and he replies, "God grant that it may do so."

The sponsor then advances with a drawn sword, extends the blade for the young squire to kiss, and gives him a sharp blow on the shoulder with the flat. This is the accolade or *paumée*,[21] a survival of the old Germanic rite. Finally, he pronounces the formula of dedication, beginning with an invocation of St. Michael and St. George, and admits the youth into the order of Chivalry. Girt with the sword, the new knight stands before the altar, stretches forth his right hand, and takes the oath.

Such was the ritual of "dubbing" a solemn mingling of military symbolism with the sacred liturgy; and there is no better illustration of the method whereby the Church introduced her spiritual ideals into what was, after all, no more in substance than a formality of incorporation. Who could be admitted to the ranks of Chivalry? Contrary to widespread belief,

---

21. *Accolade* from *colada,* the Provençal form of *colée. Paumée* because the blow was originally given with the hand.

the privilege was not dependent upon birth or fortune. "No one is born a knight" ran the adage, and in theory even commoners could be knighted[22] as a reward for courage and devotion. "Knighthood," it was said, "confers nobility" and "the means of attaining nobility without titles is to be made a knight." Moreover, the institution stirred enthusiastic longings of youth. Francis Bernardone dreamed of knighthood at the age of twenty years, before Christ called him to another service; and the kudos attaching to that title was largely responsible for the eagerness with which many a young man embarked on the crusade. Not before the second half of the twelfth century was it decided in certain countries[23] that, apart from exceptional cases, only the sons of knights should be granted knighthood. But this step perverted the very meaning of the institution, which, through lack of members who had proved their worth, atrophied and lost its essential character.

Knighthood could be lost just as it could be won. He who failed in his duties, violated his oath, or was cowardly or cruel, ran the risk of degradation. This took the form of a humiliating ceremony at which the delinquent's spurs were hacked off flush with his heels. "Honni soit hardiment où il n'a gentilesse"; nobility of soul went hand in hand with valour in the field. The higher degree of refinement represented by Chivalry took a long time to evolve and reach perfection. It began with Roland of the *Chanson*, which was written about 1120, but included traditions of much greater antiquity. Roland, however, was still a fierce fighting man who delighted to cleave his enemy in two or beat out his brains, and whose faith rested on the quiet assurance that to triumph over pagans was the most sacred of all duties. Nevertheless, there is already apparent in this crude way of thinking a definitely

---

22. I say "in theory," for in fact this was very seldom done. Until the thirteenth century, soldiers of fortune and seigniorial officers were admitted to knighthood. When the urban bourgeoisie rose to power, its members coveted the honour; but the original warrior class, fearing the encroachment of these people, gradually created an "order of Chivalry," so that *de facto* nobility gradually became nobility of right. Kings, however, reserved to themselves the privilege of authorizing a man to be knighted, and their instructions were conveyed in what was significantly called a "letter of ennoblement." In this way Philip the Fair rewarded a butcher who had fought bravely at Mons-en-Pévèle.

23. Norman Sicily was the first, c. 1160.

Christian element—the idea of sacrifice, of man offering his life to God, as
expressed by Roland in the hour of death. According to the *Chanson*, the
knight should be a powerful influence for good, and many crusaders made
it a point of honour to imitate these lofty examples. Before long, the *Cantar del Cid* put forward a new but exaggerated model in the person of that
great Spanish adventurer who had courageously done battle with the Moors
towards the end of the eleventh century. About the same time also (c. 1200)
the *Niebelungenlied* roused ancient memories of German heroism. The ideal
knight, in consequence, lost none of his nobility or purity; he became more
realistic, more concerned with results obtained than with mere gallantry. At
this date the Holy Sepulchre was once again menaced by Islam; a new generation was called upon to defend it, and the crusading spirit varied according
to the personality of individual knights. Some laid emphasis not so much
upon military qualities and temporal ends as upon loftiness of spirit; the
knight, in fact, no longer considered himself as a "Christian soldier," but as
a Christian who would serve God before all else, even in battle. Such is the
mystical type of knighthood which we find in the story of the Grail as told
by the Provençal Guyot and the German Wolfram von Eschenbach (twelfth
century). Around the mysterious vessel which had held the Precious Blood
of Christ, and which, say the poets, is really the "Grace of the Holy Spirit," are grouped the figures of Parsifal, "toute candeur et toute niceté"; of
Bohort, who expiates his sins so thoroughly that Paradise opens for him;
and finally of Galahad, the incarnation of Purity itself. These are sublime
embodiments of Chivalry, who lived almost as monks, in whom was reflected the living image of St. Bernard or the crusader-founders of the Temple,
and of whom St. Louis was the heir.

Roland, Cid, and Galahad stand for three periods and three varieties
of a single splendid ideal which dominated the political and social order
of the Middle Ages. So powerful and so enduring was this ideal, that in the
days of Luther and Machiavelli, long after Christendom had disintegrated,
it fashioned the outlook of a man who died facing the enemy as Roland died
at Roncevaux—Pierre du Terrail, Seigneur de Bayard.

7. THE CHURCH AND HUMAN LOVE

THERE was another sphere of life in which the Church played a decisive part, more decisive perhaps than in her struggle against violence. This was the sphere of human love. To the profligacy which was rife in feudal society she opposed those very principles upon which Europe was ultimately stabilized. She insisted, first, upon obedience to the commandments of God, to Christ's precept of chastity, and to that doctrine which she had made her own since the days of St. Paul. She insisted also upon respect for the human person, which led her to place woman on a level of spiritual and moral equality with man.[24] It was respect full of tenderness and mercy, of which our Lord Himself had given numerous examples; the same respect which so many heroic and saintly women had helped to implant in Christian consciousness from the time of the Persecutions down to the worst days of the barbarian epoch. Moreover, by raising the moral standard in general, the Church did much to tighten relationships within smaller groups, to strengthen the family, and to establish it as the unit of society.

She laboured with obstinate determination to give marriage its true dignity. Adultery, a veritable plague in the feudal world, was condemned time and again, even when the guilty sat in high places, even when the sin disguised itself as second marriage. "So long as his wife lives," wrote St. Anselm of Lucca in the eleventh century, "it is never lawful for a man to marry another woman." The same applied to women; in fact, the Church tended to regard adultery on the part of a woman as more serious than in the case of a man. But she never condoned the killing of an adulteress, for "two wrongs do not make a right." Wherever there was flagrant guilt, her first concern was to remove the scandal, then, if possible, to bring the parties together in repentance and forgiveness, a matter upon which one of the Hungarian councils delivered itself of much sage advice.

---

24. See Fr. Claude Schall, *La doctrine de fins du mariage dans la théologie scolastique* (Paris, 1948), and the article by Fr. Riquet entitled "Christianisme et population" in *Population*, October 1948.

Both in books and sermons the Church loved to praise marriage; she
looked upon it as sacred and indissoluble. Jacques de Vitry (d. 1240) went
so far as to say that married people "also belong to an Order, the Order of
Matrimony." His words were echoed by the Dominican Henry of Provins:
"The Order of Matrimony is by no means of recent origin, but has existed
as long as humanity itself. Our Order and that of the Friars Minor have
been recently established; indeed, all religious Orders are later than the
Incarnation. But the Order of Matrimony is as old as the world. I will go
even further: our Order is the work of a mere mortal, but God Himself
founded the Order of Matrimony at the beginning of time." And the good
Dominican concludes with this irrefutable argument: "At the time of the
Deluge, those whom God preferred to save were married people." Robert de
Sorbon (1201–1274) described marriage as a "sacred Order," of which, said
Pérégrin, God alone is the Superior; while Guillaume Péraud enumerated
the "twelve heads of honour" proper to marriage. St. Thomas Aquinas, in
his *Summa Theologica*, rounds off these eulogies of marriage with a shrewd
observation: "Although the state of virginity is better than the state of matrimony, a given person may still be more perfect in the married state than
another in that of virginity."

Theologians and canonists, however, did more than simply condemn
violations of conjugal morality or praise the merits of that state. They produced a whole body of legislation; and, from Anselm of Lucca to Gratian
and his successors, no canonical work of any importance omitted to deal
with this subject, which occupies a large section of the present *Codex*.
Marriage is a sacrament, but in what exactly does it consist? The canonists
replied: "Its essence is the consent of the parties"; they themselves administer the sacrament. The priest, they maintained, acts, so to speak, as witness
on behalf of God and blesses their union; and some went so far as to say that
his blessing is no more than an "ornament" or "flourish."

The Church also set her face against feudal marriages, whereby a man
gave his daughter to some vassal whom he desired to invest with land. They
were marriages lacking genuine consent, and were therefore considered
invalid. In order to preclude all doubt as to consent, the Church forbade

clandestine marriages, and required the presence of witnesses.[25] She likewise condemned the influence of wealth in this connection. "Are we going to publish the banns of marriage between my Lord Such-and-Such and my Lady So-and-So's purse?" cries Jacques de Vitry. The keen interest displayed by so many modern churchmen in problems of conjugal relations is nothing new; that much is quite clear from medieval documents. Some rigorists tried to limit free intercourse between husband and wife by forbidding the marital act on certain days, e.g., Friday, or during certain periods such as Lent; and the example of St. Louis suggests that these prohibitions were sometimes taken seriously. Those with more common sense protested at this undue severity in which Peter the Cantor, a twelfth-century preacher, saw "an indirect means of bringing marriage into disrepute."

The administration of the sacrament was attended with a wealth of beautiful and elaborate ceremonial which we have inherited; and even betrothal, whereby the parties bound themselves *per verba de future*, was a solemn rite. The Church blessed the ring, of which the episcopal or abbatial ring, as also that worn by nuns, is a symbolic replica. Wedding rings came into general use during the twelfth century; they were tokens of fidelity and love, "worn," says Honorius of Autun, "on that finger wherein beats the vein of the heart." The nuptial Mass, too, was accompanied with expressive symbols: a single veil was held over the young spouses, and the first loaf of bread they would eat together was blessed by the priest, together with the first measure of wine they were to share. In some countries there was even a custom of incensing the marriage-bed and sprinkling it with holy water, what time the couple sat therein side by side and prayed.

Thus hallowed, the matrimonial bond was indissoluble. Unlike Roman and Germanic Law, according to which divorce could be effected by mutual consent and even at the wish of one party, Canon Law stubbornly refused to recognize it. Even in cases of adultery, the Church repeatedly quoted St.

---

25. The Church was particularly watchful in the matter of impediments. She would not allow marriage between persons related by consanguinity up to the twelfth degree, nor (on grounds of spiritual relationship) would she recognize the marriage of a godfather and godmother who had together held a child over the baptismal font.

Augustine's famous dictum which occurs in his *De bono conjugali*: "The mar- 361
riage tie cannot be broken except by the death of either party." Nor could a
marriage be dissolved even "in the cause of religion." There were conciliar
decrees ordaining that if a wife took the veil against her husband's will she
must be returned to him, for according to St. Paul (1 Cor. 7:4) it is the husband and not she who has command over her body. Grounds for annulment
recognized by the Church were very few; there were, and still are, only three:
(1) if the husband had been ordained before the marriage; (2) if the parties
were related within prohibited degrees (and even then ecclesiastical jurisprudence hesitated to apply the letter of the law for fear it should be made a
pretext for divorce); (3) if there were "infirmity of the flesh," but in this case
an interval of two or three years was required as well as the testimony of at
least seven relatives that there had been no intercourse between the parties.

The Church, then, was at pains to honour marriage as it deserved. She
likewise undertook the training of mankind in love, and laid down rules
wherever there was danger that instinct might break loose. Important consequences followed, of which two in particular should be noted. The first
of these concerned the family, which would infallibly have been ruined by
lustful imagination and unbridled passion if Christianity had not stemmed
the tide. By this means the very framework of society was strengthened in
such a way as to endure for centuries; and it is no exaggeration to say that
the enormous increase of population during the Middle Ages was partly due
to the Christian view of marriage.

The Church's attitude towards human love had another consequence
which made a deep impression on the mind of Europe, and helped to distinguish Western civilization from those, say, of India, China, and Islam. This
was the raising of woman's status, a truly remarkable phenomenon. It is clear
that at the beginning of our period woman occupied an insignificant place
in a society where force reigned supreme; she did not count, except for her
reproductive function. She had to submit to her lord and master; and if she
criticized his behaviour she was likely to receive what the *Geste de Lorraine*
describes as "the big fist fair and square on her nose," or to be dragged by the
hair as was Blanchefleur by her husband William of Orange (a future saint).

362   As for a personal opinion, she was not supposed to have one; and if she tried to speak her mind, she was quickly sent about her business. This attitude underwent complete transformation between the eleventh and thirteenth centuries. The Church obliged man to respect the dignity of woman, who ceased to be his property, the plaything of his passions or his interests. Woman's maternal role in society was still regarded as fundamental, but society now recognized her right not to be absorbed in it. Both the slavish type of female and the virago were superseded by another kind infinitely more delicate, the kind imagined by a twelfth-century troubadour in these gracious words:

> Work of God, worthy, praised
> As is no other creature;
> Endowed with all blessings and virtue
> Both of spirit and of nature.

There is a well-known and apposite remark of Charles Seignobos: "Love? An invention of the twelfth century!" And Gustave Cohen, an expert on the medieval period, is of the same opinion. "Love," he says, "is a great discovery of the Middle Ages, especially of twelfth-century France. Before that time it had not savoured so fully of eternity and spirituality." Here we meet a question that has produced two fascinating but widely different interpretations[26]: How far was this metamorphosis of love, or rather this appearance and impressive growth of the love-passion in Christian consciousness, due to specifically Christian influence?

During the twelfth century there grew up, especially in the south of France, where manners were more refined, a new ideal known as *courtesy*. It was popularized by the Provençal poets or troubadours: Guillaume de Poitiers, Macabru, Jaufre Rudel, Bernard de Ventadour, and Arnaud Daniel, many of whose exquisite verses have come down to us. In what did courtesy

---

26. D. de Rougemont, *L'Amour et l'Occident* (Paris, 1939); P. Belperron, *Joie d'Amour* (Paris, 1948).

consist? In a code of delicacy, of politeness, and fidelity by which love was regulated. So defined, love could perfectly well be included in the Christian outlook; it constituted an advance on sexual beastliness, and it reached fulfilment in God. Thus we find the celebrated but tragic love of Abélard and Héloïse striving painfully to tear itself away from carnal temptation, and rise towards eternal consolation. In the wonderful story of Tristram and Iseult, passion seems wholly to enslave the lovers; and yet there is a sublime Christian echo in their repentance, the high light of that pathetic scene in which the compassionate hermit reveals to them the ways of God.

But did courtly love retain these Christian characteristics? In practice, it is open to doubt whether the impassioned urge that drove man towards woman was always platonic; and even when the intention was pure, we cannot be certain the devil did not play his part in their effusions—notwithstanding Macabru's uncouth assertion that "true love and sexual love cry out for one another." What part, though, did Christianity play in love's transformation on the historical and psychological plane? Denis de Rougemont maintains that "the love-passion appeared in the West as a counterblast to Christianity (and especially to its doctrine of marriage) on the part of souls inhabited by natural or inherited paganism." And he goes so far as to advance a theory, which other historians (among them Pierre Belperron) have warmly denied, that the troubadours who sang of courtly love had been contaminated by Albigensianism. On this view, the love-passion is heresy. Others believe there may have been Arab influences at work in its development, e.g., the court of Cordova, where manners had reached a high stage of refinement, or certain examples picked up by crusaders in the East. We can only say, without pretending to decide these questions, that it was precisely in the heyday of courtly love that the raising of woman's status (which was certainly the Church's doing) effected a complete reversal in the order of values, making woman, weak and helpless though she remained, no longer dependent on the warrior but the object of his veneration.

It may also be asked whether or not the Church took account of woman's glorification. There is no question of her having as it were equated courtly and mystic love, so as to treat the former as a kind of substitute for the latter. It is a fact, however, that both were developed at the same time, and that the two impulses (one spiritual, the other carnal) often met, even in speech. "The Middle Ages," writes Gustave Cohen, "drew no hard and fast line between divine love on the one hand and human love on the other, between heavenly and earthly love, between love spiritual and carnal; love was there with all its complexity, the motive power of life." Surely Christianity set its seal upon the glorification of womanhood when it offered mankind the purest and the fairest of all women, Mary, Virgin full of grace. At a time when all earthly loves were failing, it was the Church who could alone console mankind, offering them a love which knew no weakness or decay. Thibaut IV of Champagne wrote many a verse in honour of the lady whom he loved, Queen Blanche of Castile; but when about to leave her and set out on the crusade, he penned these lines:

> Lady of heaven, great and powerful queen,
> Be thou my succour in my most need.
> May I be fired to love thee aright!
> When I lose my lady, do thou, Lady, me assist.

This work of training men in love accomplished by the medieval Church culminated in the worship of Mary.

8. ST. LOUIS

To live in the presence of God: such was the ideal offered to medieval society by the Church in spite of many difficulties and setbacks. There were men and women who, without leaving the world or joining the ranks of the clergy, managed to live accordingly and practise heroic virtue. If we would learn by the example of one among the lay saints, we may do so by considering the most typical, a prince who with sovereign splendour occupied the throne of France from 1226 until 1270—Louis, the ninth of that name, whom history remembers as St. Louis. In him were assembled and expressed all those

virtues which twelve hundred years of Christianity had developed in mankind. He dominated his age, and shed upon it so much lustre that our vision
is apt to be deceived. We tend to see him as representative of the thirteenth
century as a whole, whereas those hundred years were less truly Christian
than the twelfth. In the eyes of posterity, St. Louis is not only the type of
manhood at its best, according to medieval standards, but one of those transcendent figures which, through generation after generation, vouch for the
grandeur of our race. It is impossible to speak of him otherwise than on a
note of respect mingled with affection.

The monarch's physical appearance is easily imagined.[27] He was tall and
thin, rather frail, with regular features, fair hair, and clear blue eyes. His
strength and goodness of soul were reflected in his every look. Morally,[28] he
was a saint, but there was nothing sanctimonious or bigoted about him. On
the contrary, he was gay; he could both make and take a joke, and preferred
conversation to books. There was, indeed, a patriarchal atmosphere about
his court. But he had none of those easy-going ways which often veil inherent weakness, none of that undue familiarity which is often the concomitant of bad manners. He never thrust himself on others, was never casual in
his address; and when need arose he could prove himself tough as tempered
steel. Few men have been so keenly aware of their eternal destiny; few mystics have been such accomplished men of the world or taken so active a part
in public life.

The keystone of his career was rock-like faith, critical but unshakable.
"Dear child," he warned his eldest son Philip in a testamentary letter, "I beg
you set your heart upon the love of God; for without that no one can be
saved. Avoid doing anything that will displease God." And Louis observed
these principles throughout his life; they were the source of all his merit.

---

27. From contemporary descriptions, principally that by the Franciscan friar Salimben,
who saw him in 1248 at his departure for the crusade; and also from works of art,
above all the beautiful statue at Maineville (Eure) which was no doubt inspired by
contemporary records.

28. The psychology of St. Louis is familiar from the Chronicle of his intimate friend Joinville; but also from documents used in the process of his canonization, especially the
evidence of his confessor William of Saint-Pathus.

He had grown up under the wise tutelage of his mother, Blanche of Castile, who used to tell him, almost as a truism, that she would rather see him dead than in sin. He never forgot this lesson. Despite the crushing burdens of office, he found time each day to recite the liturgical hours, to search the Scriptures, and to read the Fathers. He confessed often, and his penitential practices included fasting as well as the discipline and hair-shirt. His diet was frugal, his dress simple—except when the duties of his rank obliged him to wear ceremonial robes. One of his biographers observes that he "combined the manners of a king with the habits of a monk"; he was, in fact, a Franciscan tertiary.

It may be suggested that St. Louis was guilty of excess in this direction, and Voltaire unworthily accuses the "crowned monk" of negligence. That is manifestly absurd, when we consider the state in which he left France. "The throne shone like the sun which sheds its rays far and wide," says Joinville; and his is not the language of a courtier. Louis was a grandson of Philip II (1180–1223), whose success in consolidating his dominions had earned him the title of "Augustus" after the victory of Bouvines. He was also the son of Louis VIII, whose brief reign had sufficed to prove his courage and his intellectual gifts. St. Louis, therefore, never had to admit that his faith conflicted with his duty as trustee of the French kingdom; the wonder is that while working for his realm he was able to reconcile its best interests with the supernatural demands of religion. His outward expression of that faith may sometimes cloy; but it was only his manner of proselytizing in and out of season, of preaching, and of moralizing. We may be tempted to smile at the thought of a father sending his favourite daughter a hair-shirt and discipline for Christmas; but the gift signified a transcendent love, and Isabel accepted it as such. On one occasion, certainly, he was tempted to go beyond the requirements of his faith by shirking the responsibility laid on him by God. He talked of joining the Cistercians or Franciscans, whose humble board and labours he delighted to share. His wife, however, who acted on this occasion in a manner worthy of her dignity, reminded him that his duty lay not in withdrawing from the world, but in governing according to God's law. At once he put aside his dream.

St. Louis considered the Faith as no "garden enclosed," no remote and secret region of the soul unrelated to conduct. It should, so he believed, govern man's every act; and since to believe in Christ and to follow his example is, first, to love one's fellow men, his generosity was unbounded. "He had charity towards his neighbour," wrote William of Saint-Pathus, "*together with orderly and virtuous compassion*"—words deserving of remembrance and meditation. "He practised works of mercy," William continues, "by lodging, feeding, clothing, visiting, and comforting the poor and the infirm, whom he relieved and supported by personal service. He ransomed friendless prisoners, buried the dead, and assisted all both virtuously and abundantly." St. Louis setting out to walk through the streets of his cities and distribute alms by the handful; St. Louis at the Maison-Dieu at Compiègne tending the worst cases, oblivious of his defilement by pus oozing from lupus sores; St. Louis inviting to his table twenty poor folk whose filth and stench revolted the soldiers of his guard; St. Louis making straight for a leper, whose distant rattle had attracted his attention, and giving him a fraternal kiss: these anecdotes and many more are derived not from some "Golden Legend," but from the most reliable histories. Moreover, France was indebted to him for countless charitable institutions: the hospitals at Pontoise and Versailles, the "Quinze-Vingts" for blind people at Paris, besides guest-houses and orphanages. Nor must we forget his numerous Benedictine establishments. Joinville tells us that he "adorned his realm with many a Maison-Dieu of his own foundation," and adds by way of conclusion: "Many priests and prelates might envy the king his manners and his virtues."

Above all, these virtues, which were essentially religious, never detracted from his natural qualities or impeded the development of his character. He realized, in fact, that they were fraught with peril. Joinville records that one day when the king was in a merry mood he asked him and Master Sorbon whether it is better to be "*prudhomme* or *béguin*." He listened, smiling, and then, more gravely, said: "Well, I would prefer to be known simply as '*prudhomme*'; you can have all the rest. It is so great and grand a thing to be *prudhomme*, that even the very word itself is a mouthful to pronounce."

What did he mean? He meant what the whole Middle Ages understood the word to mean; he meant what the *Gestes* mean when they refer to Roland and Percival as *prudhommes*, viz. *integrity*. Integrity is achieved by the fulfilment of those duties arising from the situation in which God has placed one; it demands submission to the moral law, and whole-hearted striving after perfection. St. Louis, on account of his royal birth, was required not only to cultivate the inner man, but to prove himself a knight "sans peur et sans reproche," a king who realized his duty; and such indeed he was.

St. Louis was a true knight all his life, a soldier in whom courage was a second nature, because it rested on the certainty of everlasting life. He faced the enemy with fervent joy, and was always in the forefront of battle, never yielding, never resorting to guile. He might have stepped from the *Grail Quest* rather than from the pages of history. Even his enemies were affected by the radiance of his personality; and when he was taken prisoner by the Muslims, the Sultan's leniency not only did honour to a Moor but revealed the stature of a Christian. Many stories bear witness to his prestige. One day a Muslim chief, one Faress-Edin, who had brutally assassinated his master, sought out the captive king and begged him for the honour of knighthood as reward. St. Louis refused—not without irony, since he asked the murderer whether he intended first to renounce the Koran. To everyone's surprise, the criminal bowed his head and withdrew without a sign of resentment. Such was the saint's authority.

St. Louis, however, was no mere paragon of knightly valour. He never failed in the virtues of humanity and refinement, whereby the knight was recognized not only as an accomplished warrior but as a witness of God. His gentleness towards children, his longing to protect the weak, all those qualities, in fact, which are now covered by the word "chivalry," are so characteristic of him that one is apt to forget how much their practice must have cost a man so quick-tempered and so highly strung. He possessed also, to an eminent degree, that quality which the poets assign to Parsifal and Galahad: he was "single-minded"—which means to say he was a gentleman, upright in mind and heart, rejecting all that tends to drag men down into the mire.

This quality of single-mindedness is outstanding in St. Louis's relations
with his wife.[29] Unlike so many princes whose matrimonial and extra-mat-
rimonial whims fill the chronicles with scandal; unlike his contemporary Frederick II; unlike several of the Capetians too, such as his beloved
grandfather; St. Louis showed that it is possible for a king to obey the sixth
and ninth commandments without being at the same time either a prude
or physically impotent. He had no fewer than eleven children. God alone
knows the merit of his loyalty to Margaret of Provence, whom he had married while still a boy. At that time she was a pretty little girl of fourteen, but
after several years of flaming passion for his charming spouse, Louis realized she was lightheaded, coquettish, and unsympathetic towards his mystic aspirations. Although she could show herself every inch a queen, as she
did during the crusade, she was likewise capable of petty intrigue, if not of
downright treachery, which caused him some anxiety. Their union was little
more than a prolonged and often painful misunderstanding; but the saintly
king remained faithful to his marriage vows. No act on his part, whether in
the eyes of God or before the gaze of men, betrayed the motto he had had
engraved on the inside of his wedding-ring: *En cet annel, tout mon amour.*
("In this ring is all my love.")[30]

However great a man's interior virtues, they cannot be called truly
Christian unless they are in some way manifested, made apparent, in day-
to-day conduct, amid the duties of his state. St. Louis never forgot the
principles taught him by his mother, who, during her regency, had also
accustomed him to be present at council-meetings, to listen to the jurists,

---

29. See my study of St. Louis's marriage in "En cet annel tout mon amour," *Ecclesia*, July
1951, and the collective work, *Le couple chrétien* (Paris, 1951).

30. We know from evidence given during the process of his canonization, especially that
of the king's confessor, that St. Louis abstained altogether from intercourse with his
wife not only during Advent and Lent, but also on Fridays and Saturdays, vigils, and
even on feast days whenever he received communion. He was clearly something of a
rigorist; but Margaret offered no objection. Instead, therefore, of scoffing at his austerity, we should perhaps see it rather as proof of a lofty determination on the part of
both spouses to spiritualize even carnal pleasure, an outlook which is similarly reflected in the fact that so splendid a Christian communicated very seldom, four or five
times a year at the most.

and to go in person wherever his people suffered in consequence of poverty, epidemic, flood, or bad harvests. Even at the end of his life, when it was clear he desired nothing but union with Christ, to live and die in His love, he continued to fulfil these tasks with unflagging ardour because his Lord expected it of him. So great, indeed, was his sense of responsibility, that he considered himself one with his people, as sharing in their destiny. On June 4, 1249, before Damietta, he summed up his idea of a Christian king in these memorable words: "My friends and trusty subjects, we shall be unconquerable so long as we are united in charity; *I* am not King of France, *I* am not Holy Church; it is you who, because you are all the king, are Holy Church." Surely no ruler has defined his mission in more splendid terms.

The policies which these ideals led him to adopt made the reign of St. Louis one of the happiest in French history. The following short sentence may still be read in the letter of advice bequeathed to his son Philip: "You must see to it that your people, who are your subjects, live under your rule in peace and equity"; and such was the whole purpose of his government. Equity demanded, first, the repression of those who endangered public order and brought suffering to the common folk. Private wars were strictly forbidden; and although St. Louis did not succeed in preventing them altogether, at least they were the exception during his reign. Equity demanded likewise that he should recognize, and oblige others to respect, human personality even among the humblest and most destitute of men; which explains the leading part taken by St. Louis in emancipating serfs. Some words spoken by Jacques de Vitry in a sermon penetrated deep into his mind: "True nobility resides in the soul. We have not been fashioned some of us from gold or silver, others from clay; we have not come some of us from the head, others from the heel. We are all descended from the same man, all sprung from his loins." In 1246 he began the enfranchisement of serfs in his private domain; and whenever possible he encouraged his vassals to do likewise, compensating from his own resources those who were deterred by the prospect of financial loss. The working classes had no firmer friend, none more attentive to their needs or more generous to their occupations, than the king who took Étienne Boileau[31] as his confidant and appointed him to one of the highest magistracies.

Peace and equity, however, entailed a more stringent obligation. The Capetian monarchs had been long renowned as "rois bon justiciers," royal judges upon whose scrupulous fairness all were able to rely; and Joinville has left a famous description of St. Louis going straight from Mass to sit in the woods at Vincennes, where, leaning against an oak, he would hear "without impediment of court-procedure" anyone who desired to put his case. The picture is symbolic; for even though he could not always administer justice in person, it was his constant preoccupation. As a judge, however, he was by no means indulgent, as some people discovered to their cost. A cook, for example, who had committed robbery with violence thought he could escape the gallows because he belonged to the royal household; St. Louis personally sentenced him to death. Then there was a noblewoman of Pontoise who had persuaded her lover to murder her husband. Franciscans, Dominicans, ladies in waiting, and even the queen herself, all interceded on her behalf; but Louis had her burned on the site of her crime, "because it is good that justice should be seen to be done." Many cases were celebrated in his day for the firmness and independence which he showed. The affair of Enguerrand de Coucy astonished his contemporaries. An illustrious baron, connected by marriage with all the nobility of the realm, was arrested, thrown into jail, condemned to pay a heavy fine, and obliged to expiate his crime by pilgrimage—simply because he had had three boys hanged for poaching on his land. In the light of thirteenth-century customs, the sentence was unthinkable. Another case, though seldom quoted today, caused no less sensation at the time. The king's own brother Charles, Count of Anjou, had been convicted of imprisoning a knight travelling through his territory, and appealed to Louis against the verdict. Summoned to appear at Vincennes, he thought it as well to take with him a select body of jurists; but at the king's order they were opposed on behalf of the plaintiff by the most eminent crown counsel, and the result was such as might have been expected.

---

31. It was Boileau who had organized the trade-guilds in days of Philip Augustus.

The influence of St. Louis in the field of justice was as profound as it was lasting. Judicial duels were abolished by a decree of 1260, and "instead of battle, proof was to be based on evidence." Cases in which an appeal lay to the king, subject to the Parliament, were explicitly defined and their number increased. Great care was taken in the appointment of judges, who were obliged to take an oath to receive neither gold nor silver nor any other fee from interested parties, and forbidden to frequent taverns or to play at dice. The provostship of Paris had been hitherto a fief of the wealthy bourgeoisie, who sold it to the highest bidder. It was now made a salaried office and entrusted to Étienne Boileau, of whom Joinville says that "he filled it so thoroughly that no malefactor, thief, or murderer dared remain in Paris but he was soon hanged or otherwise removed; neither family connections nor gold nor silver, could save him." And the chronicler adds that "people were henceforth drawn to Paris by the fairness of its courts."

St. Louis adopted the same equitable policy with regard to money. He spent very little on himself, and, in his will, advised his son to follow his example. True, the level of taxation was not reduced during his reign; that was due partly to the wars he was obliged to undertake against rebellious vassals and the King of England, and partly to the crusades, which were financed almost exclusively by France. But in this respect also he showed himself scrupulously just; he declined the services of moneylenders, and saw to it that there was no unfair assessment. He would undertake none of those profitable currency-deals which marred the reputation of his grandson Philip the Fair.

Thus, while living up to his duties as a Christian, St. Louis attained the full stature of kingship. In his day, too, France was regarded by the whole of Christendom as "the most blessed and most happy land"; a country where, since peace and harmony went hand in hand with an effort to achieve efficiency, the "conjuncture" (as modern economists would say) was most favourable. Throughout his reign France was the scene of intense creative activity. At this period Master Robert of Sorbon, the king's chaplain, founded a still famous college—the Sorbonne. All the realm of France, indeed, and especially Mont Sainte-Geneviève at Paris, was covered with institutions,

colleges, and houses for students. At this period also, the towers and side-cha-
pels of Notre-Dame were constructed; Chartres cathedral was rebuilt after its
destruction by fire in 1194; and the scaffolding at Rheims, Bourges, Amiens,
Beauvais, and Rouen was alive with workmen. Finally, it was in the days of St.
Louis that there soared to heaven, symbolic of his reign, the Sainte Chapelle,
a marvel of delicately carved stone and mysterious glasswork, destined to
receive that most sacred of all relics—the Crown of Thorns.

In his day men were able to distinguish those among their masters who
wielded power for their own interests and those who sought to exercise
authority for the common good alone. None doubted that St. Louis was
of this latter class; and when he died, the grief of France was echoed in a
moving lay: "To whom will poor folk cry out, now that the good king is
gone, who loved them so?" Long before Boniface VIII issued his official
Bull in the Church's name, the common people had already canonized him
in their hearts.

St. Louis was the admiration not of France alone, but of all Christendom, which knew him while still on earth as a man of God. For he applied
the same principles which governed his life to the sphere of international
relations, a sphere in which they have too frequently been misinterpreted.
He believed, and on more than one occasion openly declared, that there are
not two moral codes, one for the individual and another for the community.
He considered such precepts as "Love one another" equally binding on the
international as on the personal level; and his attitude in this respect has
been falsely judged if not completely misunderstood. The extravagances of
present-day nationalism have so distorted man's sense of values that otherwise honest men are ready to embrace the worst elements of Machiavellian-
ism for the sake of quick returns, while Christian policies are denounced as
chimerical and dangerous—with results that are plain for all to see.

Did Louis's "policy derived from Holy Scripture," to quote a phrase
of Bossuet, do harm to the French monarchy? There is some difference of
opinion; but we do know that, so far as this most saintly of the Capetians
was concerned, it involved no servility towards the Church, no indifference to the welfare of France. On many occasions he adopted a policy of

374   absolute independence with regard to "Mother Church," whose most obedient son he nevertheless styled himself in his private capacity. He was once
approached by a group of bishops who wanted help from the secular arm to
enforce a sentence of excommunication. Louis replied that, in his opinion,
those penalties were often undeserved, and he would therefore not interfere.
On the contrary, he got the Pope to request that they would in future think
twice before imposing sanctions of this kind. Certain high Roman prelates,
and even some popes, e.g., Innocent IV, took such license in the matter of
ecclesiastical property as amounted almost to rapine.[32]

St. Louis gave full support to the protests of the French clergy, and
approved the terms of a memorial addressed by them to the Lateran. He acted in still more characteristic fashion during the tragic conflict between the
Priesthood and the Empire. He would not for a moment play second fiddle
to the papacy. When, in 1240, Gregory IX offered him the Roman crown
for his brother, the Count of Artois, he joined Blanche of Castile in refusing
it; and later on he tried to arrange a settlement between the two adversaries.
In 1245 Innocent IV summoned an ecumenical council at Lyons to depose
Frederick II; but St. Louis refused to attend in person, and did all in his
power to mitigate the Pope's severity. He could not prevent the sentence of
excommunication being read from the pulpits, but at least he took care to
make no comment which might suggest that he approved. When we consider the results of this unhappy quarrel, we are surely justified in believing
that his appeal for a general reconciliation and a united effort in the crusade
shows him to have been more clear-sighted than the Roman pontiff.

There is one case, however, in which St. Louis's impartiality in international affairs deserves particular attention; for the course he chose to follow
in his dealings with Henry III of England appeared contrary to the best
interests of his crown. Philip Augustus, in return for the injury done him
by his vassal John "Lackland," had seized most of that monarch's French
possessions, including the paternal estates of the Plantagenets. The English
made repeated protests against this confiscation, and prepared to resume

32. Chapter VI, section 9.

war at the earliest opportunity. St. Louis asked himself whether his ancestor
had acted fairly; "his conscience pricked him." Henry was supported by his
brother Richard, Earl of Cornwall, whose election as "King of the Romans"
had been secured by the Pope; but the title was purely nominal, and, in any
case, the English baronage were constantly at loggerheads with their sovereign. Henry, therefore, was not much to be feared; and if St. Louis had
consulted none but political interests, he need only have drawn his sword to
sweep France clear of English influence—or what was left of it. The solution
upon which he decided was altogether different. He told Henry: "If you
will unconditionally renounce your claim to Normandy, Anjou, Touraine,
Maine, and Poitou, recognizing these provinces as unquestionably French
and at the same time doing homage to me for Guienne, I will grant you as
fiefs (in return likewise for your homage) all my possessions in Limousin,
Quercy, and Périgord. Furthermore, if Alphonse of Poitiers should die without issue, I will allow you to take Saintonge and Agenais, again as my vassal."
This proposal astounded the king's advisers, who asked him what end he had
in view. The saint replied: "To establish love between my children and his
children, who are first cousins." This extraordinary arrangement has been
criticized not only by his contemporaries, but by many historians down to
the present day. In order to understand it, we must try to share the outlook
of that period, when the fact of doing homage for land was an extremely
serious matter, and when a great overlord such as the King of France exercised a very real power of control over fiefs held by his vassals. There was
not a handful of French soil which the King of England would occupy as
an independent sovereign; Normandy and all the Loire valley was restored
unreservedly to France, while distant Guienne, which would in fact have
been very difficult to conquer, was made subject to France in such a way
that Bordeaux came under the appellate jurisdiction of Paris. On December
4, 1259, in the royal orchard on the site of what is now the Place Dauphiné,
the King of England, bareheaded and without mantle, belt, or spurs, knelt
before St. Louis, in whose hands he placed his own, swearing faith and loyalty. By acting thus on Christian principles, Louis had not done badly for
France. This was proved by the English themselves, who showed the greatest

indignation: "It is beyond the bounds of reason!" exclaimed John Peckham, Archbishop of Canterbury.

Deeds such as this, at all events, raised the king's prestige by capturing the public imagination. At a time when moral principles counted in international politics to an extent which they no longer do, St. Louis enjoyed universal respect because he was a thorough-going Christian. This much is evident from the fact that he was called upon as "elder statesman" to arbitrate between one nation and another, rather as St. Bernard had done in the preceding century and for the same reason. In one sense, too, his intervention was a great deal more effective than the similar efforts of Innocent III and other great popes. For St. Louis spoke not as enjoying *de facto* authority, nor as having power to condemn and to constrain, but only by virtue of that wisdom which he had received from God. We find him adjudicating on the succession to Hainaut and Flanders, ignoring altogether the private interests of his own brother Charles of Anjou. Again, at the expense of his future son-in-law, Thibaut V of Champagne, he judges who shall occupy the throne of Navarre. Between the Count of Chalon and his son the Count of Burgundy, between Burgundy and Champagne, between Henri de Luxembourg and Thibault de Bar—in each case it is Louis who decides; and no one could suspect him of an unjust end. When his advisers suggested he should leave his vassals and their neighbours to tear one another to pieces, he was indignant and replied that by so doing he would "earn the hatred of God." He was called upon to intervene in the home politics of foreign states. Thus, in 1258, when the great barons of England defied their king, St. Louis—in a manner perhaps somewhat tactless and abrupt—condemned and rejected the Provisions of Oxford as unfair. As regards Italian politics, he had tried to prevent his brother Charles of Anjou from accepting the Sicilian crown, and having failed, he refused to send his own troops to occupy that dangerous realm.[33]

The culmination of St. Louis's Christian policy was the crusade, upon which he twice embarked. The undertaking failed on each occasion, and we

---

33. If St. Louis had had his way, the atrocity known as "The Sicilian Vespers" would never have occurred.

may ask whether this was due solely to the French king's unpreparedness and tenacity, or to the fact that the rest of Christendom, including the papacy, withheld assistance. The two expeditions have much to commend them; but they mark the one single point at which St. Louis's holiness, blinding him to a sense of reality, led him into dreamland and disaster. We might on this account harbour resentment, were it not for his heroism during the Egyptian campaign and the sublimity of his death at Tunis, which endow his portrait with an aureole of splendour.[34]

Such, then, was Louis de Poissy,[35] King of France and witness on behalf of man before the face of his Eternal Father. We cannot doubt that in whatever station of life he had been placed by birth, he would have been what we have seen him to be—a perfect Christian, a just man after Christ's own heart, a saint. Providence had ordained that, in the position which he held, he should move as a figure of outstanding influence and significance. We may recognize in him the most complete example of what Christian faith, which dominated the Middle Ages, could do with one prepared to give it his whole obedience and thereby reach the full stature of a man.

---

34. The crusades of St. Louis will be studied in Volume 2, Chapter XI.
35. This was the way he liked best to style himself, for it was at Poissy that he had been baptized.

Designed by Fiona Cecile Clarke, the CLUNY MEDIA *logo*
depicts a monk at work in the scriptorium,
with a cat sitting at his feet.

The monk represents our mission to emulate
the invaluable contributions of the monks
of Cluny in preserving the libraries of the West,
our strivings to know and love the truth.

The cat at the monk's feet is Pangur Bán, from the
eponymous Irish poem of the 9th century.
The anonymous poet compares his scholarly
pursuit of truth with the cat's happy hunting of mice.
The depiction of Pangur Bán is an homage to the work
of the monks of Irish monasteries and a sign
of the joy we at Cluny take in our trade.

"Messe ocus Pangur Bán,
cechtar nathar fria saindan:
bíth a menmasam fri seilgg,
mu memna céin im saincheirdd."

Made in the USA
Middletown, DE
14 August 2023

36719497R00219